CYCLING

100 Rides in N

£1.20

Sven Klinge

CYCLING THE BUSH

100 Rides in New South Wales

SECOND EDITION

Fully Revised

Sven Klinge

Hill of Content
Melbourne

First published in Australia 1991
by Hill of Content Publishing Co Pty Ltd
86 Bourke Street, Melbourne, Australia 3000

Second Reprint 1997

© Copyright Sven Klinge, 1994
Cover photo-The Apollo 'Comp' on Narrow Neck (Ride 37)
Typeset in Australia by Midland Typesetters,
Maryborough, Vic
Printed and bound in Malaysia by SNP Offset (M)
Sdn. Bhd.

National Library of Australia
Cataloguing-in-Publication data

Klinge, Sven, 1969-
  Cycling the bush.

  2nd ed.
  Bibliography.
  Includes index.
  ISBN 085572 250 9

  1. Bicycle touring—New South Wales—Guide-books.
  2. New South Wales—Guide-books

796.6409944

CONTENTS

ACKNOWLEDGMENTS

Thanks to the following people and companies for their generous support and technical advice: Rogan Carroll at Apollo, Steve Turner at Paddy Pallin, Martin Hanley and Jamie Beford at Hanley Trading, Alan Malone at Eureka Tents, Noel McFarlane at Bunyip Bags, and John Bazzano at Shimano. All photographs including the cover were shot on Fujichrome Velvia 50 ASA 35 mm film while note-making Digital Audio Tapes were supplied by Fuji.

Thanks also to my cycling and walking companions; Dean 'Cooper' Piggott, Frank Bichler, Linda Rodriguez, Adrian Hart, Kerrie Tambree, Joe Doyle, Sean O'Byrne, and Carmen Frugone.

Much appreciation to Bruce Patterson and Brendan Lahiff for their useful comments, allowing me to revise several rides considering other cyclists' perspectives.

INTRODUCTION

Recreational mountain biking in Australia has become one of the country's fastest growing leisure sports. Since the mid-1980s, the mountain bike (or all-terrain bicycle as it is referred to overseas) has become the dominant bicycle design in Australian shops and the subject of more cycling related articles and advertisements than racing and touring put together.

The reasons are many; some are obvious, some less so. A central part of our national identity or character revolves around some form of participation in our geographical environment. In short, we love the outdoors and we love sports. In addition, we have the natural features that deserve exploration: millions of hectares of forested mountains, varying from tropical rainforest and sandstone gorges to alpine plateaus and coastal ranges. They are largely protected in a national parks reserve totalling over seventy national parks in New South Wales, many being of world heritage importance. The majority of the larger reserves are concentrated about the Great Dividing Range which spans the entire length of the state from north to south and is fortunately close to our major cities and easily accessible in most places.

Our colonial history saw much penetration into many of these areas to supply resources, mainly timber and mineral, to rapidly growing eighteenth and early nineteenth century populations. These ventures have left a legacy of trails throughout our forests, many closed to four-wheel drive vehicles, that are ideal for the pioneering mountain cyclist.

On the hardware front, the accelerated evolution of the mountain bike has resulted in the most versatile, robust form of transport available. The universally accepted new generation suspension forks, aluminium frames, quick-shifting indexed gears, and efficient canti-lever brakes have provided bushwalkers and road cyclists with a new means of escape from the congestion of urban society.

Australians, arguably not a technologically sophisticated society, have nonetheless been eager to embrace each new advance in mountain bike design with abandon. The pace of change is so intense that continual upgrading is forced upon us by manufacturers in an increasingly more ludicrous war of gadgetry, accessory gimmicks, and fads. Ovalised cranks, cro-moly frames, and Rapidfire gears are all fashion-victims in the battle for technical supremacy, once 'in' and now long forgotten in the serious cyclist's quest for the ultimate off-road bicycle.

It is hoped that this guide can show the prospective mountain biker where to take his machine. Whether his motive is physical fitness, or testing newly acquired ATB gadgets, or simply to retreat into the wilderness, the best areas in this most diverse state are detailed in the following chapters.

The mountain bike has many advantages over walking. More luggage can be carried in panniers that can be positioned almost anywhere on the bike. In fact, with duel panniers correctly packed, almost three times as much food and other supplies can be carried which of course allows longer trips to be planned, and in the case of an emergency, an unexpected delay can be endured without hunger. Much more can be seen in the same time, for one can of course cycle at higher speeds than the walker; the perfect compromise between enjoying the scenery and arriving at your destination as planned.

There are many other advantages: because walking is slow, any wildlife ahead has time to move out of sight before one approaches. But the cyclist can surprise lyrebirds, roos, or other marsupials as one comes hurtling around a corner. Crossing streams can be done without getting your feet wet on a bike, and with its increased storage capacity, one can afford to take along a few added luxuries like some good camera gear or a bottle of red for around the campfire.

For one day rides, those not so fit can transport the bike to a high starting point and coast all the way down the mountain. This is especially convenient when public transport connects both the beginning and ending of the ride, such as exists in the Blue Mountains.

Mountain biking also beats touring by road bike in many aspects. Firstly, you are away from traffic that so often makes touring uncomfortable, if not dangerous. But more importantly, the greatest bane of cyclists everywhere is virtually non-existent—the headwind. Riding on bush trails through national parks which invariably have dense tree cover shelters one from all but the severest of winds.

Of course, one is limited to where one can ride. Most walking trails have steps and this makes riding very impractical. But by combining cycling and walking, one can have a far greater appreciation of the Australian bush without resorting to Spartan conditions.

But cycling the bush is not without its dangers. The most real hazard that continually threatens a cyclist in the mountains is a snapped brake cable. With a heavily laden bike travelling down some steep mountain pass, a broken front cable would almost certainly mean very serious injury. Consequently some knowledge of how your bike works is essential, and in this book I've included advice on how to maintain your bike and what tools to take along.

I first began bush cycling on an early fake mountain bike that soon fell apart and nearly took me along with it. Our national parks are no place for caliper brakes and thin, smooth tyres. But it lasted long enough to get me hooked. There is nothing to compare with the exhilaration of charging down a narrow cliff pass, rocks and trees a blur, with one's entire concentration focused on ducking branches, avoiding rocks, and generally keeping the bike upright.

Over the years, I have built up a collection of over one hundred 1:25 000 topographical maps and have used these to plan my trips. But planning is of little use when maps were printed in the 1970s, and trails which are marked as 4WD tracks disappear due to disuse or new trails which are have been cut recently don't exist on the map. In this book, I have attempted to correct and update much of the obsolete information contained on CMA Maps. But in no way, do the maps contained within this book offer an alternative to CMA Maps: they are only a guideline and should be used in conjunction with the topographicals, especially where walking or camping is involved.

Furthermore, many of the rides contain dangerous descents where speeds in excess of 50 kph might lead to loss of control with inexperienced cyclists. No responsibility can be accepted for any injuries or accidents resulting from the use of this book.

This book is divided into two unequal parts. The first contains information on equipment and techniques involved in touring. I've made a conscious effort to limit the amount of useless information that fills up so many cycling books and magazines: things like 'ensure your bike is well-maintained' and 'cycle in control at all times'. I believe cyclists possess quite a bit of common sense and don't need to be told the obvious.

The remaining chapters concern themselves with suggested routes divided up into specific regions. The rides are predominantly through national parks but sometimes state forests and recreation areas are included as quality cycling environments. Most rides around the Sydney area, the Blue Mountains, the North Morton, Ku-ring-gai Chase, and Royal National Parks are of one day duration (rarely more than 50 km). However, almost all other rides especially in more remote parks such as Kosciusko and the Barrington Tops require overnight accommodation. This primarily means your own tent. Some cabins, huts, and youth hostels are available, but prior bookings are essential, even in the off-peak season.

This second edition has many new features. Firstly, the introductory chapters have been almost tripled to include a history of Australian bush touring, new innovations in mountain bike technology, and new camping products. These chapters also contain additional sections such as photographic tips and mountain bike/wilderness compatibility issues. A third part has been introduced mainly for overseas and interstate visitors giving information on the state: climate, transport, and accommodation. The grading system has been overhauled and many of the more difficult longer wilderness rides of the first edition have been omitted or downscaled. The sandstone parks still have by far the largest representation, with tours through the spectacular Wollemi National Park increasing from 7 to 15. New regions are also included: the Nattai and Wadbilliga Rivers, the ACT, and Gibraltar Range National Park. The maps have been downgraded to act as a simple area guide, as it is imperative to purchase the topographicals listed in the table at the beginning of each ride. Other improvements include an expanded index, greater detail on longer rides, and a classification table of rides based on interest. The photographs, I believe, are a large improvement over the first edition, giving first timers an impression of what the terrain and views are like.

The author and publisher welcome any suggestions for amendments so that future editions of this book can be brought up to date and expanded.

As the popularity of cycling in national parks increases, the National Parks and Wildlife Service which manages these areas will have to formulate policies in their management plans to accommodate this activity. At the moment, cycling is classified as an acceptable activity within national parks and all fire trails and roads are open to them (with the exceptions of designated Wilderness Zones and Waterboard Territory). However, if sufficient correlation exists between environmental damage and mountain bikes, as has occurred in the US and Europe, the National Parks' policy-makers will have to legislate to exclude mountain bikes from many areas. This has already occurred with much controversy in Victoria, South Australia, and even certain parts of NSW. It is the responsibility of the individual to observe the code of conduct of cyclists (contained in Part 1) in order to ensure that mountain biking will not be classified together with four-wheel drives as an environmentally *un*friendly activity.

SUGAR GLIDER

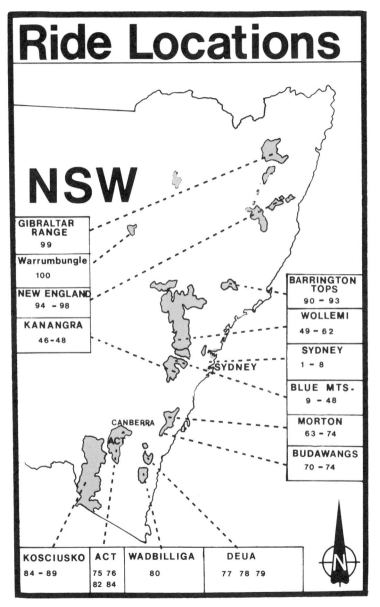

Ride Locations

NSW

GIBRALTAR RANGE
99

Warrumbungle
100

NEW ENGLAND
94 – 98

KANANGRA
46-48

BARRINGTON TOPS
90 – 93

WOLLEMI
49 – 62

SYDNEY
1 – 8

BLUE MTS.
9 – 48

MORTON
63 – 74

BUDAWANGS
70 – 74

SYDNEY

CANBERRA
ACT

KOSCIUSKO	ACT	WADBILLIGA	DEUA
84 – 89	75 76 82 84	80	77 78 79

13

CLASSIFICATION OF RIDES
ACCORDING TO INTEREST

COASTAL RIDES

   1: West Head
   2: The Basin
   3: Bobbin Head
   4: Bradley's Head
   6: Garie Beach
 82: Jervis Bay
 83: Myall Lakes

RIVER RIDES

  5: Lady Carrington Drive
 11: Bents Basin SRA
 12: Nortons Basin
 38: Six Foot Track
 43: Scotts Main Range
 47: Kowmung River (Tuglow Cave)
 48: Yerrandrie (Kowmung)
 49: Colo River (Lower)
 50: Mountain Lagoon
 58: Wolgan River (Deanes Creek)
 59: Glen Davis (Capertee River)
 64: Purnoo Lookout (Shoalhaven)
 69: Yalwal
 72: Clyde River
 77: Deua River (Lower)
 78: Deua River (Upper)
 80: Tuross River (Wadbilliga)
 90: Allyn River (Barrington Tops)
 91: Polblue (Barrington River)
 94: Styx River (New England)

WILDERNESS RIDES

(For experienced cyclists, walkers, and campers:- self-sufficiency is essential)

29: Wentworth Creek (Lawson Ridge)
32: Watershed Road
38: Six Foot Track
43: Scotts Main Range
46: Kanangra Walls
48: Yerrandrie—Kowmung River
51: Tootie Ridge
54: Six Brothers
61: Gospers Mountain
62: Capertee Gorge (Gospers Mt)
68: Meryla Pass
71: The Vines (Sassafras)
74: The Castle
80: Wadbilliga National Park
86: Mount Jagungal
89: The Pilot

HISTORICAL ATTRACTIONS

4: Bradley's Head
8: Old Great North Road
43: Scotts Main Range
45: Mount Banks
48: Yerrandrie—Kowmung
55: Glow Worm Tunnel
57: Newnes
59: Glen Davis
89: The Pilot

ABORIGINAL INTEREST

1: West Head
2: The Basin
14: Thirlmere Lakes

19: Red Hands Cave
60: Dunn's Swamp (Kandos Weir)
71: The Vines (Bora Ground)
72: Clyde River

GREAT LOOKOUTS

13: Burragorang Lookout
25: Grose River (Faulconbridge)
33: McMahon's Lookout
36: Cliff Drive (Katoomba)
37: Narrow Neck
39: Evan's Lookout
40: Perry's Lookdown
45: Mount Banks
46: Kanangra Walls
56: Wolgan Lookout
61: Gospers Mountain
67: Bungonia
73: Pigeon House
74: The Castle
75: Brindabella Range
86: Mount Jagungal
92: Barrington Tops (Carey's Peak)
96: Cathedral Rock
100: Mount Exmouth

WATERFALLS

34: Wentworth Falls Tour
39: Evan's Lookout
40: Perrys Lookdown (Govett's Leap)
44: Victoria Falls
46: Kanangra Walls
80: Tuross Falls
84: North Kosciusko Tour
85: Valentine Hut (Valentine Falls)
93: Gloucestor Tops (Gloucestor River)
98: Ebor Falls (Guy Fawkes River)

ALPINE RIDES

46: Kanangra Walls
75: Brindabella Range
84: North Kosciusko Tour
85: Valentine Hut
86: Mount Jagungal
87: Mount Kosciusko
88: Smiggin Holes
89: The Pilot
92: Polblue (Barrington Tops)
93: Gloucestor Tops

TOURING BIKE

1: West Head
3: Bobbin Head
4: Bradley's Head
6: Garie Beach
11: Bents Basin SRA
12: Nortons Basin
13: Burragorang Lookout
22: Hawkesbury Lookout
34: Wentworth Falls Tour
36: Cliff Drive (Katoomba)
41: Shipley Plateau
82: Jervis Bay
98: Ebor Falls (Guy Fawkes River)

STATE FORESTS

47: Kowmung River (Tuglow Caves)
55: Glow Worm Tunnel (Newnes)
56: Wolgan Lookout (Newnes State Forest)
61: Gosper's Mountain (Coricudgy)
68: Yalwal
72: Clyde River (Yadboro)
80: Wadbilliga National Park

90: Allyn River
94: Styx River

RIDES INVOLVING EXTENDED WALKING

25: Grose River (Faulconbridge)
29: Wentworth Creek (Lawson Ridge)
39: Evan's Lookout (Grand Canyon)
44: Victoria Falls
51: Tootie Ridge
53: Canoe Creek (Colo River)
67: Bungonia
70: Tianjara Plateau
74: The Castle (two nights to Mount Owen)
80: Wadbilliga National Park (Tuross Falls)
86: Mount Jagungal
96: Cathedral Rock
97: Woolpack Rocks
100: Mount Exmouth

GREAT DOWNHILLS

(These often involve 'great' uphills)

26: Oaks Fire Trail
38: Six Foot Track
42: Megalong Valley
43: Scotts Main Range
68: Meryla Pass
73: Pigeon House
74: The Castle
84: North Kosciusko Tour
85: Valentine Hut
86: Mount Jagungal
89: Pilot Wilderness
90: Allyn River
94: Wattle Flat
100: Mount Exmouth

CAVE ATTRACTIONS

AUTHOR'S SELECTION
(THE BEST RIDES IN THE STATE)

BOTTLEBR.

19

A KEY TO RIDE AND TRACK GRADES

GRADING OF RIDES

The difficulty of each ride is assessed from a fitness point of view. From this one can determine what the rate of progress will be. *Please note these are only averages and approximations and are very subjective.* They are included to give a more specific differentiation between rides than the traditional 'easy'–'medium'–'hard' classifications contained within many cycling guides.

A ride will vary in its difficulty due to equipment, weather, fitness, hours of daylight, track quality, and the number of cyclists in your party. Rides will naturally take longer to perform if they augment a longer NSW tour and the cyclist has to use his/her own power to travel to the staging area.

ALL DISTANCES GIVEN ARE RETURN. Some variations may alter slightly according to starting and ending points: railway depots, coach depots, car drop-off/pick-up points, youth hostels, and camping areas. To give an appreciation of vertical variations spot heights are also given. The height variations listed for each ride are calculated as the highest point on the ride minus the lowest point. This figure applies only to the cycling component of a ride, not walking. In planning all rides, priority should be given to the *tracknotes*, rather than the grade rating.

1. Predominantly downhill; some pedalling required
2. Level; easy pedalling
3. Gentle uphills
4. Short steep gradients
5. Long steep gradients
6. Above average fitness necessary to enjoy ride
7. Challenging
8. Experienced cyclists only

GRADING OF TRACKS

For each ride, the quality of the track will be graded on a scale of 1–8. The higher the number, the worse the track condition. Consequently one will need to travel slower, on better tyres, making the ride more challenging. Where different types of tracks are encountered, the grading refers to the *worst* one. For all tracks rated at 2 or less, a conventional touring bike can be used.

A mountain bike is recommended for all rides rated 3 and higher, and is essential for grades 4 and above. Fit wide knobblies and carry a pump so you can deflate and inflate pressures in accordance with terrain. Tracks along granite mountain ranges are very rocky and kevlar belted tyres and thornproof or anti-crevaison tubes are strongly recommended.

Once again, this grading index is only an average. Track maintenance could decrease for certain areas with the establishment of wilderness core zones. In recent years, unusual monsoonal climatic patterns have produced heavy rains in late summer and early autumn. These can very quickly convert a Grade 3 track into a Grade 7 making progress considerably slower and even necessitating *walking down* a hill! These accelerated erosion effects are exacerbated with steeper slopes, softer soils, and poorer track drainage construction.

1. Sealed road
2. Country road, unsealed
3. Rough dirt road (2WD)
4. 4WD track (good quality)
5. 4WD track (bad quality)
6. Abandoned fire trail
7. Overgrown track: rocks, corrugation, erosion gullies, fallen trees, sand, wash-outs, cess-pits, and potholes, vegetation
8. Walking track: narrow, overgrown, steps, and roots

1
The Bike

An Introduction

Today, mountain bikes are big business. Spearheading a new bicycle boom, they are capturing an ever increasing slice of the market. Even racing cyclists and tri-athletes have mountain bikes as their second bikes. Young teenagers responsible for the BMX craze of the early 1980s want a larger bike, but just as tough. Cycling magazines are full of articles, reviews, and advertisements for mountain bikes, and sponsorship of mountain bike racing has already entered the Australian scene in a big way.

Also known as All-Terrain Bicycles (ATBs), they are at the spearhead of rapid technological development. Aluminium, titanium, magnesium, and carbon fibre are replacing steel and Cro-Mo traditionally used for constructing the frame and forks. These materials are lighter, stronger, and ultimately have the potential to be cheaper. High-technology has also played the primary role in the rapid evolution of mountain bike components, with more efficient gear selection systems, smoother suspension, and greater reliability in braking and pedalling.

This development and level of popularity has ensured that competing manufacturers specialise their bikes to suit a variety of riders' needs. Accordingly, there is a tremendous range to choose from. Today one can pick up an imitation mountain bike with the groceries at a supermarket with ten gears and caliper brakes for about $120 or the more enthusiastic can blow $9000 for a top American imported 24-speed titanium competition model with adjustable suspension forks, rear suspension, grip shifting, up-turned handle bars, leather seat, kevlar tyres, clipless pedals, hydraulic brakes, and a spokeless rear wheel.

In Europe and the USA, where cycle-planning is extremely advanced, there are schools that teach the paying customer how to ride ATBs. Subjects include obstacle clearance, controlling descents, maintenance, falling, and navigation. In short, the mountain bike was universally become regarded as the ideal synthesis between man, machine, and nature.

HISTORY OF THE
MOUNTAIN BIKE

Although the mountain bike (MTB) boom in Australia began in the early 1980s, its origins can be traced to the inter-war years. It was in 1933 that Ignaz Schwinn introduced his Excelsior, the bicycle equivalent of the tank, to the US. It was the first production bike to come with balloon tyres, coaster-hub brakes, only one gear, and wide back-swept handlebars. It was constructed from twenty kilos of carbon steel. But unfortunately at the time, few saw its merits and its use was confined to newspaper delivery and other similar utilitarian duties.

Its potential was only discovered after groups of local teenagers 'terrorised' the country backroads with motorised trail bikes. The problem got so bad that environmental damage was being caused by the hundreds of motorbike wheels spinning in soft ground. Restrictions were consequently enforced.

Legend has it that in one particular region near San Francisco, where erosion problems and complaints by rural residents were particularly severe, the young enthusiasts looked to alternative means of descending steep hills as fast as possible. It had to be on wheels, noiseless, and incredibly strong. After many spectacular and often 'unhealthy' experiments with various types of bikes, the old Schwinn Excelsior, a motorbike look-a-like, made a comeback and remaining models in the locality were quickly bought up at as little as $5 each. It was one of the only bikes on which riders had a fairly good chance of reaching the bottom without their relatives making a life insurance claim.

But it wasn't without its faults. On one famous stretch in Marin Country on the slopes of Tramalpais, the Cascades Fire Trail was so steep (total drop: 800 m) that continual use of the brakes was needed during the 'bombing'. The coaster hub the Excelsior was equipped with had a tendency to overheat, to the extent that the grease was boiled right out of the bearings and had to be re-packed before the next descent.

This hill, now named Repack Hill, is considered the birthplace of the mountain bike, for it was here that new equipment was tested. By the process of natural selection, the bike evolved to its present form. Gary Fisher, a racer, added derailleur gears, thumb shifters, and a quick-release mechanism on the seat-post of his Schwinn so that riding *up* the hill was now possible, and indeed he was first man to demonstrate this feat.

The maturing of the mountain bike was facilitated by two men: Joe Breeze and Tim Neenan. They developed the frame geometry and, with Californian businessman Mike Synyard, they sold the first production mountain bike, the Specialised Stumpjumper for $750.

Even with a huge advertising budget, the Japanese-manufactured bike had only moderate success, and it wasn't until Tom Ritchey and Charles Kelly teamed with Gary Fisher that mountain biking came into its own. The conservative European manufacturers, initially lagged behind America, Taiwan, and Japan, but soon caught up and introduced a whole series of high quality frames and innovations. By manufacturing aluminium rims and nylon gum-wall tyres, four kilograms could be shaved off. By the late 1970s, this constant refining led to production standards required by serious competitors. But perhaps more importantly, they gave it the status that is now taken for granted: the mountain bike was no longer a device whereby some off-beat suicidal dare-devils got their thrills, but a respectable machine that everyone from businessmen to bushwalkers could use. Today, the mountain bike is generally regarded as the most efficient and versatile form of transport on the planet. It can go over more types of terrain than any other mode except walking, and requires less energy to get between any two points.

This is one of the mountain bike's greatest advantages: one no longer has to contend with hostile traffic on old ill-planned suburban streets. For decades, cyclists have had to share roads with aggressive drivers having to endure abuse, cans, bottles, and other refuse from the car's cabin. Some unfortunate cyclists have even died at the hands of hit-and-run drivers. But now cyclists can travel along trails impassable even to four wheel drives, having almost exclusive passage to remote spectacular places in a massive national parks system that ranks among the world's best.

STEEL HORSES
The Bicycle in the Australian Bush

What more hallowed turf than the MCG could hold Australia's first bicycle race in 1889? While early models were built with the aid of Americans and Europeans, it wasn't until 1875 that importation of mass-produced bicycles began, and the Melbourne bicycle club became established in 1878. Newsletters were written, rallies and exhibitions were held, and distance records were established between capital cities. The Australian capital of cycling was undoubtedly Melbourne, especially during the 1890s when significant improvements and price reductions meant thousands could afford this easy to use, cheap, efficient form of transport.

The Dux Cycle Company in Melbourne employed up to 150 labourers who constructed bikes for domestic and even international markets. Around the turn of the century there were dozens of brands (from Acme to Zimmy) on the market, selling tens of thousands, first costing around £35 each then dramatically dropping to between £4 and £10. Sounds cheap, but this was equivalent to several weeks' wages.

Bush bikes were advertised as having superior clearance, thornproof tyres, greater strength, and were 'designed to suit the rough roads of Australia'. Tall tales abounded as to the feats people had performed riding the first bicycles in the Australian bush. For example, adding springs to jump post-and-rail fences, kangaroo shooting, emergency chains made from bullock hide, races with horses, and luggage of eighty pounds on trans-continental treks. As it infiltrated the bush, the bicycle was used increasingly for rural tasks, until observers were predicting the extinction of the horse.

Cycle touring grew in popularity. Because of the rough nature of early roads and the virtual non-existence of motor vehicles, bush cycles were the ideal way to travel. However, cycling was not without fatalities: thirst, break-down, lack of efficient brakes, and being chased by dogs were all causes of death.

Early cycling gazettes and magazines are full of colourful accounts of the hazards early bush cyclists had to endure. One adventurer complained of the continual loss of spokes due to sticks being flipped into the wheels, while others encountered fencing wire in the cogs, stumps, anthills, salt lakes, mud, logs, and plagues of prickly *Emex australis*. Cyclists went out of their way to travel on anything but the appalling roads; even to the extent of travelling in between railway lines and on camel pads. The latter was claimed to be the best cycling surface and camel tracks were used extensively in the West Australian gold fields. It was here that official bicycle paths were formed with the levying of a bicycle tax.

Mountain cycling was first recorded in the late nineteenth century. Excursions to the Victorian Alps began as early as 1896, the rugged Budawangs in NSW were crossed in 1889, and the summit of Mount Kosciusko was attained by bike in 1898. The first guide for mountain cycling was written in 1897: published as the *Austral Wheel Guide to the Victorian Alps*. Tracknotes included alpine settlements, touring routes, road conditions, food, and accommodation. Mountain touring was a great contrast to cycling conditions normally: there was abundant fresh water, shade, exciting downhills, spectacular views, and little dust.

Constant improvements in the standard of bicycles broadened the spectrum whereby ordinary workers of both sexes could enjoy a ride in the country just as much as the more athletic pioneers and hermits. Pneumatic tyres, freewheeling hubs, universal wheel sizes, steel rims, front and rear brakes all were standard by the early twentieth century.

These developments were augmented by improvements in mapping and road conditions, reductions in working hours, and higher disposable incomes. Jenolan Caves in NSW was just one popular tourist attraction visited by cycling/touring clubs on weekends around the turn of the century.

Throughout the next seventy years however, the basic design of the pushbike didn't change. Interest grew in the motor car, and to a lesser extent, the motorbike. Speedwells and Raleighs became dominant leaders in the touring market: thicker tyres, strong construction, and room for saddle bags. These were used by pioneers such as Jim Smith and Gwyllam Roberts to do crossings of the Blue Mountains using the many fire trails constructed during the 1950s and 1960s.

It was only in the late 1970s that the mountain bikes that had evolved on Repack Hill in California started to be exported to Australia. The first of these were called 'Cruisers', the evolutionary link between the BMX of the early 1980s, and the modern All-Terrain Bike with 26 inch wheels and gears. Cruisers have themselves evolved in today's 'Hybrids' or 'Cross' bikes—mountain bikes with large 700C tyres that have many touring bike properties, and are often used for urban transit. Some are used by the controversial bicycle couriers seen in the Sydney CBD. The late 1980s saw a revival of the BMX, in somewhat altered form, as principally a stunt bike on which a multitude of spins, leaps, and other acrobatics could be performed. However this fad was short-lived, being replaced by mountain bike and accelerated technological improvements.

Today we see Australian companies such as Apollo and Repco competing against American models. There are annual national competitions, the most important being the MTB Titles regularly attracting hundreds of competitors; many from overseas. Australia's performance in international events is improving too, after early disappointments due to the lack of any factory-sponsored professional athletes.

Still in its infancy, mountain biking has become an economic miracle for manufacturers faced with poor 10-speed racer sales and a dying BMX fad. The market in Australia has more than doubled in the last five years from 70 000 units in 1988 to approximately 165 000 in 1994, accounting for nearly half of all bicycle sales. A quarter of these are in New South Wales. The next ten years promise even greater heights of technology—lighter components, lower costs, and a greater range of Australian bikes built for our unique conditions. For example, a young Australian, Glen Sharrock, has built and patented a 2WD mountain bike with its own front wheel gear and derailleur assembly. While the prototype definitely increased handling performance, this was unfortunately offset by the added weight of the additional crankset and derailleur. This perhaps won't be a problem once lighter alloys are used in the construction. Muddy Fox in England have even produced an interactive suspension bike, combining front and rear shock absorbers in the single system.

Already new models are coming on to the market made of lighter and stronger metals, front and rear suspension, through-the-tube cable housings, wider and knobblier kevlar tyres, hydraulic brakes, self-repairing tubes, and even in-built computers. The group-sets on today's bikes has been downsized to make it lighter while allowing a wider range in gear ratios. Componentry in the not-too-distant future has further innovations in store for us: solar powered bikes with disc-wheels, hub-less wheels, and drag-reducing fairings.

Accessories are equally innovative: smaller double-action light-weight pumps, compact tool kits that fit in a drink-bottle lid, altimeters, double-sided clipless pedal and cleat-recessed shoes, handlegrip gear selection, electric gear selection, split seats, air seats, and gel seats.

Initially new bike models are expensive, but like personal computers, mass production has ensured dramatic price reductions less than three years after first release. In the late 1980s, 21-speeds were upwards of $1500, now they're $500. Aluminium frames are falling under $1000 and it won't be long before titanium follows. Dual suspension bikes, that didn't exist a few years ago, are low less than $1500.

The average retail price is in the $299–350 price range, and this is the fastest growth range as quality parts move down the range: cantilever brakes, index gearing, alloy rims, off-road tyres, over-sized tubing, and even suspension forks. A little patience will see today's top-priced bikes, such as the hydraul-ically-braked San Andreas become affordable as subsequent models are developed. While this seems good for the con-sumer, there is a drawback: once purchased, they don't keep their price on the second hand market. But then again, regular maintenance should ensure that these new generation bikes will last for years. And as long as the pace of change is rapid, the mountain bike fad will no longer be just a trend, but a way of life: urban transport, recreation, and sport all in one activity that appeals to all.

BUYING A MOUNTAIN BIKE

Obviously, those satisfied with their bike can skip this section. For those looking for their dream machine, there is no simple answer. A bike requires a lot more interaction between rider and machine. And that's where things get complicated.

For the novice, selecting a mountain bike will prove a con-fusing experience. You will inevitably be confronted with tech-nical jargon by the salesman about frame metallurgy and componentry. See the following **Glossary** for a key to some of the most commonly used jargon.

When choosing a mountain bike, size is of crucial importance. A good bike store will let you test ride the bike. Make sure that you don't have to stretch to reach the pedals, and that you can straddle the top tube with at least 50 mm of crotch clearance with both feet flat on the ground. If not, get the salesman to adjust the seat, or try another frame size.

Mountain bike frames come in four common sizes:

RIDER LEG LENGTH	FRAME SIZE
28–31 inch	43 cm (17 inch)
32–34 inch	48 cm (19 inch)
34–36 inch	53 cm (21 inch)
35–37 inch	58 cm (23 inch)

The next most important item to consider are brakes. Make absolutely sure the bike cannot be moved forward when the brakes are applied. The same should apply if only the front is applied. The back brake should skid when applied separately.

Insist on thorn-proof tubes (26 inch $\times$ 2.125 inch) once you make your final decision. Any good bike store will fit them straight away. They cost approximately $12 each but they are worth it. Ensure that they either give you the original tubes as spares or deduct them from the cost.

If you plan to tour extensively with your new bike, you need to carry panniers for extra storage space. Accordingly, select a bike with a strong frame and adequate provisions (eyelets and lugs) to attach front and rear panniers. There's nothing worse than having one broken during your trip. A disturbing trend in top mountain bike models is that they aren't equipped with eyelets and lugs. When asked about this, sales representatives give a little laugh and say 'This is designed for racing only, not *touring*'. As if only the racers need the good stuff. A lot more stress is placed on a bike doing a five day crossing of the Blue Mountains with 30 kilograms of luggage than a 30 minute race!

A very dangerous feature on some cheaper mountain bikes are foam sponge handle grips that slide off when wet. This can result in a very serious accident. Beware!

Finally, if all this sounds daunting, a simple checklist will prevent the most inexperienced novice from getting 'ripped off', either in the bike store or buying second hand:

1. When looking from the front, with the bike vertical, the back wheel shouldn't be visible. If it is, the wheels are out of line. Either demand a lower price or go to someone else.
2. Check each wheel for sidewards movement. If there is any play, follow the same procedure as above.
3. Hold each wheel up and spin it. It should look like it will spin for three or four minutes. If it stops straight away, it needs adjusting.
4. Try to rattle the crankcase. It should be impossible.
5. Apply the brakes and try to push forwards. If there is movement in the handlebars, the headset in the neck is loose or worn. If the seller can't rectify it, leave.
6. Test-ride it while changing gears and using brakes. Does the chain stay on at extreme settings? Is the rear brake alone sufficient to stop you on short notice? If the answer to these questions is no, offer him loose change or go home.

All in all, be prepared to spend at least $500 for a new bike that will be reliable and comfortable if you intend to do any of the longer or more difficult rides suggested in this book. Any less, and you will be sacrificing safety and risking a long walk.

GLOSSARY of TERMS

The following is a brief glossary of technical terms associated with the industry:

Bottom bracket A flexible bottom bracket reduces efficiency as pedal power is wasted in moving the bottom of the frame from side to side. Kirk Precision has developed frames made of magnesium. With this light-weight stiff metal, the bottom bracket moves half as much as steel frames.

Bottom bracket height This is the height from the centre of the crankcase to the ground. If you intend to do a lot of offroad riding in rough conditions, you would be well advised to buy a bike that maximises this height so that the chainwheel or pedals don't scrape the ground every time you pass over a small crest or rock.

Cantilever brakes A very efficient braking system whereby two brake pads are mounted by pivots to the frame and contracted by means of an anchor plate connected to a centre-pull cable. For value for money, it is difficult to go past the popular *Shimano Deore* STX or XT M-system. The *Suntour* XC 9000 SE brakes are designed to give greater braking power by having the pad move in a three-dimensional arc. The energy of the rotating rim is utilised by a directional helix mechanism to enhance braking efficiency. In other words, the faster you're going the more braking power you get.

Chrome molybdenum tubing An alloy (531/653) of chrome, molybdenum, manganese, carbon, silicon, sulphur, and phosphorus. This is the most common type of steel alloy in the frame and is responsible for most of the bike's cost. In general, the thinner the grade, the higher the cost. But not all the bike will be necessarily made from Chrome-Moly: for the downmarket models the forks and rear triangle are sometimes made from high-tensile steel (1020) as a sneaky cost-cutting measure. New materials include aluminium, carbon fibre, titanium, magnesium metal matrix, and plastic! These are the bikes of the future with total weights as low as 9 kg.

Clusters This is the group of five to eight gears on the rear wheel. The market standard is Shimano's Hyperglide range which can handle changing gears even under pressure. Previously this would have meant the chain coming off or even breaking, but this remarkable gear system seems to handle the stress considerably well. The Suntour XC clusters are manufactured to be weaker than the chain, so that if something breaks due to stress, it's going to be the teeth. This still allows the bike to be ridden in the other gears.

Double-butted tubing The thickness of the frame's tubing varies from being relatively thin in the middle to thick at the ends. It is primarily used to manufacture lightweight bikes but the weight saving comes at a rigidity cost.

Drop-outs This refers to the rear triangle assembly where the wheel is secured to the frame. If one has to push the wheel forward to remove it, it is called a Horizontal Drop-Out, or if the wheel can be pulled straight down after removing the nut it is a Vertical Drop-Out. The latter has the advantage of better wheel alignment, while the former allows for superior gear adjustment.

Indexed gears Users of the old 'guess-what-gear' system will know how frustrating the hit and miss process of selecting a gear can be, especially when concentration is needed elsewhere such as negotiating a difficult corner. What indexing basically entails is an accurate and reliable means of changing gears as each setting is represented by a click and a stop. Pushing the shifter, one click up changes gear one gear lower. It's as simple as that. Top models include the Shimano XT and XTR and Suntour Microdrive XC PRO. A recent fad has been the introduction of Rapidfire 'push-button' gears. Despite their name however, gear change is slower and consequently professional competitors still use the traditional lever. Furthermore they have a relatively fast wear out rate, due to the inclusion of a complicated system of springs, and consequently are difficult, if not impossible, to repair. In recent types, grip-shifters (as used on motorbikes), have seen their way down the range of mountain bikes models. Eight-speed rear cassettes are being more standard, not necessarily giving a wider range of gears but allowing smoother shifts.

Variations on the indexed gearing system include indicators to tell you what gear you've selected, wish-bone levers that allow you to push and pull without releasing your grip, grip-selection similar to a motor bike, and electric gear selection that promises smoother, more reliable changes.

Quick-release capabilities These have been the standard in racing bikes for years and have only recently ventured on to mountain bike frames. What is referred to is a small lever that replaces the bolt on the seat and wheels so that they can be easily removed. This means that changing a tyre can be done in less time, as can changing the seat height for differences in gradients. A quick-release lever on top of the seat-post allows one to quickly adjust the angle of the seat. Testing has apparently confirmed there is no loss of safety when riding offroad. The disadvantage is that theft of the wheels and seat is made easier. Some of the up market brakes also have quick-release capabilities for brakes so that tubes do not have to be deflated to remove the wheel.

TIG welded lugless joints The majority of mountain bike frames are made of tubes which were welded together using this method. In order to prevent corrosion, the electrical welding is conducted in an inert argon-gas atmosphere. The joints are made less abrupt by applying a polyester spackling compound. Other joining methods include brass brazing with lugs, and fillet brazing (no lugs). Mongoose have their aluminium frames bonded together. This leaves a beautiful finish, in contrast, to the traditional chunky aluminium welding.

APOLLO

The Apollo Bicycle Company is an Australian brand, established by the Carroll family in Sydney in 1978. With continued growth and market penetration, Apollo has shaped the face of the Australian bicycle industry over the past 18 years. Current national distribution through 350 specialist bicycle retailers in every state makes Apollo the leading full line supplier of bicycles to the Australian consumer.

Apollo's comprehensive range of bicycles at every level is the culmination of a research and development programme which is genuinely and totally committed to producing the finest bikes in the world with innovative frame designs, integrated suspension systems, ultra lightweight space-age materials, and the latest state-of-the-art componentry. They're all researched, tested, evaluated, and refined over time and under actual race conditions at the elite level of competition throughout Australia and on the super tough American NORBA ciruit.

The latest range of MTBs from Apollo is the result of the firm's research into the requirements of competition and serious off-road riders who are finding equipment costs escalating out of reach, but still require the strength and handling of top line performance models.

Aluminium 7005 is chosen as the leading material of today's bicycles for its lightweight, stiffness, and comfort factors. Aluminium has a natural absorption, taking the road- or trail-shock out of the frame which would normally channel directly to the rider. Even with today's sophisticated suspension systems, a steel frame will still allow noticeable shock to be felt. When riding an aluminium bike, much of the road shock is absorbed in the frame, leaving the rider more comfortable after hours in the saddle.

In addition, Apollo's 7005 aluminium tubing is specially

formed to enhance frame stiffness, especially minimising lateral movement flex. By cross-ovalising the down tube, vertically at the head tube and horizontally at the seat tube, any undue stresses are dispersed out of those two key stress areas, reducing road shock, but foremost, creating a stronger frame as stiff as a steel frame.

Oversizing of an aluminium frame is essential for increasing the strength of the tube without sacrificing aluminium's lightweight property characteristics. As the tube's diameter becomes wider, the wall thickness can become proportionally thinner, and therefore lighter.

Suspension is another area where Apollo has been placing some serious research and development effort. Front suspension has become standard equipment for $1000+ models. Rear suspension is now seriously considered by consumers undertaking serious offroad riding, whether it be touring or racing. The assumed complexity of rear suspension has kept it out of reach of the average consumer, with prototype and flagship models hitting the market at anywhere between $3000 and $6500.

Through the research and development by Apollo MTB Team Racing, the average consumer can now enjoy the benefits of top line rear suspension at affordable prices. For example the Comp adjustable dual suspension mountain bike is priced at just $1595. Apollo has successfully developed a simple, yet very functional, rear suspension system, without the complex components found in the unaffordable flagship models. Apollo's active race suspension systems have been purpose designed to provide faster speed with greater control. Their systems incorporate bicycle-relevant technology drawn from the world of off-road motorcycle racing, and feature controlled re-bound damping and surer-handling. They've been tested throughout the National AMBA Cross-Country and Downhill series by Apollo MTB Team Racing, which is your guarantee that whichever Apollo competition certified suspension model you choose, you'll get the speed, handling, and suspension performance you require.

Groupsets

Many cyclists like to build a bike up themselves. That is, by purchasing or even designing their own custom-made frame and then acquiring the groupsets to match. This method is invariably expensive, as you are paying spare-part prices, rather than wholesale. The advantage is that you can get exactly the bike you want. The early 1990s trend of many manufacturers producing their own industry formats has fortunately subsided and there now exists a reasonable level of standardisation (e.g. SPD clip-less pedals) making it possible for cyclists to mix-and-match componentry from various suppliers. Suntour has led the way in innovation of mass-produced group-sets. Their features are summarised below:

Microdrive Smaller chainrings and smaller cogs lead to large weight savings without sacrificing strength. The gear ratios still remain the same, and clearance is increased. The 1994 STX componentry from Shimano has copied this idea.

Power-hanger A v-shaped arm that attaches on to the forks takes up the slack of the brake cable and gives exception leverage when correctly adjusted. This also has found its way on to Shimano rear and front braking systems.

Grease-guard The hubs, bottom bracket, headset, and pedals are equipped with grease-nipples so that one can use a grease-gun to lube the bike without disassembling it! By the use of valves and clean white teflon based grease, one simply squeezes until the old dirty grease comes out through pores. It takes about three minutes to re-grease all vitals on the bike, and better still can be done on the go as the gun and tube are quite compact.

ACCESSORIES

One can spend more on accessories than the cost of the bike itself. Many are necessary for long distance touring, most are not. National parks can be inhospitable places at times. The extreme isolation in some regions of New South Wales requires good preparation, and tough equipment. In order of priority, the following accessories are recommended:

Essentials

Air-pump Unless you're the world's slowest rider, chances are you will get a flat in the bush some time on a long ride. Since it's a long way to the nearest petrol station, a portable pump is a necessity. They are lightweight, small, and can be attached almost anywhere on the frame, the most popular place being on the upright tube below the seat. Make sure the attachment fits your valve. If not, another hose can be bought for around $2. New pumps, such as the Blackburn MP-1 Mini-pump, need no hoses and fit both schraeder and presta valves. Despite being only 29 cm long it is rated up to 180 psi and can inflate an average mountain bike tyre in a minute. An alternative to manually pumping up the tube is to carry small pressurised air cylinders. These work by screwing a plastic attachment on to your valve and then screwing the air cylinder into the attachment. These can be obtained separately or in Rema Tip Top Mountain Bike ATB Puncture Repair Kits. Some air-pumps, such as the Mt Zéfal Graph have an in-built pressure gauge supposedly accurate to ±2 psi.

Tool kit It is also inevitable that you will have to make some minor adjustments or repairs to the bike while on the go. Although somewhat heavy, a tool kit doesn't need to be bulky and can be permanently stored in a bag under the seat or in the back pocket of one of the panniers. Standard equipment includes: puncture repair kit, tyre levers, allen key set, small 5–10 cm shifter, 32 cm shifter, multi-faceted bone, pliers, screwdriver, 15 mm philips-head screwdriver, and spare tube. Some firms assemble complete compact tool sets that are designed to minimise weight. These can also save on cost.

On longer trips, one should expand this suggested kit to include spare spokes, spoke tightening key, chain link remover, spare links, grease, small lubricating oil flask (dry molybdenum or lithium based), and valve tightener. But above all, no matter how long the ride is, ensure that you have the right tools to repair a flat and tighten the brakes.

A spare tube will prevent mucking around with patches and glue on the first flat. The new Hutchinson Anti-Crevaison tube contains a self-sealing liquid for automatic sealing of small punctures. They won't however, repair tears or punctures at the base of the valve.

Water bottle Even though prices vary between $5 and $40, they do much the same job. The fashion or weight conscious might want to invest more in a fluoro-red bottle with a titanium cage, but it'll store the water no better than a K-Mart Jurassic Park special.

Water bottles can be attached via bosses to any of the three major tubes of the frame, or even to the handlebars. You can then use them as drink bottles on any walks you may do away from the bike. Don't fill them with anything but water as heat and time will make a mess of other solutions. Some have tyre repair kits attached to them while others can be used as containers for snack food or a spare tube. Some models have a specially designed spill-free pull top valve so they can be opened without using your other hand.

The Adura/Apollo bidons have a 23 oz. capacity (3 oz. larger than normal) and have wide openings, enabling easier cleaning.

Panniers Panniers come in a variety of shapes, sizes, and prices. What type you buy will depend on what length excursions you intend to go on and/or what degree of luxury you intend to travel in. Whether you carry food, clothes, camera gear, stereo, or the wine cellar, panniers should be strong and the racks likewise. People who make their decision solely on whether it matches their bike colour are asking for trouble. Remember that if your rack-stays break, you could be forced to leave your valuables behind. Other considerations besides strength are the strength of zippers and the number of compartments. The more the better, as gear can be classified into areas for ease of access. Straps at the top for a sleeping mat are convenient as are little pockets at the back where the day's snacks and repair kit can be stored.

The premier Australian brand is undoubtedly Bunyip. Although they aren't available in a wide range of fluorescent colours that imported panniers come in, experience has proven that their nearly unbreakable reputation is well founded. Designed in Australia and manufactured in Tasmania, Bunyip panniers are made from thick waterproof cotton stiffened by high density polythene. The Rear Touring models have two sizeable external pockets to store tool kits, snacks, tubes, gas cookers, etc, and stainless steel rack hooks that fit 8 mm aluminium alloy carriers, and four locking straps and adjustable shockcords that prevent the panniers from jumping off. Large

3M reflective strips ensure safety for night riding. They're adjustable, quickly detachable, portable, and have easy access to a large storage area; just one pannier can hold a sleeping bag and tent in the main compartment! There are various models in different shapes and sizes including a handlebar mounted bag. Colours are either green or black. Distribution is limited and they are only available from large specialist bike stores, or can write to the Bike Warehouse, PO Box 156, Summer Hill, NSW 2130.

An imported New Zealand pannier also deserves mention. Called the Tika Alpaca, it consists of a front and rear pannier system that can be re-assembled into a backpack with a full Tika pack harness and 85 litre capacity for overnight walking. It has 6 separate compartments, a detachable alloy frame, and is manufactured from heavy-duty cordura, weighs 4.5 kilograms, sells for about $500, and is available through Paddy Pallin camping stores. A surprising advantage is that the separate compartments also have their own straps to be used as a day-pack or even as bum bags for short walks to lookouts or rivers. An excellent idea! Even if the front panniers aren't used, they can be still be used to carry luggage by riding on your back. The Alpaca is still largely a first generation product, and reassembly from panniers to backpack takes up to half an hour. Future models will undoubtedly be even more flexible and facilitate ease of transformation.

Before going on any major trip with new panniers, test them first. Put some lead ballast or bricks in them and ride up and down a few gutters. Many NSW fire trails are very rough in places. Rocks and corrugation will cause loosely secured panniers to jump off. If they pass this, spray them down to simulate rain. Check inside for leakage. Remember your clothes and sleeping bag will be in there. If they do leak, and most cheaper ones will, one can spray them with a waterproofing compound. A more reliable method is to simply wrap up your gear in plastic bags. Pack so that the items you need during your trip are on the top.

It needs to be said that there are also disadvantages with panniers: (1) It is more difficult to ford deep rivers, (2) there is more hassle when lowering the bike down cliffs, (3) a fully laden bike becomes quite strenuous to push up steep hills, (4) panniers reduce the room available on bike racks if they are to be transported by car, and (5) front panniers reduce steering manoeuvrability. There are two ways around most of these problems: purchase panniers that are easily detachable so they can be separately carried across rivers or down cliffs. During transit they can be simply stored in the boot. The other way is to use a backpack, as many bushwalkers-turned-cyclists do. Despite what one might think there aren't any major stability problems and you will find that pushing up hills is much easier. Backpacks also have the advantage of better insulating your gear from shocks and river crossings, and you have the option of being able to take your gear down to a campsite by the river where access is often only on foot.

Tyres Choose tyres according to what terrain and climate you will be riding in. For the northern rainforest parks, knobbly tyres are recommended due to soft nature of the soils, and the high annual rainfall. For Kosciusko National Park, there are many long descents due to the mountainous terrain and knobblies such as the popular Panaracer Smokes provide that extra braking power. They are also ideal for sandy trails near the coast. Their multi-faceted knobs give good cornering on loose surfaces, but one loses performance if using them on sealed roads. If the majority of cycling is along tar roads, Avocet Cross K tyres which are a good compromise having some grip and yet being smooth enough to average 10 kph faster than knobblies. They permit sharper banking angles on sealed surfaces and contain an interwoven Kevlar composite shield for puncture resistance. They have a very low hysteresis (measure of memory time) and therefore can rebound very quickly after being compressed or deformed. This results in the Cross having longer life expectancy, and less rolling resistance. For complete off-road usage through the disused trails of the Blue Mountains and Wollemi National Parks, Hutchinson's On the Rocks are perfect. They come with sexy black strong sidewalls or a Kevlar belt and retail for about $45.

Skellerup has introduced a tube that never goes flat! They're simply made of natural rubber: nails, sharp rocks, etc can all penetrate but will have no effect on performance as the tubes are not pressurised. The disadvantages are that they're more difficult to fit as the spokes need to be re-tensioned, and they give a harder ride than normally inflated tubes: about 65–90 psi (448–620 kilopascals). Also, they're not adjustable for different riding conditions, and they weigh substantially more: about 740 grams.

Tyre liners that fit between the tube and the inside of the tyre are also an alternative measure one can employ to improve puncture resistance.

Non-essentials

Mountain bike fashion has progressed to such a point that manufacturers advertise countless gadgets as 'must-haves' such as titanium seat-post quick-release skewers, supposedly giving you the edge over others. As the cliché goes, there's no substitute for fitness.

It must be remembered that these gadgets and 'innovations' in componentry and accessories mostly come from Japanese factories and designed with the American market in mind. Mountain biking in the rough Aussie bush will take its toll on your equipment. Mountain cyclists commonly experience breakages. In fact a good overnight trip is one where you don't need to replace anything. It'll be a few years until Australian cyclists get the toughness of gear that they need to complete extended tours without hauling out the repair kit every few hours.

Air pressure gauge One can accurately measure air pressure to adjust for different riding conditions. In muddy conditions, hot weather, and sand, it would be wise to lower pressure somewhat to maximise traction. Remember that low pressures over rocky terrain will increase the likelihood of punctures. On the other hand, too high a pressure will destroy any feeling of suspension your bike has, and can also lead to punctures caused by sudden impacts. Some air-pumps, such as the Mt Zéfal Graph have an inbuilt pressure gauge supposedly accurate to ± 2 psi.

Bike rack (cars) For transporting your bike to staging areas. Many of the rides described in this book are in national parks out of reach by rail or coach. Good racks are about $100 and accommodate 3 bikes. They are secured to the rack by a plate which fastens on using two winged nuts. However, the gradual introduction of red light cameras and speed cameras have caused police to enforce licence-plate obstruction laws and consequently new racks have entered the market that have provisions to mount the licence-plate on the back. This is not a hassle if the rack is installed permanently but for hatchbacks, utility, and station wagon owners, racks would need to be detachable. This necessitates continually changing the location of your licence-plate. Alternative bike rack designs, such as the Thule 549 can mount your 'treadly' securely on the car roof. This is also a good option for four-wheel drivers who damage their pushbikes along rough trails, but has the disadvantage of susceptibility to overhanging branches. Another alternative is the *Ark* bike carrier that tilts downwards thus allowing hatchbacks, utes, and wagons to open.

Clip-less pedals Competition has developed clipless pedals where the sole of the your mountain bike shoe clicks into a specially designed pedal. There are a number of different systems on the market and one must buy the right shoe compatible with the right pedal. Shimano has developed a system called SPD (Shimano Pedalling Dynamics) specifically for the mountain bike market. It appears that this has become the industry standard in a very short time. The SPD shoes have a recessed cleat to enable you to go walking. Formerly, this was not possible. The SH-M200 shoe ($260) is a good all-round hiking/cycling shoe with Velcro straps and plenty of grip. However, it's not designed for extended bushwalks through mud, water, and over boulders. The double-sided low-profile PD-M737 pedals that goes with the shoe weigh 225 g each and cost about $300. You exit by twisting your heel outwards. Release-tension and entry-position is fully adjustable and, unlike other systems, work well in muddy conditions. For off-road cycling, an easy setting is necessary to ensure quick release when negotiating rough terrain. The novice will find the idea of being locked in uncomfortable on very rough trails, but the experienced can find the system a bonus as one has better control over the positioning of the rear wheel and therefore can manoeuvre it over rocks, logs, etc. The advantage is that it automatically positions the ball of the foot over the centre of the pedal—the optimal riding position.

Computers The Japanese have shrunk everything from cameras to cars, and cycling computers are no exception. Ever since the Cateye Velo CC-1000 set the standard for such features as digital readouts and average speed calculations, the trend has been more features in a smaller unit. Indeed, today's computers, such as the Cateye Vectra, are about half the size of the original, yet retails for about twice as much, $65–70.

Their new model is the Cateye Mity2 (CC-MT200) which comes in five colours so fashion followers can 'co-ordinate' with their frames.

Wheel circumferences can be accurately entered into the computer, taking into account tyre sizes and rider's weight. Regular functions include speed in kilometres or miles, trip distance and time, as well as an odometer, maximum speeds, a clock, and calculation of average speeds.

All are water-resistant, and should work even when the sensor is caked in mud. Battery life expectancy is about two years, the accuracy is astounding, and most can be easily detached when locking the bike up in public. Another advantage is a motivational one: when one has a constant readout about one's average speed, one is more likely to expend extra energy when climbing in order to maintain that figure.

One of the top units on the market at the moment is the Avocet 50 Altimeter. Apart from having the standard functions of speed and distance calculations, it has an in-built barometer that converts air pressure into altitude readouts. Even when ascending small hills, the readout updates altitude changes every second. Furthermore it records accumulated height gained over a longer trip and can even be useful for predicting weather. For example if one has set up camp and the readout is steadily increasing, air pressure is falling, indicating a possible front approaching. It automatically compensates for temperature differentials and wind doesn't affect its accuracy. Another advantage is that it's easily detachable and still operates in your pocket when walking. This can aid in navigational queries as one can reconcile one's altitude with topographical information on maps as to locate your position.

New models come with cadence readout and even heart rate monitor! Who knows what the future will hold? Thermometer? Compass? Mobile phone? Satellite navigation?

Gel seats All the rage during the early 1990s. One of the most common problems that mountain cyclists experience is a tender backside from the constant shifting in the saddle. The Avocet Gelflex saddle, manufactured with spenco gel, distributes vertical and lateral pressure more evenly over the contact area and, unlike other gel saddles, it doesn't lose its elasticity during the colder temperatures that a cyclist can experience in higher altitudes. Weight is kept to a minimum by varying the thickness of the gel in critical pressure points, and the nylon/

lycra cover moves with the gel so that its hydrostatic properties are not diminished. There are various models on the market comprising of various thicknesses and shapes catering for everyone from the casual weekend recreationalist to the professional competitor. The cost varies from $48 to about $80.

Other types of seats have also found their places on the market: leather, air, split. The material comprising the rails for attaching to the seat-post is also quite varied and can dramatically affect the price. Cro-Mo, aluminium, and titanium rails exist for mountain cyclists with anorexic bikes.

Lights Cycling in the bush at night, while cooler, is a little dangerous. If it's a necessity, lights will be more of a hindrance because you will be travelling too slowly for a dynamo to work effectively and it is better to let your eyes adjust to available light. An alternative are batteries, but these are, of course, expensive. Models such as the Cateye Halogen are relatively efficient. But for the specialised mountain bike market, OK Electrical has released a set of Soubitez 6 volt, 9 watt, 2.1 amp halogen lamp and battery set. Rechargeable batteries give 4–5 hours performance, up 1200 times. Cycling on roads at night has been revolutionised by the LED flashing tail light, enhancing one's visibility to drivers.

Lock While in the national parks of New South Wales, you will almost definitely have to leave your bike behind as some attractions can only be visited on foot. Since the Australian bush is vast, an infinite number of hiding places exist where the bike can be stashed for a few hours or a few days. Obviously locks are unnecessary here as the most likely thing to stumble across your bike is a kangaroo. However, if passing through a township in order to resupply or in the more popular tourist areas, it would be advisable to carry a lock; it looks as if mountain bikes will be popular for a little while longer!

A U-Lock or thick chain is most effective. For example the Rhode Gear Gorilla ATB lock is specially designed for mountain bikes being longer so that it can encompass the wider tyres. It's made of hi-tensile molychrome, has a ball-bearing behind the lock that prevents drilling, and over 700 000 combinations ensures excellent security.

Another design is the rear-wheel lock used in China that fits permanently on to the bike preventing a quick ride-away theft. However, there is a small possibility of the lock snapping shut when the bike is in motion.

Lastly, those small plastic covered four-digit combination locks on sale in supermarkets are useless and can be easily pulled apart by stepping on one end and pulling. Owners of bikes with quick release wheels are at a disadvantage and would have to disassemble the bike every time they wanted to leave it.

Mudguards Usually more of a hindrance than anything else as they can get in the way of brakes and pannier tie-downs, not to mention clogging up with mud. In any case, tri-compartment rear panniers act as pretty good mudguards.

Pannier racks The premium brand that all are based on is Blackburn. For strength and lightweight design, their alloy carriers racks are unbeatable.

Suspension forks The introduction of polyurethane elastopolymer shock absorbers on the market have raised queries about their weight and ability to perform when climbing as energy is wasted compressing the shocks as much as 4–5 cm. However along rough flat roads, kinetic energy expended perpendicular to the road surface is minimised with shock absorbers and forward momentum is maintained. In this respect, shock absorbers save energy that would normally be wasted in hitting a small obstacle such as a rock. Because the wheel moves up and over the obstacle, there is less resistance and therefore less energy loss. Magnesium shock absorbers are all the rage in the 1990s and their adjustability and low weight have made them quite attractive to top end users. Their price is still fairly hefty although it is possible to now purchase a mountain bike fitted with front shocks for under $600. Reputable shock absorber name brands include Rock Shox, Manitous, and Marzocchi. One of the best value for money shocks is the popular SR Duotracks. The tubes and lugs are built from aluminium and contain elastomer dampers. They weigh 1.4 kg and cost about $350, but unfortunately are non-adjustable. Their big advantage is their forward angle, meaning that they start absorbing the shock before the wheel has passed over the bump.

One suspension fork to get especially good reviews was locally designed and manufactured by Victorian Edwin Sachan. Called the Edsan forks, they are machined out of solid blocks of alloy. They have a maximum of 6 cm of travel, and are adjustable by the use of different combinations of elastomer bumpers. Retail price is about $600, considerably cheaper than comparable imported models.

Dual suspension frame designs are also finding their way on top end performance bikes. One of the classic designs is the Diamond Back Racing Dual Response aluminium frame that was built by Italian motorbike manufacturers, Verlicchi. It features a pivoting Posi-trac rear arm, the only link between the frame and the rear wheel. The radical shape totally eliminates lateral flexing of traditional rear suspension designs. But several thousand dollars for the frame alone is too high a price for most people. The price is the one shock they can't absorb.

Toe-straps These increase cycling efficiency as one can pull through the zero-torque point (when the pedals are in 6 o'clock position) as well as push down. They are a bit of a hassle to enter and have to be manually tightened to optimise efficiency. Furthermore they can prevent a quick escape during an accident as one needs more than a split-second to release if they are tight. Despite these drawbacks, they are making their way down the range of mountain bikes.

Clothing

Helmets Most cyclists rarely fall hard, and if they do, reflexes ensure the head is protected. But it is those lower-end statistics, those could-have-been-saved cases which makes the helmet an almost essential item. The space-helmet look is no longer necessary with new energy-dispersing impact-absorbing materials such as expanded polystyrene (EPS). It works by crushing on impact, and therefore has to be just the right density in order to reduce a 400+ G shock to under 200. If the foam is too soft, it will compress too easily, while being too hard will also damage the head during a fall or collision. Despite the controversial nature of the legislation (first introduced in Victoria in 1990) of mandatory helmet use, cycling deaths *are* down from a peak of 104 in 1983 to just 41 in the 1993 year. About a fifth of these deaths are recorded in NSW each year. Cycling organisations, protesting about being made to wear helmets, claim that better road conditions and specific bicycle path construction is the best way to lower yearly death tolls. They also point out that deaths are down because fewer cyclists are riding, and the 1990–93 recession has pushed down car use also, making it safer to cycle.

Bell are the largest manufacturer of helmets and consequently can sink a lot of time and money in research and development such as wind-tunnel testing. Their Image II weighs in at only 255 g and has a microshell bonded to the energy absorbing liner to protect it from everyday handling abuse. It sells for around $85. Other models include the Spectrum, Quest, Cruzer, and Cyclone.

Always try on the helmet before you pay for it. Remember that any small discomfort will be multiplied many times on a long ride. Also make sure it has maximum ventilation so as to minimise sweating. Heat dissipation for the skull is of utmost importance when trying to maintain one's cadence.

An important point to note is the use of soft foam adjustable fitting pads. The Traffic Accident Research Unit in NSW has found that the thicker these pads, the more pronounced is a bouncing effect which gives an additional shock to the brain. Furthermore they can result in the helmet becoming dislodged. A helmet therefore works at optimal efficiency when there is a maximum amount of surface area of the inner shell of the helmet in contact with the skull. It is important that these foam pads be kept to a minimum quantity and thickness, and where possible to match the shape of the helmet to the shape of the skull *directly* and not by the use of foam.

Multi-density helmets, such as the *Adura* LT850, have been ranked first by American university studies for deceleration effectiveness. These helmets have two densities of expanded polystyrene—a hard exterior and thick soft inner portion. The design disperses the impact around and across the surface of the inner shell to help eliminate shattering. Over the outer portion is a microshell which protects the helmet from normal handling bumps.

Legislation has made it compulsory for cyclists in New South Wales to wear an Australian Standards (No. 2063.2) Approved bicycle helmet.

Pants One can enjoy the Australian country perfectly well without spending unnecessarily on cycling pants. The advantages are that they absorb perspiration and offer some protection from grazing during a fall. I have found that a pair of ordinary corduroy beach shorts have proved themselves indestructible. Remember that if walking is on the schedule, cycling tights will be lacerated by the bush, especially if any rock scrambling is involved. For colder months, there now exists a range of thermal tights involving new hi-tech water and wind proof fabrics such as CoolMax, Supplex, Gortex, and SuperRoubiax.

Shirt Special cycling shirts allow greater perspiration evaporation but for the recreational mountain biker, any T-shirt will do. Cotton is particularly unsuitable for cycling purposes as it absorbs and retains water.

Shoes Normal sandshoes or sneakers are perfect. If some lengthy or difficult walking is involved, a good pair of walking boots will be needed. If no walking is in store, shoes are the least important of all items for hopefully your feet will never touch the ground!

Recently mountain bike shoes have been marketed which are made of materials such as carbon, nylon, and glass fibre that are supposed to be 'the most efficient tool ever designed for transferring energy from the foot to the drive chain'. Stiff soles and recessed cleats are definitely an improvement for specialised mountain biking shoes used in conjunction with SPD pedals (see previous section on clip-less pedals). However rock walking can be dangerous as often the metal cleat is the only part of the shoe in contact with an uneven hard surface. This means no grip on rock climbing and descending and the constant slipping will rapidly wear down the metal causing entry and exit problems. In short, the wilder the terrain expected to be encountered the less useful clip-less pedals and mountain biking shoes will be.

Gloves Cyclists in Kosciusko National Park, even during summer, can experience freezing temperatures. Any gloves from home are adequate if cold weather and/or strong wind is expected. You might also need a pair of gloves if your handlegrips cause blisters or chafing. They can also protect your hands from grazing during a fall. Special mountain biking gloves from Adura contain a 3 mm layer of neoprene for shock absorption and cost around $35. The disadvantage is that during hot weather your palms can become quite sweaty.

Glasses Not really necessary for the recreationalist, but if your eyes water during high speeds, in winds, or during hazy, glary days, cycling glasses definitely will be more comfortable. Make sure they are shatter-proof, scratch-resistant, reduce glare, block out all UV light as well, in order to improve contrast and reduce the risk of cancer. Some of the newer mountain bike glasses come with a lycra band for retention and

47

perspiration absorption. Like the glasses that the cricketers wear, they're expensive: expect to pay anything up to $300. The other disadvantage is that bumps, holes, and sand-patches in shadows on the trail will be more difficult to pick up.

Wet-weather gear Here prices can range from as little as $5 for a poncho (great for those brief thunderstorms) to Gortex Thermal Ski-Jackets (for settled-in rain and cold) for $700. Gortex has a well respected reputation in Australia for being waterproof, windproof, and ventilated. This is achieved by a semi-permeable microporous membrane that lets condensation and perspiration evaporate out through the fabric but prevents moisture from entering.

Whatever you choose, make sure that it doesn't impede your knees so you can ride with it on and that it has pockets for maps, food, etc. Good value lightweight foul-weather gear includes the Peter Storm 123 Cyclists Overtrouser, which has greater ventilation than Gortex without sacrificing waterproofing. Furthermore it is approximately a third of the price of Gortex.

MAINTENANCE

A new bike fresh from the shop is always going to function well, even if it's a supermarket special with caliper brakes. However, after the cables stretch, the brakes loosen, the gear-springs weaken, and the spokes re-tension, the bike will never be the same. This is why maintenance is an essential ingredient to cycling. Even if it's top of the range Suntour Microdrive XC Pro or Shimano XTR, the componentry will still break down. The Australian bush is too tough.

Maintenance is not about keeping the bike as you bought it. It's about slowing the rate of equipment failure. Despite what many sales staff, cyclists, owners' handbooks, and maintenance guides tell you, it is impossible to restore a bike to its shop condition after a few rides. Perhaps in the future, manufacturers will design bikes that don't need cables or spokes or pad-based brakes. One can only hope.

At home

Whether it is pumping up the tyres or reconstructing the rear
wheel, some degree of technical knowledge will be called for.
There are many books available which cover this subject, the
definitive one being Van der Plas' *Mountain Bike Maintenance*.
However, books like this, can quickly become useless, not only
due to rapidly changing technology, but to the wide range of
systems and group sets on the market. Shimano alone has over
a dozen componentry sets on the market, and there are several
other manufacturers. What is required are comprehensive
maintenance manuals that come specifically with your bike
when you purchase it.

Before embarking on any ride in the bush, one can quickly
carry out the following four-point check:

1. *Tyres*   Ensure the tube is fully inflated: usually
around 50–70 psi (276–344 kilopascals).
For slicks, this can be as high as 85 psi (586
kilopascals).

2. *Brakes*   The bike should be impossible to move
forwards or backwards when both brakes
are applied. Remember that if you're travelling over 30 kph, you need at least 10 m
to stop. In dirt roads or wet weather or
steep downhills, minimum braking distances are significantly higher.

3. *Chain*   Lubricate if dry.

4. *Wheels*   Tighten if there's lateral movement in the
rims.

If planning a major ride of several days duration it would be
wise to overhaul the bike by:

1. Regreasing all bearings. A lithium-based grease
will provide good protection—do not use oil).

2. Lubricating all cables and moving parts such as the
flywheel and dérailleur pivot points with a graph-
ite-in-solution lubricant. Specific ATB oils, such as
Finish Line are based on Teflon, trilinium, and paraffin that not only reduces friction but gives rust
protection, improves water resistance, and does not
attract grime.

3. Check for even spoke tension.

4. Check for wear in the chain wheels and shifting mechanism.
5. Tighten all nuts and bolts.
6. Replace brake blocks if worn.

A bike specialist would also do the above for you, but it is better that you do it yourself in order to familiarise yourself with the componentry.

In the bush

Punctures Locate small holes by filling tube with air and immersing in water. If there is no water, rotate the inflated tube next to your ear. Clean area around hole and rub with sandpaper to ensure adhesiveness of the patch. Wait 3–4 minutes to dry before replacing.

Always take a spare tube along in case the puncture is too big for a patch or is too close to the valve.

As a last resort, grass and normal bracken ferns can be stuffed inside the tyre. But they must be replaced every few kilometres for heat and friction quickly displaces any moisture in the plant and all that is left is brown dust. Shift weight off the wheel that has no tube.

If the tyre is slashed as well, cutting a small square off a foam sleeping mat and pressing it between the inner tyre wall and the tube will usually alleviate the problem until the nearest bike store is reached.

Both Specialised and Hutchinson have produced tubes which contain a built-in sealant that self-repairs small punctures.

Squeaking brakes This is probably due to a dirty or wet rim or worn pads. Now you've got a horn!

Weak brakes Worry. At best, it is just due to a wet rim, or some oil that has dripped down from the cluster. Wiping the rim and block and braking hard a number of times will remove the problem. At worst it could be due to bent braze-ons. If it's the rear brake, one could probably get away with it until the next bike store. But one should *NEVER* ride in the mountains without a properly functioning front brake.

Slipping chain This occurs when the rear dérailleur is out of adjustment usually because the bike was leaning against a tree with the gear assembly pressing against the trunk. Simply adjusting the 'high' and 'low' screws in the adjustment mechanism with a Philips screwdriver will bring the chain back into line with the gears. At worst, the slipping could be due to a worn chain, or even a worn freewheel sprocket. These would need replacing. Simply remain in low gear until civilisation is reached and avoid riding up hills.

Steering out of alignment Either you ride like a maniac or head-set bearings are loose. These can be tightened by means of a large shifter. If you don't have one, hand tighten as secure as possible and take it very easy. New headset technology from Suntour and Diacomp considerably reduces the likelihood of this happening.

Broken spoke Things are starting to get serious. Replacing a broken spoke, especially in the rear wheel, is about the equivalent of a human by-pass operation. On most bikes, specialised tools are needed. And even with these, the operation takes about half an hour for the entire hub assembly has to be taken out piece by piece, including the bearings. The new spoke then has to be inserted and tightened. Then the whole wheel needs re-adjusting so it spins without wobble.

The band-aid solution if you don't have the tools is to simply twist off the broken spoke, take as much weight off the wheel as possible by moving luggage forward or backward or giving it to your companion. Coast to the nearest bike store.

But spokes in the rear wheel might soon be outdated with the recent development of carbon/kevlar wheels that give greater suspension, durability, energy efficiency, and less wind resistance. The Tioga Disc Drive is manufactured from thermoplastic, alloy mesh, and kevlar cord arranged in a geodesic pattern of angular and tangential cords forming a continuous tensioned linkage between hub and rim. They are, however, unsuitable for the front wheel due to the possibility of a strong cross-wind making steering difficult. But some spokeless wheels have blades that actually produce lift in a cross-wind! The Tioga Disc Drive is still fantasy for many bike owners who baulk at the $1200+ price.

Bent links If some of your chain's links have become twisted, it is not as bad as it looks. A small chain-breaker or chain-removing tool and some spare links will rectify the problem easily.

Uneven pedalling A loose crankcase is usually the cause of this problem. It can be easily tightened with a shifter. If it happened just after an accident, suspect a bent chainwheel or pedal axle.

Rack stay broken Normally caused by people overloading their panniers and riding as fast as possible over branches, rocks and ledges. Usually only one of the stays would have been broken. This one can be fastened up to the bottom of the seat by some strong string. Transfer as much weight as possible from the pannier to the other end of the bike, your back, or a friend. This remedy will also solve a broken seatpost attachment, usually the weakest link between the rack and the frame.

At home again

Whether you've spent an hour or a month in the bush, it will be dirty; either from dust or mud. Usually both. Hose it down straight away and spray all moving parts with some form of WD spray to protect against rust. This is doubly important for cyclists living near the coast. Don't believe the people who tell you it is cool to have it covered in grime—unless you can afford disposable mountain bikes.

Long term

An annual service with an authorised dealer will ensure everything is tightened, greased, and oiled. They should also be able to touch up scratched paint-work. Many components, such as dérailleurs, freewheels, rapidfire gears, and the crank-case require specialised tools such as torque meters.

RIDING TECHNIQUES

The final part in this chapter will try to relate a few handy tips that can improve cycling efficiency and enjoyment. It's better to learn it the right way first, so that in a short time, the new skills will become a matter of habit. A lot of books deal exclusively with this subject—many however give useless tips like 'ride within your limits' and 'watch out for headwinds' and 'shave your legs because it gives you a 0.2% aerodynamic advantage'.

Accordingly this section will be kept to a minimum. Suffice it to say the most important technique is exercise. The fit poor cyclist on the beaten-up single geared BMX will *always* beat the unfit rich $7000 custom titanium dual-suspension bike owner.

After selecting the right bike and adjusting the handlebars and seat height for your comfort, you should be eager to try it out. People *converting* to mountain bikes from touring or racing bikes will immediately notice that greater effort is necessary to achieve high speeds. The reason is in the thicker tyres and the less crouched seating position. The higher gears will also be lower ratios, while gear levers will be positioned on top of the straight handlebars. Those accustomed to lifting their bike up stairs will also find a few extra kilos of metal separate a mountain bike from a touring bike.

Cycling in our rugged mountains is different to all other forms of cycling. New skills are required, and concentration is directed away from long distance 'rhythm' cycling to focusing on avoiding obstacles: with continual steering, braking, and gearing changes as the cyclist negotiates his way through rough, winding, and undulating fire trails, across streams, under overhanging branches, and down narrow cliff passes.

CLIMBING With the exception of the Blue Mountains, staging areas in NSW national parks are usually low. The Barrington Tops and Deua National Parks are good examples of cycling areas over 1 km higher than the surrounding land. Therefore a lot, and I might even add, the *majority* of the time will be spent climbing, and climbing, and climbing … You will indeed wonder if Australia is really the flattest continent on Earth.

Three methods of climbing exist: walking, spinning, and honking.

Walking (also known as first-gear) Trek's slogan 'Ain't no mountain you can't climb' is a lie. Many uphills just can't be conquered on a bike, no matter how many cogs you have. But even pushing a bike uphill can be faster than normal bush-walking due to the fact that you can rest your upper body on the handlebars. Experiment with different techniques: push in short bursts and rests, or one slower consistent uphill trudge. The break-even point where cycling has no energy efficiency advantage over walking is about a 1 in 5 slope. Any steeper, and walking is metabolically more productive. Another reason why climbing is so difficult relates to your blood. At about 85% of your maximum heart rate (220 minus your age), your body reaches 'the aerobic/anaerobic transition zone'—the lungs are unable to supply a sufficient amount of oxygen to the bloodstream. This means that your body switches over to glycogen to substitute for the deficient oxygen. As a by-product, lactic acid builds up in your muscles. This accumulation quickly reaches a saturation limit within 10 minutes preventing you from cycling any further. As you get fitter however, the transition zone into the anaerobic state moves closer to your maximum heart rate, preventing the need for lactic acid build-up, and you are therefore able to sustain longer periods by high-energy output.

Spinning Choose a very low gear and stay seated the entire length of the slope. Your seat has to be positioned quite high. Concentrate on maintaining your cadence (the number of pedal rotations per minute). If the rear wheel starts to spin in the dirt or mud, get up and lean back to put more pressure on it so traction increases. Although walking seems like the easier alternative, cycling up a gradual slope actually requires *less* effort but is more tiring as your muscles are required to emit much more energy per unit of time. This is the preferred method for the experts.

Honking This method is used for steeper shorter slopes and a higher gear is selected while standing up and leaning forward. But perhaps the most efficient way is a combination of honking and spinning for the variation temporarily relieves certain muscles. However, there is no substitute for fitness.

A handy water bottle is almost essential for cooling down. Expending just 74 watts of energy, a cyclist can maintain an average speed of 22 kph on level ground and the 22 kph head-wind will ensure adequate heat dissipation. But on a 1:6 slope, only 2.4 kph can be maintained at the same 74 watt power output, resulting in at least a doubling of energy used to remain stable. However heat dissipation without a regular drink will prevent this level of output from being maintained.

Attitude is also important. Think positively about the hill: it will be another obstacle out of the way, you will feel good about conquering it, you are nearer to your destination, there will be a good view on top, and best of all, there'll be a downhill on the other side!

DESCENDING As always in life, the fun things are the most dangerous. Physics defines force as proportional to the square of the bicycle's velocity. This implies that there will be a point where braking resistance is insufficient to stop a fully laden bike on a steep slope if the rider allows it to accelerate too much. Always try to use constant pressure on the rear brake *alone* to slow you down. If it is not enough, lean back to put more pressure on the rear tyre. If you still accelerate, apply the front brake gradually. Never speed up and then suddenly jam on the brakes at the last minute because you might fall further than you expect: six feet further.

When at the top of a steep, long descent, stop and quickly check your brakes and anything else that might be loose. Once you get going, you don't want to stop until you hit the bottom!

Jumping Imagine you are flying down a fantastic trail, the trees a blur, adrenaline surging through your veins. Suddenly you round a corner and there's a fallen tree lying right across the track. There's not enough time to brake, so the only alternative is to harmlessly pass over the log. How? By jumping. Begin a jump by waiting until your strongest leg is at the top. Then suddenly lean back on the handlebars, lifting the front wheel off the ground, while simultaneously pushing down the pedal. With some practice you should be able to hold a 'wheelie' for about 2–3 seconds. When you've mastered this, lift the front wheel again while standing on the pedals and throw your weight forward while raising your legs. This motion, called a bunny-hop, should raise the rear wheel off the ground for a split-second. By co-ordinating the wheelie and the bunnyhop, one should be able to clear small objects with practice. Don't worry too much if you can't actually get the rear wheel airborne; the reduced pressure off the ground will be sufficient to tackle the majority of obstacles such as sharp rocks and small branches. Bunny-hopping, of course, can *not* be done with a bike that has excessive luggage attached and descents must therefore be more controlled.

Rocks and ledges The technique when negotiating descents down platforms, ledges, and large rocks is quite simple: *lean back!* This has two effects. Firstly, it stops the bike from flipping over when the front wheel drops down to the next level, and secondly it increases your braking on the rear wheel.

Falling Instinct is to release your hands to protect your fall but statistics reveal that this often leads to a sprained or broken wrist, and so experts advise to keep one's hands on the bars, thus protecting your arms. Difficult to practise this one.

GENERAL Watch out for traffic the other way. Blind corners, especially when descending fast are just as dangerous for cyclists as for cars. Be aware that the trail you are riding on could be open to four wheel drivers, walkers, cyclists, equestrians coming the other way.

Cornering Avoid excessive leaning in on turns when the ground is loose. Rather take the corner slowly and drift from inside to outside.

Sand and mud If approaching a sandy patch in the road ahead, accelerate and coast straight through it if it can't be skirted. Avoid steering, gear, and acceleration changes when actually in sand as they can all result in a loss of momentum. If a lot of sand is to expected, deflate the tyres by 10 psi. The best condition for sand traversing is rainy weather. Wet sand is much easier to ride across—the same principle when choosing the best section on the beach to jog or cycle on.

The same negotiation techniques apply to mud. Don't worry too much about getting mud off during a ride. Most of it will come off by itself. The rest can be left as decoration until you reach public transport or a stream. Avoid skidding in soft wet ground as erosion is greatly accelerated. These bogs can just as likely occur on plateau tops as by rivers.

Fording Check to make sure there are no large river rocks across the ford when crossing streams. Don't ride too slowly as loss of momentum could be embarrassing in a strong current. Also watch out for exposed concrete mesh on fords. When riding in a group, cross large streams one at a time. If the stream is a strong one from overnight rain and debris is being washed down, it is better to walk the bike across. As a rule of thumb, any fast flowing water above 40 cm (especially if the bottom is uncertain) is potentially unsafe to ride across.

Headwinds When cycling in open country, nothing can be more frustrating than a headwind. You have the latest hi-tech lightweight bike, have trained for years, and a headwind can make you feel like a first-timer on a steel BMX with rusted hubs. Murphy's law of cycling dictates that there will always be a headwind, no matter which direction, how fast, or when you cycle. The simplest solution is make it go away.

CODE OF BEHAVIOUR (AND THE FUTURE OF MOUNTAIN BIKING)

Here in Australia, we cyclists have to be on our best behaviour in order to minimise any future hostilities and zoning of national parks. Already authorities have prevented the use of walking trails as cycling routes due to the conflict of use and fragile nature of the trails. Horse-riders have already suffered abuse for their activity here in Australia, as have four-wheel drivers and trail-bikers. Policies should address problems on specific tracks, and not be general blanket bans on cycling.

Visitor Use Surveys Often at camping grounds, the National Parks and Wildlife Service of New South Wales have placed questionnaires called 'Visitor Use Surveys' in canisters. These are an important way of letting the authorities know that mountain cyclists exist. They ask questions like your age group, frequency of visits, your origin, mode of transport, destination, numbers in your party, accommodation, walking intentions, and suggestions of management ideas. These questionnaires often have an opinion section as well asking you what you feel about the number of people at the place, camping restrictions, vehicle access, damage assessment, facilities, ranger presence, etc. Please take some time to fill these out, taking special care to mention that you did cycle there.

Code of behaviour In order not to get classified together with motorised transport in any future National Parks Management Policy, some sort of code of ethics should be adopted by commercial tour operators as well as private mountain bikers. The International Mountain Bicycling Association has adopted some simple guidelines based on United States experience:

1. Ride on Open Trails Only
2. Leave no trace
3. Ride under control
4. Always yield to others
5. Never spook animals
6. Plan ahead

Here's what the Department of Conservation and Environment in Victoria have established as a mountain bike code of behaviour:

1. *SELF-SUFFICIENCY*	Carry first-aid kit and tool set.
2. *GROUP SIZE*	Less than four in a party is considered unsafe, while ten or more will often lead to rapid track degradation and conflict with other users.
3. *CONTROL*	Always ride so you can stop in time for unexpected reasons. Keep your bike well maintained.
4. *UTILITARIAN RIGHTS*	Respect the rights of other users such as walkers and equestrians. Due to the silent nature of the bicycle, both walkers and horses easily get a shock when a cyclist flies past from behind. Always announce your presence. To avoid spooking horses, dismount when passing them and allow them wide berth.
5. *WEED PREVENTION*	Bicycle tyres have been proven to be a cause of the spread of exotic weeds and plant disease by seeds becoming trapped in the tread and dislodging later. Therefore, cleaning your bike regularly not only makes sense for your bike but also for the environment.
6. *OBEYING SIGNS*	Some tracks, while perfectly possible to cycle on, are closed to all cyclists because they are being rehabilitated. All throughout Australia, gazetted wilderness areas involve the suppression of information on closed

58

trails, revegetation, and the implementation of barriers, penalties and patrols. While the main perpetrators are four-wheel drivers, mountain biking is not a recreation recognised as being reconcilable with official wilderness areas. Likewise all walking tracks are out of bounds to bicycles due to the rapid damage to the trail and the conflict of use with walkers. If you must use a walking track, walk the bike.

Also be aware of the other regulations in regard to total fire bans, camping permits, fees, fuel stove only areas, and rubbish removal. Leave all gates as found.

7. *SENSIBLE RIDING*
Don't cut corners as this breaks up the soft soil on the road shoulders so that the next rain can easily wash it away leading to erosion. Likewise skidding is an effective way to accelerate track degradation especially if the ground is wet. However, the authorities recommend that you travel *through* mud rather than widen the track by going around large puddles.

Many of these actions will seem restrictive, unnecessary, or over-cautious. However, experience has shown even here in Australia that mountain bikes are already being excluded from large areas of the national parks system. The most controversial cases are twenty-two gazetted wilderness areas in Victoria: the Alps, the Grampians (Gariwerd National Park) and on Wilsons Promontory. Bans were placed when wilderness areas were gazetted throughout the early 1990s, much to the distress of Victorian mountain bikers. In South Australia, the legislation has limited cycling only to public access roads. In other words, where it is o.k. to drive, it's o.k. to ride. The attitude is that cyclists are being classified with high impact users such as trail-bikers and four-wheel drivers, rather than low impact users such as bushwalkers. Even in NSW, on the last section of the summit road to Mount Kosciusko and in some areas of the Blue Mountains and northern volcanic parks, cycling is prohibited. Cyclists all have to be especially careful of their actions in order to keep the great national parks open to them. All state cycling organisations agree that there should be no cycling on walking tracks. Facilities at the start of walking tracks to chain-up bikes would encourage cyclists to leave their bikes behind when walking.

At time of writing the State government is debating the boundary lines of 11 wilderness areas totalling 350 000 acres in New South Wales as well determining access rights for user groups. These are:
* Lost World (near the Border Ranges)
* Binghi (the far north)
* Washpool National Park
* Guy Fawkes River
* Macleay Gorges (Oxley Wild Rivers National Park)
* Bindery/Mann (North Coast)
* Kanangra Boyd (south-western Blue Mountains)
* Yalwal (northern Morton National Park)
* Deua National Park (upper Shoalhaven and Deua Rivers)
* Goodradigbee (far south)
* Nadgee Nature Reserve (near Eden)

THE MAN FROM YARRA RIVER

There was movement at the station, for the word has passed around
That the mountain race was on that very day,
It was worth a thousand dollars—no bigger prize was found,
And the crack riders had gathered to the fray.
There was Harrison, riding on his gleaming Cannondale,
A bike which had forty gears or so;
Few could ride beside him, for surely this bike couldn't fail
He would go wherever bike and man could go.

And Clancy of the Override was down to try his hand
No better rider held the handle bars;

For never bike could throw him while the cold steel chain
   would stand
He learnt to ride by challenging street cars.
And one was there, a loner on a small, battered bike
It was something like a dragster undersized,
With balding back tyre, no toe-clips, faulty brakes and the like
Such as by mountain bikers much despised.

They laughed at him and one said 'That bike will never do
For this ride you will not keep the pace
This country is too rugged and those hills too rough for you.'
And they all agreed he couldn't join the race.
So he undid his helmet and began to walk away
Until Clancy spoke up on his part
'No, no, let him come, he'll be with us all of the day
For this man has a mountain biker's heart.

He hails from Yarra River, down by sunny Melbourne's side,
Where the hills are twice as steep and twice as rough
His bike may be buggered but he's got rider's pride
This man from Yarra River is good enough.'
So off they set a-riding, on towards the mountain's brow
Going lazily along in low cog
Only Harrison called out, 'boys do not slacken now
Soon enough we'll face the hard slog'

Clancy took the lead of course, with Harrison on his wing
Where the best and boldest riders take their place
And one brought up the rear although he made his bike bell
   ring
The man from Yarra River just kept pace
Upward, ever upward, the helmeted pack strove to find
A path where no path had been before
It was tough, dangerous riding, for the trail was nowhere kind
They knew not what the crest held in store.

When they reached the summit, even Clancy pulled his brake
It well might make the boldest hold their breath
The drop was sheer, the rocks severe, there was no path to take
A fall would mean almost certain death.
Harrison declared aloud he could not risk his bike
He said it was too shiny new

'Lads, this is madness, a case of life and limb or the like.
I cannot risk it—neither can you.'

But the man from Yarra River pedalled past the pack
He rang his bell and gave a mighty cheer
And he raced down the mountain like a torrent down its bed
While the others stood and watched in very fear.
He skidded and bounced but the frame refused to bend
Nor the wheels to buckle 'neath his weight
He sent the flint stones flying in a mad dash to the end
How grand to see a biker tempting fate.

Now in bike shops round this nation and in pubs and cafes too
The tale of his daring is held dear
How he rode where none could go, on a bike which would not
   do
Tis the reason his face flogs every-bloody-thing
From roll-on deodorants, superannuation, and beer
His legend has grown and been embellished on the way
The gap 'tween truth and fiction has got wide
The man from Yarra River is a household name today
And the bikers tell the story of his ride

> *John Amy & Chris Darwin*
> *Australian Adventure Guide*
> *(With apologies to Banjo Paterson)*

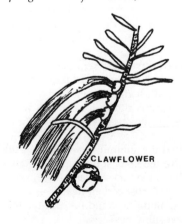

CLAWFLOWER

2
The Bush

An Introduction

NSW offers an amazing variety of environments to cycle in: from the sandstone plateaus of the Blue Mountains to the world heritage rainforests of the north, from the alpine ranges of Kosciusko National Park, to the spectacular state forests on the slopes of the Barrington Tops, from one of dozens of large coastal parks, to the gorges and canyons of rugged Wollemi.

Cycling is a fantastic way to see these places. You have the advantage of not being sealed off in the cabin of the car, and yet you can still see vastly more than the walker during the same time. It's not as tiring as walking, yet one still gets very fit. While the walker is limited to little more than a fly and a groundsheet for accommodation and freeze-dried powder for food, the cyclist can roll into the campsite, set up his waterproof tent, and start cooking dinner: French onion soup, spaghetti bolognaise, and tropical vegetable salad served with a sparkling rosé, followed by some canned pears for dessert. He can then proceed to take some photographs of the surrounds with his 35 mm camera outfit complete with collapsible tripod and zoom lens, then decide whether to proceed with the journey the next day, or just read a book by the stream ...

CAMPING EQUIPMENT

After some preliminary day rides around your area or in the nearest national park you might like to try camping overnight. The times immediate before, during, and after sunset really give the bush an atmosphere unparalleled anywhere in the world. The gum tree's silver leaves glow a brilliant red, the wind stops, and the only sound audible is the crackling of logs in the campfire.

As with bike equipment, only the *essential* gear can be purchased at first for camping, with the cyclist updating his inventory once experience and ambition take hold.

Sleeping bag Cyclists have the advantage that they're not restricted to expensive small lightweight models, but can choose more according to comfort and warmth rather than size and weight. Prices start at around $100 for synthetic Thermofill, Hollofil, Lite Loft, polyester Puradown models that weigh close to 2 kg. These are good for all summer camping in relatively warm climates such as by the coast. Slightly upmarket are synthetic Quallofil bags that are relatively warmer than down even when wet. The disadvantage is that they're bulky. Expect to pay around $135–229.

However, it is difficult to go past a fill that is comprised mainly of duck or goose down. Coming mostly from China, down is by far the best insulator due to its air-trapping qualities. Furthermore, down bags are light (1–2 kg) and can compress to incredibly small sizes. The damage? From $249–799 depending on the amount and ratio of the fill. The up-market models have waterproof Gortex exteriors but unless you plan to cycle Antarctica or camp underwater, they're not necessary.

Australia's leading camping equipment suppliers, Paddy Pallin, have a complete range of down sleeping bags that are treated with 3M Scotchguard which enables the down to resist the effects of condensation and moisture in general. A light and breathable fabric called Pertex is used to further protect the down from moisture that can seep up through the tent floor. Paddy Pallin rate their bags on a scale of 2–6, with 2–3 being for mild climates, and 4–6 designed for multi-season, extreme latitudes, and high altitude use. For alpine conditions, a Grade 4 Gingera with 700 g of down gives effective warmth for its low weight (1.40 kg). It's compactability makes it perfect for the mountain cyclist with luggage and weight constraints. Its price is about $500. The ultimate sleeping bag for all conditions is Paddy Pallin's Jagungal (Grade 5). It has 900 g of down, with a total weight of 1.65 kg and costs around $560. The ratio of down is 95% fine down, and 5% small feathers, thus giving the bag optimal lofting characteristics. Other features included wrap-around contoured adjustable mummy hoods, velcro-Posilock close of the top zipper to prevent the bag opening when in use, independent adjustment of neck and hood, and reverse zipper models giving one the potential to create a double bag.

Accessories also exist for sleeping bags; Paddy Pallin sell large storage bags as down should not be compressed when

A one day touring configuration: dual suspension, and easily accessible bidons

An overnight configuration: panniers, front suspension, kevlar tyres

Some assorted accessories for mountain biking

The Tika Alpaca backpack can be disassembled and transformed into a front & rear pannier system

not in use, silk and cotton inner sheets for extra warmth, Gortex outer lining, and sleeping mats.

Tent A simple fly will do perfectly to keep the dew off on clear nights by the coast in summer. However when venturing into uncertain territory such as the Budawangs, Kosciusko, or New England tablelands which are notorious for unpredictable appalling weather, a sealed tent is highly recommended.

Price depends on the material, design, name brand, and size. If cycling in a group, the weight of the tent can be shared. Water-resistance can be improved by the application of a seam-sealant and the use of a group sheet, preferably a space blanket.

Eureka manufacture Australia's most popular tents. A variety of styles and sizes are available that range from 1-person bivvy style tents to models designed for use in snow-expeditions. The *Bike and Hike* design, featured in the photos in this book, weighs under 2 kg, has a floor area of about 3.5 square metres, and a frame of shock-corded 7000 series aircraft aluminium which compacts to a small enough size of fit easily inside any pannier, and a design that reduces buffeting if pitched with its longitudinal axis aligned with prevailing winds. The cost is approximately $260, is fast to erect, sleeps 2 with room for small packs, and comes with a fly that can be zipped open on mild nights. Two entrances ensure cross-ventilation. Compactability ensures that it can be taken to the longest cycling and walking expeditions. Eureka's other cycling/walking models for Australian conditions include the Moonshadow and the one-person Gossamer. For cyclists venturing into rugged high altitude terrain on extended excursions, the Expedition Caddis offers superb protection with ease of erection. It is a comfortably 180 cm wide with two vestibules and allows you to pitch it with or without the fly. The Expedition Caddis weighs in at 3.5 kg and costs about $450. For northern coastal summer conditions, Eureka manufacture a Tropical Screen which is basically a tent fly made from fly-screen supported by a fibreglass frame.

Recent tent designs have taken advantage of new light-weight materials and technology. The classic new age tent is the self-supporting dome. Gone are days of carrying heavy steel frames, canvas, plastic ground floors, pegs, ropes, etc. No more drilling in through hard surfaces and tripping over ropes. The self-supporting dome tent needs no pegs and no ropes! It also has many other advantages: it's lightweight, has an excellent space-to-weight ratio, good headroom, stability, ease and speed of erection, the ability to pitch on rock, as well as the fact that once set up, it can be simply picked up and placed elsewhere. The only disadvantage with these self-supporting tents is that they can be blown away when no one is lying in them so it's always a good idea to throw in your sleeping gear immediately. Multi-pitch tents allow you the flexibility of setting up the fly first in the event of bad weather, or to set up the main tent first and have the fly on stand-by if it does get wet.

The tunnel-style tent (sometimes cross-bred with the dome forming a 'dunnel') is also popular, incorporating vestibules (an area between the tent wall and the fly), and is very light and suitable for exposed high-altitude conditions. These are what the 'experts' use, and indeed some models are priced as high as $800.

Sleeping mat Foam closed cell sleeping rolls are unbeatable for their price. Supermarkets sell them for about $15, although some models can cost up to $65. However for cold conditions such as can exist in the Alps, the ground will drain heat away during the night because the sleeping bag filler directly underneath you will be compressed. Proper insulation can be provided only with self-inflating foam mattresses that are smaller than their closed-cell counterparts, but about five times the price. They provide a cushion of air that shields the body from the ground. The disadvantage (beside their cost) is that they can puncture. There are various manufacturers of these now on the market, but Therma-a-rest has the strongest reputation. Their models (varying in size and material) cost from approximately $89 to $110, while cheaper brands come as low as $60. All are available at Paddy Pallin.

The traditional lilo air mattress is far too heavy and bulky for extended cycle touring, but of course has the advantage of being far cheaper ($10–30) and one can explore lakes and rivers and even go surfing with it!

Ground sheet The common space blanket can be bought at disposable stores everywhere and are by far the most popular groundsheet. Uses include: a floor when using a fly so sleeping bags don't get dirty; an extra floor when using a tent to help prevent heat escaping and water leaking in; a picnic blanket for meals where cooking utensils and food can be spread out, and an emergency blanket for victims of hypothermia and heat exhaustion. With the silver side out, the blanket will reflect some 70% of external radiation keeping the body cool. The dark side is placed outside in the event of hypothermia so all external radiation is absorbed, and internal radiation is reflected back.

Pack towels A very useful multi-purpose 68 cm × 25 cm cloth made from 100% Viscose that can hold up to ten times its weight in water. This water can be 92% wrung out by hand and the remainder quickly air dries. Weighing just 42 g, it's the ideal towel for the bushwalker and cyclist. Use it to dry yourself, as insulation for hot pots, cleaning the dishes, neckerchief for sweat absorption, compress, and so forth. These have proven extremely popular and are available in the *Australian Geographic* shops as well as camping stores.

Backpack As mentioned before, when luggage is stored in back packs as opposed to a pannier, you have the advantage of easier up hill pushing, easier lifting of the bike, extra storage space, and the option of overnight walks. There are many quality brand names on the market. When choosing, make sure there is plenty of padding on the lower back so that when adopting the forward cycling position, the harness is not digging into your spine. Although external compartment packs are becoming out of fashion, most good packs now have several internal compartments for dividing up your gear. The Burghaus range have detachable compartments that become day packs and bum-bags.

Your pack should be waterproof, and accommodate enough equipment for at least a four day walk away from the bike. The combination of a 65–80 litre pack and rear panniers should allow you the greatest flexibility in cycling and walking so that one can explore the furthest corners of NSW.

The New Zealand made Tika Taranaki has a fully adjustable comfortable 'Expedition' harness system and five compartments. It weighs under 2 kg, has 80 litre capacity, and costs about $350 (available from Paddy Pallin).

General camping equipment

The following is a checklist of equipment (both necessary and unnecessary) that one may need in the bush. It is by no means comprehensive, and individuals may want to add or delete items according to taste. It is wise to draw up a list so you don't forget anything in the last minute packing rush. What could be worse than realising after a long day's ride that you've forgotten the can-opener?

Cooking	Hygiene	Miscellaneous	Bike
Billy	Toothbrush/paste	Lighter/matches	Spare tubes
Frying pan	Soap (natural)	Candle	Puncture repair
Pots/saucepan	Toilet paper	Maps	Tools
Plate	Insect repellent	Pocket knife	Computer
Cutlery	First aid kit	Sleeping bag	Oil, grease
Small fuel stove and fuel	Tissues	Sleeping mat	Spare chain links
Can opener	Trowel	Tent and/or fly	Spare spokes
Scouring pad	Clothes (warm)		Water bottle
Cup	Water		

Despite the long list, the above shouldn't weigh more than 12–15 kg. Add another 1 kg of food per day and one is looking at about 20 kg of luggage for a week's trip. While this may seem a lot, properly packed panniers, saddle bags, and a back-pack can carry up to 40 kg of supplies!

For those owners of racing and conventional touring bikes who are switching to mountain biking, you will most likely already have panniers and a rack and these of course can be easily and costlessly transferred to your new bike. Allocate your luggage in the ratio of 2:3 with the majority of gear at the back for maximum stability. As previously stated, the optimal system for many mountain bikers is to have no front panniers or front rack at all—one simply carries any excess on one's back.

FOOD

The following is a list of calorie, carbohydrate, and protein content per 100 g or 100 ml of common food types:

Type	Calories (k)	Carbo-hydrates (g)	Protein (g)
White rice	103	23	2
Beef steak	396	0	26
Chicken	150	0	30
Baked beans	110	21	6
Mushrooms	165	4	3
Potatoes	77	18	?
Apples	55	13	0.4
Cheese	400	0.5	26
Corn flakes	363	79	8
Eggs (2)	150	1	11
Red wine	95	0.5	0.3

The freeze-dried food from New Zealand that is commonly found in camping stores is popular for long wilderness expeditions. It is extremely expensive, and despite being reasonable quality, is not of adequate quantity. For each meal additional food has to be prepared, especially after a long tiring day cycling. Cans and fresh fruit/vegies are recommended but should be consumed as fast as possible in the first few days to save weight. For lunches and cold snacks, dried fruit and nut mixes give long-lasting nourishment. A quick top-up can be supplied by confectionery.

Drink For drinks, a little sweetener such as a barley sugar in a drink bottle will flavour water. However, mountain streams are quite often so fresh and pure, that their taste is entirely different from home tap water, and no sweetener is needed. A problem with sweeteners in drink bottles is that heat will breed fungus in the sugar residue after the first day.

Recently a trend in isotonic sports drinks has arisen and there are now quite a few to choose from. They are similar to soft drinks but are not carbonated and contain certain fluid and energy replenishing nutrients such as electrolytes, sodium, chloride, potassium, and phosphorus, as well as the usual sucrose and glucose. Brand names include Lucozade, Gatorade, Powerade, Isosport, and Sport Plus Still. Some even come in powder or tablet form and are recommended for drinking before, during, and after strenuous exercise. The drinks themselves come in unbreakable plastic 500 ml containers, perfect for throwing in the panniers or even the bidons. These can be insulated by the use of a wet sock. Sports scientists tell us that it is good to consume such drinks no more than 45 minutes before the ride. As you are cycling, top up every 15–20 minutes, consuming about a litre an hour on a hot day. The advice is not to drink when you are thirsty, as by that stage you're already dehydrated and fatigue starts to set in.

Around the campfire one might like to take a bottle of red wine, port, mead, or flask of Drambuie to 'help with sleep'. However, it must be added that, despite popular belief that a couple of nips warms you up, alcohol ultimately makes one more susceptible to cold.

When camping at lookouts and ridgetops, obviously large supplies of water must be taken, not only for drinking, but for cooking and washing. There is no better container than empty plastic soft drink bottles. They come in a range of sizes and are recyclable, disposable, resealable, flexible, lightweight, cheap, and clear.

MAPS

The Lands Information Centre the state government's official supplier of maps, have their main outlet located at:

    Map Centre
    Department of Lands
    33 Bridge Street, Sydney 2000
    Phone (02) 228 6111
    Fax (02) 221 5980

The LIC's headquarters and postal map ordering department is located at Bathurst:

Map Sales Counter
Land Information Centre
PO Box 143
Bathurst NSW 2795
Phone (063) 32 8245 or (063) 32 8246
Fax: (063) 31 8095

The NSW LIC have agencies all over the state where specific maps can be purchased; for example camping stores, disposal stores, service stations, visitors centres, rangers headquarters, and information kiosks in the national parks themselves. The standard map that covers NSW from the coast to the Great Dividing Range is the 1:25 000 topographical. This is the most useful to the cyclist and walker, being detailed with contour intervals of 10 and sometimes 20 metres. For the majority of rides in this book, these detailed topographical maps are essential. Some rides are in extremely remote areas, such as the Wollemi National Park. For these expeditions and with most of the walks that are detailed in this guide, it is imperative that one knows how to interpret these maps. Relying on route notes can lead to frustration especially in forestry areas where new trails are being forged all the time and old ones rehabilitated, signs get taken down and tracks get renamed, upgraded, downgraded, closed or re-routed. In these circumstances, close-scaled topographical maps will show you the best way to get to where you want to go.

A scale of 1:25 000 means that 8 cm on the map equals 2 km in reality. For many areas, however, this detailed scale is not yet available and cyclists will have to make do with the 1:50 000 series or even the 1:100 000 NATMAP series. This calls for expertise and experience in navigation and self-sufficiency.

Despite being rather old (most were surveyed in the 1970s), the coverage is just about complete. This feat is something other states have yet to achieve. At present, the NSW LIC is working on producing a digital database of maps whereby new information can be updated immediately and user needs can be met more specifically. Towards 2000 we will hopefully see new updated editions of the state's topographical coverage.

Besides their topographical coverage, the LIC has also released two series of Tourist Maps, with emphasis on national parks and their environs. Called the Red and Green Series, they are of a larger scale, often 1:100 000, and depict four-wheel drive tracks, camping areas, picnic facilities, lookouts, watercourses, etc. At present these maps are available:

GREEN SERIES	RED SERIES
Barrington Tops and Gloucester Districts Including Chichester, Barrington Tops, Avon River, Stewarts Brook, Mount Royal, Masseys Creek, Bowman, Copeland Tops, and Coneac State Forests	Albury/Wadogona Armidale & Districts Including New England, Oxley Wild Rivers, Guy Fawkes River National Park, Serpentine Nature Reserve, Styx River, Hyland, Nulla Five Day, Oakes, Clouds Creek, Ellis, Marengo,
Kosciusko National Park Ku-Ring-Gai Chase National Park Royal/Heathcote National Parks Wollemi National Park Including Newnes, Lidsdale, Hampton, Nullo Mountain, Coricudgy, Putty, Comleroy, and Kandos State Forests, Goulburn River National Park, Dharug National Park, Marramarra National Park, Cattai State	Thumb Creek, Mistake, Lower Creek, and Pee, Dee State Forests Bateman's Bay/Ulladulla Bathurst/Orange Bega/Eden Blue Mountains Including Kanangra Boyd National Park Thirlemere Lakes National Park Nattai National Park Lake Burragorang Bents Basin State Recreation Area Norton Basin reserve Jenolan, Vulcan,

72

GREEN SERIES	RED SERIES
Recreation Area,	Gurnang State
Patoney Crown	Forests
Nature Reserve,	Broken Hill/Menindee
Blue Mountains	Lakes
National Park	Central Coast
(northern area)	Coffs Harbour
Warrumbungle National	Dubbo/Wellington
Park	Grafton
	Hunter Valley
	Inverell/Glen Innes
	Kempsey
	Lightning Ridge
	Lismore
	Mudgee
	Murrumbidgee Irrigation
	Area
	Port Macquarie
	Port Stephens
	Taree/Wingham
	Tweed/Byron
	Wagga Wagga

There is also a Waterways series (Light Blue) containing detailed coverage of Myall Lakes, the Hawkesbury River, the Snowy Mountains lakes, Central Inland Lakes, and Sydney Harbour.

Other producers of maps include the Forestry Commission of NSW. They have produced a series of state forestry maps. Although they aren't topographical, they show watercourses, reserves, roads, four-wheel drive tracks, picnic facilities, and camping areas. The coverage is confined to the following areas:

Tenterfield	Walcha	Nowra
Casino	Port Macquarie	Bateman's Bay
Glen Innes	Barrington Tops	Eden
Coffs Harbour	Bulahdelah	Tumut
Pilliga	Newcastle	Central Murray Valley
Kempsey	Bathurst	NSW Map

NATMAP have produced a complete 1:100 000 topographical coverage. There are about 270 of these that cover the whole state. Contour intervals are 20 m. However many of these maps are more than 10 years old are quite inadequate for areas such as state forests where new logging trails are being created all the time. Their price is around $7 each and can be ordered through AUSLIG Sales, PO Box 2, Belconnen ACT 2616.

Other types of maps include historical sketch-maps that are still useful today. They were drawn up by bushwalking pioneers such as Myles Dunphy in the Blue Mountains and the Budawang Committee members in the Morton National Park. These are available through larger camping stores such as Paddy Pallin. There is no topographical information but the maps show negotiable routes: rough walking tracks showing passes through cliffs, on ridge-tops, and camping spots by rivers in wild area.

For access to National Parks, the NRMA have state wide coverage of road maps. They augment this by including Tourist Maps of specific areas, for example, the Blue Mountains, the Southern Highlands, and Coffs Harbour. Some fire trails are included. The LIC also has a Dark Blue Series of eleven broad scaled regional maps giving an overview of a particular area: New England tablelands and adjoining coast, the Outback, Murray Riverina, Snowy Mountains and Canberra, the South Coast, the Hunter, the Golden West (centred on Dubbo), and Lord Howe Island.

A Word about this Guide's Maps

The regional maps that appear in this guide are only to give cyclists an idea of where the rides are located. The decision not to include detailed maps arises out of lack of space. For a walking book, full detailed mapping is possible as the average day walk is only about 15 km, therefore making it possible to fit the entire length on to one page. But for mountain cycling, one needs almost the same level of detail but average day trips can be up 50 km needing several maps. For a 100-ride book, with many tours being extended overnight rides, I would have needed to produce about 400 maps, resulting in an 800 page book!

Planning your own rides

The best method for planning a route is to purchase the maps that cover the area you want to cycle and work out a route along the fire-trails (or vehicular tracks as they're represented on the map's legend) that go the most scenic way to where you intend to visit. The distance of the trail can be measured in centimetres with a piece of string. Simply divide the length of the string by four to obtain the distance of the journey in kilometres. One can also purchase a simple mechanical gadget called a 'map meter' that you roll along your intended route and it'll tell you the horizontal distance. They're available at most camping stores. Either way, one would then simply add on 20–30% to account for altitudinal fluctuations and to be conservative.

The average cycling speed on moderately hilly country on dirt is about 7–10 kph, so try not to plan day-trips longer than about 50 km unless you are very fit or the terrain is predominantly downhill, especially if you are laden with panniers. This will leave plenty of time for rest breaks, sightseeing, walking, and unexpected delays. Ridge and plateau riding is the fastest as a good momentum can be maintained both ways. Cyclists travelling for many days will find that their fitness increases over the duration of the excursion and distances on the last day can be more easily accomplished than on the first day. Having less to carry also helps. Very rough tracks, great uphills, and navigational errors will reduce cyclists' average in mountainous country to that of walking or sometimes even slower.

The best and simplest tip one can follow is to *leave early*— 6–7 a.m. If everything goes according to plan, then you arrive at your destination early. If things don't, you've still got time up your sleeve to deal with problems. One of the main problems with mountain bike touring is running out of daylight hours.

Learn to recognise features on the map using contour lines (lines that joins all places of equal height). This will allow you to check your progress. Orthodox navigation skills involving conversion of bearings and resection are totally unnecessary. One simply has to familiarise oneself with how contour lines represent the landscape. After the first few times in the bush, you should be able to recognise simple and common features on the map: mountains, valleys, ridgelines, saddles, cliffs, etc. Cycling computers also enable you to monitor your progress, giving confirmation as to where you are. When calibrated correctly, they are amazingly accurate.

FIRST AID

The most likely cause of injury faced by the cyclist is a fall. A simple medical kit with disinfectant and bandages is adequate for most types of grazing. For minor scrapes, bumps, and small grazes it will be perfectly all right to continue in accordance with the initial plan.

However for any major loss of blood there will be a loss of stamina, shock, and a risk of infection. At this point the planned route will have to be altered to the easiest and quickest way back to civilisation. Infection can also be caused by serious cases of saddle soreness where the combination of chafing and perspiration cause cracks in the skin where bacteria can enter.

First aid kits can be obtained from camping stores, the Red Cross and chemists. One can do worse than the Thursday Island Tea Tree First Aid Kit containing many substances based on the famous all-purpose tea-tree oil. Medical kits can also be home-made from individual items purchased from a pharmacy or supermarket (this is the cheaper and sometimes better approach). For cycling, the following is recommended:

Sterilised bandages (about 15 m)
Aspirin
Large gauze dressings (non-adhesive)
Small scissors
Disinfectant/antiseptic powder
Cotton wool
Plaster adhesive tape
Tea tree oil

Grazes

The aim here is to minimise loss of blood and risk of infection. Clean wound with water. Make sure there aren't any pieces of gravel caught in the open area. Then simply cover with some antiseptic powder or tea tree oil, apply a large gauze dressing and bandage. Treat shock by giving warm liquids and resting the patient. If it is late in the day, and statistics confirm that risk of an accident increases dramatically with time spent on the bike, start looking for a campsite nearby so the injured can rest overnight.

Bites

If bitten by a fully grown taipan in the neck two days' ride from the nearest telephone, there is little one can do. However the majority of bites are treatable and the accepted procedure is surprisingly simple to learn (the old days of cutting the wound, sucking out poison, and tourniquets are over):

1. Apply pressure on the wound.
2. At the same time, starting from the top of the limb (shoulder or thigh) bandage tightly and steadily downwards. Several bandages might be needed.
3. Keep the limb *lower* than the heart.
4. Immobilise the limb by splinting it to a straight branch.
5. Treat for shock: tell victim that it wasn't a poisonous snake, or that most of the venom went outside the wound, etc. If one acts calm and collected, chances are the patient's heartbeat will start to fall. This will limit the spread of the venom to the central nervous system. Treat spider and scorpion bites much the same way. Keeping the bite area cold helps deaden the pain.

Heat exhaustion

Symptoms are a loss of blood in the facial area causing it to turn white. The skin will be wet and cold. If there is a salt deficiency, cramps will also be a symptom. Rest in the shade is the best treatment, followed by drinking water with a touch of salt in it. If there is no shade, for example, if you have been travelling on treeless plateau tops, set up a fly or groundsheet over some bushes. Make sure there is adequate ventilation.

Hypothermia

Travelling through Kosciusko in winter without adequate clothing is perhaps the best way to get hypothermia. The cure is to get out of the wind, replace your wet clothes with dry ones, and put something in between the ground and you, use a space blanket to reflect internal heat and eat plenty of food. Drink *no* alcohol as it only makes you colder. It will be a time to become closer to your companions—literally. Shared body warmth can cure all symptoms of hypothermia, but body reserves will still have to be built up after normal body temperature is reached.

PHOTOGRAPHY

Cycle touring allows increased storage and weight capacity, enabling one to carry a good camera outfit. Photographing the Australian bush can be rewarding due to the outstanding variety of landscape and the availability of direct sunlight.

Camera A 35 mm camera is recommended that has manual settings so that one can compensate for measuring inaccuracies of the light meter. Fog, high contrast, direct sunlight, position of subject, and long shadows can all lead to incorrect exposure evaluations. Furthermore, a manual mode gives the photographer more control over his pictures with respect to waterfalls and other time exposure shots.

Tripod In addition to a camera, one needs a tripod. Rainforest canopies, narrow valleys, flowing rivers shots, and waterfalls all require time exposures of anything up to 30 seconds. A tripod should naturally be lightweight and compactable. There are numerous models that cater directly for the outdoor trekker. Tripods are also an advantage to the solo adventurer to enable self-portraits. If there is no space for a tripod, you may be lucky and have a forked tree or well-placed boulder to set up the camera on.

Lenses Ideally a standard lens, a macro, and a telephoto will give optimal results as the number of glass elements in the lens is kept to a minimum, thereby allowing maximum resolution. But a cost-benefit analysis dictates that a good zoom lens will do the job of all three and still give more than adequate definition. All the photographs in my guidebooks were taken on a 28–200 mm (f3.5–f22) zoom lens.

Filters Polarising filters are generally unnecessary as they reduce the amount of light entering the camera by up to 2 stops and they become less useful when there is diffused light. Windy, fresh conditions ensure a minimum of haze over landscapes, so most of time a skylight (UV) filter is also unnecessary. The Blue Mountains however, with its covering of eucalypt trees can get extremely hazy on hot calm days. Consequently, a polarising filter will help to make features more defined.

Film Although the quality gap between negative and slide film is narrowing, transparency (reversal, slide, or positive) films still produce the best results in terms of colour saturation and resolution. Australia's topography is a photographer's paradise and the use of a low-ASA rated film gives it the best justification. An award-winning high resolution 17-layer emulsion film from Fuji called Velvia 50ASA enhances greens superbly in both direct and indirect light as well as giving very fine detail.

The disadvantages with slide films are that they're usually more expensive, the results are more difficult to view, and there is limited scope for corrections in processing. Exposures have to be spot-on, whereas with negative film, one can make alterations up to two stops.

Tips Good results are the product of three factors: skill, equipment, environment.

- For most types of photography, direct sunlight will give better colour and contrast.
- Early morning and evening are best times to photograph. This is because the lower angle of the sun's rays through the atmosphere removes blue light giving a warmer shift.
- Prevailing misty conditions are good for mood shots: calm lakes, trunks of beech trees, dew droplets on spider webs, moss, etc.

- Avoid using a flash as this washes out colours. Cave formations are best captured using a tripod and a long exposure using the installed coloured lights. Back-lit shawls and curtains especially come out well using this technique.
- For landscapes, include a foreground where possible—whether it be a person, boulder, or shrub. This gives the picture depth of field, highlighting distance.
- Avoid having the horizon passing through the middle of the frame. Make a habit of angling the camera slightly down, so the horizon is only a short distance from the top of the frame. The only exceptions would be in unusual cases where cloud formations are particularly dramatic.
- When using a polarising filter, photograph as much 'with' the sun as possible, although good polarising effects also occur when shooting at 90 degrees to the sun.
- For shots of cyclists fording water crossings, choose a fast exposure and follow the cyclist into the water while taking the shot. This will blur the background thereby enhancing the sensation of speed.
- For shots of cyclists/walkers at lookouts, choose a smaller aperture so that there is more depth of field, i.e. both the foreground and background will be in focus. This implies longer exposure speeds, forcing the subjects to remain as still as possible.
- Rivers, seascapes, cascades, and waterfalls can have the classic softened effect by slowing the exposure to as much as 10 seconds. However, too long an exposure will start to produce a blue-shift without the suitable correction filter.

Not all that looks good to the eye will look good on film. Only experience will improve your judgement of what will make a good photograph. Comparing results to records of exposure settings will also improve the accuracy of your compensation adjustments so that a smaller percentage of film is wasted.

CAMPING

The National Parks and Wildlife Service policy on camping is decentralised. Naturally rules and regulations depend on the specifics of an area. In some parks, for example the Blue

Mountains and Ku-ring-gai Chase, fees will apply at certain areas, and restrictions on aspects such as fireplaces and length of stay are enforced. These campgrounds require advance booking especially during school holidays. Other places, such as Wollemi and Budawang National Park, use is limited and one can camp where one wants.

Like cycling, there is a code of behaviour for walking/camping. Much of it is common sense. Studies into the effects of camping have concluded that the following practices should be adhered to:

- Washing your dishes and your body should be done at least 50 m from streams as soap, detergents, and food scraps are all harmful to aquatic life. Bio-degradable organic soaps are preferable to commercial chemical-based varieties.

- Human waste should be well buried at least 100 m from streams with the use of a trowel (15 cm deep). This reduces the incidence of gastroenteritis (diarrhoea and vomiting) caused by exposed faecal matter. 'Gastro' and 'giardia' (human bacterial parasite) exist in watercourses contaminated by faecal waste. The sicknesses are quite common in popular camping sites in the USA and New Zealand, and have recently spread to Australia. The most prone areas are in alpine regions. The symptoms include severe diarrhoea and vomiting that can last a month. Always use pit toilets if they're provided. Some camping stores now import heavy duty sealable bags for actually carrying out your waste—drastic measures for particularly sensitive areas.

- Camp at low impact sites at least 30 m away from watercourses. Sand and hard surfaces are better than wet, soft, boggy, vegetated areas. Choose existing campsites rather than making your own. This can be achieved by proper planning.

- The use of modern tents is encouraged. Pitched properly they are mostly waterproof and don't require the digging of perimeter trenches. They come with fibreglass or aluminium frames so saplings do not need to be cut down for poles, and foam/inflatable mats make obsolete the traditional practice of cutting fern fronds for bedding.

- Carry rubbish out with you. Remove the ends off tins and flatten. Buried rubbish can be dug up by animals.

- Where fires are allowed, use existing fire places, do not encircle them with rocks, use only fallen dead wood, don't use it as a rubbish tip, and extinguish it completely when leaving. There is a year-round fuel-stove only area for camping above the tree-line in Kosciusko National Park (1700 m). This means strictly no campfires. In remote places such as isolated river valleys, leave some kindling for the next party.

- Keep group sizes to a minimum (4–8).
- Spread out in open untracked country, rather than walking single file, so the impact on vegetation is minimised. A plant trampled on once has more of a chance of surviving. Keep on rocks where possible.
- Wear lightweight walking boots or soft sandshoes rather than heavy-duty GPs.
- Choose a different route each time you visit a trackless area, and camp at different sites whenever possible.

The above code of minimal impact bushwalking and camping is supported by the national parks administrative bodies of New South Wales, the Australian Capital Territory, Victoria, and Tasmania.

GREY
SPIDER
GREVILLEA

3
The State

An Introduction

No other state packs the variety of New South Wales. Australia's most populous state has an astonishing range of geographical environments within its borders. Surrounded by water to the east and three states in other directions, New South Wales occupies about 10% of Australia's land mass. Mount Warning, near the Queensland border, is the first point on the mainland to receive sunlight each morning for the cooler months. The volcanic peak is surrounded by lush rainforest parks that have all been declared as world heritage for their age and diversity of species. The Great Dividing Range parallels the coast to its southern border with Victoria. Here at Cape Howe, the summer sun first shines on mainland Australia. About one-third of the state's coast is protected in reserves, comprising coastal ranges, sand dunes, beaches, peninsulas, lakes, and estuaries. The majority of the state's population lies in the narrow corridor between the coast and the Great Dividing Range. These mountains contain virtually all the state's major national parks. But even within this environment exists enormous variety: the gently sloping ancient Kosciusko snow highlands with Australia's highest mountain, the rugged valleys of Deua and Wadbilliga regions, the spectacular Budawang escarpment, the sandstone mesa formations and cliff-lined gorges of the Blue Mountains, the maze of steep canyons and ravines of Wollemi, the lofty alpine plateau of the Barrington Tops, and the wet forests of the New England tableland.

To the west lies the wheat belt and the volcanic parks of the Warrumbungles and Mount Kaputar, islands of dramatic geological features. Beyond is the desert. Australia's oldest world heritage area is located near Broken Hill, the Kinchega National Parks with its dry lakes containing some impressive anthropological sites. Underground, New South Wales boasts some of the most extensive cave systems in Australia, while off-shore Lord Howe Island is one of the country's true idyllic paradise get-aways.

In addition there are Aboriginal, historical, and cultural attractions. Native cave paintings, pioneering monuments, and colonial buildings are all evidence of the land's rich past. The struggle to tame it is the cornerstone of Australia's conservation history. New South Wales has the second oldest national park in Australia. The Royal, in Sydney's south, was declared in 1879, only seven years after Yellowstone in the USA, and was the first reserve to be officially called 'national park'. Furthermore, the state's percentage of preserved land is the highest on the mainland.

What often surprises overseas visitors is that one can travel from the state's capital in any direction on land, and one will soon come to a national park. Indeed, a satellite view of Sydney confirms this. Surrounded by the blue ocean on one side and the Blue Mountains on the other, the Hawkesbury lined river parks and the Royal National Park to the south, Sydney's four million residents are provided with more recreation space than just about any other city in the world. This can be a problem too, as the great bushfires of January 1994 demonstrated.

The capital of mountain-biking is undoubtedly the Blue Mountains, fifty kilometres west from Sydney. A terrific freeway and railway line provides direct access to the central plateau of the mountains, allowing cyclists to set off north or south for their rides. Because of their extreme vastness, the Blue Mountains allows novices to the sport to undertake short one day rides around the small towns of the Blue Mountains, while experienced adventurers can embark on epic two week tours down the spine of the mountains, camping at lakes, rivers, caving resorts, and old ghost mining towns!

In all, New South Wales offers the owner of a mountain bike the opportunity for limitless exploration of spectacular scenery. The climate is largely mild, the access to staging areas is generally good, and accommodation exists to suit every taste.

CLIMATE

Sydney's climate, being close to the coast, is generally mild. Temperatures rarely exceed 30°C in summer with average maximums being about 27°C. In winter average minimum is about 13°C during the two coldest months, July and August. Rainfall is distributed fairly evenly throughout the year, with the first half receiving slightly more: about 100 mm a month. Rainfall on the coast increases as one moves north and south from Sydney. The proximity of coastal ranges causes moist air from the sea to mix with colder air pushed into higher altitudes. This causes condensation resulting in fog and usually settled in rain. As a consequence of these meteorological conditions and geographical environments, the far north of the state, the area around Lismore and Murwillumbah, receives the most rain. The south coast as well is notorious for its likelihood of long periods of precipitation. This is made evident by the distinctly greener countryside than the central to mid-north coast.

The upper Blue Mountains, centred on Wentworth Falls also receive a lot of rain, but in summer months conditions on the plateau tops can get extremely hot, and cycling should be avoided on these days. Generally anything west of the Great Divide is a safe bet for a holiday due to prevailing dry conditions. To the south, Kosciusko can get freak blizzard conditions in summer and even snow falls at times through the hottest months of December and January, so cyclists should be prepared for all conditions.

TRANSPORT

Mascot airport at Sydney is the main gateway for international and national visitors to New South Wales. Daily train services run from Brisbane, Adelaide, and Melbourne to Central Station at the edge of the central business district, as do coaches. In the latter half of the decade, the Very Fast Train (VFT) linking Sydney and Melbourne will allow Victorians to make the 1000 km trip to Sydney within a few hours, permitting long weekend cycling tours around Sydney, if it is ever constructed.

WITHIN NEW SOUTH WALES

(1) Sydney The metropolitan State Rail Authority *CityRail* network services most areas of Sydney. The main lines are Hornsby, Epping, Carlingford, Hornsby, Eastern Suburbs (Bondi Junction), Sutherland, Cronulla, Campbelltown, Bankstown, Richmond, and Emu Plains. Bikes can be taken on trains at the cost of a child's ticket. During off-peak rates (out of business hours in week days), the price is quite cheap. There are about 2000 services daily.

(2) Country In the late 1980s, there was an unfortunate trend by the state government to close many of the inter-city railway services. The shift to coaches has frustrated cyclists, and even now lobbying continues for the re-instatement of country lines. There are some 1700 kilometres of track. The main *CityRail* and *CountryLink* lines that extend to or past the electrification limits are:

> Blue Mountains Line (Lithgow is the terminal station)
>> No reservations needed until Lithgow
>> Rail continues to Bathurst, Dubbo, and Broken Hill
>> Bus services to Mudgee
> Newcastle line (Dungog, Scone)
> Wollongong line (Bomaderry—Nowra is the terminal station)
> Goulburn line (Campbelltown, Mittagong, Moss Vale)
>> No reservations needed until Goulburn
>> Bus services to Thirlmere and Hilltop

Extended services include Armidale, Dubbo, Canberra, Cooma, and the far North Coast. For information concerning *CityRail* fares and services, phone (02) 13 1500. For information concerning *CountryLink* fares, services, times, and reservations, phone Central Terminal on (02) 217 8812 or (008) 028 384. Cyclists who use the silver double-storied electrified trains such as the hourly Blue Mountains service to Lithgow should note which side their bikes are stored in the vestibules. With all stations until Lapstone, the platforms are on the outside (left) as you travel towards Lithgow. From Glenbrook on, the platforms are in the middle (right) and the bikes will have to shifted to the other side so other passengers may enter and exit the carriage. Some carriages have empty guards quarters which are an ideal storage place for your bikes.

Occasional *CityRail* and *CountryLink* services involve buses. As in Victoria, there is no set policy on this and the transport of bikes will be up to the driver's discretion, depending on passengers and luggage room.

The use of *CountryLink* rail to access remote places can be a little frustrating for cyclists. One must pre-send their bike using the State Rail Authority's *Trackfast* system. Bikes are no longer able to be carried with you as part of luggage. It is preferable that the bike is packed. This is for two reasons: (1) it helps protect your bike against damage, and (2) it's a lot cheaper. An unpacked bike costs a flat rate of $60 regardless of distance, whereas a packed bike gets charged according to mass, and averages between $15 and $20 for medium distances. For packing, State Rail requires the bike to be partly dissembled in a flat cardboard box: pedals removed, handlebars turned sideways, tyres deflated, etc. When bikes are presented in the correct fashion, State Rail will accept some responsibility for damage if the bike is insured. The value must be declared when you send off your bike at a *Trackfast* depot. You are advised to do this about one week before you plan to start your ride as the State Rail Authority (SRA) do not guarantee delivery.

ACCOMMODATION

Camping by tents

The New South Wales National Parks and Wildlife Service manages several dozen official camping grounds throughout the state. These can have little or no facilities, or be quite well developed with kiosks, toilets, showers, power, water, firewood, tables, bins, and fireplaces. Camping fees sometimes apply and a ranger usually checks up on this with an early-morning wake-up call, as we discovered. For the more popular areas bookings are essential as they can be packed out, especially in holiday seasons.

In addition there is an almost infinite amount of 'bush camping' available (divided into preferred and dispersed sites) where you find any suitable natural clearing, so long as it's not immediately adjacent to a watercourse or lake. You are unlikely to find these sites occupied and therefore can enjoy the wilderness atmosphere. Wild camping areas involve a higher degree of responsibility—one must keep observe the correct fire management procedures, bury human waste, and take all garbage with you. Some of the higher graded rides in this book feature these natural bush settings and complete self-sufficiency is integral to this mode of camping. Many hard-core campers prefer this mode of accommodation. Self-supporting tents or flies are 'in' for the environmentally conscious. Old methods of perimeter trench digging and fern cutting are definitely 'out'. See the section on **Walking** in the previous chapter for currently acceptable camping practices.

Camping by Youth Hostel
One of the most popular forms of accommodation for cyclists is the Youth Hostels Association (YHA) network, especially for those touring from overseas. There are over 30 such hostels in New South Wales, with the headquarters being in Sydney:

Youth Hostels Association of New South Wales
422 Kent Street
GPO Box 5276
Sydney NSW 2001
Phone (02) 261 1111
Fax (02) 261 1969

There are also regional offices at Newcastle and Canberra.

The YHA began before World War II in Victoria and is now one of the largest accommodation networks in Australia with over 140 hostels distributed among the country's most scenic spots. Worldwide, Youth Hostels are found at 5300 places in sixty countries. The membership fee is $40 initially, then another $24 to renew each year.

LOCATION	PHONE	BEDS	BIKE HIRE	AREA ACCESSED
Armidale	(067) 72-6470	40	Yes	New England National Park Cathedral Rock National Park Dorrigo National Park Oxley Wild River National Park

LOCATION	PHONE	BEDS	BIKE HIRE	AREA ACCESSED
Ballina	(066) 86 6737	27	Yes	Guy Fawkes River National Park Styx River State Forest Coastal and rainforest national parks of the far north-east Including Bundjalung, Nightcap Mount Warning, and the Border Ranges National Parks
Bega	(064) 92 3103	18	Yes	Mimosa Rocks National Park Wadbilliga National Park
Blue Mountains (Katoomba)	(047) 82 1416	76	Yes	Upper Blue Mountains Kanangra Walls, Jenolan Caves Megalong Valley, Wollemi National Park
Blue Mountains (North Springwood)	(047) 54 3046	16	Yes	Lower Blue Mountains South-east Wollemi National Park
Broken Hill	(080) 88 2086	76	Yes	Kinchega National Park
Bundanoon	(048) 83 6010	76	Yes	Northern Morton National Park Bungonia State Recreation Area Fitzroy Falls, Kangaroo Valley
Byron Bay	(066) 85 8788	110	Yes	Coastal and rainforest national parks of the far north-east Including Bundjalung, Nightcap Mount Warning, and the Border Ranges National Parks
Canberra	(062) 489 155	124	Yes	Namadgi National Park Budawangs, Brindabellas Deua National Park

LOCATION	PHONE	BEDS	BIKE HIRE	AREA ACCESSED
				North Kosciusko National Park
Cessnock	(049) 90 1070	25	Yes	Hunter Valley
				Northern Wollemi and Yengo
				National Parks
Coffs Harbour	(066) 52 6462	56	Yes	North coast national parks
				Including Yuraygir, Hat Head
				Dorrigo National Park
Coonabara-bran	(068) 42 1832	10	No	Warrumbungle National Park
				Siding Spring Observatory
				Mount Kaputar National Park
Deniliquin	(058) 81 5025	14	Yes	Southern Central NSW
				Murray River
Dubbo	(068) 82 0922	45	Yes	Western Tablelands
				Western Plains Zoo
Garie Beach	(02) 530 5617	12	No	Royal National Park
Gerrigong	(042) 34 1249	32	Yes	Seven Mile Beach, Kiama
Girvan	(049) 97 6639	12	Yes	Barrington Tops National Park
				Myall Lakes National Park
Mount Warning (Murwillum-bah)	(066) 72 3763	24	Yes	Coastal and rainforest national parks of the far north-east
				Including Bundjalung, Nightcap
				Mount Warning, and the Border
				Ranges National Parks
Narranderra	(069) 59 1768	50	Yes	Central Southern NSW
Newcastle	(049) 29 3324	60	Yes	Myall Lakes National Park
				Central Coast, Hunter Valley
				Barrington Tops

LOCATION	PHONE	BEDS	BIKE HIRE	AREA ACCESSED
Nimbin (Murwillum-bah)	(066) 89 1333	30	No	Coastal and rainforest national parks of the far north-east Including Bundjalung, Nightcap Mount Warning, and the Border Ranges National Parks
Nowra (Bomaderry)	(044) 23 0495	38	Yes	Morton National Park Kangaroo Valley, Ettrema Seven Mile Beach, Budawangs
Port Macquarie	(065) 83 5512	32	Yes	Hat Head National Park Crowdy Bay National Park Werrikimbe National Park
Scone	(065) 45 2072	24	Yes	Barrington Tops, Allyn River Chichester State Forest Hunter Valley Goulburn River National Park
Shoal Bay	(049) 84 2315	18	Yes	Myall Lakes National Park Port Stephens
Sydney Hereford	(02) 660 5577	250	Yes	Ku-Ring-Gai, Sydney Harbour Parramatta, Botany Bay
Sydney Glebe Point	(02) 692 8418	150	Yes	Ku-Ring-Gai, Sydney Harbour Parramatta, Botany Bay
Sydney Pittwater	(02) 99 2196	32	No	Ku-Ring-Gai, Sydney Harbour
Tenterfield	(067) 36 1477	35	Yes	Bald Rock National Park Boonoo Boonoo National Park Girraween National Park (QU)
Thredbo	(064) 57 6376	52	Yes	Kosciusko National Park (south and central regions)

LOCATION	PHONE	BEDS	BIKE HIRE	AREA ACCESSED
Wauchope	(065) 85 6134	30	Yes	Hat Head National Park Crowdy Bay National Park Werrikimbe National Park

CYCLING

Books Before 1990, there were only a few Australian cycling publications. Jim Smith's guide to the Blue Mountains in 1980 was among the first modern day books that dealt with off-road touring in the country. Over the last five years, however, a profusion of touring guides have hit the market. The best retail outlet for cycling publications is Bicycle New South Wales.

Other Publications
Cycling periodicals are Australian based and dominated by:
   Australian Cyclist (including PUSH-ON)
   Published by the Bicycle Federation of Australia
   15 000 copies, bi-monthly

   Cycling World (Freewheeling)
   Published by Mason Stewart Pty Ltd
These magazines feature articles on touring, equipment reviews, new guide releases, readers' experiences, product advertising, etc. A standard inclusion is a list of cycling club addresses so people can join various groups interested in the same activity. Editors of all the magazines pursue commentary on interesting cycling adventures and will consider articles and photographs of local and international mountain biking tours for publication.

Organisations
Representing cyclists' interests in a whole range of issues and activities is Bicycle New South Wales. The headquarters contains a shop which stocks the largest collection of cycling books available in Australia. It's located at:

Bicycle House
82 Campbell Street
GPO Box 272
Sydney NSW 2001
Phone (02) 212 5628
Fax (02) 211 1867

In addition there are numerous local Bicycle Organisations, normally operated by a few individuals, that have cycling as their common ideal. They're called BUGS (Bicycle User Groups) and would only be too interested to attract new members. Activities including tours (both MTBs and other), petitioning councils on urban planning issues, and race meetings.

Issues

The ultimate aim of cycling organisations is the institutionalisation of cycling in the legislative policy-making of our governments, on a federal, state, and local level. Countries such as the Netherlands are model examples of how effective an all-encompassing cycling policy can be. If public transport access points and local shopping centres have bicycle locking/ security facilities, and urban areas are inter-laced with exclusive bicycle path networks, then a dramatic decline in motor vehicle use is experienced. The end result is a greater level of health and fitness for society, reduced pollution, reduced petroleum imports, less traffic congestion, longer vehicle life expectancy, and a cleaner overall environment. In general, Europe and Asia make good use of bicycles. The fact that Australia doesn't is a result of government subsidisation of the motor vehicle. This situation results from our unfortunate adoption of American lifestyle.

Mountain biking is a safe, clean, and green way of exploring natural areas. The MTB's multi-purpose construction allows people to use it as an efficient means of urban transit: most urban commuting tasks that are traditionally used by the motor vehicle can be done on a bicycle. The aim of Bicycle New South Wales is to have just 1% of road construction budgets allocated to the development of general cycling facilities.

Cycling and the law The following are bookable offences if caught by the police:

• Cycling without a helmet (unless there are medical or religious reasons)

93

- Cycling abreast on a road (cyclists must ride in single file)
- Cycling without lights at night (after sunset, before sunrise)
- Cycling through a red light
- Cycling on a footpath
- Failing to give way at an intersection
- Riding dangerously or incorrectly

Organised Tours

Bicycle New South Wales also promotes and organises very successful mass tours for cyclists. By far the most popular of these is the famous Gong—Sydney to Wollongong. Fund-raising is a by-product with distributions to charities. In addition, other more adventurous rides have been conducted: Kosciusko to Sydney, Mudgee, and the North Coast. Their organisation is legendary—support vehicles carry your luggage, so all you do is concentrate on enjoying yourself.

Commercial tour operators also are starting to cash in on the mountain bike craze. Lithgow and Katoomba are both centres for organised mountain bike touring with support teams. Paddy Pallin has also started it in the Snowy Mountains. $30–$40 will get you a 21-speed Apollo bike and helmet hire, transport, food, and a guide for a day. For longer tours, panniers and racks are also provided.

OTHER RECREATIONAL ACTIVITIES

Walking

Many of the most spectacular places are located in wilderness areas and on top of rugged peaks, kilometres from the nearest road. A cycling tour of New South Wales' rugged highlands, whether it be in the Blue Mountains or the Kosciusko Main Range is never complete without a few day walks. An overnight walk will exercise different muscles as well as offering some variety.

The definitive walking guide is undoubtedly Tyrone Thomas' 319 page *100 Walks in New South Wales* containing detailed topographical maps and suggesting a wide range of interesting walks predominantly through the highlands and national parks ranging from easy, one-day family walks to overnight hard-graded treks. He has also augmented the New South Wales coverage by two other smaller guides:

50 Walks in Southern New South Wales and A.C.T.
50 Walks Coffs Harbour Gold Coast Hinterland

Horse-riding Much has been said about the impact of equestrian activities in national parks. In summary, it boils down to management policies recognising fragile environments in certain areas and then determining what forms of recreation are most compatible there. Horses have hard hooves and repeated travel on wet, soft soils undoubtedly causes damages, just as mountain biking does. Horses do more, however, like facilitating the spread of floral pests. Grazing leads to eating exotic weeds which can be then dropped through faeces in new virgin wilderness. A classic example is the alarming spread of Scotch broom in the Barrington Tops. Today, in many national parks, horse-riders need either an annual permit, or a day-ticket, so park authorities can monitor the activities of equestrians.

Four-wheel driving No recreational outdoor activity is more controversial than four-wheel driving. All around the country, off-road driving associations have had to battle national parks administrators for access into natural areas. They argue 'what's the use of having national parks if you can't see them'. Members of associations claim they act responsibly and due to their great carrying capacity, can actually clean up a campsite by removing the garbage. Once again, the impact of vehicles on soft, steep, wet slopes has to be assessed.

Canoeing The most popular areas for canoeing in New South Wales are the Hawkesbury and Shoalhaven Rivers. The former has excellent access points for staging areas and pick-up points, but unfortunately suffers from overuse and canoeists have to compete with power boats and commercial vessels for water space. The Shoalhaven, by contrast, is far more remote, and winds its way through a 500 metre sandstone gorge. Other 'canoeable' rivers include the Colo, Clyde, Deua, Murray, and Snowy.

Caving Most cave systems in New South Wales are found in the south along the Great Dividing Range. Starting from Wellington in central west, there's a line that extends south through Jenolan, Tuglow, Colong, Wombeyan, Bungonia, Deua (Bendethera, Wyanbene), and Yarrangobilly caves in

Kosciusko. Popular tourist facilities exist at Wellington, Jenolan, Wombeyan, and Yarrangobilly. With the exception of the cave systems in the Deua National Park near Braidwood, all other wild caves in NSW need a permit for exploration. This can be obtained at the local NPWS District Office. The Deua caves have been partially developed and are open for self-guided tours. Unfortunately, this inevitably leads to vandalism through graffiti and souveniring. It is important to remember that speleological formations are created over thousands of years and are extremely fragile.

KEY TO RESERVE CLASSIFICATIONS

National Parks In 1978, New South Wales adopted the definition of the International Union for the Conservation of Nature and Natural Resources (IUCN) in classifying national parks as 'a relatively large area where one or several ecosystems are not materially altered by human exploitation and occupation ... and where visitors are allowed to enter under special conditions, for inspiration, education, cultural, and recreational purposes. Another simpler definition is an extensive area public land of nation-wide significance because of its outstanding natural features and diverse land types, set aside primarily to provide public enjoyment, education, and inspiration in natural environments. These reserves have high conservation, scenic and recreational values and are usually larger than 4000 ha. Despite the prefix 'national', they are state managed. The 'special conditions' include the prohibition of pets, firearms, and cutting equipment, fire regulations, and the requirement of vehicle registration. Rangers have the authority to evict people and impose penalties on those who do not observe the regulations. At the time of writing, there are 76 national parks totalling 4 million hectares in New South Wales, the largest being Kosciusko, Wollemi, and Sturt.

State Recreation Areas (SRAs) These are smaller reserves that often protect only a particular feature, rather than a self-sustained ecosystem. There are only about seven SRAs in the state managed by the NPWS, others are administered through other government departments. Regulations are less restrictive than national parks with the emphasis being more towards public

Some various types of topographical maps necessary for mountain biking available through the Lands Information Office

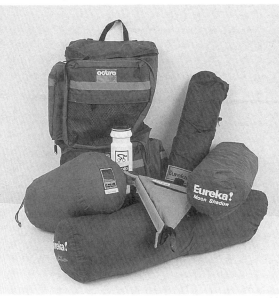

Some overnight touring equipment: panniers, Eureka Tents, Paddy Pallin sleeping bags

When all equipment is working properly, some remote locations can be accessed. (Above) Cooleman Caves in Kosciusko, and (Below) Sassafras in Morton National Park

recreation rather than conservation. One of the most popular is Bungonia near Goulburn.

Nature Reserves These reserves are the highest level of protection that can be awarded in the state. Usually a particular type of rare environment is preserved: e.g. coastal rainforest in Broken Head Nature Reserve. Facilities are very limited—in many, camping is prohibited altogether.

State Forests These are managed by the Forestry Commission of NSW for the purpose of timber production which generates about $100 million income. The forests can either take the form of softwood *radiata* pine plantations or native eucalypt hardwoods. There are just over 3.5 million hectares of state forest in NSW, 95% being native. Recreation activities are well catered for in state forests—roads are generally more widespread and of better quality than in national parks. There is an abundance of picnic and camping areas in popular regions, and restrictions are usually less severe. While the general scenery is normally not as aesthetic as in national parks, the sheer scale and relative ease of access of state forests make them ideal for extended mountain bike exploration.

Flora, Fauna, Forest Reserves These small reserves are often found along tourist drives in state forests and preserve particular sensitive or aesthetic areas for conservation and recreational purposes. There are about 140 reserves totalling about 220 000 hectares, and act as a control against which to judge the effects of logging elsewhere. Despite popular belief, these have full legislation-backed protection and can only be revoked by parliament. Often picnic and camping facilities exist here.

Water Board territory Because catchment areas for urban water supplies need to be in relatively wild areas in order to maintain purity, the Water Board jointly administers a reasonably large proportion of the sandstone parks surrounding Sydney. In the Blue Mountains, the construction of Warragamba Dam in 1960 blocked the Coxs River and Wollondilly River valleys forming a massive stored water build-up known as Lake Burragorang. A three kilometre circumference around this 7500 hectare lake is totally prohibited to bushwalkers and cyclists. Certain corridors have been opened through this zone, allowing access through to other areas of the Blue Mountains. One example, is White Dog Ridge from Medlow Gap to the Coxs River. Another is to the south from Yerrandrie to the

Wollondilly River (Belloon Pass—Sheepwalk Road Track). For other restricted areas, permission *may* be granted by a written request to the Water Board.

To the south, the Shoalhaven Scheme centres on Tallowa Dam. Here restrictions are less formal and one may cycle in any of the trails in the catchment scheme, even to the extent of camping on the lake's foreshore.

World Heritage Areas Areas of outstanding and cultural significance are registered with UNESCO in Paris. New South Wales has Kinchega National Park near Broken Hill and its northern rainforest parks dedicated as world heritage. Land tenure is determined by state legislation, but international agreements and commonwealth legislation regulate management frameworks. A related reservation status is the UNESCO Biosphere Reserve which act as controls against which human impact on pristine areas is monitored and recorded. Kosciusko National Park is an example of this type of reserve. The closest world heritage park to Sydney is the Barrington Tops.

DISTRICT OFFICES: NATIONAL PARKS AND WILDLIFE SERVICE

HEAD OFFICE

43 Bridge Street
PO Box 1967
Hurstville NSW 2220
(02) 585 6444

REGIONAL OFFICES

Central
10 Valentine Avenue
PO Box 95
Parramatta NSW 2124
(02) 895 7420

South-Eastern
Level 1, 34 Lowe Street
PO Box 733
Queanbeyan NSW 2620
(02) 297 6144

Northern
49 Victoria Street
PO Box 97
Grafton NSW 2460
(066) 42 0593

Western
183 Argent Street
PO Box 459
Broken Hill NSW 2880
(080) 88 2488

DISTRICT OFFICES

NATIONAL PARKS ADMINISTERED

Armidale .... Oxley Wild Rivers, Warrabah, Werrikimbe
87 Faulkner Street
PO Box 402
Armidale NSW 2350
(067) 73 7211

Bathurst .... Conimbla, Nangar, Weddin Mountains
154 Russell Street
Bathurst NSW 2795
(063) 31 9777

Blue Mountains .... Blue Mountains, Wollemi, Kanangra
Walls, Nattai
Blue Mountains Heritage Centre Also an office at Glenbrook:
Govetts Leap Road   Bruce Road
PO Box 43   PO Box 6
Blackheath NSW 2785   Glenbrook NSW 2773
(047) 87 8877   (047) 39 2950

Broken Hill .... Kinchega, Mootwingee
5 Oxide Street
PO Box 459
Broken Hill NSW 2880
(080) 88 5933

Coonabarabran .... Warrumbungles
56 Cassilis Street
PO Box 39
Coonabrabran NSW 2357
(068) 42 1311

Dorrigo .... New England, Guy Fawkes River,
Dorrigo Rainforest Centre   Cathedral Rock, Dorrigo
Cnr Dome Road & Lyrebird Lane
PO Box 170
Dorrigo NSW 2453
(060) 57 2309

Eden .... Ben Boyd, Nungutta, Mount Imlay, Bournda
Rear Twofold Arcade
Imlay Street
PO Box 186
Eden NSW 2551
(064) 96 1434

Glen Innes .... Bald Rock, Gibraltar Range, Washpool,
404 Grey Street   Nymboida, Boono Boono, Kings Plain
PO Box 281
Glen Innes NSW 2370
(067) 32 1177

Grafton .... Nymboida, Yuraygir
50 Victoria Street
PO Box 361
Grafton NSW 2460
(066) 42 0613

Griffith .... Cocoparra, Willandra
105 Banna Avenue
PO Box 1049
Griffith NSW 2680
(069) 62 7755

Hawkesbury .... Dharug, Yengo, Brisbane Waters,
Suites 36-38   Bouddi
207 Albany Street
PO Box 282
Gosford South NSW 2250
(043) 24 4911

Hunter .... Barrington Tops, Myall Lakes, Woko, Yengo,
Lot 5 Bourke Street   Wollemi, Booti Booti
PO 270
Raymond Terrace NSW 2324
(049) 87 3108

Kosciusko .... Kosciusko
Kosciusko Visitors Centre
Sawpit Creek
Private Mail Bag
via Cooma NSW 2630
(064) 56 2102

Lismore .... Nightcap, Mount Warning, Border Ranges,
Suite 9, Colonial Arcade   Bundjalung, Broadwater
75 Main Street
PO Box 91
Alstonville NSW 2477
(066) 28 1177

Narrabri .... Mount Kaputar
55 Maitland Street
PO Box 72
Narrabri NSW 2390
(067) 92 7234

Narooma .... Wadbilliga, Deua, Mimosa Rocks,
36 Princes Highway   Wallaga Lake
PO Box 282
Narooma NSW 2546
(044) 76 2888

North Metropolitan .... Ku-ring-gai Chase, Lane Cove,
Bobbin Head   Marramarra
Turramurra NSW 2074
(02) 457 9322

Nowra .... Morton, Budawang, Budderoo, Macquarie
24 Berry Street   Pass, Seven Mile Beach,
PO Box 707   Murramarang, Tarlo River
Nowra NSW 2541
(044) 23 9800

Port Macquarie   Crowdy Bay, Hat Head, Werrikimbe
Macquarie Nature Reserve
Everard Street
PO Box 61
Port Macquarie NSW 2444
(065) 83 5518

South Metropolitan .... Royal, Heathcote
Royal National Park Visitors Centre
AUDLEY
PO Box 44
Sutherland NSW 2232
(02) 542 0666

Sydney .... Sydney Harbour
Greycliffe House, Nielsen Park
Vaucluse
PO Box 461
Rose Bay NSW 2029
(02) 337 5355

Captain Cooks Landing Place .... Botany Bay
Kurnell NSW 2231
(02) 668 9111

ACACIA

DISTRICT OFFICES: FORESTRY COMMISSION OF NEW SOUTH WALES

Head Office
95–99 York Street
Sydney NSW 2000
(02) 234 1567

Batemans Bay Region
Cnr Princes Highway and
Crown Street
Batemans Bay NSW 2536
(044) 72 6322

Bathurst Region
Cnr Browning and William
Streets
Bathurst NSW 2795
(063) 31 2044

Coffs Harbour Region
Cnr High and Hood Streets
Coffs Harbour Jetty NSW
2451
(066) 52 8172

Eden Region
Twofold Arcade
Imlay Street
Eden NSW 2551
(064) 96 1547

Glen Innes Region
134–136 Meade Street
Glen Innes NSW 2370
(067) 32 2111

Newcastle Region
117 Bull Street
Newcastle NSW 2300
(049) 26 9783

Port Macquarie Region
1st Floor
109 William Street
Port Macquarie NSW 2444
(065) 83 7100

Please note: it is strongly recommended to purchase the relevant maps listed in the beginning of *each* ride. This is imperative for *all* overnight tours, extended walking, and mountain bike rides.

4
Around Sydney

Few cities in the world are so fortunate to have so many large areas of reserved land so close to their metropolitan area as Sydney. No fewer than nine national parks are easily accessible from Sydney by a short drive or even by public transport. Sydney Harbour National Park lies near the centre of the city. Another, the gigantic Blue Mountains complex is only an hour to the west. Besides the national parks there is a plethora of park land, state recreation areas, and large tracts of crown land scattered all throughout the city's outskirts. The next chapter deals with this region including Thirlmere Lakes, Bents Basin, Wollemi, and Kanangra Walls. This chapter will concern itself with five of the major national parks to the immediate north, south-east, and north-west of the metropolitan area: Ku-ring-gai Chase, Sydney Harbour, Royal, Heathcote, and Dharug National Parks.

All five of these are well visited, popular parks due to their close proximity to Sydney. Accordingly, the National Parks and Wildlife Service has taken special measures to accommodate the large numbers of people in order to minimise the impact on the environment. Already there are traces of damage: the classic case of loving it to death.

Most of Sydney's perimeter parks have trains running near them, so convenient day rides are possible linking stations as to avoid unnecessary car shuttles and backtracking. Because the parks are close to the coast, they are relatively flat and therefore contain great cycling country. This fact, combined with the good condition of many of the trails, make them perfect 'training' grounds for the inexperienced, or the young cyclist. Yet both are rugged and challenging enough to adequately prepare any cyclist for the more demanding and larger national parks along the Great Dividing Range. Many biking clubs recommend that this type of 'springboarding' be done in order to familiarise the cyclist with what bush-riding is all about before he or she tackles the rugged maze of sandstone gorges to the west.

Another advantage of these parks is the fine facilities which are made available to the public. Roads are well signposted, tracks are regularly graded, and everywhere there are picnic spots and camping places complete with fireplaces, tables, and toilets. A common feature of Ku-ring-gai and Royal National Parks is the ocean: with the exception of Myall Lakes no other large 'cyclable' parks are located so close to beaches and some of the following rides take full advantage of this. One must remember, however, that sea-water and salt-laden air is not too healthy for steel and bikes would be preferably left at the back of the beach. A lock is also advisable due to extreme popularity of both parks.

The best time to go is between July and October when it is cool and dry, with the added advantage of a spectacular wild-flower display. Also in these months, the threat of bushfires is lower, and the influx of tourists is not as high as for example, the Christmas-New Year holidays. Swimming is less comfort-able but the overall ride will be better appreciated.

KU-RING-GAI CHASE NATIONAL PARK

Size: 15 322 hectares
Enactment: 1894
Visitors: Approximately 1.6 million per year
Aboriginal Sites: 383 known; many interesting engravings of fish, whales, and mythical beings.
Flora: Over 1000 species in 24 recorded communities
Fauna: 28 recorded native mammal species, 139 bird species, 20 reptile species
Camping: The Basin Camping Area only
Visitors Centre: Kalkari (NPWS District Office Bobbin Head: (02) 457 9322)
Adjoining Parks: Marra Marra National Park, Muogamarra Nature Reserve, Dharug National Park, Brisbane Water National Park, Bouddi National Park, Lion Island Nature Reserve, and Davidson State Recreation Area.

The name Ku-ring-gai is derived from Guringai, the collective title of several Aboriginal tribes who spoke a similar dialect and occupied the waterways and sandstone region to the north of Sydney and to the east of the Dharng tribe which inhabited the lower northern Blue Mountains and plains. Although evidence of Aboriginal occupation only dates back 5000–6000 years, it is commonly believed human occupation of the area has existed for well over 30 000 years.

The geological history goes back slightly longer: 280 million years. Sydney was under water then, with mud and sand being washed down from the highlands and dumped in the area. As more and more deposits were piled on top of one another, the sands underneath compressed into rock: sandstone. Around 150 million years, this was uplifted in the same process that formed the Snowy Mountains. Since then the Hawkesbury River has eroded its way through the newly formed plateau. This created other streams and creeks as water had a new low point to travel to and consequently formed their own valleys. The ice ages that lasted until just 10 000 years ago locked up a lot of water in the polar ice caps, lowering sea levels and accelerating the erosion process. After the last ice age, these new valleys became flooded, creating present day *drowned* inlets such as Jerusalem Bay, Cowan Water, and the Coal and Candle Creek channel.

Then just over 100 years ago, a man named Eccleston du Faur from the Royal Geographic Society proposed to the Minister of Lands (Henry Copeland) that the 13 500 hectare region around Cowan and Smith Creeks be made into a national park for North Sydney, which it promptly was in 1894. Although du Faur's intention of a reserve with non-utilitarian motives, the idea of a 'national park' was only in its infancy (the world's first, Yellowstone in the USA, was only formed in 1872) and development still continued: mainly around the Lambert Peninsula, Cottage Point, and Bobbin Head. In the late 1800s, there was even a proposal by certain politicians and developers to construct the nation's capital in the vicinity. To be named *Pacivica*, it was to be designer city with fountains, statues, trams, castle homes, and fortress-citadels.

Many roads were built, which are only now being rehabilitated. Some can still be used for cycling and walking. But the trustees of the park were largely able to limit the spread of residential property and limit the impact of logging, hunting, and wildflower collection. Over the course of the twentieth century, the size of the park was enlarged. In 1951, West Head was included in the park's boundaries, sixteen years before the entire region became administered by the National Parks and Wildlife Service.

Today there are three main entry points by road: Ku-ring-gai Chase Road which leads from the railway line at Mount Colah to Bobbin Head and the Visitors Centre at Kalkari, Bobbin Head Road from North Turramurra, and the Coal and Candle Creek Road near Terry Hills that branches out to Cottage Point and West Head.

Of interest to the cyclist, there is a growing trend of tourist activities being water based rather than on land. Boating is perhaps the primary recreation in Ku-ring-gai with navigatable waterways extending all the way to Richmond and up the Colo River in the Blue Mountains. This leads to reduced activity throughout the park and makes cycling and walking that much more enjoyable. Due to its proximity to Sydney's metropolitan area, the park is very well suited for one day rides, which is fortunate because camping is limited only to The Basin.

The fire trails throughout the park are well graded and relatively flat because they are confined to ridge tops and the odd spur. This allows relatively easy riding, but unfortunately means that some backtracking is necessary. Only one map is necessary to cover the whole park: the CMA *Ku-ring-gai Chase National Park Tourist* Map available either from the Kalkari Visitors Centre on Bobbin Head Road, or any of the Central Mapping Authority agents around Sydney.

In January 1994, a large section of the area including the majority of the adjoining Davidson Park State Recreation was burnt out by severe bush fires. Accordingly the scarring will remain for many years, but at the time of writing, there is abundant lush re-growth due to good late summer rains.

The Mount Ku-ring-gai and Mount Colah railway stations lie on the Central Coast Line and are just under an hour from Central (express trains less than 30 minutes). Since they are normal inter-urban trains, bikes are permissible at the cost of a children's ticket and can be stored in the vestibules.

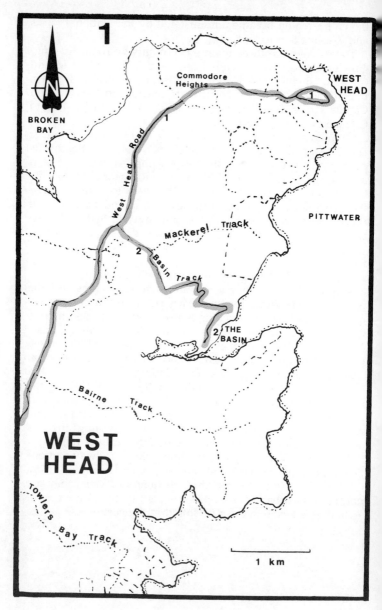

1

BROKEN
BAY

Commodore
Heights

1

West Head Road

WEST
HEAD

1

PITTWATER

Mackerel Track

2

Basin Track

2 THE
BASIN

Bairne Track

WEST
HEAD

Towlers Bay Track

1 km

RIDE 1:   WEST HEAD

FROM: Pymble Train Station
TO: West Head (Commodore Heights) (return)
VIA: Terrey Hills
LENGTH: 66 km
TIME: Full day
RIDE/TRACK GRADE: 2/1
WALKING: Optional short tracks around Commodore Heights area
HEIGHT VARIATION: 210 m
TRANSPORT: Rail (North Shore Line)
FACILITIES: General picnic facilities at West Head
SPECIAL EQUIPMENT: Bike lock, swimming gear
MAPS: Ku-ring-gai Chase National Park 1:40 000 Tourist Map (or Hornsby, Mona Vale, and Broken Bay 1:25 000 topographicals) or a Sydney street directory)

The best part of the eastern half of Ku-ring-gai Chase National Park can be covered on this ride, which is both relatively flat and easy cycling along ridgetops. Due to its popularity, however, some traffic can be expected on weekends and school holidays. For people new to cycling this is a great way to start off, but remember to start early to allow plenty of time for exploring the many short walking trails and attractions around West Head.

After alighting at Pymble Station, cycle up Alma Street which soon connects with Station Street. Continue north and turn right at Telegraph Road. At the traffic lights, turn left and follow Mona Vale Road up through leafy St Ives and into bushland. Right of Mona Vale Road is the Davidson Park State Recreation Area centred on Middle Harbour Creek. This point was the closest that the great bushfires of January 1994 got to Sydney inner suburbs. Once past Terry Hills, turn left into the Ku-ring-gai Chase National Park. This turn-off is the highest point of the trip and it is level cycling from here on through dry sclerophyll (hard leaved) forest. The vegetation in this area, for example the numerous species of heath, has adapted very well to the very sandy soils. Also growing here are banksias, needle bushes, and tea trees.

Two kilometres later, turn right to West Head enjoying a

nice downhill to McCarrs Creek. After crossing the creek, there's another turn-off left on to West Head Road. The traffic can get heavy on weekends, and drivers have a habit of looking in the bush, so don't rely on them seeing you. A bit of a climb takes you past the entrance booth and on to the Lambert Peninsula. Sydney siders and tourists have been travelling along this road to visit the lookout since 1927.

The length of peninsula should take about an hour to cover. At the end there is a good lookout on 70 m cliffs where one can see the length of the Palm Beach peninsula, Bouddi National Park, Lion Island, and out to sea. More picnic facilities are provided here and it is a good spot to have lunch. During World War II, this area once housed military fortifications for the defence of Botany Bay, before being converted to a holiday/sports camp.

Just behind the Garigal Picnic Area, there are some Aboriginal engravings depicting a fishing scene. There are many groups of these etchings to see, but most are approached by walking trails. If one is interested, one can consult the Rangers at the Visitors Centre at Kalkari or West Head for the location of others. Commodore Heights is one of the only areas in Ku-ring-gai Chase that has protrusions of volcanic rocks. These result from dykes and diatremes that date back 160 million years.

From Commodore Heights, a number of smaller walks can be conducted to the south of the Peninsula descending down to Resolute Beach and back up via the Headland Track. These take no more than an hour return, where different muscles can be exercised. Due to the popularity of the area, it is best to lock up your bikes rather than hide them.

Returning to the lookout, one backtracks the 16 km to McCarrs Creek Road where it is only another hour to the train station. An alternative way out is the Centre Fire Trail that starts several hundred metres down the Liberator San Martin Drive (formerly known as the Coal and Candle Drive) from West Head Road. It is marked on the map as a walking track, and follows a ridge line, coming out at another entrance booth.

If there is time left in the afternoon, one could cut through the Davidson Park State Recreation Area on their way back to Pymble, omitting the North St Ives section of Mona Vale Road.

RIDE 2:   THE BASIN

FROM: Pymble Station
TO: The Basin (return)
VIA: Lambert Peninsula
LENGTH: 64 km
TIME: 1 day (Optional overnight camping)
RIDE/TRACK GRADE: 3/4
WALKING: None
HEIGHT VARIATION: 210 m
TRANSPORT: Rail (North Shore Line)
FACILITIES: Picnic/camping area and general facilities at
The Basin
MAPS: CMA (LIC) Ku-ring-gai Chase National Park 1:40 000
Tourist Map (or Hornsby, Mona Vale, and Broken Bay 1:
25 000 topographicals and a Sydney street directory)

For the cyclist who has never slept outside four walls, here is
the perfect place to begin. The Basin is a popular, well developed camping ground with the full range of amenities: toilets,
drinking water, showers, tables, etc. Those just wishing to go
on a one day ride to see this beautiful place, can do so in an
easy day's cycling to and from Pymble Station.
As in Ride 1, follow the Mona Vale Road up past Terrey
Hills. But instead of turning at the official entrance, the traffic
can be avoided by taking the Duckhole Track. This 4WD trail
can be reached by two approaches. The first is just past the
turn-off to Kanangra Avenue. The fire trail swings around to
the right after you pass an assortment of concrete blocks in
the centre. After swinging left again it reaches a T-intersection
with the Terrey Hills track. This is shown as a walking trail
but the CMA have got it wrong: it is little more than scrub
bashing. Turn right and you soon come up to the Duckhole
Track (Grade 7).
The second approach is to pass this abovementioned
entrance and turn left a few hundred metres further at a clearing on the side resembling an abandoned DMR construction
site. The trail isn't signposted, but shouldn't be too hard to
find, as it is the only one leading north. The trail, descending
at first, soon gets better as it joins up with other tracks. Don't
forget to look over your right shoulder as you cycle along the

ridge here, as there are good views up to a dramatic temple (Baha'i) on top of Addison Hill. Be careful of horse-riders who use the numerous tracks in the area.

Ignore turnoffs to the left as you continue down, dropping 70 m to meet McCarrs Creek. At the barrier, turn right on to the sealed McCarrs Creek Road and then take the first on the left. This is West End Road, and it starts by passing the official entrance booth (even though you've been in the park boundaries for the last half-hour). Stay on the sealed road for much of the next hour passing numerous trails left and right until you reach I.D. Post 12. In order to save The Basin from extinction, the access road has been closed for motorised traffic, and the campers can arrive either by foot, private or hire boat, or the ferry from Pittwater Park at Palm Beach. Turn right at the indicated place on the map, immediately descending. On the right hand side, not more than 300 m, is an orange boomerang sign indicating an Aboriginal site, not marked on the map. A large bed of rock has a number of clear and distinct engravings of a woman carrying a coolamon (bark dish), some animals such as several fish and a kangaroo, sketches of weapons, and a male figure. They are some of the finest examples of engravings to be found within the Park and can be best photographed in the early morning or late afternoon sun when shadows accentuate the outlines.

Before mounting the bike once more, quickly check the brakes for there is quite a steep 160 m descent ahead. Continuing south-east, follow the ridge top ignoring the Mackerel Track on the left which leads to private property at Currawang Beach. Two other small trails are ignored further on after a minute or two of descending. The track momentarily levels out before plunging down a steep slope into wet woodland and the Basin Camping Area.

The Basin would have to rank with Euroka Clearing at Glenbrook and Bonnie Vale on Port Hacking as one of Sydney's most popular camping spots. It is the only legal camping spot in Ku-ring-gai Chase National Park and has all facilities available. Fees do apply and it is advisable to book ahead [phone (02) 919 4036 between 9.30 and 10.30 a.m.] if planning to stay the night.

If planning just a day trip, one can swim in the shark-proof inlet or simply explore the area. But remember the railway station is about 3 to 4 hours away and extra time should be

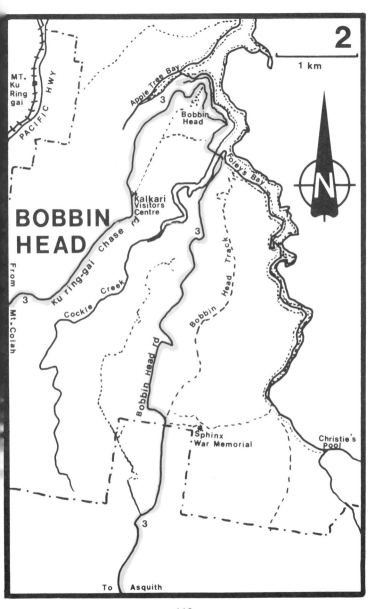

BOBBIN HEAD

allowed for the steep climb up again. Otherwise the ferry can be taken across to Palm Beach where you cycle to the nearest railway station via the Pittwater Road.

RIDE 3:   BOBBIN HEAD

FROM: Mount Colah Station
TO: Asquith Station
VIA: Kalkari Visitors Centre, Appletree Bay
LENGTH: 19 km
TIME: One easy day
RIDE/TRACK GRADE: 4/1 (steep uphill from Appletree Bay to Kalkari Visitors Centre)
WALKING: Optional walk to Christies Pool (12 km return)
HEIGHT VARIATION: 210 m
TRANSPORT: Rail (North Shore Line)
FACILITIES: Kalkari Visitors Centre, picnic areas/kiosks at Apple Tree Bay and Foleys Bay
SPECIAL EQUIPMENT: Bike lock
MAPS: Ku-ring-gai Chase National Park 1:40 000 Tourist Map (or Hornsby 1:25 000 topographical and a Sydney street directory)

Here a short ride to the beautiful Cowan Creek allows one to spent the middle hours of the day fishing or swimming. It is an excellent introductory ride, especially for people who haven't been to the Ku-ring-gai Chase National Park.

From Mount Colah Station, head south until the Ku-ring-gai Chase Road. Turn left, over the freeway and past the official park entrance. It is worthwhile taking a look inside the Kalkari Visitors Centre. The park is quite unique for its very rich Aboriginal history and quite a detailed documentary record of the evidence is available. There is also an elaborate enclosed nature walk within the fenced area on the left. From the centre of the ridge, the road diverges left and down to a sharp turnoff that leads left into Appletree Bay. Many facilities are provided here: kiosk, picnic tables, bins, and toilets. There's enough secure metal to chain up your bikes.

One can either remain here for the rest of the day exploring the Mount Ku-ring-gai Walking Track or one can backtrack around the corner to Foleys Bay where Cockle Creek meets with Cowan Waters. The picnic area is just before the bridge. Opposite the turn-off is a wildlife shop. Across the bridge, the Warrimoo Track, one of the longest walking tracks in the park, leads all the way to St Ives Chase. If the day is not suitable for swimming and you're not into fishing, an interesting side detour is to Christies Pool. Leave the bikes chained at Foleys Bay, cross the bridge, and from the car-park a road briefly follows the bank past the large boating complex on the left before turning into a walking trail. The track keeps to the right bank of Cowan Creek for several kilometres, passing patches of mangroves. Finally it crosses and zig-zags up a spur before turning into an Electricity Commission service road not marked on the map. Continuing up the ridge, turn left where the base of a pylon tower can be found about 500 m further on. From here, there's a rough track or 'negotiable route' in bushwalking jargon which begins on the left side of the clearing around the pylon and descends down to the pool. It is a 60 to 70 m descent to the beautiful pool where one can feel totally alone not far from the centre of the busiest city in Australia. The whole walk shouldn't take more than four hours. Return to bikes via the same route.

From Appletree Creek, it's a steep 150 m uphill push back up to the Kalkari Visitors Centre and easy cycling back to the freeway crossing. Turn left down Royston Parade where you soon come to Asquith Station.

FURTHER TOURING IN THE KU-RING-GAI CHASE NATIONAL PARK

The Lambert Peninsula offers the most extensive cycling opportunities. Most trails branching either side of West Head Road follow the centres of spurs and ridges. Some, like the Towers Bay and Elving Tracks even make it down to the water. While most involve simply backtracking, others allow round trips to be made—an example is the Salvation Track which loops around connecting West Head Road with Wallaroo Track. It ends at an unofficial lookout over Castle Bay and Want Spur.

Cyclists can experiment with different approaches into the

park. From Duffys Forest, one can access the beautiful Christies Pool via Slade Lookout. Just to the north of the Waratah Park Wildlife Reserve, the Long Track leads to the Peach Trees, a huge array of Aboriginal carvings not marked on the map. Walking access can then be made down to Cowan Water for a swim.

RIDE 4:   BRADLEY'S HEAD

FROM: North Sydney Station
TO: Sydney Harbour National Park
VIA: Military Road and Neutral Bay
LENGTH: 20 km
TIME: 1 easy day
RIDE/TRACK GRADE: 2/1
WALKING: Optional short tourist walks, e.g. Clifton Gardens
HEIGHT VARIATION: 70 m
TRANSPORT: Rail (North Short Line)
FACILITIES: Picnic facilities in Sydney Harbour National Park
SPECIAL EQUIPMENT: Bike lock
MAPS: Street directory

Despite being on the harbour foreshores, not too many people from Sydney's east, south, and west know about this fragmented national park in the centre of the state's capital. It can only be described as an oasis in the residential sprawl. In addition to natural bush settings and city skyline views, the park has a number of historical attractions, such as defence fortifications from early last century and the mast from the HMAS *Sydney*.

Start by alighting at North Sydney, and cycling north up Miller Street before turning right at Falcon Street which becomes Military Road. One has the quick option of following this busy road to the Taronga Zoo turn-off, or one can take the long way through the maze of inner suburb roads and lanes to Bradley's Head Road, thereby avoiding the traffic.

Bradleys Head Road continues south, ending at the HMAS *Sydney* mast and lighthouse pylon at the head of the peninsula. Note the trench galleries between the gun-pits, and direction of the cannons. The objective was the defence of New South Wales from nineteenth-century maritime colonial powers such as France and Russia.

One can lock the bikes at the jetty around the other side of Athol Bay and spend the afternoon at the zoo before returning home.

THE ROYAL NATIONAL PARK

Size: 15 014 hectares
Enactment: 26 April 1879 (the world's first reserve to be called 'national park')
Visitors: Over 1½ million a year
Aboriginal Sites: The Dharawal tribe left many remains: rock engravings, axe-grinding grooves, charcoal drawings, and hand stencils. All are protected.
Flora: The environments alternate between coastal heath, woodlands, and rainforest. On the plateau tops alone are 700 species of flowering plants.
Fauna: Swamp wallabies, rat kangaroos, koalas, gliders, echidnas, New Holland mice, ring-tailed possums, numerous ground dwelling animals, and over 200 species of birds are recorded.
Camping: Developed camping ground at Bonnie Vale. Bush camping is permitted anywhere else with a free permit.
Visitors Centre: NPWS District Office, Audley: (02) 542 0648.
Adjoining Parks: Heathcote National Park, Garrawarra State Recreation Area

The area known today as the Royal National Park is a significant part of Sydney's heritage. Seeing the Royal National Park is seeing into the past. Being only 30 km from Sydney, its history has been interwoven with the state's capital since the late eighteenth century. Before Europeans settled Australia, the land was occupied by the Dharawal tribe, who used the sandstone caves for shelter and fished the coast, estuaries, and inland streams.

It was in 1796 that Bass and Flinders sought shelter from a thunderstorm at Coote Creek lagoon just inland from Wattamolla Bay at Providential Head. The first survey of the

Hacking River was made by Lord Audley in 1864. Before then, areas of the land especially to the south-west were logged. Evidence of this can be seen not only in the deprivation of larger trees but of tracks which were built and later developed into roads. A prime example of this is the Lady Wakehurst Drive.

The most significant event in the region's history, however, was the formation of the national park under the inspiration of Sir John Robertson (Premier of NSW). It was the first national park in Australia, created to satisfy the need for a 'sanctuary for pale-faced Sydneyites—fleeing the pollution— physical, mental, and social, of that densely packed city'.

The National Park, as it was simply called until 1954 when the Queen visited, has a poor history of conservation. Just after establishment, a Javanese rusa deer park was established opposite Gymea Bay where the Hacking River flows around Lightning Point. Due to poor security, however, the deer escaped into the park. Until recent times, the deer could be seen while cycling in the south of the park mainly along the Garawarra Ridge road. In 1992 park authorities began a con- troversial program of culling or deporting the deer, as they were not native and therefore did not belong in the park's ecosystem.

In 1886, a railway line was built from Loftus to Audley for the purposes of accessing the Hacking River at the confluence with Kangaroo Creek. The construction of Lady Carrington Drive allowed further access to the very south of the park, along the upper Hacking River. After that boating became very popular.

Logging continued until 1922 when the State Crown Solici- tor prevented the Trust from obtaining finance for park works from timber-felling revenue. Unfortunately this came too late, for most of the large blackbutt and turpentine trees were gone.

Fortunately, due to pressure from bushwalkers in the 1930s and 1940s, the state government took an interest in the park and bought a lot of private land off former residents. Some estate owners, like E. J. Coote, found themselves surrounded by national park and donated their land.

Further extensions are now impossible due to residential land to the immediate north and south and the Woronora Catchment Area in the west. But now with the loggers shut out, as well as the army, a new menace is destroying the park:

118

the tourist. Commercialisation of the beaches has led to thousands migrating to the coast on a sunny weekend to participate in surfing carnivals and the like. Like Ku-ring-gai Chase, picnic areas and popular camping spots have suffered and the situation is now intolerable to the national parks authorities. Common problems include defoliation of the flora, car-dumping, vandalism, crime, defacing of Aboriginal paintings, and four-wheel driving.

Although the picture painted above makes it sound like the Bronx of national parks, there are still large areas of pleasant cycling available, and the park's popularity to cyclists confirms this. Height variations are rarely more than 50 m so there is a minimal amount of climbing. The only exception is where trips are made down to the many beaches, a maximum of 200 metres of height must be regained.

All sealed roads and four-wheel drive tracks are open to bicycles. Cycling on walking trails is prohibited by National Parks authorities and if the situation becomes out of control, proposals for the specific zoning of bicycles will be enacted. This will mean that cyclists will be restricted to only a handful of trails enforced by a fine if caught elsewhere. In extreme cases, permits may be obtainable or cyclists excluded altogether. Therefore it is our duty to mitigate any possible blame that the national parks authorities could put on cyclists in order for such extreme measures to be taken.

Like Ku-ring-gai, both the Royal and Heathcote National Parks lend themselves well to one day rides, as they can be conducted by use of the Illawarra railway line. During the day, cooking fires are only permitted at authorised picnic grounds in steel fireplaces. The cutting down of live wood is illegal. Camping fees apply at Bonnie Vale on the Hacking River, and bookings are essential during holidays. Elsewhere, fees are not charged, but the disadvantage is that (1) a permit must be obtained from the Rangers Headquarters at the visitors centre, Audley and (2) no wood fires are permitted at all when camping—only fuel stoves may be used.

In January 1994, over 90% of the park including the majority of the adjoining Heathcote National Park was burnt out by severe bush fires. Accordingly the scarring will remain for many years, but at time of writing, there is abundant lush re-growth due to good late summer rains.

The stations of Loftus, Engadine, Heathcote, Waterfall, and

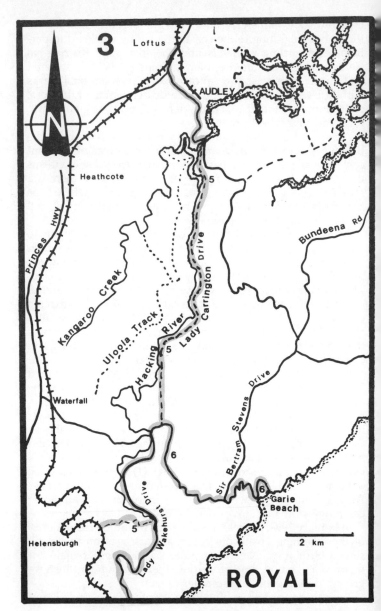

3

Loftus

AUDLEY

Heathcote

Princes Hwy

Kangaroo Creek

Uloola Track

Hacking River

Lady Carrington Drive

5

5

Bundeena Rd

Waterfall

Sir Bertram Stevens Drive

6

Helensburgh

Lady Wakehurst Drive

5

6

Garie Beach

2 km

ROYAL

Helensburgh are all good staging points, with Waterfall being especially popular as it services the Heathcote National Park too and takes only 50 minutes from Central. For the really lazy, one can catch the train right into the park. The old spur railway track built over 100 years ago still operates. It has the advantage of being close to the Audley visitors centre, and it is just a short downhill ride to the Hacking River and the start of the Lady Carrington Drive. Consult the Sutherland Time-table for train schedules.

RIDE 5:   LADY CARRINGTON DRIVE

FROM: Helensburgh Station
TO: Loftus Station
VIA: Lady Carrington Drive
LENGTH: 32 km
TIME: Full day
RIDE/TRACK GRADE: 3/3 (steep uphill climb from Audley required)
WALKING: Palona Cave, Uloola, and Karloo Tracks
HEIGHT VARIATION: 150 m
TRANSPORT: Rail (Sutherland Line)
FACILITIES: Numerous picnic areas along the Hacking River. Audley has most general facilities, including a kiosk
MAPS: CMA (LIC) Royal National Park 1:30 000 Tourist Map

This is one of the classic bike rides, being on a par with the Oaks Fire Trail in the Blue Mountains. For those who want to minimise uphills (and who doesn't?), this ride starts at the southern end of the Park (150 m) and finishes at the northern end. It also goes against the majority of the traffic on Lady Carrington Drive.

Start at Helensburgh and ascend up the main road through the township until the start of the numerous fire trails leading east. The track swings north momentarily before continuing down over the railway line and into the Garawarra State Rec-reation Area. This trail provides access to the Burgh Track which contours around the hill before joining up with the sealed Lady Wakehurst Drive just after crossing a ford. The

Hacking River here marks the boundary to the Royal National Park. One then follows the river downstream proceeding predominantly north and ignoring the causeway turnoff on the left. One then climbs slightly and the barrier to the Lady Carrington Drive entrance is on the left. The trail is of very good quality and one can easily maintain speeds of 20 kph. However, the rainforest here is far too beautiful to race through.

The 9.6 km long trail, was completed in 1886 and promoted as one of the most picturesque in the world. It was named after the wife of the governor of the colony of NSW at the time, Baron Carrington. Previously the large trees that lined the Hacking River were logged, and much of the majestic turpentine species is now gone.

The first diversion from the drive is at the confluence of the Hacking and Palona (Aboriginal for hawk) Creek. Here there is a walking track which leads east (right) for a kilometre ending at a large limestone overhang called Pagona Cave where some stalactites and stalagmites are being formed. The bikes have to be hidden or chained up at the start of this little track as riding on walking trails is illegal in the Royal National Park.

Three kilometres into the drive is a picnic ground on the left past the prominent bend in the river. The odd tree out here is an English oak tree standing in the middle of the ground and planted about 100 years ago. Not much further on, the Hacking River widens as a few smaller creeks flow into it. All the creek names in this area were named after Aboriginal birds by the original trustees of the park around the turn of the century.

The river here is effectively at sea level and has cut a valley some 140 to 170 m deep leaving a lot of rock exposed on the slopes. The drive hugs the river, and one passes some examples of early stonework. At Kobardo (Aboriginal for parrot), there is an old drinking trough. Further on, where Karoga Brook enters the Hacking, two stone basins dating from 1892 trap the water from Jersey Springs. One kilometre further, the stone remains of the old ranger's cottage are to be found. The river then bends west and one passes through Gibraltar Rock before leaving Lady Carrington Drive. After the locked gate, it shortly joins up again with Sir Bertram Stevens Drive at Ironbark Flat.

Here the Hacking gets dramatically wider as the Kangaroo and Engadine Creeks flow into it. This place is known as Audley and is one of the more developed areas in the park. The visitors centre, ranger's headquarters plus a number of facilities including a kiosk can be found here. It is recommended that one takes a rest, maybe lunch, and strolls around the banks of the Hacking River via the lower Uloola Track.

For those wishing to walk the Uloola Falls to Karloo Pool circuit, another four hours must be allowed, as the distance is some 15 km. Cross the bridge to Robertson Grove and just 30 m along the road a track branches off to the right. Walk straight up the slope and south along Gurrumboola Ridge, avoiding a turn-off to the right. Near the top is a junction, and one should proceed left or south along the ridge separating the Hacking River from Kangaroo Creek. This ridge should take about an hour to walk and a full water bottle is essential in hot weather. Vegetation here includes the beautiful waratah. Not shown on the tourist map is the Peach Trees Trig point just where the Uloola Track turns west. The turn-off is on the left, and is less than 100 m long where good views over the scenery you have just ridden are obtainable. However this track is getting increasingly overgrown and if you do not feel too confident diverging off the main track, then it should be ignored. Back on the Uloola Track, one descends to Uloola Falls which drop some 15 m into rainforest where water gums and black wattle are to be found.

One crosses above the first of the three drops of the falls and proceeds up the Karloo Track along another ridge and then down into Karloo Pool. Here there are numerous examples of unusual rock outcrops called 'Whalebacks'. According to the information pamphlet they resemble whales surfacing for air, although this has to be left to the imagination. Also on the way up are two rock stacks known as The Turrets hidden by low bush on the right. If you enjoy rock scrambling and exploring, you might like to inspect the views from the top.

The track then crosses Uloola Ridge and descends over 100 m into Karloo Pool. This is a beautiful place to spend an hour or so swimming, eating, or just lying around. From here, there are two ways back to Audley, one being simply along the creek and the other along the fire trail that leads back to Heathcote and thence along the Engadine Track. Both are straightforward, and take approximately the same time.

However one has to be on the southern side of Kangaroo Creek once Engadine Creek joins with it, otherwise crossing it will involve a major bath. At the confluence a track leads up the ridge and back to Audley.

Here the bikes have to be simply taken across the causeway and up the steep slope. On the top of the ridge is the Royal National Park station, although trains only run 3–4 times a day. On weekends there are two afternoon services and the Sutherland Line timetable has to be checked for these. The alternative is to cycle along Farnell Avenue past the toll booth where it is only a short distance along the Princes Highway to Loftus.

RIDE 6:   GARIE BEACH

FROM: Otford Station
TO: Loftus Station
VIA: The Cliff Track
LENGTH: 41 km
TIME: Full day
RIDE/TRACK GRADE: 4/1 (200 m climb uphill required)
WALKING: From Otford lookout to Garawarra Ridge (with bikes)
HEIGHT VARIATION: 210 m
TRANSPORT: Rail (Illawarra Line)
FACILITIES: General facilities at Garie Beach and Audley
MAPS: CMA (LIC) Otford 1:25 000 topographical (or Royal National Park 1:30 000 Tourist Map)

Because the railway stations of Loftus and Otford are the same height above sea level, it doesn't really matter from which end you start. I've chosen to end the ride at Loftus due to the greater frequency of trains from there back to the metropolitan area. It is strongly recommended leaving very early so that the late morning hours can be spent at the beach before the inevitable afternoon on-shore wind starts.

From Otford Station, push the bikes up the eastern embankment on to a small dirt road. Turn left, continuing up, and contouring around into Fanshawe Road. This leads over the crest to Lady Wakehurst Drive. It is just a short ride north-east to Otford Lookout. From here a foot track leads due north to up a ridge. Some scrambling with the bikes will be called for as 100 m will have to be gained. But at the top the track broadens into a proper 4WD trail. It runs at the top of cliffs for much of its way north coming out at Sir Bertram Stevens Drive just before the turn off to Garie Beach. Watch for the inevitable traffic as you descend down this road losing all of the previously gained height. There are good views and a few constructed lookouts along the way down.

The alternative to staying the day at Garie Beach is to continue another 5 km along the main road to the turn off at Wattamolla Road. Here one simply descends to Wattamolla Lagoon. This is the spot where Bass and Flinders took refuge from storms. Clear, calm waters in the inlet or the lagoon make for safe, enjoyable swimming. Walking up and down the coast is also possible along the well developed Coastal Track. Towards the end of the day, one can ride to Loftus via Audley, or one can catch the ferry from Bundeena.

From Garie Beach, it is possible to exit the national park by backtracking or via Lady Carrington Drive where cool rainforest provides a pleasant contrast to the hot beach.

RIDE 7:   WORONORA DAM
(HEATHCOTE NATIONAL PARK)

FROM: Waterfall Station
TO: Engadine Station
VIA: Woronora Dam
LENGTH: 33 km
TIME: 1 day
RIDE/TRACK GRADE: 3/3
WALKING: Optional walks to the centre of the park
HEIGHT VARIATION: 240 m
TRANSPORT: Rail (Sutherland, Illawarra Lines)
FACILITIES: General picnic facilities
MAPS: CMA (LIC) Royal National Park 1:30 000 Tourist
Map (or Campbelltown and Appin 1:25 000 topographicals)

The Royal National Park's kid sister, Heathcote National Park is a triangle over 2000 hectares large bordered by the Woronora catchment area to the south, the Holsworthy field firing range to the north, and the Royal National Park to the east. A popular picnic spot is the flat peninsula that sticks out into Lake Woronora. The road to here is the only road where motorised transport is allowed therefore the return journey via Sydney Water Board management trails fortunately can be made free from traffic.

From Waterfall station, cross the highway and turn right at Warabin Street. Follow this to the end where a fire trail branches off left, passes a gate and swings down south past Yellow Pool. As you cross Heathcote Creek there is a sign on the right which indicates the start of the Bullawarring Track, one of the more popular walking trails through the centre of the park. The main fire trail, however, follows some powerlines adjacent to the creek, and leads back to the highway. About half way down this trail, you come to a gate not marked on the tourist map. Just before this gate, there is a small walking trail marked by white paint up to Mount Westmacott, the second highest peak in the park. Here there are excellent views for almost 360 degrees. The first on the right is the Woronora Dam Road which is only half an hour away. The road is of good quality and undulates along a ridge line which marks the boundary of the catchment area. To the left there is a restricted access zone to protect the catchment area of the reservoir.

WORONORA DAM	
Completed	1941
Height	66 metres
Capacity	71 790 megalitres
Catchment Area	75 square kilometres
Lake Area	380 hectares

At the dam itself, one can rest here enjoying the views over the lake. From here it is a simple ride back along the pipeline service trail to Heathcote or Engadine. It starts just two kilometres back, marked as a minor unsealed road over Sarahs Knob. Along the way, there are a number of walking diversions. Tracks lead to Lake Eckersley and a cave nearby, as well as south along the Heathcote Creek to several beautiful natural swimming pools including Minda, Myuna, and Kingfisher. It is even possible to do round trips of various lengths if the time is available. Camping is also possible at some areas but permits are required.

The walking tracks are all well defined and signposted so detailed descriptions here are not necessary. Suffice it to say that riding bikes on them is prohibited by park officials. However, due to the illegality of car-access to the northern part of the park, there aren't many people here even on the busiest days. For this reason, cyclists can hide their bikes in the scrub knowing with reasonable confidence that they'll still be there when they return. In other Sydney national parks, for example Sydney Harbour, Ku-ring-gai, and Royal, this confidence is not really possible without a good lock.

The Pipeline Service Trail comes out under the Heathcote to Liverpool Road. The nearest station is Engadine, and can be accessed by crossing the recreation reserve to Woronora Road and turning right until you come to Waratah Road. The second on the right is Boronia Avenue which shortly connects to the Old Princes Highway. Travelling north, one comes to the top of Station Street. From here one simply rolls down to the end, across the highway and on to the platform.

FURTHER CYCLING IN THE ROYAL AND HEATHCOTE NATIONAL PARKS

Limited scope exists for further off-road mountain bike touring in these two parks. The majority of management trails of the Royal National Park are dead ends, while service trails in the Heathcote National Park and adjoining Holsworthy military area are strictly out of bounds. However, touring bike rides to destinations such as Bundeena can still provide enjoyment for cyclists who have not been to the area before.

RIDE 8:   THE OLD GREAT NORTH ROAD

FROM: Windsor Station
VIA: Old Great North Road (return)
LENGTH: 130 km (55 km to Mills Creek)
TIME: 2 days with overnight camping at Mills Creek

RIDE/TRACK GRADE: 5/6
WALKING: Mill Creek Grass Tree Circuit
HEIGHT VARIATION: 270 m
TRANSPORT: Rail to Windsor (Emu Plains/Richmond Line), and two ferries across the Hawkesbury. Alternatively, private transport can taken to the Mills Creek picnic area where the bikes can be used to complete the off road part of the trip. This reduces the ride by some 100 km, making it a simple one-day excursion
FACILITIES: Toilets, barbecues, firewood are provided at the Mill Creek camping area
MAPS: CMA Lower Portland, St. Albans, Mangrove, Wilberforce and Gunderman 1:25 000 topographicals

The Dharug National Park was named after the major Aboriginal tribe that inhabited the whole of the north Sydney region. Together with the Yengo, Marra Marra, Brisbane Water, and Bouddi National Parks, it forms a nearly complete protection zone for the Hawkesbury River to flow undisturbed from Wisemans Ferry to the sea. The 14 801 hectare park is bordered by the Great Old North Road, private agricultural land along Mangrove Creek, and the Hawkesbury River to the south. Swamp wallaby, wombats, and possums are common within these boundaries. A pocket of warm temperate rainforest is also a feature of the park around the Spencer area, supported by volcanic soils. But the dominant tree species are the eucalypts: grey gum and yellow bloodwood.

Like the Royal and Ku-ring-gai National Parks, Dharug is rich in history. The demand for flat pastoral land led to exploration of the surrounding Sydney regions by the turn of the nineteenth century. The fertile Hunter Valley was discovered and work began by Howe at the instigation of Governor Macquarie to find a pass through the rugged gorges and cliffs that make up the Hawkesbury region. He discovered a rough way through Putty which took some four years before the public could use it.

Even before the road was completed, demand for a better communications route between Sydney and Newcastle grew. Governor Brisbane commissioned a man named Finch to find one. He found a ridge that led to Wollombi and construction began in 1826 employing some 520 convicts who worked for two years carving the road out of solid rock. The road was the

128

Ku-Ring-Gai Chase National Park (Ride 3)

The Hacking River, Royal National Park (Ride 5)

The Nattai River (Ride 15)

most popular access route between the Sydney and the north for half a century, before the new MacDonald River–Mogo Creek Road provided better protection from bushrangers and water to replenish horses and other livestock. Steam boats along the coast further led to the disuse of the road. Today however, there is a revival of walkers, cyclists, and four-wheel drivers along the road, for its significance becomes apparent when seeing the incredible feats of nineteenth-century engineering along the way.

Few facilities have been installed inside the park since its declaration in 1967. There is a well developed picnic and camping area east of Wisemans Ferry at Mill Creek. Car camping is permitted, but at a price of $5 per site for two adults. Additional adults are $1.20 and children (5–15 years) are half price. Since there are only 33 sites (13 of which are for pack camping), reservations are recommended and can be made by phoning the Hawkesbury District Office in Gosford on (043) 24 4911. Fees must be paid in advance. Bush camping is permitted at Ten Mile Hollow near a Buddhist monastery, but this site has suffered from overuse and accordingly portable fuel stoves are necessary. The is a ranger's station at Hazel Dell, situated roughly between Wisemans Ferry and the Mill Creek camping area.

Here is a good opportunity to get accustomed to bike camping on an interesting route within public transport reach from Sydney. The first half follows the wide, slow Hawkesbury River from Windsor winding through pleasant agricultural land and holiday resorts before crossing at Wisemans Ferry. The second half traces the original route of the Old Great North Road for approximately 15 km before branching along another ridge to the Mill Creek camping area. For those who never ride their mountain bikes on sealed roads, one can drive to the camping area and cycle a round circuit via Wisemans Ferry.

After alighting at Windsor (about an hour from Central), follow George Street down to the lights where Richmond Road connects with Macquarie Street. Continue down and turn left at the end. This is the start of the Putty Road (also called the Wilberforce Road or Singleton Road depending on which map you've got) which provides one of the principle access points to the massive Wollemi National Park. Cross the bridge and continue through flat agricultural land, following the river.

At King Road (later called Sackville Road), turn right and proceed for about 9 km where a ferry provides a crossing. There is no fee and the ferry runs throughout the year from sunrise to sunset. The trip takes about seven minutes. Once across, the first real bushland is entered. The road passes a turn-off to North Sackville. For a great ride along the river, one should take the first sealed road on the left after climbing slightly. The alternative, and shorter route, is to follow this road until it meets with the Old Northern Road. This however is through boring pastoral land and a great deal of fast traffic makes this an uneventful road, the monotony only broken up by the Cattai State Recreation Area.

The better choice joins with the river and has little traffic on it, although you will be bound to meet the odd cyclist. It winds its way through the small hills on the southern side of the Hawkesbury, but never rises or lowers more than 50 m. It is a good quality sealed road for the first half, but then turns to short patches of loose gravel past Upper Half Moon Bend. A good place to stop for a rest is where the mighty Colo River flows into the Hawkesbury at Lower Portland. The water here comes from as far away as Capertee, on the road to Mudgee.

Continue following the river past Webbs Creek Ferry to Wisemans Ferry. This peninsula is named after an ex-convict called Solomon Wiseman who supplied the convicts with food during the construction of the road. He was granted a lease to operate a ferry in 1827, and it became the primary crossing point of the Hawkesbury River for almost a hundred years. He died a very wealthy man in 1838, but today the ferry is free, and waiting times are minimal for the cyclist has the incomparable advantage of being able to push in. There are also shops for people wishing to fill up on supplies before entering the national park. On the other bank, one can proceed straight to the Mill Creek camping ground only a half hour to the right. This option has the advantage of being able to leave the majority of your gear at the camp site before undergoing the strenuous climb up to the Old Great Northern Road.

For those wishing to continue on, turn left and the start of the trail is signposted and fenced off to four-wheel drivers almost immediately on the right. No matter how many gears you have, you will have to push up this first stretch, due to the extremely steep gradient. This however is a blessing in disguise, for along the way are amazing examples of convict engineering. The man supervising this section of the work was Percy Simpson. Ascent of the rocky ridge was enabled by the building of gigantic stone buttresses, bridges, run-off drains, and retaining walls. The first 2 km of this trail are the most spectacular, with huge hand-carved blocks of sandstone lining the road. Information boards give details of the construction processes, quarry sites, and interesting statistics. It is easy to imagine the gruelling conditions almost 200 years ago, carving blocks out of solid rock. There are also occasional views over the MacDonald River valley.

The trail starts to level out around the 200 m mark and here is where cycling can be resumed again. Ignore turn-offs to the left and right and pass over several saddles before climbing again. The road quality is reasonable but progress will be hampered by the continuous undulations between knolls. As the map indicates, a well graded road intersects just past the top of the last hill. This is an electricity service trail. Turn right here and it is predominantly downhill along another ridge to the Sackville Road, coming out just west of the rangers station. It would be wise to check the brakes before making this descent for it is easy to get tempted into speeds in excess of 30 km an hour. Close to the end, where the grade starts to get steep, there is a fine lookout over the Hawkesbury River next to an electricity pylon.

Back on the main road, it is less than 2 km to the turn-off into the Mill Creek camping area. For those who wish to use private transport, parking is on the left hand side immediately before and after the brook. It is still recommended that you cycle up the Old Great North Road and return via the closed 2WD road. If one goes anti-clockwise, one will race past the best features of the road, and see nothing.

The nature walking trail starts at the picnic ground (500 m north of the camping ground past a helicopter landing ground). The walk is at the far side of the grassy cleared area. Follow the creek for several kilometres before ascending up on to a ridgetop and down a hanging valley at the base of massive cliffs. It is not marked on the Gunderman map, but it's well defined and regularly upgraded. Allow about 3 hours as the length is some 11 km through hilly terrain. Vegetation along Biamea Creek includes epiphytes and sassafras, but most characteristic of the area are the grass trees.

The next day simply cross the Hawkesbury River via Wiseman's Ferry again and cycle to Windsor. You can afford to leave late, for trains leave from Windsor to the city at least every half hour, even at night.

FURTHER CYCLING IN THE DHARUG NATIONAL PARK

Variations of this ride include staying up on the ridge and camping at Ten Mile Hollow. The advantage is that there are fewer people, due to the lack of conventional car access. But the disadvantage is that one must sacrifice luxury with few facilities being provided. Just past the campsite, there is a convict built bridge.

Another ride is to continue up the Old Great North Road, along the Judge Dowling Range avoiding the turn-off to Mangrove Mountain. Three kilometres further you will exit the Dharug National Park. However land to the north is now part of the 140,000 hectare Yengo National Park and the Mangrove River catchment area. After crossing through Sampsons Pass at the base of the prominent Mount Lockyer (317 m), it is only half an hour before the road comes out just south of Bucketty along the St Albans to Bucketty Road. From here, turn left where a pleasant cycle along a ridge top takes you to the start of the Mogo Creek Valley. It is downhill all the way to the MacDonald River where there is flat, easy cycling to the next campsite at Mills Creek. The road is well graded but with some corrugation that can make saddle soreness just that little more uncomfortable. The Mogo Creek on the right was the water source for travellers to Newcastle in the nineteenth century who preferred this route to the dry ridge tops of the Old Great North Road.

Shops and general tourist facilities are available at the small picturesque township of St Albans. From here one can take either of the two roads down the MacDonald River, swimming wherever one wants to. Another half hour must be allowed for if choosing the right hand bank road as two ferries have to be crossed to get the Mills Creek camping ground. Along the way is a cemetery with some very old dates on the tombstones, and a mysterious old church. Be careful not to avoid missing the last ferry which leaves around 6.00 p.m. depending when the sun goes down.

For those with limited time, this ride can be done in two days by driving to the Mills Creek picnic area and parking there. This would also have the advantage of saving weight by carrying less food. The best route is clockwise so one can enjoy the Old Great North Road's wonders, camp up the top, cycle the ridge, and coast down again. Start very early on the second day for the journey is some 80 km long.

FURTHER CYCLING IN THE SYDNEY AREA

There is a lot of scope for introductory mountain biking in the many parks and reserves in and around the Sydney metropolitan area. Day ride starting points can be easily accessed by public transport. Proper planning will limit backtracking by ending the tour at another rail station. For further touring bike rides, consult *Cycling around Sydney with hang-ten*, published by Bicycle New South Wales, or *Seeing Sydney by bicycle* by Julia Thorn. Parramatta Park is a popular training ground for cyclists.

MYRTACEAE

5
The Blue Mountains

BLUE MOUNTAINS
NATIONAL PARK

Size: 236 932 hectares
Enactment: 1959
Visitors: Over four million a year
Aboriginal Sites: 100+ dating back 22 000 years
Flora: Well over 1000 species in 40 separate communities
Fauna: 27 marsupial species, 2 monotremes, 17 other
mammal species, 98 types of reptiles, and over 200 bird
species have been recorded
Camping: Official car-camping ground at Euroka Clearing
(fees apply). Elsewhere bush camping is permitted any-
where—no fees and permits required
District Office: Bruce Road, Glenbrook and Govetts Leap
Road, Blackheath
Adjoining Parks: Kanangra Boyd National Park, Wollemi
National Park, Nattai National Park, Thirlmere Lakes
National Park, and numerous state forests on the western
perimeter

This chapter outlines rides through the best and largest cycling
area in the state, if not, the best in the country. Four major
national parks, state recreation areas, and several state forests
make up well over a million hectares of eucalypt forest covering the rugged Great Dividing Range. Not only is it in a
central position, easily accessible from Newcastle, Sydney, and
Wollongong, but public transport allows the car to be left at
home. The Muswellbrook Line services the northern Wollemi
National Park, the Lithgow line provides direct access to the
central Blue Mountains plateau, while the Kanangra Boyd
National Park, the Nattai Wilderness, and the southern Blue
Mountains is best approached via the Goulburn train line.
Each area takes no longer than three hours, the heartland of

the Blue Mountains taking just two. As in the *CityRail* network, bikes are permitted in the vestibules of the interstate trains.

Those who cycle the length of Narrow Neck (Ride 37) will pass a small track on the right towards the end named Dunphy's Pass. It was named after the extraordinary man whose vision it was to protect the Blue Mountains from logging, mining, commercialisation, agriculture, urbanisation, and other forms of development. Myles Dunphy (1891–1985) had to wait almost thirty years after he first formally proposed the idea, and it wasn't a minute too late, for the first advances by progressive man were already in evidence.

But today, the mining towns are ghost towns, agricultural land is slowly being bought back, mine shafts are closed, and the coal and shale railway lines have been dismantled. There are many thousands of hectares of untouched land, the closest true wilderness areas to Sydney.

The rich history of the land deserves to be told. Before there were even mountains in the area, rivers deposited sand up to 1 km thick. The lower half of this sand was compressed into sandstone that was consequently uplifted about 1 000 000 years ago. Rivers flowing down on either side of the central plateau (where the train and highway now are) formed spectacular gorges especially where the uplift was most pronounced in the west.

Two tribes have lived in the area for at least 20 000 years leaving many examples of their culture: archaeological deposits, engravings, rock paintings, stencils, grinding grooves, and stone arrangements. Only a fraction are formally documented, and there have been unconfirmed reports of literally hundreds of sites all throughout the park, especially the central portion around the Jamison and Burragorang Valleys. This area, and land to the west was occupied by the Gandangara tribe. Further to the south: along the Kowmung and around present day Yerrandrie was the territory of the Duruk tribe. With the steady encroachment of European civilisation, they soon died out.

But it took white man a quarter of a century to conquer the Blue Mountains. Legends of what was on the other side are famous: inland seas, China, the coast. As settlers began to establish farms along the Nepean River, the pressure for a way across grew. Numerous attempts were made: in 1793, William Patterson explored the lower Grose River but had to give up due to slow progress. George Bass, in the same year that he was stranded in the present day Royal National Park, made his way towards Kanangra Walls via the Burragorang Valley but also had to turn back because of sheer cliffs. Another explorer, Barrallier almost made it via the same way but was forced to return due to the same reason. The problem in crossing the mountains was that the early pioneers followed rivers as this was the tradition in Europe and Asia. Since dense scrub surrounds both banks of any river, while the water itself is blocked by huge boulders, progress was limited to just 20 km a day. One must remember that there were no tracks or even maps of the area, and freeze dried food and other examples of modern technology that bushwalkers enjoy today didn't exist.

In 1804, another assault was conducted on the Grose River by a man called George Caley. He found the top of the Bell Range but despaired when he topped the crest of the ridge at Mount Banks and saw nothing but cliffs ahead of him. But in less than ten years, a new strategy was adopted and instead of walking along valleys, Blaxland, Lawson and Wentworth worked their way in a predominantly west-north-west direction along ridges, almost reaching Lithgow. The same year, George Evans followed the route and ended up at Bathurst. On the other side they found millions of hectares of some of the most fertile agricultural land in the world!

One century later, when the Royal and Ku-ring-gai National Parks were established as reserved land, Myles Dunphy saw the threat from progress and began his famous campaign to save the Blue Mountains. He formed the Mountain Trails Club in 1914 after three years of extensive exploration of the southern wilderness, one of the first bushwalking clubs in Australia. Much of the land from Jenolan Caves in the west to the Burragorang Valley in the east was investigated and documented in sketch maps and notes. After the First World War, the proposal for the national park was first discussed at one of the club's meetings. Ten years later, with support from other bushwalking groups, a formal submission was made to the Surveyor-General in 1932. Collaboration between various clubs had previously succeeded in the saving of the blue gum forest from two Bilpin farmers who had started ring-barking it. The going price? £150!

But it was another twenty years until the State Government

submitted to pressure from the public in order to enact the proposal. Ironically, the best persuasion came from the commercial sector, who saw potential profits in the tourist trade.

> We cannot live for commerce alone, nor will our civilisation be deemed great until we thoroughly recognise the fact the bushlands and all they naturally contain are gifts of Nature far transcending in value all monetary and commercial considerations. The humanising gifts of Nature are necessary for our interests, education, adventure, romance and peace of mind. All the Glory of canyons, caves, and rolling plateaux of our great Blue Mountains is not nearly so much a commercial asset as it is Nature's heritage for legitimate enjoyment, and our own gift to prosperity.
>
> Myles Dunphy
> *Katoomba Daily* (Supplement)
> 24 August 1934

The national park grew dramatically in stages. It took another decade for the south-west extension to be added on, and yet another two decades for the remaining area: the southeast. In 1992, Terry Metherill the then Liberal MP invited Myles Dunphy's son, Milo Dunphy who heads the Total Environment Centre to parliament and formerly introduce the last section of the original proposal: Nattai National Park. Today, over 1 000 000 hectares of continuous bushland will exist from the Hunter Valley in the north to Mittagong in the south, and improve what is already one of the world's greatest parks complexes.

Opportunities for cycling in the Blue Mountains are limitless. The variety can accommodate those who are inexperienced and prefer to be closer to civilisation on their first few rides, as well as hardcore mountain biking fanatics who abseil into rugged gorges with bikes strapped to their back.

The beauty about the Blue Mountains is that it is the only place in New South Wales where one can catch a train up to a height of 1000 m above sea level and cycle all the way down to a railway station at just 30 m altitude. These rides, where pedalling is hardly required, were my first experience of cycling. But beware: they're addictive. If you would prefer to witness something of the landscape rather than racing down fire trails with your hair on fire, you can take it easy and stick

137

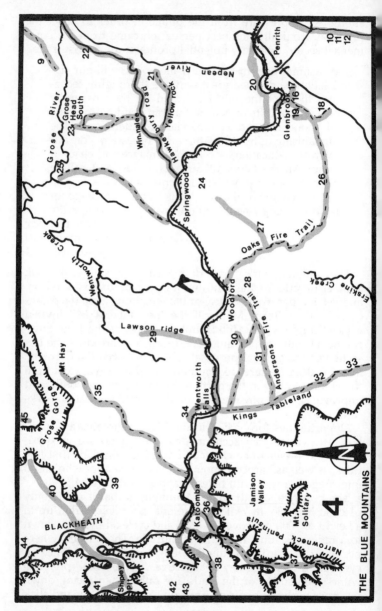

THE BLUE MOUNTAINS

4

N

Penrith
Nepean River
Grose River
Grose Head South
Winnalee road
Hawkesbury road
Yellow rock
Glenbrook
Springwood
Oaks Fire Trail
Erskine Creek
Wentworth Creek
Woodford
Lawson ridge
Andersons Fire Trail
Mt Hay
Grose Gorge
Wentworth Falls
Kings Tableland
Jamison Valley
Mt. Solitary
Narrowneck Peninsula
Katoomba
BLACKHEATH
Shipley Plt.

9
22
21
23
25
10
11
12
20
19, 16, 17
18
24
26
27
28
29
30
31
32
33
35
45
34
40
39
44
41
42
43
36
38
37

138

mainly to the flat plateaus and cliff tops around Katoomba, Leura, and Blackheath. You can then return to the station without having to push the bike at all. On the other hand, you can drop down into the valleys, camp by a river and cycle down to the plain where you can catch a train home again. For the more adventurous, you can cycle south right along the spine of the mountains, and close to the real wilderness areas. Here numerous walking tracks go down to the beautiful Kowmung River, one of the only unpolluted rivers in New South Wales. From the abandoned silver mining town of Yerrandrie in the south, one can easily continue to Mittagong and catch a train home, the whole excursion taking less than a week.

Whatever your fancy, the Blue Mountains fire trails are open to all cyclists. The only exception is the 3 km restricted access zone which constitutes the Lake Burragorang catchment area, the source of Sydney's drinking water. The rides listed in this chapter are by no means a comprehensive list of the trails available for cycling. Get some experience, then buy some maps and design your own plans. The state forests on the western boundaries and Kanangra Boyd National Park are criss-crossed with hundreds of kilometres of disused trails which offer limitless opportunities for custom-made adventures.

1. THE FOOTHILLS

RIDE 9: VALE LOOKOUT

FROM: Richmond Station
TO: Vale Lookout (return)
VIA: Grose Vale
LENGTH: 40 km
TIME: 1 day
RIDE/TRACK GRADE: 4/3
WALKING: None
HEIGHT VARIATION: 240 m
TRANSPORT: Rail (Richmond Line)

FACILITIES: None
MAPS: CMA (LIC) Kurrajong 1:25 000 topographical

Although no train line services the Kurrajong area, the hills are sufficiently gentle to allow easy cycling from Richmond to some scenic places north of the Grose River. One such is the Vale Lookout, sitting upon high cliffs which tower over the Grose River.

From Richmond Station, head north-west up Kurrajong Road and cross the bridge over the Hawkesbury River. Turn left at the first set of traffic lights on to Grose Vale Road. This climbs gradually to the scattered township of Grose Vale and turn left at Cabbage Tree Road. This deteriorates into a loose gravel road all the way to the lookout. The final section is steep and wet weather can produce many water-filled potholes. The informal rock-platform lookout is the highest stage of the trip and there are several points which give views up and down the Grose River. The lookout is almost directly opposite the massive Grose Head South mountain (see Ride 23). The Grose River was once thought to be a viable thoroughfare to the other side of the mountains. The sheer ruggedness of the gorge however prevented anyone from exploring further than the junction with Wentworth Creek. An early explorer, William Patterson (1755–1810) actually tried to take canoes up the rapids but was prevented from going further by heavy thunderstorms making progress upstream impossible. In 1857, the lesson was forgotten and an attempt was made to build a railway line up the Grose Valley. A survey track was built alongside the river taking some three years to build with sixty labourers. Eventually someone decided that the track would be impractical and the whole project was abandoned. Today, little remains of the Engineers Track due to floods, landslides, boulders, undergrowth, and erosion.

Return to Richmond via the Grose Wold Road which has less traffic on it enabling you to enjoy the downhill.

RIDE 10:   THE ROCK

FROM: Penrith Station
TO: Mulgoa Trig (return)

VIA: Rileys Mountain
LENGTH: 54 km
TIME: 1 day
RIDE/TRACK GRADE: 4/5
WALKING: None
HEIGHT VARIATION: 213 m
TRANSPORT: Rail (Emu Plains Line)
FACILITIES: None
MAPS: CMA (LIC) Penrith 1:25 000 topographical

This region is one of the few parts of the national park east of
the Nepean River and The Rock Lookout offers dramatic views
of the gorge cut through by the river. Being formerly private
property, the eastern bank of the Nepean Gorge was annexed
on to the national park in 1978.

From Penrith cycle up Station Street, past the mall and showground to the intersection with Jamison Street. Turn right
and then left again at the traffic lights. This is Mulgoa Road
and it is easy cycling south past Panthers through open agricultural land to Fairlight Road. The turnoff is just after a park
on the left and a school ground on the right and is signposted
as Mount Schoenenstatt. Turn right and climb about 100 m
before levelling out. Some great houses are passed with occasional views over the lower Blue Mountains and Penrith. As
the road deteriorates into dirt, it turns north and soon after a
locked gate marks the beginning of the national park. A car
park at the end of the road is where most people have to walk
from, but fortunately for the cyclist, a well graded fire trail
runs parallel to the river for another 4 km. Along the way is
the Rock Lookout. A well signposted walking trail leads down
some steps and up again to a ledge where one can look both
up and down the 200 m gorge. In the background on the
northern side is Emu Plains. A high pitched call will be return
from the opposite cliffs a few seconds later. The Nepean River
was first discovered by Europeans on 27 June 1789. A party
led by Captain Watkin Tench (1759–1833) reported bark huts
and bird traps in the area made by an Aboriginal tribe. It has
named by Governor Arthur Phillip after the Undersecretary of
State for the Home Department, Sir Evan Nepean. The township of Penrith, formerly Evan, was named after an English
town in the district of Cumberland. Vegetation in the area

includes scribbly gum, tea trees, banksias, and the round-leaved bossia.

Another lookout not marked on the map is from Rileys Mountain near the Mulgoa Trig on the left. The track here is rough in patches as it passes through swamp heath and open eucalypt forest. Further along there is another lookout just opposite Mount Portal. Past this point, the eastern bank of the Nepean River is private property once more.

RIDE 11:   BENTS BASIN

FROM: Penrith Station
TO: Bents Basin State Recreation Area (return)
VIA: Mulgoa Road
LENGTH: 58 km
TIME: 1 long day
RIDE/TRACK GRADE: 3/2
WALKING: Optional short walk up to Caleys Lookout on the western side
HEIGHT VARIATION: 120 m
TRANSPORT: Rail (Emu Plains Line)
FACILITIES: Picnic ground at Bents Basin
MAPS: CMA (LIC) Penrith and Warragamba 1:25 000 topographicals

Even though not a national park, the Bents Basin State Recreation Area is a very scenic and secluded green 'oasis' which has long been popular with locals. It is practically an island being surrounded on three sides by the Nepean River, and is located 25 km south of Penrith or 14 km south of Wallacia. The preserved area is 405 hectares and was named after Justice Ellis Bent who had leased the area from the Crown. Today it is administered by a non-NPWS government department.

Catch an early train to give you as much time as possible swimming in the basin. From Penrith cycle up Station Street, past the mall and showground to the intersection with Jamison Street. Turn right and then left again at the traffic lights. This is Mulgoa Road and it is easy cycling south past Panthers through open agricultural land to Wallacia. Cross the Nepean River at Blaxlands Crossing. Just past the other side, take the first on the left, signposted as Bent Basin Road. From here it is 8 km to the destination. It is hard to imagine when cycling along here through uneventful agriculture land that a beautiful forested oasis exist just at the end. Along the way is a site for a controversial new skirmish ground. At the very end, the road turns to dirt and there's a gate before one drops down to an informal carpark.

The road through the recreation area leads left from the carpark down to a bridge over the river. The area's beauty is made by the wide bend in the river around Little Mountain bordered by two beaches. Facilities include bins, picnic tables, and fire places. The water here is generally pleasant and relatively clean, and some excellent platforms exist on the far right hand side next to the rapids. A walking track leads from the back of mowed recreation grounds. Stories exist as to the depth of the river in the middle of the basin, some rumours hint at a volcanic vent. Whatever the reason, when diving near the centre, one experiences a rapid decrease in water temperature suggesting great depth.

Picnic grounds are also located on the southern side, across the river. Here there are toilets, a kiosk, the Richard S. Venables Education Centre, and camping ground (fees apply). The day can be spent swimming and relaxing, or exploring the Nepean Gorge. The resident ranger experiences much difficulty in enforcing the no after-hours entry rule, but generally will allow one to stay after sunset if they do not intend to camp on the northern picnic area. Allow about four hours for the journey back to Penrith.

RIDE 12:   NORTONS BASIN

FROM: Penrith Station
TO: Nortons Basin (return)
VIA: Mulgoa Road
LENGTH: 46 km
TIME: 1 day
RIDE/TRACK GRADE: 4/2
WALKING: None
HEIGHT VARIATION: 159 m
TRANSPORT: Rail (Emu Plains Line)

FACILITIES: None
MAPS: CMA (LIC) Penrith 1:25 000 topographical

The destination of the ride is a beautiful valley near the confluence of the Nepean River and the largest river in the Blue Mountains: the Warragamba. Although located very close to Bents Basin, it is more isolated and set in wilder setting. Once again the river curves in a wide gentle bend, making it ideal for swimming.

Catch an early train to give you as much time as possible swimming in the basin. From Penrith cycle up Station Street, past the mall and showground to the intersection with Jamison Street. Turn right and then left again at the traffic lights. This is Mulgoa Road and it is easy cycling south past Panthers through open agricultural land to Wallacia. Cross the Nepean River at Blaxlands Crossing and climb up a long steep hill through residential land. The turn-off is on the right near the top of the crest and is signposted by a small sign on the opposite side. The sealed road soon turns to dirt leading past more private property before deteriorating further. At the end is a car park. A track continues past a barrier down a short steep embankment to the prominent curve in the river where you can pick any of the numerous spots to relax in this oasis. Many birds inhabit the area, no doubt living off the picnic food scraps left by visitors. There is not as much sand as Bents Basin, but one can find some rock platforms or grassy areas on the other side of the rapids.

Allow about four hours for the return trip to Penrith.

RIDE 13:   BURRAGORANG LOOKOUT

FROM: Picton Station
TO: Burragorang Lookout (return)
VIA: Oakdale, and Nattai
LENGTH: 62 km
TIME: 1 long day
RIDE/TRACK GRADE: 4/1
WALKING: None
HEIGHT VARIATION: 410 m
TRANSPORT: Rail (Goulburn Line)

FACILITIES: Kiosk and general picnic facilities at Burragorang Lookout
MAPS: CMA (LIC) Picton, Burragorang, and Camden 1:
25 000 topographicals (or Blue Mountains National Park
1:150 000 Tourist Map)

A spectacular feature in the south-eastern Blue Mountains is near located near Nattai. From Burragorang Lookout, dramatic views can be obtained north and south along the massive cliff-lined drowned Burragorang Valley, the source of Sydney's drinking water. Despite the long distance, it is a comfortable day's cycling along sealed roads. A touring bike would allow especially good averages to be maintained along the flat straight country roads.

From Picton, cross the Nepean River via the Victoria Bridge and turn right on to Argyle Street (Remembrance Drive). After crossing under the railway line, head left on the road to The Oaks. The road winds its through lush green pastoral hills. Ignore the turn-off to The Oaks and continue straight where the road becomes Barkers Lodge Road. Within 10 kilometres, you'll arrive at Oakdale where you should turn left to Nattai and the signposted Burragorang Valley. This section can be uncomfortable at times due to the frequency of coal trucks from the Oakdale and Nattai Collieries and the Wollondilly Washery. The road soon enters pleasant bushland and begins to climb. On the other side of the small village of Nattai, a gate on the right leads up to Burragorang Lookout. This is one of the few public access corridors the Sydney Water Board allows people to enter the restricted three kilometre zone around Lake Burragorang. It is a gruelling climb but the views from the top are worth it. A cap park, kiosk, and picnic ground exist near the edge before the lands falls dramatically away to the gigantic cliff-lined lake 400 m below. The lookout has good photographic potential, especially in the morning when mist is quite common almost half a kilometre below you, and the massive cliffs on the opposite glow bright red as they reflect the early sun. The land immediately west of the lake contains the rugged Tonalli and Lacy Tableland plateaus, the largest trackless wilderness area in the Blue Mountains National Park.

The stored water here is only one section of the massive Lake Burragorang, formed by Warragamba Dam. Two main water courses flow into the lake, forming the Warragamba

River that flows into the Nepean. One is Coxs River, that starts north of Lithgow near the Wolgan Valley. The other is the Wollondilly River with a massive catchment area that extends all the way south of Goulburn almost to Lake George. This latter river is the southerly arm that the lookout presides over. Lake Burragorang, with an area several times that of Sydney Harbour, is the primary lake that supplies Sydney's drinking water, and will soon be augmented by extensions to the Shoalhaven scheme (Welcome Reef) due to the city's rapidly expanding population.

LAKE BURRAGORANG

Area:	7500 hectares
Foreshores:	354 km
Capacity:	Over 2 million megalitres (2 billion tonnes)
Maximum depth:	105 metres

WARRAGAMBA DAM

Length:	351 metres
Height:	142 metres
Width:	Up to 104 metres
Volume:	3,000,000 tonnes of concrete

The road down to the lake from Nattai is restricted by gates and notices. Return to Picton via the same route.

RIDE 14:   THIRLMERE LAKES

FROM: Tahmoor Station
TO: Thirlmere Lakes National Park
VIA: Thirlmere Railway Museum
LENGTH: 24 km
TIME: Easy day
RIDE/TRACK GRADE: 2/2–3
WALKING: None
HEIGHT VARIATION: 70 m
TRANSPORT: Rail (Goulburn Line)

FACILITIES: General picnic facilities inside the national park, and shops at Thirlmere. No camping permitted.
MAPS: CMA (LIC) Picton 1:25 000 topographical (or Blue Mountains National Park 1:150 000 Tourist Map)

At 630 hectares, this national park is one of the smallest in the state. For the cyclist, the five lakes that form the central feature of the park make an interesting detour from the scenically uninteresting pastoral land around the Picton area. The park lies adjacent to the Nattai wilderness area and the Lake Burragorang catchment area in the foothills of the Blue Mountains south of Penrith. The lakes are popular for passive recreational water sports and are well populated by locals on a hot summer's day. This tour involves a round trip with no backtracking. It is recommended to spend the middle hot part of the day in the water. If time allows, one can also visit the famous Thirlmere Railway Museum for a look into our pioneering past.

The Gungungurra tribe are believed to have first inhabited the area and the region was called 'Couridjah' meaning honey, because of the abundance of nectar in the vicinity. A corruption of this word, 'coradgery' was later applied to the lakes and they became known as the Coradgery lagoons. Rock shelters surrounding the lakes contain fine examples of artwork, the most interesting being the hand stencil.

The lakes were first discovered by an ex-convict named Wilson in 1798. Nearby, he had stumbled upon some cows and bulls which had escaped from Sydney Cove a decade earlier. The entire region was reserved by the government, and a grant was given to Macarthur near Camden. In 1867, the lakes were included in a recommendation for supplying Sydney with water. The lakes underwent a series of name changes, before the railways department finally settled on Thirlmere after the source of Manchester's water supply. At least twice in the last century the lakes have run completely dry due to droughts, and the plan to supply drinking water to new urban areas was abolished. Recently, however, wide channels were cut between the lakes allowing power boating and other recreations. The deliberate use of chemical poisons to kill the aquatic plantlife was also used in order to make the lakes more useable. Fish were introduced in the early 1970s, namely trout and perch.

147

However, their significance is their geomorphological value, and it became a national park in April 1972. Research shows that the depression containing the lakes was formed by an ancient watercourse some three million years ago. Faulting and uplifting called the Lapstone Block forced that particular basin to be cut off from the main flow and a lake system consequently formed. Because of its isolation from running water, the lakes were able to support some interesting and rare species of flora and fauna, including aquatic jellyfish, plankton, and mussels.

The Thirlmere Lakes Boat Club has imposed stringent rules on its members. Only a very limited number of boats are allowed to use the lakes and boats must proceed in an anti-clockwise direction. Lake 2 is the largest one, being a kilometre long and its banks are endowed with several standard recreational facilities such as picnic tables, bins, and a car-parking area. The other lakes (except number 4) are used for canoeing, swimming, and research. Camping is not permitted in the park.

Commence the ride by alighting at Tahmoor Station. The rail journey takes just under 90 minutes from Central and trains run quite regularly. Cycle up Pitt Street and turn left at Tahmoor Street. This leads all the way to Thirlmere where the old train tracks can be crossed. It is flat pastoral land here, and fast cycling speeds can be easily maintained. Once on the western side of the disused Picton-Mittagong loop line, head south past the Railway Museum (stop in for a look if there's time) along Barbour Road before turning off right at the signposted Slades Road (unsealed). The entrance to the Thirlmere Lakes National Park is also signposted together with the usual *Pets Prohibited* sign. The whole bike journey should take about an hour. The road comes to a turn-off and one should keep left, following the lakes around to the south before arriving at Lake 2 where general facilities are. This is the largest of the five lakes and the only one where boating is permitted. As a consequence, swimming is not permitted. Cyclists must continue on to the third lake, which has a jetty and is quite popular for passive water sports.

The fourth lake is completely suffocated with reeds and is surrounded by swampland while the fifth lake marks the start of private property again. If one follows the road along Blue Gum Creek, one soon comes to the edge of the Nattai National Park and the Lake Burragorang catchment area.

After spending the majority of the day relaxing at the third lake, head back to Tahmoor via the alternative steep road from Lake 3. After a 50 m climb, you come out on the Barbour Road about a kilometre south of the Slades Road entrance. Turn left and then immediately right crossing the tracks near the old railway station of Couridjah. The Bargo River Road then leads over the main railway line where Remembrance Drive leads north back to Tahmoor. If one has time to spare, it is worthwhile examining the Bargo River Gorge nearby, but unfortunately much of it is enclosed by private property now.

RIDE 15:   NATTAI RIVER

FROM: Tahmoor Station
TO: Mittagong Station
VIA: Hilltop and Point Hill
LENGTH:
   Day 1: Tahmoor to Nattai River: 32 km cycling, 6 km walking
   Day 2: Nattai River to Mittagong: 6 km walking, 31 km cycling
   Total distance is 63 km cycling, 12 km walking
TIME: 3 days with rest day in the middle
RIDE/TRACK GRADE: 3/3
WALKING: Starlights Trail from Point Hill to Nattai River, camping overnight
HEIGHT VARIATION: 330 m cycling, 420 walking
TRANSPORT: Rail (Goulburn Line)
FACILITIES: None (self-sufficiency important)
SPECIAL EQUIPMENT: Bike lock, camera, camping gear, back-pack.
MAPS: CMA (LIC) Picton and Hilltop 1:25 000 topographicals (or Blue Mountains National Park 1:150 000 Tourist Map)

One of the most attractive rivers in the Blue Mountains is the Nattai. It flows from Mittagong northward into Lake Burragorang and unlike many of the watercourses in sandstone country, has wide flat grassy banks, ideal for camping. If you have detachable panniers or a proper backpack, this short, relatively easy mountain bike adventure will provide the perfect introduction to longer off-road tours outlined later in this book. The idea is to cycle along little used country roads and good quality unsealed tracks to a staging area where a short 90 minute walk takes you to a fantastic little visited camping area by a truly picturesque river.

Start by catching the train to Tahmoor via Campbelltown. The rail journey takes just under 90 minutes from Central and trains run quite regularly. From the station, head for the eastern side of the railway tracks and cycle south down Remembrance Drive, turning right on to the Bargo River Road just over a kilometre out of Tahmoor. Head west until you cross the disused Picton-Mittagong Loop Line before turning left on to West Parade. Cycle through Buxton and Balmoral before you cross the old railway line again. Stop on the bridge when crossing the railway and marvel at the depth of the cutting. This incredible cutting corridor through solid rock was constructed using quite primitive technology. Next, marvel at the ugly concrete obelisk on the other side of the road one hundred metres further up. This is the world's largest monument to a railway cutting!

After recovering from the spectacle, proceed south to the quaint township of Hilltop. Cross the tracks at the first road and giggle at the platform that once constituted Hilltop's railway station and contact with the outside world. It must surely be one of the most obscure platforms in New South Wales.

Turn right along Wattle Ridge Road, once again paralleling the railway tracks cycling north. You pass through some new housing estates, vivid proof of the encroaching suburban sprawl upon the Blue Mountains wilderness. The road is unsealed but of good 2WD quality and is very flat, allowing easy pedalling. Hilltop once made the news in the early part of the decade when some munitions accidentally exploded at the nearby Commonwealth firing range. You pass the well signposted gate on the left. Continue cycling north-west branching left to an outpost of private property called 'Camelot'. The trail deteriorates slightly as it follows the perimeter of the property before climbing steeply over drainage humps to a turn-off to Starlight's Trail. This land has only been national park a short time, being former vacant Crown Land.

The bikes must be left just below Point Hill (666 m) where the trail ends and the walking track begins. Those anxious about their new $7000 mountain bikes might want to lock them as well as hide them. Except for holiday weekends, the area is usually not heavily frequented. Starlights Trail gradually descends down the side of a gully temporarily reaching the small feeder creek before levelling out for some great views over the cliff-lined Nattai gorge. The final zig-zag descent to the water section is quite steep and slippery. Beware of snakes in the undergrowth near the river. You emerge at a wide open grassy camping area with direct access to a tranquil swimming pool. Opposite some old four-wheel tracks lead to Macarthurs Flat. Camp where you want. It is suggested you spend a day here enjoying the isolated bush atmosphere.

When exiting the area, make sure you take all rubbish with you. The 420 m climb back up to the bikes is gruelling and plenty of water should be taken. Allow about 120 minutes for the return. Backtrack to Hilltop and continue cycling south to Mittagong to complete a fantastic three days in the bush.

FURTHER CYCLING IN THE BLUE MOUNTAINS FOOTHILLS

Much of the foothills are private property and therefore not much scope exists for mountain bike riding. Touring bikes are better able to traverse the long distances of private roads for people wishing to do tours between Richmond and Mittagong. The primary avenues for further off-road exploration exist in the Kurrajong area to the north and the Nattai River catchment to the south. The first section can be accessed from Richmond and includes a vast labyrinth of gorges bordered by the Grose River to the south and Bells Line of Road to the north. The land between Bowen Mountain and Devils Wilderness is particularly wild and warrants careful planning and preparation. The main attraction would be to camp on cliff-tops overlooking the Grose River. Consult the CMA Kurrajong 1:25 000 topographical.

The second area involves remote camping opportunities in huge cliff-lined gorges centred on the beautiful Nattai River. The access would be through Hilltop and Thirlmere Lakes

National Park, camping on the Little River or in Martins Creek Canyon. Once again, such terrain is reserved for the tenacious hard-core off road adventurer who is fit, self-sufficient, and energetic. Consult the CMA Picton, Nattai, and Hilltop 1:25 000 topographical maps.

2. THE LOWER BLUE MOUNTAINS

I have specified the lower Blue Mountains as all the area between Glenbrook and Wentworth Falls. The most popular places for cycling here are to the south of the Great Western Highway, down Kings Tableland, Williams Ridge, Notts Ridge, and the legendary Oaks Fire Trail. This region is generally known as the Blue Labyrinth, centred on Erskine and Bedford Creeks. One day or extended overnight rides are possible either camping on cliff tops and lookouts or down in a valley. North of the highway, around the Lawson and Springwood areas, trails follow narrow ridge tops and spurs to Wentworth Creek and the Grose River which have cut gorges into the sandstone plateau. The cyclist usually has these trails to himself as walkers and four wheel drivers are rare in these parts. Many rides have been selected as they exploit height differentials, therefore minimising any unnecessary pedalling. All of them involve the use of public transport to the start and returning from each ride.

RIDE 16:   EUROKA CLEARING

FROM: Glenbrook Station
TO: Euroka Clearing (return)
VIA: Glenbrook Creek
LENGTH: 15 km
TIME: 1 day
RIDE/TRACK GRADE: 4/2 (several medium length steep ascents)
WALKING: Optional short walk to the Nepean River
HEIGHT VARIATION: 150 m
TRANSPORT: Rail (Blue Mountains Line)

FACILITIES: Well developed picnic and camping facilities.
Visitors centre at park entrance (Bruce Road), shops at
Glenbrook
MAPS: CMA (LIC) Penrith 1:25 000 topographical

Euroka Clearing is one of the most popular destinations in the
Blue Mountains. Centred on Euroka Creek a few kilometres
south of Glenbrook, it offers an introduction to mountain bike
one day excursions or overnight camping.

Euroka, meaning 'warmth' in the native language, is a volcanic neck, evident from the rich dark soils contrasting with
surrounding sandstone. In the natural clearing are giant eucalypt specimens: blue and red gums. The area was occupied by
the original Aboriginal inhabitants of the lower Blue Mountains, and last century much evidence remained of the Dharug
tribe's camp sites. After settlement, the clearing was used for
cattle grazing, timber felling, and wheat growing, having been
granted to Francis Forbes, the Chief Justice of NSW in the mid-
1820s. Since then, the clearing has changed hands many
times—some even deduced that diamonds were present and
sank some preliminary shafts revealing nothing. In the 1950s,
when bushwalking began to take off, Euroka was used as a
staging area for many expeditions into the Blue Labyrinth,
especially in the Erskine Creek vicinity and Burragorang
valleys. Reservation under national park status largely halted
commercial exploitation but increased the construction of
tourist facilities and today Euroka Clearing is one of the most
developed camping areas in New South Wales national parks.

From Glenbrook Station, climb the stairs to the street and
turn right. A sealed road passes a park on the left hand side
where a giant oak tree resides. It winds its way down briefly
into residential property before levelling out, crossing a small
bridge over the railway tracks and entering the national park.
Cycle past the visitor centre on the left and entrance booth,
following a steep road down through hairpin turns to Glenbrook Creek. Ignore a turn-off to the left to Jellybean Pool.
Watch out for blind corners where vehicles coming the other
way are obscured by rock. Cross a ford at the bottom and it
is a steep climb back up the other side. Even though the road
here is still sealed, the bikes may have to be pushed due to
the grade of incline. Once up the top, the road deteriorates
into dirt road rising only very gently and a signposted turn-

off on the left leads to the popular Euroka Clearing. Turn here on a short descent into the camping area.

On the opposite side is an (unmarked) walking track down Euroka Creek to the Nepean River coming out opposite the Mulgoa Trig Point. This is a popular place for a swimming on a hot day. Allow about an hour for the return walk. The Euroka Creek Walking Track leaflet gives information concerning the highlights around the trail. Other walking tracks around the clearing are not marked on the topographical map and include a short-cut to the causeway via the turn-off to Portal Waterhole and another leading from an old bridge directly up to a northern embankment where some rocky ledges give excellent views over the clearing.

For those wishing to camp, the fees (1994) are $12.50 for the first two people for the first night. A detailed matrix leaflet available from the visitors centre gives hundreds of prices based on combinations of nights stayed and number of people. For example, 40 people staying 6 nights costs $574.50.

Return to Glenbrook via the exit road. One nice side trip is to Blue Pool, accessible from the first hairpin bend on the northern side of the causeway. The bikes would either have to be locked or carried down the walking track. From here, the railway station is less than 30 minutes away.

RIDE 17:   PORTAL LOOKOUT

FROM: Glenbrook Station
TO: Portal Lookout (return)
VIA: The Oaks Fire Trail
LENGTH: 18 km
TIME: An easy day
RIDE/TRACK GRADE: 4/5
WALKING: None
HEIGHT VARIATION: 160 m
TRANSPORT: Rail (Blue Mountains Line)
FACILITIES: General supplies can be bought at Glenbrook. Picnic facilities and water are located at Euroka Clearing. There's a visitors' centre at the park entrance (Bruce Road).
MAPS: CMA (LIC) Penrith 1:25 000 topographical

When catching the train up to the Blue Mountains, you will see a white obelisk high up on a cliff on the left hand side as you enter Glenbrook Gorge. This is the destination of the day's ride. From Glenbrook Station, climb the stairs to the street and turn right. A sealed road passes a park on the left hand side where a giant oak tree resides. It winds its way down briefly into residential property before levelling out, crossing a small bridge over the railway tracks and entering the national park. Cycle past the visitor centre on the left and entrance booth, following a steep road down through hairpin turns to Glenbrook Creek. Ignore a turn-off to the left to Jellybean Pool. Watch out for blind corners where vehicles coming the other way are obscured by rock. Cross a ford at the bottom and it is a steep climb back up the other side. Even though the road here is still sealed, the bikes may have to be pushed due to the grade of incline. Once up the top, the road deteriorates into dirt road rising only very gently and a signposted turn-off on the left leads to the popular Euroka Clearing. Turn here and a few hundred metres further a 4WD track turn-off to the left through flat ground leading to Portal Lookout.

Another steep climb must be endured up a rough road to a plateau. The bikes will probably have to be pushed up this section. The trail gets a bit sandy on top, but generally makes for good cycling to the round circuit at the end. From here there are outstanding, unobscured views over the entire metropolitan area. Centrepoint Tower and the Harbour Bridge can be easily made out on the horizon if it's not too hazy.

On the way back, investigate the Tunnel View Lookout which gives good views along Glenbrook Gorge and might be a nice spot to have lunch. Remember there is no water here, so a drink bottle must be taken. One can simply retrace the route back to the station, or take a long cut back to the Oaks Fire Trail through the lovely Euroka Clearing.

On the opposite side is an (unmarked) walking track down Euroka Creek to the Nepean River coming out opposite the Mulgoa Trig Point. This is a popular place for swimming on a hot day. Allow about an hour for the return walk. The Euroka Creek Walking Track leaflet gives information concerning the highlights around the trail. Other walking tracks around the clearing are not marked on the topographical map and include a minor footpad leading from an old bridge directly up to a northern embankment where some rocky ledges give excellent views over the clearing.

From Euroka Clearing, Glenbrook Station is about 40 minutes away. One nice side trip is to Blue Pool, accessible from the first hairpin bend on the northern side of the causeway. The bikes would either have to be locked or carried down the walking track.

RIDE 18: ERSKINE CREEK

FROM: Glenbrook Station
TO: Nepean Lookout (return)
VIA: The Oaks Fire Trail
LENGTH: 34 km (including 6 km walking)
TIME: 1 easy day
RIDE/TRACK GRADE: 4/3
WALKING: Jack Evans Trail to Erskine Creek
HEIGHT VARIATION: 210 m
TRANSPORT: Rail (Blue Mountains Line)
FACILITIES: General supplies can be bought at Glenbrook. Picnic facilities and water are located at the Oaks Picnic Ground.
MAPS: CMA (LIC) Penrith 1:25 000 topographical

Erskine Creek is within a short ride of Glenbrook and the cyclist is rewarded with a charming little valley with some remote and little known swimming spots. From Glenbrook Station, climb the stairs to the street and turn right. A sealed road passes a park on the left hand side where a giant oak tree resides. It winds its way down briefly into residential property before levelling out, crossing a small bridge over the railway tracks and entering the national park. Cycle past the visitor centre on the left and entrance booth, following a steep road down through hairpin turns to Glenbrook Creek. Ignore a turn-off to the left to Jellybean Pool. Watch out for blind corners where vehicles coming the other way are obscured by rock. Cross a ford at the bottom and it is a steep climb back up the other side. Even though the road here is still sealed, the bikes may have to be pushed due to the grade of incline. Once up the top, the road deteriorates into dirt road rising only very gently. Continue cycling until you come to the picnic ground about 8 km from the causeway. Turn left on to the Nepean Lookout Fire Trail which is sometimes closed to vehicles although the road is well graded.

Walking trails to Pisgah Rock, Attic Cave, and Machins Crater branch off the main road before you come to a car park not marked on the map. Machins Crater is not of meteoric origin as the name suggests. It is the eroded remains of an ancient volcanic neck discovered by Machin Hall. At the end of the road is a spectacular rock ledge called Erskine Lookout where you can preview where you are heading as well as survey the Nepean River gorge. However the most interesting feature of the day is the walking track to Erskine Creek and downstream to Word Cave where the creek flows in the Nepean River. The beginning of that track starts at the carpark 500 m back from the lookout on the left. The bikes have to be hidden in the scrub at the top, and a well defined walking track leads down the side of the valley to the wide pools and sandy beaches at the bottom.

At the bottom, walk downstream along the creek as it does a big arc around a knoll. Steep cliffs surround the valley. Anywhere along here is a good spot for lunch and the many gentle rapids here are good for a massage. Word Cave at the end is really nothing of note: the main feature is the Nepean Gorge, almost 200 m high at this point. Towards the end of the day one can backtrack along the shore and follow a partially obscured walking track as it heads up a saddle rejoining the Jack Evans Track where it starts climbing steeply. This shortcut isn't marked on the CMA map, but can be found at the point where the creek bends from south to east near a small oval pool indicated on the map. Vegetation in the area here includes banksias, yellow bloodwoods, wattles, waratahs, and smooth barked apple trees.

From here, the trains are about an hour away. One nice side trip is to Blue Pool, accessible from the first hairpin bend on the northern side of the causeway. The bikes would either have to be locked or carried down the walking track.

RIDE 19:   RED HANDS CAVE

FROM: Glenbrook Station
TO: Red Hands Cave (return)
VIA: The Oaks Fire Trail
LENGTH: 28 km
TIME: 1 easy day
RIDE/TRACK GRADE: 4/3
WALKING: A very short walk down some stairs to the cave
HEIGHT VARIATION: 210 m
TRANSPORT: Rail (Blue Mountains Line)
FACILITIES: General supplies can be bought at Glenbrook.
Picnic facilities and water are located at the Oaks Picnic
Ground
MAPS: CMA (LIC) Penrith 1:25 000 topographical

Red Hands Cave is perhaps the best visited Aboriginal site in
the Blue Mountains. The numerous Aboriginal hand stencils
are thought to be signatures: perhaps a form of ancient graffiti.
They were made by mixing ochre from ground coloured sandstone, mixing it with water and putting the solution into one's
mouth. The paint is then spat out over the hand pressed on
the wall in a motion similar to an air brush or spray can. Consequently, the outline of the hand remains, and they have been
remarkably preserved.

From Glenbrook Station, climb the stairs to the street and
turn right. A sealed road passes a park on the left hand side
where a giant oak tree stands. It winds its way down briefly
into residential property before levelling out, crossing a small
bridge over the railway tracks and entering the national park.
Cycle past the visitor centre on the left and entrance booth,
following a steep road down through hairpin turns to Glenbrook Creek. Ignore a turn-off to the left to Jellybean Pool.
Watch out for blind corners where vehicles coming the other
way are obscured by rock. Cross a ford at the bottom and it
is a steep climb back up the other side. Even though the road
here is still sealed, the bikes may have to be pushed due to
the grade of incline. Once up the top, the road deteriorates
into dirt road rising only very gently. Continue cycling for
several minutes until you come to the picnic ground as marked
on the map. Turn right on to a reasonably graded dirt track

that leads to a car park just above the cave. A short walking trail descends down to the site.

Retrace the trails back to the causeway. From here, one can hide the bikes and spend the rest of the day swimming in either the Blue Pool on the left, or Jellybean Pool on the right. Both are about 300 m upstream or downstream from the ford. Allow about 30 minutes back to the train station.

RIDE 20:   GLENBROOK CREEK AND LOOKOUTS

FROM: Blaxland Station
TO: Emu Plains Station
VIA: Glenbrook Creek, Bluff Reserve, Marges Lookout, Mount Sion, and Lennox Bridge
LENGTH: 16 km
TIME: 1 day
RIDE/TRACK GRADE: 3/4
WALKING: For swimming, there is a short walk down to an unnamed pool in Glenbrook Gorge
HEIGHT VARIATION: 200 m cycling, 110 m walking
TRANSPORT: Rail (Blue Mountains Line)
FACILITIES: None
MAPS: CMA (LIC) Penrith and Springwood 1:25 000 topographicals

Variety is the key description for this ride. Great downhills, great lookouts, a great swimming hole, a first class housing estate, and oldest bridge on the Australian mainland! All this is within easy riding distance ideal for either summer or winter. Start by alighting at Blaxland, which is the very next station after Glenbrook (just over an hour from Central). Head up the stairs and turn right, cycling down the Great Western Highway to Glenbrook. Turn right just after the real estate agent, following the signs to the shops and into the Blue Mountains National Park. At Glenbrook Station, turn right and cross the tracks at the first bridge on the left. Turn right on the other side. The road continues through residential property until coming to a dead end. At the last house, the track veers off into the bush on the right hand side along the fence. This leads along the top of a ridge covered by open woodland.

At the end, another trail from the right joins up and this is where the bikes must be left. A walking track, not marked on the map, heads straight down the side of the embankment descending about 100 m to a kidney shaped pool with a very wide sandy beach. The track is fairly well defined, and some rock scrambling is necessary at times. It takes about 10 minutes to get to the bottom. Either stay here, or explore up and down the creek following the walking track that periodically switches banks because of rock or dense scrub. A number of other pools exist upstream, none of which are well known and you might even be lucky to find them vacant on sunny week-ends. One particularly large one is dammed by boulders and is situated between The Duckhole and the unnamed kidney shaped pool at the bottom of the walking track. Backtrack to Glenbrook shops and cross the highway, cycling west to the traffic lights. Turn right and follow the street up to Levy Street where you should turn right and then follow it along a roller-coaster part to a T-section at the end. Turn left and follow the dirt trail directly ahead of you. Head right on to a good quality dirt road. Numerous minor turn-offs branch right and left and should be ignored. A signposted turn-off right leads to Marges Lookout where you have awesome views over Sydney. The lookout is particularly special at night. One can also check-out Elizabeth Lookout further north, but the views are more restricted to the Richmond area. However, it's a good spot for a break.

Backtrack to Levy Street and follow it to a major intersection and turn right passing the very dirty Glenbrook Lagoon. There are some speed humps along this section and the road is quite narrow. Immediately on the other side of the lagoon is another intersection. Continuing straight ahead will take you to Mitch-ells Pass Road, to the Lennox Bridge and then down to Emu Plains. But if there is still time and you're interested in admir-ing some exquisite mansions in the new Mount Sion estate, turn right after the lagoon and follow the road through the old park of Glenbrook. Suddenly you come into a completely new section and the houses and properties dramatically increase in size. Keep to the right at any turn-offs to get to the premium section. Some of the hills are quite steep, just like the real estate prices.

Backtrack to the lagoon and then head right to Mitchells Pass, then down to the Lennox Bridge (also called the Horse-

Grose Head South near Winmalee (Ride 23)

Ingar Picnic Ground near Bedford Creek (Ride 30)

Overlooking the Grose River from Faulconbridge Point (Ride 25)

shoe Bridge) where the two-way road ends. The pass was constructed by Thomas Livingstone Mitchell (1792–1855) and was opened in 1834. He employed an engineer and stonemason called David Lennox (1788–1873) to build the bridge and work began with convict labour in November 1832. It is the oldest stone arch bridge on the Australian mainland, being second only to the convict bridge in Richmond, Tasmania (1823–26). It was used until 1926 when another pass up the mountain was built along an abandoned railway line. A plague commemorates the work of Mitchell, while an old inscription on the southern side of the bridge reads 'David Lennox'. The equivalent keystone on the northern side reads 'A.D. 1833'.

Mitchells Pass continues until it rejoins the highway at Emu Plains, which is sometimes closed to vehicular traffic due to a massive landslide into Brookside Creek. The Great Western Highway here receives little traffic due to the freeway extension connecting the F4 with Lapstone. Follow the highway over the railway and down into Emu Plains until you come to the station on the left.

RIDE 21:   YELLOW ROCK

FROM: Springwood Station
TO: Blaxland Station
VIA: Yellow Rock lookout
LENGTH: 26 km
TIME: 1 day
RIDE/TRACK GRADE: 4/6
WALKING: None
HEIGHT VARIATION: 240 m
TRANSPORT: Rail (Blue Mountains Line)
FACILITIES: Picnic ground at Yellow Rock
MAPS: CMA (LIC) Springwood 1:25 000 topographical

This is another ride not officially in the Blue Mountains National Park but the lookout deserves mention due to its impressive views over the rugged cliff-lined Frasers Creek and over the lower Nepean River. From Springwood Station, climb the stairs and turn left down the ramp to the shops. Follow Macquarie Street up past the bus shelters to a turn-off where a bridge crosses over the railway tracks and Great Western Highway. This is the start of Hawkesbury Road that leads all the way to Richmond via Hawkesbury Heights. Follow it generally uphill past a golf course to Winmalee. A turn-off on the right is signposted as Singles Ridge Road and undulates slightly for the 5 km to the lookout. Beside a shelter, there aren't any real facilities here and cyclists must carry their own lunch and water. Good photographs can be taken from the rock platforms where one contrasts the flat pastoral land of the eastern side of the Nepean River with the craggy valley of Frasers Creek.

Back track about half of the way to the Hawkesbury Road and follow a 4WD track down Long Angle Creek where it meets Fitzgeralds Creek. A steep climb takes you back up to the ridge top where the track comes out at Blaxland. Be careful of trail-bikers and four-wheel drivers who frequent this area of the Blue Mountains. If there is sufficient time, one can swim in Glenbrook Creek by cycling down the Great Western Highway to Glenbrook. Turn right just after the real estate agent, following the signs to the shops and into the Blue Mountain National Park. At Glenbrook Station, turn right and cross the tracks at the first bridge on the left. Turn right on the other side. The road continues through residential property until coming to a dead end. At the last house, track veers off into the bush on the right hand side along the fence. This leads along the top of a ridge covered by open woodland. At the end, another trail from the right joins up and this is where the bikes must be left. A walking track, not marked on the map heads straight down the side of the embankment descending about 100 m to a kidney shaped pool with a very wide sandy beach. The track is fairly well defined, and some rock scrambling is necessary at times. It takes about 10 minutes to get to the bottom. Either stay here, or explore up and down the creek following the walking track that periodically switches banks because of rocks or dense scrub. A number of other pools exist upstream, which are not well known and you might even be lucky to find them vacant on sunny weekends. One particularly large one is dammed by boulders and is situated between The Duckhole and the unnamed kidney shaped pool at the bottom of the walking track. Backtrack to Glenbrook.

RIDE 22:   HAWKESBURY LOOKOUT

FROM: Springwood Station
TO: Richmond Station
VIA: Hawkesbury Road
LENGTH: 28 km
TIME: 1 easy day
RIDE/TRACK GRADE: 2/1
WALKING: None
HEIGHT VARIATION: 350 m
TRANSPORT: Rail (Blue Mountains and Emu Plains Lines)
FACILITIES: Nearest shops at Springwood, picnic ground at the lookout
MAPS: CMA (LIC) Springwood and Kurrajong 1:25 000 topographicals

This is one of the few rides in the Blue Mountains which can be done on a touring bike, principally because it follows a major road. Another feature of the ride is the lengthy downhill from the lookout to Lynchs Creek where 200 m are lost. And best of all for the cyclist: altitude doesn't have to be regained.

From Springwood Station, climb the stairs and turn left down the ramp to the shops. Follow Macquarie Street up past the bus shelters to a turn-off where a bridge crosses over the railway tracks and Great Western Highway. This is the start of Hawkesbury Road that leads all the way to Richmond via Hawkesbury Heights. Follow it generally uphill past a golf course, and past the small township of Winmalee to the little village of Hawkesbury Heights which was badly hit by the great bushfires of early January 1994.

The popular lookout is on the right hand side next to the main road. The entire north metropolitan area can be seen here. Below, the Nepean River widens where it meets huge sand banks. It should have taken about an hour to ride here, and Richmond lies another hour away to the north-east. From the bottom of the slope, the cyclist has several options. One can turn right on to a dirt road that crosses the Nepean and leads to the district of Castlereagh. From here one can either cycle to Penrith or Richmond. Both are approximately the same distance away. Another option is to continue along the Hawkesbury Road and turn left at Mountain Avenue which leads all the way to the Grose River where lunch can be eaten. Where the Grose River officially flows into the Nepean River is where its name changes to the Hawkesbury. Once you are on the Kurrajong topographical map, follow the Hawkesbury Road across the river over a very low bridge and turn left at Agnes Banks to the Castlereagh Road. This leads into the city of Richmond. The station lies just off the map on March Street which can be accessed by cycling south-east along Kurrajong Road. The railway line rejoins the main western line at Blacktown. From Richmond, Central is exactly 90 minutes away.

RIDE 23:   GROSE HEAD SOUTH

FROM: Springwood Station
TO: Valley Heights Station
VIA: Winmalee, Grose Head South Lookout
LENGTH: 37 km
TIME: 1 day
RIDE/TRACK GRADE: 4–5/5–6 (one particularly long steep hill to climb)
WALKING: None
HEIGHT VARIATION: 240 m
TRANSPORT: Rail (Blue Mountains Line)
FACILITIES: Picnic areas along the way
MAPS: CMA (LIC) Springwood 1:25 000 topographical (since the lookout is on the very edge of the map, the Kurrajong map is optional to identify features from the viewing point, although it is not necessary for the ride itself)

This is probably one of the most scenic cycling routes in the lower Blue Mountains due to its diversity and spectacular lookout. Expect to find other cyclists and walkers along the popular trails. Rainforest and a beautiful fern covered grotto are features along Blue Gum Swamp Creek. A bit of a climb must be endured to the lookout itself but the views at the end make it worthwhile.

From Springwood Station, climb the stairs and turn left down the ramp to the shops. Follow Macquarie Street up past the bus shelters to a turn-off where a bridge crosses over the railway line and Great Western Highway. This is the start of

Hawkesbury Road that leads all the way to Richmond via Hawkesbury Heights. Follow it generally uphill past a golf course towards the small township of Winmalee. After you pass Winmalee Post Office on the left, ascend slightly and turn left at the village shopping centre on to White Cross Road. Pass a school on the right to the end where a sign marks the boundary of Blue Mountains National Park.

After following the trail left and down for a short time, you are presented with a turn-off. Head right and up on to Shaws Ridge (also called Lynch's Ridge) passing a barrier at the very beginning preventing vehicular traffic. You soon come to another junction, where you head left. The trail is relatively flat, undulating only slightly, through typical dry sclerophyll forest. There are no navigational problems, no views, only fast cycling. The track has a few sand patches to cause a few anxious moments but rocks are not much of problem. Suddenly the trail falls dramatically down to the left as it quickly loses 100 metres past rocky ledges down to Blue Gum Swamp Creek.

It is now pleasant cycling through ferns along the creek past some picnic areas to a crossing. A signpost points the way up to Grose Mountain Lookout. The trail rises steeply immediately and most of the sections will have to be walked by the average cyclist—only some gentler parts are rideable. Near the top are some drainage humps, dividing up the trail into rocky sections.

A T-intersection awaits you on top with signposts to St Columbas College (left) and the lookout (right). This short section to the lookout makes easy cycling, the track featuring some lengthy rock platforms on the left, useful for dodging the rocks and sand traps. The trail ends at the informal ledge lookout with obscured views to Richmond through the gap. Two gorges meet here: that of Springwood Creek and the Grose River. The latter has cut its way down to bedrock almost the same height as sea level from uplifted sandstone nearly 500 m high. In January 1994 much of the mid-Grose area around Springwood, Winmalee, and Hawkesbury Heights was burnt out by savage bushfires originating from Mount Tomah. There are numerous great lookouts like this one in the area, and while the Three Sisters at Echo Point are done to death, these lookouts are relatively unknown.

A steep walking track then heads north over more rock platforms, across a saddle and up to the Grose Head South Trig point itself, but because of trees and 16 year old regrowth on the summit, the view isn't that good and one has to follow a very rough unmarked service trail further north to get partially obscured glimpses of Richmond to the east. There are no walking tracks that I know of down to the water due to the cliffs along the rim, some being over 100 m of vertical rock!

Backtrack to the lush green banks of Blue Gum Swamp Creek, taking extreme care on the steep hairpin corners of the descent, and turn right to parallel the creek completing a round trip to Springwood. There is a pleasant picnic spot called The Grotto, but since it is only about two hours from Springwood, it's up to you where you want to have lunch. The gully here is popular for spotlighting nocturnal animals. Prolonged rain can cause water-filled pot-holes to form, especially near the crossing of Blue Gum Creek Swamp. Lookout out for waratahs if cycling late in the year.

An alternative way back to Springwood from the lookout is to keep on Springwood Ridge. The trail undulates slightly but makes easy cycling. It comes out on the St Columbas College grounds behind the tennis courts. The land here was once owned by William Lawson (1774–1850), the oldest of the three explorers who found the way to Lithgow, although he didn't actually reside here. It was bought by Cardinal Moran who built a training college for priests here in 1909. The stonework from the older buildings was actually quarried on the property. A year later, 26 students were admitted. Today, it is a private high school.

Retrace Hawkesbury Road to Great Western Highway where you can cycle down to Valley Heights. Another option is to continue north-west along Hawkesbury Road from Winmalee and cycle down to Richmond as in Ride 22.

RIDE 24: MARTINS LOOKOUT

FROM: Springwood Station
TO: Magdala Falls
VIA: Glenbrook Creek
LENGTH: 12 km (with 2 km walking)
TIME: 1 day

RIDE/TRACK GRADE: 2–3/3
WALKING: Along Glenbrook and Magdala Creeks
HEIGHT VARIATION: 260 m
TRANSPORT: Rail (Blue Mountains Line)
FACILITIES: None
SPECIAL EQUIPMENT: Bike lock, day pack
MAPS: CMA (LIC) Springwood 1:25 000 topographical

In order to add some variety, this ride involves some walking to reach the destination as the view from Martins Lookout isn't quite dramatic enough to deserve being the ride's main attraction. The goal is some pools and falls in a feeder stream of the rugged Glenbrook Creek.

Cycle along Macquarie Road once you have descended the ramp from Springwood Station and follow it east until it swings around and becomes Burns Road. A mirror marks a dangerous intersection into Farm Road and this then turns into a well graded dirt road to a car park at the end. A short walk leads to a rocky ledge which gives modest views over a deep tree-covered valley. On the opposite side are two lookouts in the Lost World area which can be accessed via the Oaks Fire Trail.

The bikes must be hidden or locked up in the scrub at the top of the ridge, and the walking track (short or long) taken to descend down to Glenbrook Creek. This idyllic watercourse which has its origins at Woodford, finds its destination in the Nepean River, near Portal Lookout. Head upstream at the bottom to Perch Ponds through lush forest teeming with wildlife. Once past the small pools, the rocky lined gully of Magdala Creek runs into Glenbrook Gorge, and another walking track branches off at a sign pointing to Homedale Street. Follow the left bank of the creek upstream to the first set of falls: Martins Falls which are about 10 m high and make good slow exposure photography if the sun is on them. The next feature is about 400 m away called Blue Pool, which has another set of 10 m falls at the far end. Getting down to the pool can cause difficulties because it is surrounded by rock but once in the swimming is quite good due to the attractive scenery, the surrounding sandstone, and the falls. It is quite difficult to imagine that the major township of Springwood is just a few kilometres upstream. The water here is not the cleanest because of this very reason, and the best is to BYO together with a snack lunch.

Towards the end of the day retrace your steps to the bikes and then back to Springwood or Valley Heights. For walkers, Martins Lookout is a popular staging area for hikes right down to Glenbrook, the Nepean River, and upstream to the gorgeous Sassafras Creek via the Victoria Track.

RIDE 25: GROSE RIVER
(FAULCONBRIDGE POINT)

FROM: Faulconbridge Station
TO: Springwood Station
VIA: Faulconbridge Point Lookout
LENGTH: 29 km (including 2 km walking)
TIME: 1 day (optional overnight camp by river)
RIDE/TRACK GRADE: 3/4
WALKING: Grose River Walking Track
HEIGHT VARIATION: 40 m cycling, 400 m walking
TRANSPORT: Rail (Blue Mountains Line)
FACILITIES: None
MAPS: CMA (LIC) Springwood and Kurrajong 1:25 000 topographicals

Many trails in the Blue Mountains follow ridge tops over knolls and down saddles, making the track not too far off a roller coaster ride. This of course has to be expected, for these are the mountains. However, Grose River Road runs for nearly 13 km along the flattest ridge I know of. In fact, on the CMA Blue Mountains Tourist Map it doesn't pass through a single contour line! Therefore this trail is perfectly suitable for bikes with limited gears.

From Faulconbridge Station, turn back along the highway and left at Meeks Crescent. This curves around from north to east until it ends at Grose Road. Turn left and ignore a major turn off on the right to Chapman Ridge. The road then deteriorates into a rough dirt road that undulates very slightly throughout its entire length. Almost all the uphills are easily rideable without the need for bottom gear. Despite deterioration initially, the road stays in reasonable quality, still being regularly graded. However there are some rocky and sandy sections to cause some anxious moments every now and then. The flat ridge separates Linden Creek and Faulconbridge Creek which have already cut quite deep gullies into the sandstone. The entire distance takes about an hour. The vegetation, being burnt in early 1994, alternates between dry eucalypt forest and stunted heath. The ridge is known for an abundance of brown and copper head snakes, so beware.

The informal lookout is on the far side of the turning circle car park at the end, situated on a large flat rock platform. The immediate area has suffered from overuse, with graffiti quite evident on the rocks, making the former picnic area unattractive. The worst impact came in January 1994 when the Blue Mountains bushfires, originating at Mount Tomah, swept through the area.

The views from the lookout feature the Grose River valley, of course, as well as the prominent landmarks of Mount Wilson and Mount Tomah to the north-west, as well as Grose Head South almost due east. Particularly fascinating is the ravine country all around, where the soft sandstone has been dissected by numerous creeks and even small streams that have cut hundreds of sheer cliffs. The bushfire-induced regrowth adds to the atmosphere of another world.

Backtrack slightly to the beginning of the walking track which is marked by a clearing on the left (when travelling south) and it is quite a steep descent to the river. To give some idea of the height lost, the Grose River valley at this point would easily swallow Centrepoint Tower: the tip of its lightning conductor would be over 100 m below the lookout. Allow a good hour each way for the hike down. If camping overnight, some pack hauling may be necessary over the rock ledges near the bottom. Swimming, walking, photography, and abseiling are all activities that can be done here depending on the time available. Firewood can be easily obtained by washed up debris during floods.

About two to three hours should be counted on for the return journey from the river to Springwood Station.

RIDE 26:   THE OAKS FIRE TRAIL

FROM: Woodford
TO: Glenbrook
VIA: The Oaks Fire Trail
LENGTH: 31–59 km depending on options
TIME: 1 easy day
RIDE/TRACK GRADE: 3/4–5
WALKING: Optional walks to Red Hands Cave, and to swimming holes at Glenbrook Creek
HEIGHT VARIATION: 444 m
TRANSPORT: Rail (Blue Mountains Line)
FACILITIES: Shops at Glenbrook and visitors centre at park entrance (Bruce Road)
MAPS: CMA (LIC) Penrith and Katoomba 1:25 000 topographicals

This tour is one of the all time great rides, and would have to rank as the fastest fire trail this side of Repack. It allows the perfect opportunity to exploit height differentials in catching the train to Woodford (607 m) and descending down to Glenbrook (163 m). The entire second half of this journey requires no pedalling at all. In this section, speeds well in excess of 40 kph are possible without sacrificing too much in safety due to the good condition of the track and the straight, gradual downhill slope.

From Woodford Station, go down the stairs and turn left down Railway Parade, right at the Appian Way, left at Parker Street, and left on to Taylor Road. The Oaks Fire Trail begins on the right hand side and is marked by a sign which says that it is 18 miles to Glenbrook. Recently the trail has been permanently closed to vehicular traffic by means of a barrier. The road starts off as quite rough with a profuse scattering of large rocks. After initially remaining flat, the track quickly loses height as it winds down to The Circles. On a rocky platform on the right hand side you will see unusual concentric circles formed by Aborigines. From here it undulates giving occasional views to Sydney from rocky clearings on the centre of the ridge.

Just after one prominent steep long downhill, a turn-off left to Tobys Glen branches off and is signposted. This is a short steep scrubby track that descends down into an eroded volcanic vent/neck. It emerges at a dammed waterhole and camping/picnic ground, surrounded by wet sclerophyll forest containing some massive blue gums that are worth seeing. In dry weather, the water from the waterhole can be unsuitable for drinking. There are several isolated and sheltered camping areas further downstream among more giant blue gums. Because of the dense vegetation coverage, this place does not receive much sunlight and gets dark quite early especially on overcast days. However, it's a nice spot for a break or even lunch, but unfortunately involves a bit of an arduous climb back up to the Oaks Fire Trail.

Continuing on the ride, the track climbs very steeply for a couple of kilometres before the long downhill starting just after a helipad called The Wheel. You swing east again through dry eucalypts, and several steep downhill corners are encountered before the track levels out in a gradual long descent. Because the trail is relatively smooth and flat, incredible speeds can be achieved. The downhill becomes steadily more gradual and soon comes to a gate where the road quality increases to two-wheel drive standard. There is also a turn-off to the right here to Erskine Creek (see Ride 18). From this point, one must be aware of traffic coming from either direction. Traffic to and from the popular Euroka Clearing could be a problem during summer weekends.

There is an interesting diversion if anyone hasn't seen it. On the first real left hand branch since Tobys Glen, a trail branches off at a picnic ground with two concrete water tanks. Water is usually fairly reliable here, but you have to wait for it as it runs extremely slow. This track, the Red Hands Fire Trail is a slightly poorer quality road, staying approximately level for 5 km. At the end, the bikes must be left at the top a rocky ledge, and it is two minute walk down to the Red Hand Cave. Here numerous Aboriginal hand stencils can be viewed. These Aboriginal hand stencils are thought to be signatures: perhaps a form of ancient graffiti. They were made by mixing ochre from ground coloured sandstone, mixing it with water and putting the solution into one's mouth. The paint is then spat out over the hand pressed on the wall in a motion similar to an air brush or spray can. Consequently, the outline of the hand remains, and they have been remarkably preserved. It is easily the most popular Aboriginal site in the Blue Mountains, however lacks the variety of other famous sites such as Carnarvon Gorge, Queensland.

From the shelter, double back to the Oaks Fire Trail and continue east, ignoring various turn-offs to the right. The trail has been known to become somewhat corrugated between gradings, making frustrating cycling for the unfortunates without good shock absorbers. After a particularly flat section, the track gets steeper and turns into a sealed road before the final drop to the Glenbrook Creek causeway. This involves a number of tight hairpin turns. Cool your rims by crossing the creek of a shallow ford and it is up to you if you want to go home or spend the rest of the day swimming in the two beautiful pools nearby.

If choosing to stay, you have the option of Blue Pool or Jellybean Pool. On weekends, both of these could be crowded due to their easy access from Sydney. Jellybean Pool involves walking downstream along the rocks for ten minutes and the bike will probably have to carried for most of the way. Blue Pool is about the same distance but upstream, and is best accessed by climbing up the road to the first hairpin bend. A walking track then leads down via some stairs and once again the bikes would have to be carried. Blue Pool, in my opinion, is the most picturesque and we have had the fortunate luck to relax here a number of times without anyone else in sight. Mind you, these occasions were not on weekends.

Glenbrook Station involves a climb of about 100 m. If catching a predetermined train, leave the swimming pools about 25 minutes before it is due to come. There is a short cut which leads along the railway line. Once past the rangers' station and visitors centre you cross a small bridge over the tracks and a gate on the immediate left leads along the back of houses to an embankment. It isn't on the map but it avoids the narrow winding main road. Climb the dirt embankment or exit the service trail via a gate on the right and the station is on the left hand side over the crest. Stairs lead down to the platform. If time is available (trains usually leave every 30 minutes), drinks and the usual assortment of munchies can be bought from the milk bar just up the road.

RIDE 27: LOST WORLD
(OAKS FIRETRAIL OVERNIGHT)

FROM: Woodford
TO: Glenbrook
VIA: The Oaks Fire Trail
LENGTH: 39 km
TIME: 2 easy days
RIDE/TRACK GRADE: 5/7–8
WALKING: Optional walks to Red Hands Cave, and to swimming holes at Glenbrook Creek
HEIGHT VARIATION: 444 m
TRANSPORT: Rail (Blue Mountains Line)
FACILITIES: Shops at Glenbrook and visitors centre at park entrance (Bruce Road)
MAPS: CMA (LIC) Penrith and Katoomba 1:25 000 topographicals

This is an extended variation of Ride 26 where a detour is taken from the Oaks Fire Trail to Bunyan and Lost World Lookouts via St Helena Ridge. These lookouts lie over Glenbrook Creek opposite Martins lookout and due south of Valley Heights. A good camp clearing ground exists on the remains of a volcanic plug called St Helena. Although the ride is relatively short, it allows you to camp out under the stars in a particularly wild part of the Blue Mountains. The gorge of Glenbrook Creek separates you from civilisation. Watching the sun set from Lost World is a very moving experience as not only the lights from Springwood can be seen, but a sea of sparkling pinpoints all the way to Sydney. With a campfire and good conversation, this is the stuff movies are made from.
From Woodford Station, go down the stairs and turn left down Railway Parade, right at Appian Way, left at Parker Street, and left on to Taylor Road. The Oaks Fire Trail begins on the right hand side and is marked by a sign which says that it is 18 miles to Glenbrook. The trail has been permanently closed to vehicular traffic by means of a barrier. The road starts off quite rough with a profuse scattering of large rocks as you enter the Blue Mountains National Park. After initially remaining flat, the track quickly loses height as it winds down to The Circles. On a rocky platform on the right hand side you

will see unusual concentric circles formed by Aborigines. From here it undulates giving occasional views to Sydney from rocky clearings on the centre of the ridge.

The turn-off to St Helena Ridge is on the left hand side on an uphill and is very easy to miss. The trail is of particularly poor quality and is quite overgrown. Despite being predominantly downhill, many fallen trees and branches make the last 10 km of the first day slow progress, in contrast to the Oaks Fire Trail. If you find the trail too overgrown, or if progress is too frustrating, then one can always camp at Tobys Glen, detailed later.

About 6 km along St Helena Ridge, branch left off the ridge and across a saddle. Near the end of the trail, a turn-off on the left leads to the camping ground set in large grey gums via a rough road. I found water here to be fairly unreliable especially after long periods of no rain, but a scramble down to Western Creek will almost definitely result in a finding a permanent flow. However, camping is also possible at one of the lookouts but water is definitely not reliable due to the limited catchment area. Rock pools sometimes collect water at the edge but it shouldn't be drunk unless immediately after rain. Carry about 2–3 litres of water per person for cooking, drinking, and cleaning purposes. The next clean water source is at the Oaks Camping Ground where two concrete tanks give a reliable but slow supply. Despite the great hassle getting here, the views over Glenbrook Creek, the isolation, and the sight of the Sydney metropolitan area at night has appeal to many hard-core off-road cyclists. In the morning, the way out involves simply backtracking to the Oaks Fire Trail and continuing south.

At the bottom of one downhill soon after returning to the Oaks, a trail leads left to Tobys Glen and is signposted. This is a short steep scrubby track that descends into an eroded volcanic vent/neck. It emerges at a dammed waterhole and camping/picnic ground, surrounded by wet sclerophyll forest containing some massive blue gums that are worth seeing. In dry weather, the water from the waterhole can be unsuitable for drinking. There are several isolated and sheltered camping areas further downstream among more giant blue gums. Because of the dense vegetation coverage, this place does not receive much sunlight and gets dark quite early especially on overcast days. However, it's a nice spot for a break or even

174

lunch, but unfortunately involves a bit of an arduous climb back up to the Oaks Fire Trail.

Continuing on the ride, the track climbs very steeply for a couple of kilometres before the long downhill starting just after a helipad called The Wheel. You swing east again through dry eucalypts, and several steep downhill corners are encountered before the track levels out in a gradual long descent. Because the trail is relatively smooth and flat, incredible speeds can be achieved. The downhill becomes steadily more gradual and soon comes to a gate where the road quality increases to two-wheel drive standard. There is also a turn-off to the right here to Erskine Creek (see Ride 18). From this point, one must be aware of traffic coming from either direction. Traffic to and from the popular Euroka Clearing could be a problem during summer weekends.

There is an interesting diversion if anyone hasn't seen it. On the first real left hand branch since Tobys Glen, a trail branches off at a picnic ground with two concrete water tanks. Water is usually fairly reliable here, but you have to wait for it as it runs extremely slow. This track, the Red Hands Fire Trail is a slightly poorer quality road, staying approximately level for 5 km. At the end, the bikes must be left at the top a rocky ledge, and it is two minute walk down to the Red Hand Cave. Here numerous Aboriginal hand stencils can be viewed. The numerous Aboriginal hand stencils are thought to be signatures: perhaps a form of ancient graffiti. They were made by mixing ochre from ground coloured sandstone, mixing it with water and putting the solution into one's mouth. The paint is then spat out over the hand pressed on the wall in a motion similar to an air brush or spray can. Consequently, the outline of the hand remains, and they have been remarkably preserved. It is easily the most popular Aboriginal site in the Blue Mountains, however lacks the variety of other famous sites such as Carnarvon Gorge, Queensland.

From the shelter, double back to the Oaks Fire Trail and continue east, ignoring various turn-offs to the right. The trail has been known to become somewhat corrugated between gradings, making frustrating cycling for the unfortunate ones without good shock absorbers. After a particularly flat section, the track gets steeper and turns into a sealed road before the final drop to the Glenbrook Creek causeway. This involves a number of tight hairpin turns. Cool your rims by crossing the creek by means of a shallow ford and it is up to you if you want to go home or spend the rest of the day swimming in the two beautiful pools nearby.

If choosing to stay, you have the option of Blue Pool or Jellybean Pool. On weekends, both of these could be crowded due to their easy access from Sydney. Jellybean Pool involves walking downstream along the rocks for ten minutes and the bike will probably have to carried for most of the way. Blue Pool is about the same distance but upstream, and is best accessed by climbing up the road to the first hairpin bend. A walking track then leads down via some stairs and once again the bikes would have to be carried. Blue Pool, in my opinion, is the most picturesque and we have had the fortunate luck to relax here a number of times without anyone else in sight. Mind you, these occasions were not on weekends.

Glenbrook Station involves a climb of about 100 m. If catching a predetermined train, leave the swimming pools about twenty-five minutes before it is due to come. There is a short cut which leads along the railway line. Once past the rangers station and visitors centre you cross a small bridge over the tracks and a gate on the immediate left leads along the back of houses to an embankment. It isn't on the map but it avoids the narrow winding main road. Climb the dirt embankment or exit the service trail via a gate on the right and the station is on the left hand side over the crest. Stairs lead down to the platform. If time is available (trains usually leave every 30 minutes), drinks and the usual assortment of munchies can be bought from the milk bar just up the road.

RIDE 28:   MURPHYS GLEN

FROM: Woodford Station
TO: Bedford Creek (return)
VIA: Murphys Glen
LENGTH: 22 km
TIME: 1 day (with option of an overnight camp by Bedford Creek or at Murphys Glen
RIDE/TRACK GRADE: 6/4
WALKING: Optional Turpentine walk (1.5 km)
HEIGHT VARIATION: 250 m

TRANSPORT: Rail (Blue Mountains Line)
FACILITIES: Good camping facilities including picnic tables, toilets, and fireplaces
MAPS: CMA (LIC) Katoomba and Jamison 1:25 000 topographicals

Majestic turpentine trees and blue gums form a very picturesque backdrop to a beautiful little enclosure south of Woodford called Murphys Glen. This ride, like the previous suggestion can be done in one day but the option of overnight camping is available either at Murphys Glen where good facilities are provided or at Bedford Creek where there are no facilities. The choice is yours: if you are of similar character to the author and detest crowded picnic areas, then the sandy beaches of the serene Bedford Creek are highly recommended. Because car camping is permissible at Murphys Glen, it is quite popular and has inevitably suffered from much abuse.

Take the Bedford Road from the station south through residential property. It immediately turns into a dirt road as it leaves civilisation and descends all the way to the picnic area. The road is open to cars and so care must be taken on blind corners. The glen is set in a diatreme or volcanic vent. The rich soils support large strands of turpentines and angophoras, as well as several species of eucalypts. A walk down a gully through dark and secluded rainforest is awe inspiring. It is amazing to think that the first Europeans found the Australian bush dull and monotonous after completing this short stroll to Bedford Creek.

On return, one can then ride down the very steep fire trail to the ford across Bedford Creek and the start of the Andersons Fire Trail. On the right hand side as you approach the water is a large wide beach, around which curves the creek. Firewood is scarce here. The water is deep enough for swimming in some spots and is certainly slow enough not to be dangerous. Surprisingly, it is quite clear. Have lunch here if you are not camping, and backtrack to Woodford. This inevitably involves an uphill slog for almost an hour.

RIDE 29:   LAWSON RIDGE

FROM: Lawson Railway Station
TO: Hazelbrook Railway Station
VIA: Lawson Ridge Fire Trail
LENGTH: 25 km
TIME: 1 day
RIDE/TRACK GRADE: 4/7
WALKING: Bushbashing down to pools along Wentworth Creek
HEIGHT VARIATION: 150 m cycling, 250 m walking
TRANSPORT: Rail (Blue Mountains Line)
FACILITIES: None
MAPS: CMA Katoomba 1:25 000 topographical

This is the longest of the three ridges that extends north from the railway line and east of Wentworth Creek. It loses altitude more than the other ridges, dropping some 150 m therefore making enjoyable riding for the first half. Ridgetop walking along here is also fairly fast, but the scrub-choked valley walls can reduce speeds to 3 and even 2 kph. The maze of valleys, gullies, and canyons near the confluence of Mount Hay Creek and Wentworth Creek is truly impressive from the top of the spur. It's as if any small trickle of water can erode gigantic gorges through solid rock. Massive knolls hundreds of metres high jut out from the valley floor forcing watercourses to meander and reverse direction every few kilometres.

From the station, turn right at the tunnel underneath the platform and right again at the first road reached. This leads into Badgerys Crescent which follows the railway line east, down and then up a steep hill. One briefly meets up with the Great Western Highway before turning left onto Queens Road marked by the Kilhilla Convention Centre. The road is sealed and flat for about two kilometres before you hit the gravel and the bush. Head right down to a sign marking the entrance to the national park and a gate barring all vehicular traffic. The traffic parallels private property to the right as it descends into saddle. Up the other side is an overgrown branch right to Blue Mountain. Ignore this and head left, descending as the trail quickly deteriorates. Unlike other trails in the area, sand does not present much of a problem.

178

The trail winds around, avoiding gullies on the left and cliffs on the right. The slopes are quite rocky and eroded, while the saddle depressions are overgrown. The best cycling is when the trail is on the centre of the ridge. Whenever you are presented with a fork, head right. The first option occurs at the bottom of a particular steep rocky slope where the right trail heads over an old bridge under some scrub and towards a small range of sandstone knolls. A bit of a climb must be endured here.

Once back on the ridge it is pleasant cycling to a turn-off marked by a small clearing. Head right off the ridge. At once the trail becomes overgrown and cycling will involve dodging, ducking, and pushing aside branches of shrubs. At the next turn-off, head right again. It descends gradually before coming to a fallen tree which previous walkers and cyclists have cleared a track around. The trail descends and then contours around another range of small knolls, marked by cliff ledges near their summit. The trail is particularly overgrown here but still is possible to cycle. In the mornings, there will be many spider webs to negotiate but fortunately their makers are not large or venomous.

The trail then drops off the end of the ridge into a prominent saddle and shortly comes to a large flat rocky platform and resembles a car-park of sorts due to its unexpected openness. Traces of past camp fires exist here and there are obscured views to the west. Unlike the information given on the topographical map, the trail ends here. The bikes must be hidden in the bushes for ahead is no place for wheels. Barring no major equipment failures, it should have taken no longer than two hours to arrive at the rock platform. The objective is to descend west to the closest corner of Wentworth Creek. Be careful to avoid heading into the gully to the north. The best route is to head left as one is descending maintaining the centre of a wide spur. There are occasional open patches between the hard dry shrubs and several rock ledges or 'mini-cliffs' must be negotiated. The very last section is the steepest and most densely vegetated and presents the only real difficulty in finding a route. It is recommended that you wear trousers and long sleeves for the walk.

The pool at the bottom where Wentworth Creek changes direction from east to north west is not the deepest or most attractive, especially if the water is low. However, ten minutes of boulder scrambling upstream will be rewarded by a much more picturesque pool flanked by flat sandy banks on the southern side. It is located just before a major block-up of giant moss-covered boulders. By contrast the northern bank is almost sheer for 100 metres creating a small canyon. Safety is of crucial importance in such an isolated place as the overgrown banks can harbour the odd red-bellied black snake while the boulders can shelter some large spiders. It is suggested to spend several hours here swimming, sunbaking, and relaxing in this incredibly wild remote place before returning to the bikes.

The only difference on the return journey is that there are a few more uphills and a great descent along the footpath to Hazelbrook Station. Hard core campers will find the area tempting if they prefer the natural setting. Firewood, of course, is unlimited. When camping in this forsaken valley, one has the overwhelming feeling of being in another world. All sounds and sights of civilisation are non-existent. This is the true bushcamping experience: Euroka Clearing and Murphys Glen seem like cities in comparison!

RIDE 30:   INGAR

FROM: Wentworth Falls Station
TO: Woodford Station
VIA: Ingar Picnic Ground
LENGTH: 29 km
TIME: 1 day
RIDE/TRACK GRADE: 2/4
WALKING: None
HEIGHT VARIATION: 487 m
TRANSPORT: Rail (Blue Mountains Line)
FACILITIES: Fire places, and a large dam for swimming
MAPS: CMA (LIC) Katoomba and Jamison 1:25 000
topographicals

For those wishing to exploit height differentials, this route starts at Wentworth Falls (867 m) and finishes over 200 m lower at Woodford where a train can be caught back to the metropolitan area. Alight at Wentworth Falls, climb the stairs

and head back along the highway. The turn-off to Kings Tableland is well signposted just before the Brown Horse Inn restaurant. The road briefly undulates for a kilometre passing
through a residential area. The Murphys Fire Trail turn-off is
on the left, marked by a standard street signpost ('Ingar Picnic
Ground') with a distance of 10 km although it is actually closer
to 12. Along the way is a turn-off up to Kings Table (884 m)
upon which Aboriginal axe grinding grooves are etched into
the rock cap on the northern side of the trig. Aboriginal occupation in this area is believed to extend back some 22 000
years. Back on the Murphys Fire Trail, head south and then
east. The trail is of good quality down to the camping ground.
Ignore two turn-offs on the left before a final steep descent.

Ingar is quite a popular camping ground matching the
nearby Murphys Glen. At the site, there is a large dam which
is great for swimming, although water has to be boiled if you
intend drinking it. Its only feeder creek has a waterfall where
clean drinking water can be obtained.

After having a break and/or swim at Ingar, backtrack up
the steep hill where the Murphys Fire Trail continues down
and crosses Bedford Creek. This section is marked as a
walking track on the topographical map. The first part to the
locked gate is quite comfortable through pleasant forest. All
of a sudden, the track plummets down to Bedford Creek and
can be quite slippery due to the leaf cover. The last section in
particular may even be too steep to ride down as the track is
quite rough.

At Bedford Creek that you join up with the Andersons Fire
Trail. At the crossing, on the left, is a wide sandy beach where
lunch can be taken if the picnic ground is too full. The water
is deep enough for swimming in some spots and is certainly
slow enough not to be dangerous. Surprisingly, it is quite
clear. From here it is a very steep climb back up to Woodford.
The bike will most likely have to be pushed up this section. If
time is available, one can check out Murphys Glen, another
popular camping ground set in a hollow surrounded by beautiful turpentine trees. See Ride 28 for details.

RIDE 31:   ANDERSONS FIRE TRAIL

FROM: Wentworth Falls Station
TO: Woodford Station
VIA: Notts Ridge, Bedford Creek
LENGTH: 31 km
TIME: 1 day
RIDE/TRACK GRADE: 4/5–6 (one very steep section from
Bedford Creek to Woodford)
WALKING: None
HEIGHT VARIATION: 487 m
TRANSPORT: Rail (Blue Mountains Line)
FACILITIES: None
MAPS: CMA (LIC) Jamison 1:25 000 topographical

Andersons Fire Trail is the twin sister of the Oaks Fire Trail
(Ride 26). Both allow great cycling due to considerable height
differences, both cross a lovely creek where lunch can be
taken, both are popular with cyclists, and both have long fast
downhills. Of the two, Andersons winds its way through
wilder terrain and consequently some navigation and riding
skills will be called for.
   Alight at Wentworth Falls Station, climb the stairs, turn left,
and head back along the highway. The turn-off to Kings Tableland is well signposted just before the Brown Horse Inn restaurant. The road briefly undulates for a kilometre passing
through a residential area. There are impressive views over
the Jamison Valley and east to the Sydney metropolitan area
here. This part of the tableland is quite exposed and can get
very windy. The residential property is soon left and a long
very fast downhill leads to the Queen Victoria Memorial Hospital grounds. This was originally one of three sanatoriums in
the area and was first opened in 1903. The very tidy European
style setting and associated gardens contrasts with the standard Australian bush as a backdrop. The road diverges here:
to the right leads to a car-park and eventually to Kedumba
and Jamison Valleys, but keep left following Kings Tableland.
As you pass the hospital, the road immediately deteriorates
into a very rough and loose dirt road, before recovering into
quite a well graded and wide unsealed road. This leads even-

182

tually to Warragamba Dam, about 41 km away, but that's another story (Ride 32).

The national park is entered but if you're like the author, you'll be too busy hanging on to the handlebars to notice. The road here has some very good downhills and it basically alternates between two gradients: steep down and not-so-steep down.

Be warned: private vehicles, Water Board patrol and NPWS rangers all travel the road so don't be completely reckless. Just after one uphill that bends sharply left around a hill, a clearing on the right offers good views over the Jamison Valley. Continue south, and during another great downhill, a signposted turnoff leads up an embankment to the beginning of Andersons Fire Trail. There is a barrier on top of the hill just out of sight of the main road. This trail winds its way generally north-east, and a number of turn-offs can cause some navigational difficulties. Head right at the first fork. Some sandy parts are encountered along the way but shouldn't cause difficulties if you ride fast and keep the handlebars straight. Parts of the trail have also been washed away by erosion gullies and these can cause problems especially when speeding around tight hairpin corners.

There are occasional glimpses of Queen Victoria Creek to the north, but the thick undergrowth on the trail generally makes this a thrilling high speed mountain biking trail rather than a scenic cycle in the country. A dam and another barrier are encountered along the way but aren't marked on the map. On the final steep descent down to Bedford Creek, the vegetation has grown very profusely since the last grading and now actually forms a tunnel over the trail. Tall cyclists would have to duck and there is just enough room for a person's head to pass through. This is quite an unusual effect, speeding down this dark tunnel. The last section in particular can be quite slippery due to the leaf cover and may even be too steep to ride down as the trail has deteriorated considerably. The softer soils, steep slope, and frequent rainfall and track-use all contribute to accelerate the effects of erosion.

Cross Queen Victoria Creek and then rise steeply up only to descend down again and cross Bedford Creek. Although it is quite wide, it is possible to cross it without getting your feet wet. The wide sandy beach on the left hand side is a good place to have lunch and possibly even a swim if the weather is hot. The water is deep enough for swimming in some spots and is certainly slow enough not to be dangerous. Surprisingly, it is quite clear. What lies ahead is then a very steep climb back up to Woodford and will inevitably involve walking the bike up for all but the very strongest riders. A turn-off to the right just past the gate at the top leads to the beautiful Murphys Glen if you still have energy left.

RIDE 32:   THE WATERSHED ROAD

FROM: Wentworth Falls Station
TO: Penrith Station
VIA: McMahon's Lookout, Rocky Knob, Warragamba Dam, Bents Basin
LENGTH:
    Day 1: Wentworth Falls to McMahon's Lookout 26 km
    Day 2: McMahon's Lookout to Ripple Creek 25 km
    Day 3: Ripple Creek to Bents Basin 33 km
    Day 4: Bents Basin to Penrith 25 km
    Total distance is 109 km
RIDE/TRACK GRADE: 5/4–5
WALKING: None
HEIGHT VARIATION: 847 m
TRANSPORT: Rail (Blue Mountains Line)
FACILITIES: None
SPECIAL EQUIPMENT: Water containers, extensive repair kit, spare night's food
MAPS: CMA (LIC) Jamison, Bimlow, Warragamba and Penrith 1:25 000 topographicals

This ride is perhaps the most eventful in the lower Blue Mountains. Featured on this medium graded route are spectacular views, fabulous downhills, the dramatic McMahon's Lookout over beautiful Lake Burragorang, wild terrain, Warragamba Dam, and the picturesque Bents Basin.

The majority of the route is along the Watershed Road which marks the boundary between restricted Water Board territory on the right and national park on the left. I've inquired several times about the legality of this trail and I am told by the Water Board that walkers are permitted on it, but

184

cyclists are discouraged. Apparently this is due to the dangerous blind corners where Water Board rangers would be in
danger of wiping out anyone on two wheels. This excuse was
a relief, for I was beginning to believe the Water Board considered all cyclists to be filthy animals whose only aim was to
poison the catchment area. In any case, you won't be arrested
for cycling along here, and so long as you don't urinate on the
Water Board side of the road, you should be OK.

The first night is spent camping on a lookout and therefore
has no water. Cyclists are recommended to take at least 2 litres
per person per day for the first two days until the Ripple Creek
camp site. A camera is also recommended for the views are
too good to be recorded only by memory.

Alight at Wentworth Falls Station, climb the stairs, turn left,
and head back along the highway. The turn-off to Kings Tableland is well signposted just before the Brown Horse Inn restaurant. The road briefly undulates for a kilometre passing
through a residential area. There are impressive views over
the Jamison Valley and east to the Sydney metropolitan area
here. This part of the tableland is quite exposed and can get
very windy. The residential property is soon left and a long
very fast downhill leads to the Queen Victoria Memorial Hospital grounds. This was originally one of three sanatoriums in
the area and was first opened in 1903. The very tidy European
style setting and associated gardens contrast with the Australian bush as a backdrop. The road diverges here: to the right
leads to a car-park and eventually Kedumba and Jamison
Valleys, but keep left following Kings Tableland. As you pass
the hospital, the road immediately deteriorates into a very
rough and loose dirt road, before recovering into quite a well
graded and wide unsealed road.

The national park is entered but if you're like the author,
you'll be too busy hanging on to the handlebars to notice. The
road here has some very good downhills and it basically alternates between two gradients: steep down and not-so-steep
down.

Be warned: private vehicles, Water Board patrol and NPWS
rangers all travel the road so don't be completely reckless. Just
after one uphill that bends sharply left around a hill, a clearing
on the right offers good views over the Jamison Valley. Continue south past the residential island of High Valley.

Fortunately there are many landmarks to check your progress along this section: prominent knolls such as Notts, Warrigal, and Harris Hills make good navigational markers. Towards the end several uphills are encountered, but none are very long or steep. A signpost points right to McMahons Lookout. The track deteriorates somewhat this turnoff between the Rocky Knob Trail and Kings Tableland Road. This finally descends down a hill a large car-park. The picnic/camping ground is on the right hand side.

From the southern end of the car-park, the road continues over a large log. It would still be possible to ride your bike for most of the way to the lookout as it follows the original road, but it is very overgrown in some places, and the bike would have to be pushed back up again, so it is recommended you leave it around the start of this last section. The track continues around to the west descending through some beautiful forest. You shortly come to the first lookout that has a safety fence for protection. It looks west and only gives limited views of the lake. Continue left down the track to a section resembling a glen covered in a rich display of green ferns. It has as its central feature a gigantic bare tree that towers over all others. At the bottom, the track then climbs up on to a small hill where it becomes a multitude of minor footpads. At the crest, head left to the end of the knoll. All around are vantage points over the lake and it is up to you to find the best ones. One particularly good spot lies at the very southern end of the ridge, and down about 20 m below, at a large rock ledge on the left. Here absolutely no trees obscure the view and all of the Coxs River arm and much of Wollondilly River arm of the lake can be seen in one vista. Some rock scrambling is necessary to get here, but the view is worth it. The skyline features the Broken Rock Range and the rugged Bimlow Tablelands with its multiple 'roller-coaster' knolls.

On the western side of the last crest is a small patch of pine forest with a rough campsite in it. There are good views from here also to the Kowmung River and Mount Cloudmaker. One of the two prominent islands down below has a red telephone booth on it. When you've finished taking in the spectacle, head back to the car-park. There is another lookout just beyond the picnic/camping ground looking along the Coxs River valley. From up here, this entire region looks surprisingly flat. The only real bumps are the Wild Dog Mountains south of the Narrow Neck Peninsula.

Here the sunset can be witnessed as you set up camp. Early next morning, you might like to go down to the end again, for there is usually a high probability that the lake will be covered by a carpet of clouds. When this occurs, there is no better place to take photographs. After breakfast, head back north to the first turn-off to Rocky Knob.

The trail immediately descends and close to here is a brilliant patch of beautiful red waratahs. I've also sighted kangaroos here a number of times. This road serves as a central service line to the overhead high voltage power lines. Accordingly it is very open territory due to the wide cleared corridor underneath the lines. If water is low by this stage, you might want to get some from Pelham Creek. It can be reached by turning left just before Brereton Bend at the very top of a crest. The track is extremely overgrown and has numerous fallen logs over it. The first part can be ridden, but the second half (just past the fork marked on the map) contains quite thick scrub in the middle of the trail. It stays flat for a while before descending further. At another junction there is a clearing and another trail branches left down a washed out section of the trail. Erosion gullies are quite large here and the bikes would probably have to be wheeled the last 100–300 m. There is a makeshift campsite is on the right hand side at the end, surrounded by cut logs. The place is not completely forgotten as there was evidence of recent use when we camped there. The very last section to Pelham Creek after the road ends is completely overgrown and involves negotiating prickly bush and some large, slippery, moss-covered logs. Leeches could be a problem here after rain, so remember the salt.

If there still is sufficient water, continue cycling east along the Watershed Road as it winds its way through the maze of ridges in a relatively little known area of the lower Blue Mountains. Cross under the powerlines one last time. There are occasional views north to Mount Hall and the Erskine Creek valley. The road also passes beside some impressive rock formations on the right. It was here that I first got the inspiration to write this book as I wondered why more people don't explore the many trails in our national parks.

All of a sudden, the road tops a crest and descends suddenly into a steep valley. Along here some standard Water Board signs are passed but the restricted area is quite a few kilometres to the south. There are no official campsites at Ripple

Creek so one has to find one's own flat area to pitch a tent. The narrow valley here resembles a canyon. Unlike Erskine Creek a few hundred metres to the north, the water here is quite pure as it originates from a wild source.

The next day, head up the other side of Ripple Creek negotiating some steep hairpin turns to the top of the Erskine Range once again. The gradient is so steep that most cyclists would have to walk this section. At the top, surprise. The vegetation and the road really open up and some fantastic speeds can be achieved. Numerous kangaroos inhabit the grasslands on either side of the road. Through a small gap on the right, a very short turn off leads to a clearing. A track then enters some bush to a ledge called Fred's Lookout. From here it is a sheer drop down to Ripple Creek which has developed considerably. Five kilometres further on the left is a signpost marking the beginning of the Jack Evans Track. It proceeds up slightly and then flat along two ruts through very high grass. At the end are some good views over Erskine Creek. If the day is hot and someone is dying for a swim, a 15 min walk down negotiating a series of rock ledges takes you to some nice swimming spots and rapids.

To exit the Watershed Road, simply follow it for another 4 km past the Jack Evans Track turnoff to Warragamba Dam. A gate must be negotiated, then it's across the dam wall, through the picnic grounds and on to Farnsworth Avenue to the round-about intersection with Silverdale Road. Continue past the Nortons Basin Road and down the hill to the Nepean River. Shortly before the bridge is a road right signposted as Bents Basin Road.

From here it is 8 km to the third day's destination. It is hard to imagine when cycling along here through uneventful agricultural land that a beautiful forested oasis exists just at the end. Along the way is a site for a controversial new Skirmish ground. At the very end, the road turns to dirt and there's a gate before one drops down to an informal carpark.

The road through the recreation area leads left from the carpark down to a bridge over the river. The area's beauty is made by the wide bend in the river around Little Mountain bordered by two beaches. Facilities include bins, picnic tables, and fire places. The water here is generally pleasant and relatively clean, and some excellent platforms exist on the far right hand side next to the rapids. A walking track leads here from the back of mowed recreation grounds. Stories exist as to the depth of the river in the middle of the basin, some rumours hint at a volcanic vent. Whatever the reason, when diving near the centre, one experiences a rapid decrease in water temperature suggesting great depth.

Picnic grounds are also located on the southern side, across the river. Here there are toilets, a kiosk, the Richard S. Venables Education Centre, and the camping ground (fees apply). The day can be spent swimming and relaxing, or exploring the Nepean Gorge.

Penrith can be accessed the next day by backtracking to Silverdale Road, crossing the Nepean River to Wallacia and following Mulgoa Road all the way north.

Note: Until the year 2000, the Water Board will be upgrading the strength of Warragamba by reinforcing the spillway and raising the height of the dam to withstand a worst-case scenario 1 in 100 000 years flood. There will probably be times when the road on top of the wall will be closed, so it's best to check with the dam authorities first.

RIDE 33: McMAHON'S LOOKOUT (LAKE BURRAGORANG)

FROM: Wentworth Falls Station
TO: Bullaburra Station
VIA: McMahon's Lookout, Kings Tableland Road
LENGTH: 48 km
TIME: 1 long day, or 2 easy days of 24 km each
RIDE/TRACK GRADE: 3/4–5
WALKING: 1 km to the viewing points
HEIGHT VARIATION: 267 m
TRANSPORT: Rail (Blue Mountains Line)
FACILITIES: Picnic ground at the end with tables and toilets
SPECIAL EQUIPMENT: Water containers
MAPS: CMA (LIC) Jamison and Bimlow 1:25 000
topographicals

The spectacular scenery around the water supply for Sydney is largely monopolised by the Water Board. However, they have allowed an access corridor through the restricted area so that one may view Lake Burragorang. This is the lake formed by Warragamba Dam and is fed by the Wollondilly, Nattai, and Coxs Rivers. Before the dam was built, Kings Tableland Road used to go all the way to Picton, an incredibly scenic drive of over 100 km.

This ride can be done in one day, but it is recommended that you camp overnight at the picnic/camping ground next to the carpark at the lookout. This will allow you the splendour of seeing Lake Burragorang in the early morning when it is often enshrouded in mist.

Alight at Wentworth Falls Station, climb the stairs, turn left, and head back along the highway. The turn-off to Kings Tableland is well signposted just before the Brown Horse Inn restaurant. The road briefly undulates for a kilometre passing through a residential area. There are impressive views over the Jamison Valley and east to the Sydney metropolitan area here. This part of the tableland is quite exposed and can get very windy. The residential property is soon left and a long very fast downhill leads to the Queen Victoria Memorial Hospital grounds. This was originally one of three sanatoriums in the area and was first opened in 1903. The very tidy European style setting and associated gardens contrasts with the Australian bush as a backdrop. The road diverges here: to the right leads to a car-park and eventually to the Kedumba and Jamison Valleys, but keep left following Kings Tableland. As you pass the hospital, the road immediately deteriorates into a very rough and loose dirt road, before recovering into quite a well graded and wide unsealed road.

The national park is entered but if you're like the author, you'll be too busy hanging on to the handlebars to notice. The road here has some very good downhills and it basically alternates between two gradients: steep down and not-so-steep down.

Be warned: private vehicles, Water Board patrol and NPWS rangers all travel the road so don't be completely reckless. Just after one uphill that bends sharply left around a hill, a clearing on the right offers good views over the Jamison Valley. Continue south past the residential island of High Valley.

There are fortunately many landmarks to check your progress along this section: prominent knolls such as Notts, Warrigal, and Harris Hills make good navigational markers.

Towards the end several uphills are encountered, but none are very long or steep. A signpost points right to McMahons Lookout. The track deteriorates somewhat this turnoff between the Rocky Knob Trail and Kings Tableland Road. This finally descends down a hill to a large car-park. The picnic/camping ground is on the right hand side.

From the southern end of the car-park, the road continues over a large log. It would still be possible to ride your bike for most of the way to the lookout as it follows the original road, but it is very overgrown in some places, and the bike would have to be pushed back up again, so it is recommended you leave it around the start of this last section. The track continues around to the west descending through some beautiful forest. You shortly come to the first lookout that has a safety fence for protection. It looks west and only gives limited views of the lake. Continue left down the track to a section resembling a glen covered in a rich display of green ferns. It has as its central feature a gigantic bare tree that towers over all others. At the bottom, the track then climbs up on to a small hill where it becomes a multitude of minor footpads. At the crest, head left to the end of the knoll. All around are vantage points over the lake and it is up to you to find the best ones. One particularly good spot lies at the very southern end of the ridge, and down about 20 m below, at a large rock ledge on the left. Here absolutely no trees obscure the view and all of the Coxs River arm and much of Wollondilly River arm of the lake can be seen in one vista. Some rock scrambling is necessary to get here, but the view is worth it. The skyline features the Broken Rock Range and the rugged Bimlow Tablelands with its multiple 'roller-coaster' knolls.

On the western side of the last crest is a small patch of pine forest with a rough campsite in it. There are good views from here also to the Kowmung River and Mount Cloudmaker. One of the two prominent islands down below has a red telephone booth on it! When you've finished taking in the spectacle, head back to the car-park. There is another lookout just beyond the picnic/camping ground looking along the Coxs River valley. From up here, this entire region looks surprisingly flat. The only real bumps are the Wild Dog Mountains south of the Narrow Neck Peninsula.

Here the sunset can be witnessed as you set up camp. If staying the night, water would have to be taken. In an emergency however there is a small gully down the bottom on the east side of the car-park. Since this is technically within the 3 km restricted radius around Sydney's water supply, campers must be on their best behaviour. Early next morning, you might like to go down to the end again, for there's usually a high probability that the lake will be covered by a carpet of clouds. When this occurs, there is no better place to take photographs.

The fastest way back to civilisation is to backtrack all the way to the Great Western Highway and turn right cycling down to Bullaburra.

OTHER RIDES IN THE LOWER BLUE MOUNTAINS

The main avenues for further mountain bike exploration in the Lower Blue Mountains are:
• Linden Ridge
  Attractions: wild bush camping by Wentworth Creek
• Red Ridge (accessible from Kings Tableland)
  Attractions: wild bush camping by Erskine Creek.

3. THE UPPER BLUE MOUNTAINS

Between Lithgow and Wentworth Falls are the two famous valleys: the Jamison and the Grose. This is where most of the tourist trade is centred, and most of the development has taken place. People escaping the busy city for a day flock to Katoomba, but strangely enough on most weekends the township is far more crowded that Sydney during peak hour! It's a case of experiencing the solitude with 100 000 other people.

However, with a map and a little experience, the wiser of us can find better places with no one around at all. In the following suggested rides, the cyclist can discover plateaus that all vehicles are banned from, gorges too far for the walker to travel in one day, and beautiful valleys that are perfect venues for a picnic. The central plateau can also be used as a staging point for longer tours: Blackheath to Mittagong, Katoomba to Jenolan Caves, and Mount Victoria to Singleton.

Whatever the occasion, cycling the upper Blue Mountains will be an unforgettable experience. It is here that the first commercial bicycle tour operators in Australia are conducting their rides. Even if you don't have a mountain bike, you can hire one, or bring your own road/touring bike for there are still plenty of sealed roads and well graded tracks.

RIDE 34: WENTWORTH FALLS TOUR

FROM: Wentworth Falls Station
TO: Bullaburra Station
LENGTH: 17 km
TIME: 1 easy day
RIDE/TRACK GRADE: 2/2
WALKING: Valley of the Waters (optional but recommended)
HEIGHT VARIATION: 40 m cycling
TRANSPORT: Rail (Blue Mountains Line)
FACILITIES: Picnic grounds at the Valley of the Waters and shops at Wentworth Falls
SPECIAL EQUIPMENT: Warm jumper on windy days, and a lock for the bike
MAPS: CMA (LIC) Katoomba 1:25 000 topographical

Wentworth Falls is a charming township set right in the heart of the Blue Mountains. It blends the atmosphere of a European village with that of an Australian country town, all within the spectacular backdrop of one of the state's most scenic places. The actual waterfalls that it was named after were first discovered by one of Governor Macquarie's party on 15 May 1815. They were originally called Campbell's Cataract. Charles Darwin visited the township in 1836 when there was little more than an inn called 'The Weatherboard'.

Alight at the station, which is exactly an hour from Penrith, or two hours from Sydney. The platform was called 'Weatherboard' and this as is far as one could go up the mountains when the line was opened on 3 July 1867. Climb up the stairs and left down to Station Street where the shops are. Turn right on to the highway, then down and left at Falls Road. Follow this road to the very end over some crests. Along the way are some very fine old English-style houses with luxurious front gardens. A lot of Australian celebrities have their hideaways in either Leura, Wentworth Falls, or Mount Wilson.

At the end is a lookout right on top of the cliffs with views to the Kings Tableland escarpment on the left. The cliffs along here are well over 200 m high. Wentworth Falls are on the left, where water tumbles uninterrupted into the Jamison Valley. On windy days however, the water often falls *up* due to the extreme exposure to south-westerlies channelled into the valley. Walking tracks lead from here to the top of the falls, Weeping Rock, and down to the National Pass. Cycle right down Sir Henry Burrell Scenic Drive to another lookout over the Jamison Valley, this one giving views south to Mount Solitary which juts out of the valley like an impenetrable fortress. The road then curves back up again to join Falls Road. Turn left at Fletcher Street and head west to the very end. Residential property is left behind and you enter a nice picnic area with a hut at one end. On weekends and public holidays this will almost certainly be crowded: even on rainy days.

The hut is now a shop catering for tourists and is run by the Katoomba and District Wildlife Conservation Society. It has displays and some food and warm drinks can be bought here. It is suggested that you chain the bikes (thieving is becoming quite rampant in the national park) and do the Valley of the Waters walk down to a waterfall nestled in glen and surrounded by rainforest. A nature track leaflet is available outlining information on the vegetation and local fauna. Some ladders are provided for the steep descent but the walk itself is an easy grade. A diversion leads past Lilians Bridge to Lilians Glen, which makes a nice spot for lunch. The creek disappears through a narrow cleft in the rock that can be explored upstream, but only by those willing to get wet. In all, the Valley of Waters is well signposted and because of the short distances involved along well graded tracks, shouldn't provide any difficulty in navigation. A map board is provided at the start of the walk on the left of the Conservation Hut. There is also a lookout here to the Inspiration Point peninsula. Allow about 2 hours for walking to the waterfall, the glen, and back up again.

Head out again and take the first on the left. This, like any other north-south road in this part of Wentworth Falls, leads back to the highway. Head left further up at an angle on to Valley Road to access the main road further west. Travel up the highway momentarily and take the first on the right after crossing under the railway tracks. This road follows the railway tracks to Wentworth Falls Lake. If you desperately hate traffic, you can lift your bikes over the railway line directly into Sinclair Crescent on the opposite side of valley road. Alternatively you can ride down the hill to the School of Arts and turn left into Adele Avenue, a small side street that serves as the main entrance to the Blue Mountains Grammar School. Turn right at a three way junction on to a council road past a cricket oval and down to the railway tracks. This gives direct access to the lake.

Wentworth Falls Lake was created in 1878 as a reservoir for the railway until the line was electrified in 1957. The picnic grounds on the south side provide a pleasant relaxation venue for the locals, and the lake is used for swimming, sailboarding, and fishing.

Sinclair Avenue continues across Jamison Creek and up to Henderson Street. From here you can either cross the bridge where you arrive back at the train station or you can cycle down Boddington Hill via the unsealed Railway Parade on the northern side of the tracks to Bullaburra. The station is 5 km away on a well graded and predominantly downhill road.

RIDE 35:   MOUNT HAY

FROM: Leura Station
TO: Wentworth Falls Station
VIA: Mount Hay Road
LENGTH: 39 km
TIME: 1 day
RIDE/TRACK GRADE: 3–4/4
WALKING: 3.5 km return walk to the summit
HEIGHT VARIATION: 170 m
TRANSPORT: Rail (Blue Mountains Line)
FACILITIES: Picnic ground at the end

Formerly called Round Hill, this was the destination in 1789 for an expedition led by Dawes, who unfortunately only got as far as Mount Twiss north of Linden. Now a well graded road leads almost to the base of the summit where a one hour 1.7 km walk leads to the summit. Mount Hay is one of the most prominent landmarks north of the main plateau. In geological terms it is a basalt capped residual, meaning that it is covered with volcanic rock as opposed to ordinary sandstone. This layer is about 55 m thick, and was liquid about 17 million years ago. The pie-shaped mountain sits right on top of the plateau and overlooks the spectacular Grose Gorge opposite Explorers Wall. This area features the highest cliffs anywhere in the Blue Mountains. Other examples of basalt capped mountains include Mount Banks and Mount Wilson. A couple of water bottles would be handy here as there is no water along the way.

From Leura Station, head up to the overhead bridge and cross the highway taking the first on the right. This is Britain Street and marks the highest stage of the trip. Turn left at the next intersection on to Mount Hay Road and follow this past the national park entrance sign for another 16 km. Over this distance, the road drops about 200 m with the only significant rise occurring at Flat Top where an eroded 4WD track gives good views east to the Wentworth Creek gorge and associated feeder streams. Just a few minutes further on is a turn-off to Lockley's Pylon on the left which should be ignored. This is a staging point for extended overnight walks into camping areas by the Grose River such as Acacia Flat servicing the very popular Blue Gum Forest.

From here the road swings east and then north-east to the picnic ground. Ignore the track to the right that continues to Hurley Heights—there is nothing of interest at the end. However, it can be useful if you plan to stay the night and find the small campsite at the base of Mount Hay crowded.

In any case, leave your bikes at the picnic/camping ground to the left, 300 m after the last turn-off. You will most likely find other bikes here as well on a summer weekend. Walk north through some rugged and rocky country to the summit.

On the way is a short detour to Butterbox Point not marked on the map. The Grose Valley gorge is over 600 m below.

Some scrambling is necessary in places to attain the summit of Mount Hay but generally doesn't provide any problems. The best views, surprisingly, are not from the top but from the approach. For photographers, the best time to capture this area is very early in the morning when the gigantic golden Explorers Wall turns a deep bronze colour and the rim is highlighted by rays coming through the trees. Because of the angle, some dramatic shadows are enhanced in the cliff face. Shots can be taken from the summit if you are willing to bushbash through the scrub to the rocky edges. Return via the same route. For something different, head left where Mount Hay Road reaches the Great Western Highway and cycle down to Wentworth Falls Station, enjoying some height loss.

RIDE 36:   CLIFF DRIVE

FROM: Katoomba Station
TO: Leura Station
VIA: Cliff Drive
LENGTH: 16 km
TIME: 1 easy day
RIDE/TRACK GRADE: 2/1
WALKING: Numerous options to explore lookouts
HEIGHT VARIATION: 60 m
TRANSPORT: Rail (Blue Mountains Line)
FACILITIES: Many well developed picnic grounds and shops
MAPS: CMA (LIC) Katoomba 1:25 000 topographical or
NRMA Blue Mountains Holiday Map

There are well over thirty official lookouts along this ride, so bring plenty of film. Because of the short and easy grade of this suggestion, there is plenty of time to dismount from the bikes and investigate certain prominent features such as the Devils Hole and Boars Head.

Start from Katoomba Station and follow the railway lines on the southern side along the shops until you join up with the highway. Turn left on to the beginning of the famous Cliff Drive, called Narrow Neck or Valley Road at this point.

Turn right at the turn-off to Cahills Lookout on the Peckmans Plateau. There are some interesting features along here: the first is Cahills Lookout which overlooks the Megalong Valley, and is a popular horse-riding area. The start of the short track to Boars Head is marked by the point where the road swings east. To see the actual distinctive boar head formation on the rock tower, you must head north-west along the cliff top following a rough track. In the background is the cliff-lined Narrow Neck peninsula.

Further along is another short walking track to Devils Hole, a very narrow and dramatic cleft in the sandstone. A rocky walking track descends through this cleft before disappearing. Have a look at the chasm and then head back up to the bikes. Follow Cliff Drive around until it overlooks the exact centre of the long cliff lined Narrow Neck plateau. This prominent peninsula ends at a lookout over the Coxs River valley and the mountain bike tour along it is detailed in Ride 37. Further on, a short track leads to a dramatic lookout over a massive landslide that occurred in 1932 where an entire section of cliff collapsed. This is a classic example of the erosion process in action. One day, many million years in the future, the Blue Mountains will have eroded completely into the Pacific Ocean via the Hawkesbury River, leaving just a flat plain.

Then pass the Scenic Skyway and Railway and then down the next peninsula where the Three Sisters stand. Here is the famous Echo Point, possibly the most famous lookout in Australia. At night the Three Sisters formation is even illuminated. Cliff Drive then heads north again to Leura and Linda Falls. These and many other falls in the area were how Katoomba got its name, as a corruption of the Aboriginal word 'Kedumba' which means falling water. From Linda Falls, several walking tracks branch out linking with the Federal Pass walking track at the base of the cliffs. More cliff tops are visited as the road heads east with fantastic views over the Jamison valley with the very high cliffs of Sublime Point on the left and Mount Solitary in the middle. If the day is still early one can head around to the end of this peninsula via Watkins Road. If not, Leura Station lies due north along Leura Mall and through some exquisite real estate. For walking tracknotes in this area, consult Tyrone Thomas *100 Walks in New South Wales* or Neil Paton's *Walks in the Blue Mountains National Park*.

RIDE 37:   NARROW NECK

FROM: Katoomba Station
TO: Clear Hill (return)
VIA: Narrow Neck Plateau
LENGTH: 35 km
TIME: 1 day
RIDE/TRACK GRADE: 3/4
WALKING: Short walk to lookout at the end
HEIGHT VARIATION: 110 m
TRANSPORT: Rail (Blue Mountains Line)
FACILITIES: None
MAPS: CMA (LIC) Katoomba and Jamison 1:25 000
topographicals

Narrow Neck is a very long peninsula completely skirted by high cliffs that form the western boundary to the huge Jamison Valley that Mount Solitary resides in. The plateau on top is quite flat and makes fantastic cycling country. Furthermore, most of the peninsula is closed off to motorised traffic. The stunted heath on top of the plateau is testimony to the high winds that blow across from the west. For this reason it is recommended to take a jumper along. A couple of water bottles would also be handy here as there is no water along the way. This ride has become one of the most popular bike tours in the upper Blue Mountains, especially after Andrew Eddinghousen did a tour here for a network television holiday program.
From Katoomba Station, cycle up to the shops and over the crest down the main street. Just before the very end is the turn-off to the Scenic Railway and you should turn right and head past numerous parks and picnic places. On sunny weekends, these will be teeming with people while the Narrow Neck itself will be relatively empty. Once past the Scenic Skyway, head left down an unsealed road that descends steeply at an angle to the road. Beware of cycling too fast along this first drop as cars can be coming the other way from the Golden Stairs car-park. Once past the car-park, there is a very steep uphill but this is the only one of its kind for the whole journey. To the right are expansive views over the Megalong Valley (Megalong is an Aboriginal word meaning 'valley under the

rock'. This becomes apparent when entering the valley via the Six Foot Track or the Megalong Valley Road from Blackheath). A number of other features are passed along the way: including a locked Water Board gate barring cars, the actual very thin 'neck' with sheer cliffs on either side of the road, some wide open amphitheatres with some very weathered rock formations, and a fire tower. Some rough camp sites are also found along the way in the forested part. The peninsula thins once more before the road comes to an end amidst some low heath. A walking track then heads off on the right down a cleft past a plaque paying tribute to Walter Taro, a pioneer bushwalker in this area who died in 1969.

A thin rocky shelf leads to the top of Taro's Ladders. It is here that panoramic views of the southern Blue Mountains can be obtained. In the distant south-east is Lake Burragorang, directly south is the massive Mount Cloudmaker complex with the Wild Dog mountains in the foreground. Further west is the Megalong Valley with Kanangra Walls in the distance. In fact you would need at least six to seven other topographical maps to cover and identify the features in this panorama. Despite the spectacular view, photographs unfortunately do not come out too well from here because of the thick haze. Only around dawn and dusk or on extremely windy days that can something worthwhile be captured.

Narrow Neck is a popular staging point for more ambitious expeditions across the Great Dividing Range to Mittagong. For cyclists, there is an easier way down to the fire trails around Medlow Gap at the base of Narrow Neck, and that involves a spectacular descent from Blackheath (See Rides 42 and 43).

However, after the view is taken in, have lunch and return to Katoomba so you can plan your next trek in the magnificent area you've just witnessed. Allow about two to three hours for the return journey.

RIDE 38:   THE SIX FOOT TRACK

FROM: Jenolan Caves Road
TO: Katoomba Station
VIA: The Six Foot Track
LENGTH: 46 km

TIME: 1 long day or 2 short days
RIDE/TRACK GRADE: 6–7/6–7
WALKING: None
HEIGHT VARIATION: 950 m
TRANSPORT: Private transport to Jenolan Caves and Rail (Blue Mountains Line) from Katoomba
FACILITIES: Camping ground at Old Ford Reserve
MAPS: CMA (LIC) Jenolan, Hampton, and Katoomba 1:25 000 topographicals

The Six Foot Track is another one of those classic bike rides with a massive downhill that'll give your brakes a workout. Private transport must be arranged so you can be dropped off in the Jenolan State Forest about 12 km north of Jenolan Caves. This is the Great Dividing Range and lies at 1200 m above sea level. The entire first half of the day will be spent cycling down to the Coxs River at 250 m. To get up to the train line requires a considerable climb up either via Nellies Glen to Katoomba, or leaving the Six Foot Track and cycling along the Megalong Valley Road to Blackheath.

The track was built in 1884 at the instigation of the Premier of New South Wales, Alexander Stuart. It was built as a horse-riding or bridle track from Katoomba to Jenolan Caves. Today it has been superseded by a standard fire trail for much of its way and therefore is the perfect venue for cyclists. The result is that you are likely to see one or two parties of cyclists on summer weekends. Please note that the track is also heavily used by walkers and due regard should be paid: no wild over-taking manoeuvres. The track is quite rough in parts and sometimes pushing the bike through eroded sections will be necessary. The ride is also physically challenging as pushing a fully laden bike up long steep hills is extremely tiring even for relatively fit persons.

The Six Foot Track passes through state forest, national park, and private property. Camping, if you plan an overnight trip, is available at the Old Ford Reserve. However, it is still possible to do the ride in one day. This has the advantage of avoiding hauling a heavy overnight pack/panniers around, but the disadvantage is that you'll have to rush. The ascent to Katoomba or Blackheath takes about three hours alone.

The trail is easy to follow has it has been extensively marked by the Orange Lands Office. For more information on the history of the track, consult Jim Smith's book *From Katoomba to Jenolan Caves: The Six Foot Track*. The Lands Department has also published a small fold-out pamphlet of the track.

Start where the Six Foot Track leaves Jenolan Caves Road opposite a picnic ground. The spot is on the border between the Jenolan and Hampton topographical maps. Head through pine forest down Black Range along one of the best downhills in the Blue Mountains. Turn left at the rain gauge and roll down to Little River. This section is particularly steep. Don't go too fast down here for there's a locked gate just before the river. You then follow the watercourse downstream and then over a small crest before another long descent to the Coxs River via Murdering Creek Gully. Although the topographical maps don't actually mark the trail as 'Six Foot Track', the area is well signposted. Cross the river and pass through private property. Public access has been permitted here by arrangement with farm owners provided that walkers and cyclists stick to the track. Due to the rough condition, the bike might have to be wheeled over certain sections before arriving at Old Ford Reserve. From here Katoomba and Blackheath stations are about three hours away. The route to Blackheath is slightly longer (15 km) but makes easy riding for most of the way as it is a sealed road. The Six Foot Track continues up to Nellies Glen along Megalong Creek and coming out at Explorers Tree. The station can then be found along the highway to the right about 12 km from the Old Ford Reserve. The bike will definitely have to be pushed for most of the uphill section due to the bad condition of the track. It is however the more scenic of the two exit routes.

If camping at Old Ford Reserve, the best places are on the north-eastern side of the ford. However, these can be crowded on weekends. More secluded places exit on the north-western side, where good swimming holes exist in the Megalong Creek. Firewood is a problem and it's best to carry gas or metho fuel stoves.

RIDE 39:   EVAN'S LOOKOUT
(INCLUDING GRAND CANYON WALK)

FROM: Blackheath Station
TO: Medlow Bath Station
VIA: Govetts Leap, Evans Lookout
LENGTH: 19 km cycling, 6 km walking
TIME: 1 full day
RIDE/TRACK GRADE: 2/3–4 (mostly 1)
WALKING: 6 km medium difficulty walking through the
Grand Canyon
HEIGHT VARIATION: 110 m
TRANSPORT: Rail (Blue Mountains Line)
FACILITIES· Blue Mountains National Park visitors centre at
Govetts Leap, picnic facilities at Govetts Leap and Evans
Lookout
SPECIAL EQUIPMENT: Bike lock, camera
MAPS: CMA (LIC) Katoomba 1:25 000 topographical

Blackheath is a small township sitting on top of a narrow
plateau and surrounded by cliffs to the east and west. This
ride tours the eastern side of the town where several lookouts
give some of the most spectacular views in the Blue Mountains. Cycling is particularly pleasant here as the tracks and
roads are flat and of good quality. Even on cloudless days, the
high altitude of Blackheath and gentle south-westerly breezes
make sightseeing conditions very comfortable.
   Start by alighting at Blackheath Station. One doesn't have to
climb up the stairs, but can cross the tracks directly via a ramp
at the end of the platform. The station was originally called
Govetts Leap in 1869, but changed to Blackheath two years
later. The station master's building was constructed in 1883
and it was the only stop between Wentworth Falls and Mount
Victoria for about five years.
   Cross the highway and head left at the intersection on to
Govetts Leap Road. Follow this to the end to access one of the
best lookouts in Australia. Just before the end is the District
Office of the NPWS, administering the entire Blue Mountains.
It doubles as a Visitor Centre. Displays give information concerning wildlife and the geography of the mountains. Leaflets
can be obtained here on walking tracks throughout the Grose

River area, and maps can be purchased. Govetts Leap lookout is Blackheath's pride and joy and the principal source of its tourist trade: Govetts Leap. From here, a waterfall forms a foreground to the sheer grandeur of the very rugged Grose Gorge and those seeing it for the first time will always remember that experience. This is one of the few lookouts that you can actually ride your bike up to the very edge. The place was named after William Romaine Govett (1807–48) who first discovered the waterfall when he was commissioned to survey the Blue Mountains in June 1831. Contrary to popular belief, the legend of the bushranger named Govett who jumped himself and his horse from the edge is almost certainly fiction. The falls were once named Govett's Leap Falls but have recently been renamed as Bridal Veil Falls.

To see the Grose Gorge from another angle, head back up the main road and turn left up Cleopatra Street. This swings around and deteriorates into a rough dirt road before descending down into the gully of Govetts Leap Brook that forms the falls. The track then climbs back up to joins Evans Lookout Road. Turn left and cycle to the car-park at the very end. A short rideable walking track leads to the actual lookout which has been fenced off for the public's protection. The view is as astounding as Govetts Leap and makes for excellent photographs.

It is recommended that you lock the bikes here and do 6 km round tour of the Grand Canyon. Along the way are some swimming holes and lush fern dominated vegetation. Head down the track to Beauchamp Falls and then upstream along Greaves Creek through the Grand Canyon to Neates Glen where an exit track climbs 100 m up again to Evans Lookout Road. Simply follow the road east back to the bikes.

Access Medlow Bath Station by heading west along Evans Lookout Road to the Great Western Highway and turn south.

RIDE 40:   BLACKHEATH TOUR
(PERRYS LOOKDOWN)

FROM: Blackheath Station
TO: Hanging Rock, Perrys Lookdown, and Govetts Leap (return)

LENGTH: 24 km
TIME: 1 day
RIDE/TRACK GRADE: 3/4
WALKING: Optional hard graded walk to Blue Gum Forest
HEIGHT VARIATION: 85 m (600 m doing the Blue Gum Forest walk)
TRANSPORT: Rail (Blue Mountains Line)
FACILITIES: Blue Mountains National Park visitors centre at Govetts Leap, picnic facilities at Govetts Leap and Perrys Lookdown.
MAPS: CMA (LIC) Katoomba and Mount Wilson 1:25 000 topographicals

Blackheath is a small township sitting on top of a narrow plateau and surrounded by cliffs to the east and west. This ride tours the eastern side of the town where several lookouts give some of the most spectacular views in the Blue Mountains. Cycling is particularly pleasant here as the tracks and roads are flat and of good quality. Even on cloudless days, the high altitude of Blackheath and gentle south-westerly breezes make sightseeing conditions very comfortable.

Start by alighting at Blackheath Station. One doesn't have to climb up the stairs, but can cross the tracks directly via a ramp at the end of the platform. The station was originally called Govetts Leap in 1869, but changed to Blackheath two years later. The station master's building was constructed in 1883 and it was the only stop between Wentworth Falls and Mount Victoria for about five years.

Travel up Hat Hill Road along a ridge to Perrys Lookdown 8 km from the station. On the way is Hat Hill where panoramic views of all the mountains can be seen. From here, the city of Sydney is perfectly visible. Horse-drawn coaches used to come out here in the 1890s to bring tourists to Anvil Rock. Check out Anvil Rock first, taking the left option at the fork near the end of the Hat Hill Road. There is a water tank here for anyone who needs to fill up their water bottle. To the right is Perrys Lookdown where car camping facilities are provided. This is a staging post for walks down into the gorge. The views of the gigantic Mount Banks massif are particularly dramatic. The cliffs are the highest in New South Wales. A tour to the summit of this prominent landform is featured in Ride 45. For the ultra-fit, a short walk down into Blue Gum Forest is very rewarding. Although it's only about 30 minutes to get down, allow at least two exhausting hours on the return as 600 m of altitude have to be regained. At the bottom is an information plaque featuring the Myles Dunphy led Mountain Trails Club's successful bid in saving the forest from ringbarking in 1932.

Return to Blackheath and turn left into Wentworth Street thereby avoiding the traffic of the Great Western Highway. Cycle down past a restaurant on the right and turn left at the shops and post office on to Govetts Leap Road. This leads all the way to the NPWS rangers headquarters and visitors centre. Displays give information concerning wildlife and the geography of the mountains. Leaflets can be obtained here on walking tracks throughout the Grose River area, and maps can be purchased. Further down is Blackheath's pride and joy and the principal source of its tourist trade: Govetts Leap. From here, a waterfall forms a foreground to the sheer grandeur of the very rugged Grose Gorge and those seeing it for the first time will always remember that experience. This is one of the few lookouts that you can actually ride your bike up to the very edge of. The place was named after William Romaine Govett (1807–1848) who first discovered the waterfall when he was commissioned to survey the Blue Mountains in June 1831. Contrary to popular belief, the legend of the bushranger named Govett who jumped with his horse from the edge is almost certainly fiction.

Simply head back to Blackheath along Govetts Leap Road to complete an eventful day's cycling.

RIDE 41:   SHIPLEY PLATEAU

FROM: Blackheath Station
TO: Mount Blackheath Lookout (return)
VIA: Shipley Road
LENGTH: 24 km
TIME: 1 easy day
RIDE/TRACK GRADE: 3/2
WALKING: To Panorama Point
HEIGHT VARIATION: 70 m
TRANSPORT: Rail (Blue Mountains line)

FACILITIES: Sheltered picnic table at lookouts, shops and pool at Blackheath
MAPS: CMA (LIC) Katoomba and Hampton 1:25 000 topographicals

The western side of Blackheath also has much to offer cyclists. The Shipley Plateau is a cliff lined peninsula jutting out from the main plateau at Blackheath directly above the Kanimbla and Megalong Valleys. Where much of the tourist traffic is centred around Glenbrook and Katoomba, this section of the Blue Mountains remains relatively peaceful. Two prominent lookouts feature here: Panorama Point and Mount Blackheath.

From Blackheath station, head south along the line to the railway crossing and take the very first road on the left after crossing the tracks. This road briefly runs parallel to and below the railway line before the Shipley Plateau turn-off on the right. Follow this road all the way to the end avoiding the hair pin turn-off down to the Megalong Valley. You can visit any of the two lookouts first, and both are well signposted.

Hargreaves Lookout is about 3 km from the Shipley Road and some small steps are the only obstacle to prevent one from cycling all the way to the very lookout. In any case, they are nothing a mountain bike can't handle. From here a short walking track leads to Panorama Point via a very narrow ridge. The bikes will have to be left at the top near the shelter. The walk descends at first over some rocks and then levels out with very steep slopes on either side. A fenced rock ledge at the end marks the lookout. Every time I've been here, I have found it extremely windy so a jumper or parka might come in handy. There are views from here to the Radiata Plateau near Katoomba. On it sits the Explorers Tree where the etched initials of William Lawson provide the only remaining evidence of the original crossing.

The Shipley Road is the only way back to Blackheath. The afternoon can either be spent cycling some of the roads outlined in the previous ride suggestion, or the pool can be visited in the beautiful Memorial Park.

RIDE 42: MEGALONG VALLEY

FROM: Blackheath Station
TO: Katoomba Station
VIA: Old Ford Reserve
LENGTH: 31 km
TIME: 1 full day
RIDE/TRACK GRADE: 6/6 (one very steep long uphill to Katoomba)
WALKING: None
HEIGHT VARIATION: 530 m
TRANSPORT: Rail (Blue Mountains Line)
FACILITIES: None
MAPS: CMA (LIC) Katoomba and Hampton 1:25 000 topographicals

Megalong Valley is a popular weekend retreat for motorists and horseriders. Despite being largely cultivated rural/grazing land, it is surrounded by the Blue Mountains National Park. The name originates from the Aboriginal language and translates as 'valley under the rock'. From most points in the Megalong Valley, the cliffs of the Katoomba–Blackheath plateau are visible. Only two roads allow entry through these cliffs and this ride makes use of both of them. The object is to enjoy a terrific sealed road downhill losing around 400 m altitude and then spend the middle hours of the day swimming in the Megalong Creek at the Old Ford Reserve. The Megalong Valley can then be exited via the Six Foot Track through picturesque Nellies Glen. This ride is for experienced and fit cyclists only and the topographical map coverage is highly recommended. Some cyclists might prefer to do this ride in reverse, cycling down the rough track from Katoomba and using the sealed road to Blackheath as the exit. There is no real net height gain or loss from doing this as both Katoomba and Blackheath are on similar altitudes. Another option is to camp at the popular Old Ford Reserve, splitting the ride into two days.

From Blackheath station, head south along the line to the railway crossing and take the very first on the left after crossing. This road briefly runs parallel to and below the railway line before the Megalong Valley/Shipley Plateau turn-off on the right. This is Shipley Road and further on, a signpost on the left shows distances to the Megalong Valley. The turn-off is easy to miss as it cuts back at an angle. Still a sealed road, it descends down a fantastic mountain pass, one of the best downhills in the Blue Mountains. Along the way are views to the ever declining cliffs above where some interesting rock formations are. Several short walking tracks are passed on the left hand side, and the rock on the right is permanently dripping with moisture. Lyrebirds and whip birds can be heard through the grumble of cars carrying picnickers to the Megalong Valley.

At the bottom the road levels out and it is easy pedalling through this very popular valley. On the right are the cliffs of the Shipley Plateau while the main plateau forms the eastern boundary of the valley. Many homesteads and cattle ranches are located in the valley. There are some very gentle uphills and downhills to the Megalong Creek where you intersect the Six Foot Track. Hopefully the day is warm and you can enjoy a swim before leaving.

The Six Foot Track continues up to Nellies Glen along Megalong Creek and comes out at Explorers Tree. The station can then be found along the Great Western Highway to the right about 12 km from the Old Ford Reserve. The bike will definitely have to be pushed for most of the uphill section due to the bad condition of the track and steep gradient.

If camping at Old Ford Reserve, the best places are on the north-eastern side of the ford. However, these can be crowded on weekends. More secluded places exit on the north-western side, where good swimming holes exist in the Megalong Creek. Firewood is a problem and it's best to carry gas or metho fuel stoves.

RIDE 43:   SCOTTS MAIN RANGE

FROM: Blackheath Station
TO: Mittagong Station
VIA: Coxs River, Mount Cookem, Yerrandrie, Wollondilly River
LENGTH:
    Day 1: Blackheath Station to Cox River 37 km

Day 2: Coxs River to New Yards Huts 25 km
Day 3: New Yards Huts to Yerrandrie 33 km
Day 4: Yerrandrie to Fowlers Flat 36 km
Day 5: Fowlers Flat to Mittagong 58 km (can be split into two)
Total distance is 189 km
TIME: 5–7 days
RIDE/TRACK GRADE: 8/8
WALKING: Up Mount Cookem (allow six hours)
HEIGHT VARIATION: 880 m
TRANSPORT: Rail (Blue Mountains and Goulburn Lines)
FACILITIES: None
MAPS: CMA Katoomba, Hampton, Jenolan, Jamison, Bimlow, Kanangra, Yerrandrie, Nattai, Barrallier, Bindook, Hilltop and Mittagong 1:25 000 topographicals

This is the ultimate bike ride. Included in this package are steep mountain passes, wild rivers, dramatic cliffs, a ghost mining town, wilderness country and an infinite variety of vegetation, scenery and wildlife. However it also rates as the most difficult tour in this guide. Then again, quite often the worst rides are remembered with the most pride. A few warnings must augment this introduction:

1. This ride is graded maximum difficultly. Only very fit and experienced cyclists should consider undertaking it.
2. Due to the rugged terrain and the distances between campsites, it is strongly recommended to leave each day before 8 o'clock, even earlier if not in summer.
3. This ride is impossible to do if has just been raining. The Coxs River can swell up in a few hours making fording impossible.
4. The climb up Mount Cookem is extremely steep and very strenuous with fully laden packs. If possible, use detachable panniers. Practise beforehand carrying your bike on your back. Many cyclists prefer to do this tour in reverse, as the Mount Cookem–Coxs River section becomes infinitely easier. However if it did rain during the trip, then crossing would be impossible and one would have to backtrack all the way to Mittagong.
5. Scotts Main Range has little water, so provision must be made to carry large amounts of water (5 litres+). Side trips

210

to cycle down to the Kowmung River can be taken but this involves an extra day.

6. Water Board catchment area is crossed when exiting the national park from Yerrandrie. No permits are required to cross Murphys Flat but it might be advisable to quickly phone the Water Board Rangers headquarters at Guildford on 681 0313 or Warragamba Dam on (047) 74 1001 before setting out.

7. Be prepared to spend an extra one or two days if storms hit and the Wollondilly River becomes uncrossable.

8. If planning variations of this trip, for example exiting via the Oberon to Colong Stock route, remember that no more than 50 km a day can be ridden in such rugged country.

9. Bush camping experience and complete self-sufficiency is essential.

10. All 12 topographical maps listed above are essential for this ride. Laid out on the floor, the maps form a carpet over 4 m long and 2 m wide, and cost about $80.

Alight at Blackheath Station and head down along the tracks to the railway crossing. Cross the tracks, take the very first on the left, and then the first on the right. This is Shipley Road and further on, a signpost on the left shows distances to the Megalong Valley. The turn-off is easy to miss as it cuts back at an angle. Still a sealed road, it descends down a fantastic mountain pass where about 400 m of altitude are lost. Along the way are views to the ever declining cliffs above and some interesting rock formations are. Several short walking tracks are passed on the left hand side, and the rock wall on the right is permanently dripping with moisture. Lyrebirds and whip birds can be heard through the grumble of cars carrying picnickers to the Megalong Valley.

At the bottom the road levels out and it is easy pedalling through this very popular valley. On the right are the cliffs of the Shipley Plateau while the main plateau forms the eastern boundary of the valley. A lot of homesteads and cattle ranches are located in the valley and camping is restricted to Old Ford Reserve where the Six Foot Track is passed. There are some gentle downhills to the Megalong Creek. From here however is a seemingly endless uphill that is easily rideable under normal conditions but because of its length and a fully laden bike and backpack, quickly wears out the unfit cyclist.

At the top of the hill, after several false crests, is an intersection with a private road on the right and a locked Water Board road on the left. Keep straight ahead and roll down the second of the three great descents on this day. Open pastoral land is replaced by densely forested timberland the road soon joins a stream and follows it down to Packsaddlers. It is marked on the map as Green Gully. This is a horse stud which has gone commercial and it hires out horses to people conducting expeditions in area. There is a small shop here which sells drinks and sweets. They also have a wide selection of lollies.

Some very old farm machinery lines the road as you continue south. Over the crest is a long cleared gully. The road cuts through the left side and heads up to a junction. Turn left into another small valley that supports cows. Things can get confusing here: a new road which has been left off the map has been constructed here and it contours around the side of this valley, while the original road which is marked on the map is almost completely overgrown. However if you follow the fence service trail up on the right, the trail soon gets better on top once you enter natural woodland. The bikes will most likely have to carried due to the condition of the tracks and the enormous erosion gullies here. Once on top it is easy cycling along open woodland to join up with the Electricity Commission service trail and Water Board road. Turn right at the base of Carlon Head and pass underneath the powerlines. This is the border of the Blue Mountains National Park which you will exit and enter repeatedly for the next three days.

The trail leads all the way to Medlow Gap. Along the way are good views of the southern end of the massive Narrow Neck peninsula and the prominent Wild Dog Mountains. You pass through a small valley where Breakfast Creek is forded. Just before the crossing on the left is a fantastic grassy campsite where lunch can be taken. Breakfast Creek has formed a small pool just upstream from the ford and a swim could be appropriate on a hot day. Head up the other side to Medlow Gap and turn right. This is the start of the corridor which the Water Board has opened up in recent times to walkers. Cyclists are also allowed to pass. There is a locked gate here and Water Board Rangers patrol these roads, looking mainly for people such as trail-bike riders and hunters. At this point, the Water

Board has asked me to add warnings saying that you can't venture off the road and you must not bring any kind of firearm into the catchment area.

The base of Mount Mouin is passed after a gradual climb. The road then stays level before descending slightly. At the fork, there is no need to brake and check the maps, just head left down the best downhill of the day, and indeed the whole ride. The road literally plummets down the side of White Dog Ridge with one tiny 3 metre uphill interrupting a 600 m drop. A hut is passed towards the end and should be ignored. Keep right and down a final very steep descent where the road dies out by the bank of the Coxs River. The bank is covered with large cobblestones. It is recommended that you camp on the other side of the river for an early start is needed on the second day for the Mount Cookem ascent. The bikes will need to be walked, pushed, and carried for two kilometres to the base of the Mount Cookem spur. Unfortunately this is the only access point between the northern and southern Blue Mountains. This distance is small but the rough nature of the river banks will make progress slow and strenuous. You may need to cross many times depending on the nature of the river. There are a few sections where rocks have to negotiated. By the way, notice the type of rock predominant here; it of Devonian origin and includes much quartz, the oldest stone in the Blue Mountains and a common source of gold veins.

On the southern side you will see the fast flowing Kowmung River joining the Coxs River, resulting in the latter swelling considerably. Unless there has been a protracted period without rain, fording the Kowmung River could prove dangerous due to its fast flow. The alternative is to ford the Coxs River before its confluence with the Kowmung, and then ford it again to access the southern bank well after the confluence. At normal depth, the Coxs is quite flat but the bikes may need to be lifted if they have panniers with luggage that can't get wet.

Camp on this side as close to the base of Mount Cookem as possible. The rest of the evening (if there's anything left of it) can be spent panning for gold or fishing. Make sure however that you've located the start of the Mount Cookem trail. It begins on the most northern part of the ridge and is marked by the usual Water Board sign and some amateur spray painting reading 'Trail' just below. In front of the tree is a large rock inscribed with a white arrow. However do not rely on these markers as they existed in the early 1990s, and due to fading or erasure, may not be there any more. The centre of the spur where the river curves to the south-east is the most reliable navigational aid.

There has been much talk over the purity of the Coxs River with cases of dysentery and other milder forms of sickness resulting from drinking the water. The reason is apparently due to the farms around the Lithgow area dumping fertilisers and farm waste products in the river. It might be wise to take chlorine tablets or to boil the water. Otherwise water can be taken from Breakfast Creek which harmlessly runs off Narrow Neck. The Kowmung River to the west is also pure.

Next day, rise early, have a big breakfast, and begin the mighty ascent. Although not technically difficult it is very strenuous with bikes and could take anything up to half a day depending on fitness and the weight of the bike. The top is especially steep but this is the price the cyclist has to pay for all the fine downhills the day before.

Once this is accomplished the worst part of the trip is over and your mountain bike will have been truly christened. It's nothing but fire trails and roads from here to Mittagong. A large rock cairn marks the top and you might like to add to it if you have any energy left. In any case, have lunch up here before descending along the Cookem Fire Trail to New Yards (the huts are run by the Catholic Bushwalkers Club). Water is obtainable here but chlorine tablets are recommended.

On day 3, cycling becomes easier as you are now on the Old Cedar Road which used to join up with the road from MacMahons Lookout via Butchers Creek before the Burrago-rang Valley was flooded. Wildlife is quite profuse along this section of road and you will almost definitely see kangaroos, emus, and wild cattle. To the right is the very beautiful Kowmung River valley and left are the cliffs of the narrow Broken Rock peninsula. For those willing to spend an extra day out here, a very rough and tremendously steep fire trail leads down to the pristine Kowmung River where unlimited campsites can be found.

The road undulates in certain places but generally allows good fast cycling. Because of its central position and high altitude, there are views almost all the way along Scotts Main Range. Byrnes Gap is especially wild where numerous cliff-lined plateaus break up the horizon. There is a good descent here to the Tonalli River where a brief steep climb takes you into Yerrandrie. The bikes may have to be pushed here. On the northern side of the landing strip is a large camping ground managed by the Water Board. The silver mining town, which once supported several thousand people, was closed shortly after the Wall Street crash in 1929 when metal prices fell, making operations unviable. Luxury accommodation (compared to camping) is available at a guest lodge. There are six rooms here of a twin share basis. You have to bring your own linen and food, but rates are reasonable. For more information and bookings, ring the lodge itself on (047) 59 6165. Some informal tours are available at a low price—inquire at the Post Office. All the buildings in the ghost town are classified by the Heritage Commission as National Trust. A cemetery near here has graves dating from 1908–1919.

Spend some time exploring the ruins before camping the night. Some extra days can be spent here by cyclists who don't consider time as a constraint. Walks to Yerrandrie Peak and the massive Mount Colong complex are popular but difficult. Rideable 4WD tracks lead to the base of both of these peaks. Inquiries should be made at the Yerrandrie Lodge. A short popular side trip is to Silver Peak Mine located to the west.

The next day, cycle east out of Yerrandrie (the national park is left behind for the last time) and down a long hill to first cross the Jooriland River and then the very wide Wollondilly River at Murphys Flat. Sheepwalk Drive leads to another access corridor for walkers and cyclists. On the other side is a short uphill and a locked gate. Continue along the well graded road until you come to a fork. To the left a road by the lake comes out near Thirlmere Lakes National Park. The closest railway station at this point is Picton but unfortunately the flat thoroughfare is strictly closed to cyclists and even walkers. Only people lucky enough to obtain a permit can proceed to Picton.

Head left to descend into the Wollondilly Valley once again where another locked gate must be negotiated. One would think that most of the rangers' time is spent searching for keys when they patrol these areas. This is Douglas Flat and it proceeds through heavily undulating country at the base of Douglas Scarp until a turn-off leads down to Fowlers Flat. Camp by the Wollondilly River.

On the last day, head back to the main road and continue through private property to the Wombeyan Caves Road via The Oranges. A final steep climb must be endured. This uphill is especially rocky preventing cycling. Once on the road head west through the tunnel along the road to Burragorang Lookout where lunch can be eaten while you survey the country you've just travelled. Mittagong lies two to three hours away where you'll be able to collapse in the train on the way home!

RIDE 44: VICTORIA FALLS

FROM: Mount Victoria Station
TO: Victoria Falls Lookout (return)
VIA: Victoria Falls Road
LENGTH: 15 km
TIME: 1 easy day
RIDE/TRACK GRADE: 2/3
WALKING: Medium–hard graded walk to the bottom of the falls
HEIGHT VARIATION: 80 m cycling, 400 m walking
TRANSPORT: Rail (Blue Mountains Line)
FACILITIES: Shops at Mount Victoria
SPECIAL EQUIPMENT: Bike lock, swimming gear
MAPS: CMA (LIC) Mount Wilson 1:25 000 topographical

The object of this short exercise is quite simple. You catch a train up the mountains, cycle along a flat ridge to a good lookout, then walk down and spend the day lazing by a beautiful stream next to some impressive waterfalls with a wide pool surrounded by rocks and ferns at its base. The disadvantage is that Mount Victoria is a long way from Sydney so an early start must be taken. Take a water bottle per person for the strenuous climb back up to the bikes.

Mount Victoria was originally named 'One Tree Hill' until 1876 when it was used as a horse resting place and a military outpost. Also located here was one of the first schools in the mountains.

From the railway station, cycle down the highway and cross the railway tracks after passing an old restored toll house. At this very point, a minute gully on the left hand side marks the absolute beginning of the Grose River. It is difficult to imagine how such a small trickle eventually cuts out a massive gorge 20 km long, 2 km wide and 650 m deep.

Take the first turn on the left (signposted to Victoria Falls) and follow a well graded dirt road over a couple of crests and then downhill to the end. From the lookout you can see north along the plateau where features were all named after Nordic mythology: Asgard Head, Odin Head, Thor Head, and Valhalla Head. The cliff-lined Grose River gorge is particularly impressive here.

The bikes should be left here, preferably locked or well hidden in the undergrowth. It is then a steep walk down through a cliff pass to the waterfall. The water is always cold but the middle of the day will see the sun shining down the north-south aligned gorge enabling you to warm up quickly.

If any time is left at the end of the day once you return to Mount Victoria, you can watch the sunset from Mount Piddington. A road leads directly up to the summit trig point/ lookout and is signposted just over 1 km south of the Mount Victoria. At 1094 m, it is one of the highest mountains on the main plateau and a popular venue for abseiling.

RIDE 45: MOUNT BANKS

FROM: Bell Station
TO: Mount Banks (return)
VIA: Bells Line of Road
LENGTH: 42 km (14 km if driving to the Mount Banks carpark)
TIME: 1 day
RIDE/TRACK GRADE: 4/6
WALKING: None
HEIGHT VARIATION: 200 m
TRANSPORT: Rail (Blue Mountains Line)
FACILITIES: Picnic area with toilets
SPECIAL EQUIPMENT: Parka or warm jumper as the lookout can be very windy
MAPS: CMA (LIC) Mount Wilson 1:25 000 topographical

Mount Banks (formerly known as Mount King George) is cut by 500 m cliffs, well over one and half times the height of Centrepoint Tower. A sign at the base reads: '*MOUNT KING GEORGE. GEORGE CALEY (1770–1829) WAS A BOTANIST EXPLORER WITH COMPANIONS TRAVELLED VIA KURRAJONG AND ASCENDED THE MOUNT ON 15TH NOVEMBER, 1804. HE NAMED IT MOUNT BANKS AFTER SIR JOSEPH BANKS. THERE ENDED HIS HEROIC ATTEMPTS TO CROSS THE BLUE MOUNTAINS*'.

The story is tragic. Caley's party walked from Mount Tomah and camped at the base of Mount Banks. The next morning, he climbed the summit of the mountain and saw for the first time the impenetrable gorge of the Grose Valley. Finding no way around it, he had to turn back to Parramatta. You can relive this ascent by means of a fire trail that climbs right up to the summit. However the best part of this ride is the view obtainable from the top of Banks Wall. Together with Govetts Leap and Kanangra Walls, this would have to rank as the best view in the Blue Mountains. Furthermore it is directly accessible from the seat of a mountain bike, needing no walking!

From Bell Station head back east along the Bells Line of Road ignoring the Mount Wilson turn-off on the left. In January 1994, a lot of this area was burnt out by savage bushfires and enthusiastic backburning. There are occasional glimpses of the cliffs that line Grose River gorge along this section that sometimes distract drivers from the road. The turn-off to Mount Banks is signposted on the right hand side as the road begins to swing north shortly after the Pierces Pass turn-off. The road winds around through some small hills and Mount Banks looms up ahead dominating the horizon. A very well developed and pleasant camping ground is on the left hand side and includes a water tank, fire places, picnic tables, and toilets. On the right is a large rock with the commemorative inscription quoted above. In between the plaque and the cleared picnic ground, a locked gate bars motorised transport.

The trail undulates around the base of the mountain, predominantly climbing. It is in fairly poor condition, the surface being dominated by many large sharp rocks in it. Shock absorbers are definitely an advantage here. The vegetation is often low, dry, and stunted allowing expansive views to the east. A turn-off leads steeply up to the King George Trig point well over a kilometre above sea level and should be attempted later. For now keep left, following the trail as it skirts around the southern side of the mountain, undulating as it swings in and out of side gullies. One in particular is quite overgrown and moist, but the track condition soon improves. Less than 30 minutes after the summit turn-off, the terrain suddenly opens up and you arrive at the most amazing view one can witness from a mountain bike.

Directly opposite is Perrys Lookdown, accessible from Blackheath. On either side the Grose Gorge recedes majestically into the distance with 300 m cliffs on either side creating an impenetrable barrier. Directly below is the beautiful blue gum forest, a very popular walkers' destination.

Backtrack to the summit track. It is suggested you climb to the top via the overgrown fire trail for more views over the Grose River gorge. One either can take the bikes to push up enjoying a steep rough downhill or simply leave the bikes at the bottom, to be picked up on the return. The approach trail is very narrow and eroded in places, the last section being quite overgrown. On top of the basalt-capped mountain lie a few picnic tables and some pleasant grassy woodland. From the trig point on the second of the two humps, a very small foot pad leads down a steep rocky slope to a narrow ridge. Notice the rocks here are not sandstone but of volcanic origin.

The vegetation changes once more, reverting back to traditional dry Aussie bush, as you walk along the centre of the spur to some prominent rock outcrops and unusual weathered formations. The rocks too have reverted back to sandstone as you are now just below the 50 m erosion-resistant basalt cap. Because of its height, Mount Banks is one of the first peaks in the mountains to receive sunlight in the day. Watching the sun hit the cliffs over a mist covered Grose River will inspire new life into the would-be suicidist.

Return to Bell Station via the same route.

OTHER RIDES IN THE UPPER BLUE MOUNTAINS

The main areas offering mountain bike riders further opportunity for off-road touring are:
• Hartley valley (between Mount Victoria and Lithgow)

219

Attractions: places of historical interest, Mount York, down-hills to Lithgow
- Mount Wilson detailed in the first edition of *Cycling the Bush: 100 Rides in NSW* and in Ride 52 of this guide.
  Attractions: lookouts over wilderness, old English gardens, walks to wild rivers
- Burramoko Ridge (accessible from Blackheath)
  Attractions: Baltzar Lookout, Hanging Rock

4. KANANGRA BOYD NATIONAL PARK

Size: 68 276 hectares
Enactment: Kanangra Tourist Resort 1891
            Kanangra Walls National Park 1969
            Significant additions 1977
Visitors: Unknown
Aboriginal Sites: No detailed survey conducted. The Gandangara tribes left some evidence of occupation: rock art and axe grinding grooves
Plants: Snow gums and mountain gums are among the hundreds of species of diverse vegetation that the inhabits the slopes of the Boyd Plateau. In the valleys, rainforest provides a pleasant alternative to the dry heath and swamp on the tops
Animals: Wombats, wallabies, pademelon, sugar gliders, water rats, koalas, among others plus 100 observed species of birds
Camping: Anywhere further than 800 m from the main road. A formal site exists 8 km from the lookout on the Boyd River.
District Office: Govetts Leap Road, Blackheath
                   (047) 87 8877
                   Oberon NPWS office (063) 36 1972
Adjoining Parks: Blue Mountains National Park, Jenolan State Forest, and Lake Burragorang catchment area.

Remarkably few people have heard of Kanangra Walls, let alone been there. It is just twenty minutes by car from Jenolan

Caves and the views rate with Mount Owen and Govetts Leap as the best in the state. The best way to approach the area is to ride the Six Foot Track to the Jenolan Caves and then regain the plateau top to the unsealed road that connects Oberon to Kanangra Walls. From here it is only an hour by bike to the camping ground, and a further 8 km to the actual look-out.

Kanangra derived its name from the Aboriginal words for 'beautiful view'. On the right of the lookout are the actual walls: sheer golden banded cliffs. On the left are the heavily folded Thurat Spires made from extremely tilted white Devonian sandstone some 350 million years ago. In fact the whole place is a geologist's paradise: the sheer variety of formations created by complex uplifting and erosion resulted in hundreds of unusual landforms comprising shale, volcanic basalt, quartzite and other metamorphic rocks, coal seams, and granite.

Because of the rugged wilderness nature of the area, cycling is limited only to the main plateau as no fire-trails exist in the narrow valleys. Self-sufficiency is essential due to the isolation of the national park and difficulty of access. Rides from Blackheath or Katoomba will require overnight camping due to the sheer distance rather than difficulty. Alternatively, private transport can be taken to the car-park at Kanangra Walls and the whole plateau explored by a series of cycling and walking combinations.

RIDE 46:   KANANGRA WALLS

FROM: Boyd River Crossing Camping Area
TO: Kanangra Walls (return)
VIA: Thurat Tops
LENGTH: 24 km
TIME: 1 day
RIDE/TRACK GRADE: 4/6
WALKING: Exploring Kanangra Walls lookout area
HEIGHT VARIATION: 220 m
TRANSPORT: Private transport to Boyd River Crossing via Jenolan Caves

Jenolan
Caves

COXS
RIVER

46

Tuglow
Caves

47

Boyd
River
Camp

46

47

KANANGRA
WALLS

KOWMUNG   RIVER

Colong Stock Route

N

KANANGRA
WALLS

Batsh
Camp

5

To   Yerranderie

FACILITIES: Good camping facilities at Boyd Crossing (no kiosks)
MAPS: CMA (LIC) Kanangra 1:25 000 topographical

Although there seems little point in driving to a camping area just 8 km before a major lookout and cycling the remainder of the distance, this ride allows a circuit to be completed keeping to locked four wheel drive tracks on the Kanangra Plateau. The highlight is of course the spectacular lookout over Kanangra Walls and Mount Cloudmaker, but good high altitude off-road cycling through snow gums on Thurat Tops makes an interesting contrast to the traditional dry Aussie bush.

Access by private vehicle is best through either Oberon or Jenolan Caves from Mount Victoria. The camping ground is on the main 2WD road at the river and is usually populated on summer weekends. In the morning, cycle along final section to the lookout. The cyclist can keep going past the car-park, cycling directly to the lookout. Keep left at the first fork and the rock platform is on the right, marked by a small warning sign. At sunset, when the west-facing cliffs glow bright golden, this is the place to be. Admire one of nature's finest spectacles, perhaps having a late breakfast here. The feature that impresses me the most is not so much the Walls themselves, but the way they contrast with the extreme folding of the Thurat ridgelines on the left. The gigantic mountain at the far end of the gorge is Mount Cloudmaker. It is really a whole series of mountains as each knoll and peak struggle to get on top of one another. The walk out to the summit where a visitors book can be signed takes about three-quarters of a day and camping is possible just on the other side at Dexs Creek.

The day can be spent exploring the area with walks to the left down to a fresh mountain pool at the base of Kalang Falls, or to the right where the plateau tops can be accessed directly. There are many things to do using Kanangra Walls as a staging area: climbing the Cloudmaker massif (overnight), checking out an exposed coal seam at Murrarang Head, walking to Crafts Wall, abseiling down jagged cliffs, liloing the pristine Kowmung River, or camping in a large cave which drips fresh water into your billy overnight (Blacks Pass). Sounds like a travel brochure, doesn't it? The difference is this is all true and absolutely free.

The next feature to see is Kanangra Brook and from here on the bikes must be hidden in the surrounding scrub. Keep heading left down the trail. There are some steps as a slippery embankment is descended. There is a lot of extremely loose rock here. Looking up you'll see the top of a waterfall. The trail then levels out before descending further into a sort of glen. A series of small pools have formed here. There are also some views out into the gorge. It is not very often you find that you can have a swim high up over such a spectacle as Kanangra Walls. One of the best experiences in my life was swimming here very early in the morning with the sun rising over the massive cliffs in the background.

A large cave can be inspected by heading back up the slope, past the bikes and turning left on the walking track that winds down into a gap between the two plateaus. Some large twisted eucalypts obscure more views of the gorge. At the lowest point, just before it climbs up again on to Seymour Top, a track heads through the trees to the right. The cave is about 50 m further on the left hand side. Behind one of the walls is an open concrete cylinder which captures and stores continually dripping water that seeps through the rock.

One can then continue up to Seymour Top and view the waterfall on the other side of the gorge in its entirety. The walking track passes through thick low heath and small water-courses have formed ruts in the soil. Some rocks on top allow access to the very edge of the cliffs where the unusual white strata of Thurat Walls can be studied. When you've finished exploring the tops, head down to the bikes again and cycle back towards the Boyd River Camping Ground. About 2 km along, turn right on to an unmarked fire trail. The terrain undulates gently in contrast to the rugged terrain just witnessed. Cross over Kanangra Brook and then ascend Kittani Ridge. It is then a gentle downhill over pretty rough surfaces to Kanangra Creek. This is a pleasant place for lunch. You then have 200 m to climb to access Thurat Tops. The vegetation opens up here. Snow falls often in winter around these parts. Kanangra plateau was formerly used for grazing and the Forestry Commission planned to establish pine plantations here before concerted conservation campaigns prevented this. Some evidence of clearfelling still exists in the woodlands.

Ignore the Baldy Bill Fire Trail turn-off to the right. It is easy cycling west back to Kanangra Road where you should turn

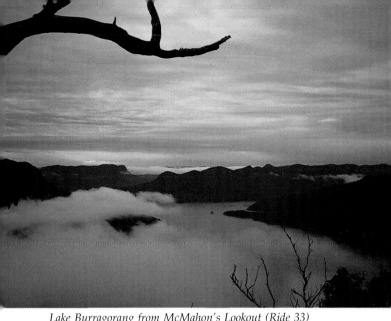

Lake Burragorang from McMahon's Lookout (Ride 33)

The view over the Grose Gorge from Mount Banks (Ride 45)

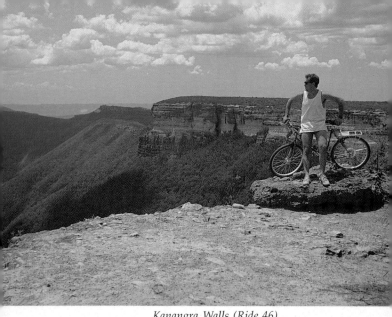

Kanangra Walls (Ride 46)

Inspecting old mine shafts at Yerrandrie (Rides 43 & 48)

left (south) to reach the Boyd River Crossing, completing an eventful day's cycling and walking.

RIDE 47:   TUGLOW CAVES

FROM: Boyd River Crossing Camping Ground
TO: Dingo Dell
VIA: Kowmung River, Tuglow Caves
LENGTH:
   Day 1: Boyd River to Dingo Dell Camping Ground 22 km
   Day 2: Dingo Dell Camping Ground to Boyd River via Morong Creek 29 km
   Total distance is 51 km
RIDE/TRACK GRADE: 6/6 (long steep uphill from the Kowmung River valley)
WALKING: Exploring caves area
HEIGHT VARIATION: 420 m
TRANSPORT: Private transport to Boyd River Camping Area via Jenolan Caves
FACILITIES: General camping facilities. Car camping permitted
MAPS: CMA (LIC) Kanangra and Shooters Hill 1:25 000 topographicals

Despite its isolation, several one day rides can be undertaken in the Kanangra Boyd National Park where car camping is based at the Boyd River Camping Ground about 8 km from Kanangra Walls. The drive is about 3 to 4 hours from Sydney via Penrith, Mount Victoria, and Jenolan Caves. Caravans have to be taken via Oberon. There are only a handful of fire trails which allow cycling access to this very beautiful and unspoilt river, one of the most pristine in New South Wales.

If you leave Sydney very early, you can be at Kanangra Walls by late morning and spend the afternoon exploring the magnificent Echo Head area before driving back and setting up camp. The next day cycle north along Kanangra Road and left at the signposted Kowmung River Fire Trail. Follow the signposts for 14 km to Dingo Dell. The drop into the Kowmung River Valley is quite steep and slippery. Cyclists have a surprise here—the entire downhill is punctuated by huge drainage humps. One can use these to help slow down or accelerate over them for some aerobatic action. Either way, one arrives at the Kowmung within minutes and your rims should be quite warm.

A walk-in campsite exists just upstream at the crossing, and the cyclist has the option of camping here if the day is late or proceeding on to Dingo Dell to share a large camping area with 4WD vehicles. The Kowmung River is not quite mature at this stage, yet it will always provide a reliable source of fast flowing fresh water.

If proceeding, cross the Kowmung here ascending steeply up to a saddle between two knolls and then down to Horse Gully Creek to the Tuglow Cave turn-off. If the day is late, one can walk up the steep track to explore some of the cave entrances in the karst area. One major entrance is sealed by a locked grille, while another gives access only to experienced cavers with all the appropriate equipment and a permit. The main cave is 1420 m long and 66 m deep. A caving permit is required here, like all the undeveloped caves in the area. However it is interesting enough to note that these caves are only one system of dozens in the area. In addition there are caves near Mount Colong, Billys Creek, Hollanders River, and Church Creek besides the more well known Jenolan and Wombeyan Caves. Permits need to be applied for about 3 months in advance. Allow about 2 hours for the return walk back to the bikes. Walkers will notice an extensive area of private property with sheep on the western perimeter of the sinkhole area.

After another saddle, the Kowmung Fire Trail drops down into the Tuglow Hole Creek valley, also known as Dingo Dell. This is a huge clearing with an infinite amount of camping areas, many close to watercourses. Some swimming holes exist to the right after the ford. The best camping is to be found left. Keep an eye out for kangaroos.

The next day, backtrack up out of the Kowmung Valley. This unfortunately involves a long strenuous push uphill, paying the price for the terrific descent the previous day. Head right at Boyd Hill (1255 m) on to the Boyd River Fire Trail. There's another excellent descent to Morong Creek, a good spot for lunch. Another option is to take a detour to where Morong Creek plummets into the Kowmung Valley. Take the first on the right after fording the creek to access the area near the top of the 83 m falls. It is then easy flat cycling along reasonably good quality fire trails back to the Kanangra Road via Dingo Swamp and the Boyd Range Track. This is the start of the Uni Rover Trail that ends at Colong Caves. Some informal campsites exist along this section, something to keep in mind for future reference if the Boyd River Camping Area is crowded. Simply head north to the Boyd River to complete the round trip.

RIDE 48:   KOWMUNG RIVER

FROM: Yerrandrie
TO: Kowmung River (return)
VIA: Mount Armour Track
LENGTH: 32 km (28 km cycling, 4 km walking)
TIME: 2 days (Day 1 and 2: 16 km each)
RIDE/TRACK GRADE: 6–7/7
WALKING: Armours Ridge
HEIGHT VARIATION: 210 m cycling, 320 m walking
TRANSPORT: Private transport to Yerrandrie
FACILITIES: Accommodation at Yerrandrie Lodge. Otherwise car camping at Water Board camping ground near landing strip.
MAPS: CMA (LIC) Yerrandrie and Bindook 1:25 000 topographicals

The Kowmung, being the only unspoilt major watercourse in the Blue Mountains, is the pride and joy of bushwalkers in the area and the main destination for hard-core campers relaxing on long weekends by this very special river. An interesting and unused approach involves a cycling-walking combination based at the ghost silver mining town of Yerrandrie. The only vehicular access here is via Oberon and Shooters Hill along a road called the Oberon to Colong Stock Route. From Sydney, it takes the best part of a day. Luxury accommodation (compared to camping) is available at a guest lodge. There are six rooms here of a twin share basis. You have to bring your own linen and food, but rates are reasonable. For more information and bookings, ring the lodge itself on (047) 59 6165. Tours are available at a low price—inquire at the Post Office. All the buildings in the ghost town are classified by the Heritage Commission as National Trust. A cemetery near here has graves dating from 1908–1919.

There are several approaches down to the Kowmung River. On the Yerrandrie map, the Inglis Selection Track is marked as providing access from Scotts Main Range to the river, but I found this impossible to follow for more than a few hundred metres due to the thick undergrowth. Because of the difficulty of the terrain and poor quality of the track, I had to turn back. A far easier descent to the Kowmung, and a much more enjoyable bike ride is via Mount Armour. A fire trail leads right along the top of the ridge before the bikes must be left about 45 minutes before the river is reached.

From Yerrandrie head up the old fire trail from behind the Guest House past more abandoned mine shafts. The trail winds around through fairly dry eucalypt trees on the slopes of Yerrandrie Plateau to the south. It then rises for about 200 m before entering Tonalli Gap and crossing through Colong Swamp. There are some nice camping sites here and it would be a good spot for a break. The views, however, are not that good because you are surrounded by low cliffs and forest. Head right through another gap and ignore a walking trail turn-off on the left to Colong Caves. The trail then descends down to the narrow Armours Ridge and should be followed to the end. There is no real defined walking trail down to the river but it is an open cleared slope which presents no difficulties at all. Camp anywhere you want along the river's banks. Black snakes are common around here but there is no need to panic as they are shy and will take off when they 'hear' a footstep through ground vibrations. The return route involves backtracking.

OTHER RIDES IN KANANGRA BOYD NATIONAL PARK

Many rides can be conducted from bases at either Yerrandrie or the Boyd River area at Kanangra Walls. Scotts Main Range can be explored from the south although this involves backtracking. A short round one day trip is from Yerrandrie to Colong Swamp, as described above and back again via the southern side of the Mootik Plateau. Nearby are the Colong Caves, a horizontal system containing one of Australia's longest caves: Lannigans Cave has been followed underground for more than 6000 m!

Also omitted in this guide is Wombeyan Caves. There are over 270 caves there including Junction Cave which is 760 m long. Most are developed and public access is permitted. There are numerous backroads around the Mount Armstrong region, and not all of them are private property. I've left this out purposely because it is too far from the nearest station, making it impractical to undertake excursions via public transport. Furthermore car camping and accommodation are only possible at the caves themselves which are situated deep down in a valley so that any exploration of the area involves a long push uphill. However there are rideable trails directly to the north of the caves, and the Wombeyan Caves Road itself can be followed east to the Wollondilly River, where large camping grounds exist. This is far to the south of the national park and therefore beyond the scope of this book. For anyone who is interested, get hold of the Richlands and Barrallier topographicals.

What I've also completely neglected are the plantations to the west of Kanangra Boyd National Park: Gurnang and Vulcan state forests. There are interlaced by literally hundreds of roads, most of which aren't even of the map resulting in some confusion. Depending on time available and temperament, this all can add to the fun of exploring the Great Dividing Range.

GREVILLEA

6
Wollemi National Park

Size: 486 536 hectares
Enactment: April 1979
Visitors: Mainly small walking groups
Aboriginal Sites: 35 recorded sites
Flora: Over 700 species in diverse communities such as rainforest, heath, swamp, and mallee, including 40 rare and endangered species
Fauna: Dingoes, eastern grey kangaroo, red-necked wallaby, numerous nocturnal animals, many endangered species, and increasing numbers of feral animals
Camping: Anywhere—no permits required. Office sites at Kandos Weir, Newnes and Bowen Creek.
District Office: Govetts Leap Road, Blackheath and Wilberforce
Adjoining Parks: Yengo National Park, Goulburn River National Park, Blue Mountains National Park and numerous state forests including Putty, Newnes, Coricudgy, Bylong, Comleroy

Although officially designated a wilderness area, there is still excellent cycling available to anyone wanting to experience one of the greatest national parks in Australia. In fact, Wollemi the largest forested area in the country and the closest wilderness area to Sydney! The most approachable part of the national park is north of Lithgow, about 3 hours from Sydney along the scenic Bells Line of Road. Places to see include the magical Glow Worm Tunnel, the abandoned mining towns of Glen Davis and Newnes, as well as one of the longest uninterrupted fire-trails in New South Wales.

The area was first explored by white man in 1817, 12 000 years after Aboriginals first occupied the region. However it was found to be as impenetrable as the Blue Mountains and consequently was left alone. The battle to save the area from hydro-electric schemes and mining was a fierce and surprisingly recent one. Now the national park, just over fifteen years old, will get even larger as more land leases expire along the Putty Road and to the east of Rylstone and Capertee.

Like the Blue Mountains, Wollemi National Park consists of a dissected plateau with the distinction of having large volcanic basalt caps on many of the peaks. Some of these peaks, most notably Mount Coricudgy (1257 m) and Mount Monundilia (1108 m), contain some pleasant rainforest, although walking is necessary to see these. The sandstone is primarily from the Hawkesbury and Narrabeen groups some 250 million years old and is being slowly eroded by the Wolgan, Capertee, and Wollemi Rivers which all eventually flow in to the mighty Colo. To the north, Wildin Brook and Greigs Creek flow into the Goulburn River.

The western border was quickly surveyed and settled by 1840 with farmers making full use of the rich alluvial soils along the Cudgegong and Capertee Valleys. But in the Wolgan and Bacrami Valleys, a new resource was discovered: oil shale. By the turn of the century, mine shafts were sunk, refineries built and railway tracks laid through the rocky mountains to Lithgow.

Today the shafts are closed and the railways dismantled. Even the townships which were built to accommodate the industry are derelict. What's left is being preserved by the national parks authorities and can be inspected by cyclists interested in our cultural past. Both Glen Davis and Newnes are used as staging areas for extended ventures into the park.

The national park is popular for horseriding as there is little conflict with other types of activity. Another popular activity is canoeing. Sometimes this is the *only* way to venture into some otherwise inaccessible areas. Canoeists use the park's water 'highways' flowing from west to east. All roads in the southern part of the park lead to the rugged Colo River gorge: some 69 km long and taking about a week to complete. This sport also comes with its dangers: rain upstream can turn the Colo River into a swirling mass of 150 Grade 6 rapids that would almost certainly result in death or at the very least, destruction of the canoe.

Cycling the park is already being commercialised by tour operators in Lithgow. The Glow Worm Tunnel is a frequently visited venue due to its close proximity to rail and highway in Lithgow and its relatively easy grade ride through the beautiful scenery of the Newnes State Forest.

As in the Blue Mountains chapter, the following rides are listed from east to west with more difficult overnight cycling/walking expeditions listed at the end.

WOLLEMI NATIONAL PARK

6

N

60

61

RYLSTONE

PUTTY

54

53

62

GLEN DAVIS
59

NEWNES
57   58 56
55

COLO HEIGHTS

51

52   50   49

LITHGOW

WINDSOR

1. EASTERN WOLLEMI NATIONAL PARK

RIDE 49: THE COLO RIVER

FROM: Colo
TO: Kurrajong (return)
VIA: Comleroy Road and Blaxland Ridge
LENGTH: 45 km
TIME: 1 day
RIDE/TRACK GRADE: 4/3
WALKING: None
HEIGHT VARIATION: 112 m
TRANSPORT: Private transport to Colo via the Putty Road
FACILITIES: Picnic area at Wheeny Creek
MAPS: CMA (LIC) Lower Portland, Mountain Lagoon and Kurrajong 1:25 000 topographicals

This is one of the rides officially endorsed and even encouraged by the NPWS. Start early and drive down to the tranquil Colo River from Windsor via the Putty Road. I've chosen this as the starting point as it allows a final downhill at the end of the day and one can swim in the middle of the day. However, depending on which direction you are coming from, it is perfectly possible to start this ride from any point on the round circuit as all of it is accessible by conventional transport.

At Colo, the Putty Road crosses the river on a long bridge. There is a car parking area on the right hand side just before the bridge. It is situated on a grassy bank of the river where it makes a sweeping curve. Canoeing around here is very popular, and a caravan park is situated on the other side.

Start cycling upstream along the river on its southern bank. Being used to the deep interiors of wild national parks, I normally find open agricultural land boring. However this stretch to Upper Colo is very pleasant. Along the way you can swim in the river any time you like. Even though the road is going upstream, the slope is extremely gradual making the gradient hardly noticeable. Both river banks are comprised of sand, some even being in dune formation. A poplar plantation on the right makes an interesting landmark.

Towards the end you pass a signposted turn-off to Colo Heights on the right. Keep on the southern bank and turn left up a steep hill and down the other side to Wheeny Creek. At the top is a lookout, but the best views are obtained cycling down the other side. A national park sign at the top announces you are entering Wollemi. One of the most amazing engineering feats in the Blue Mountains is electrification—specifically the overhead powerlines crossing the huge gorges and cliffs. The Wheeny Creek valley is a prime example. At the bottom is a pleasant picnic ground. A sandy trail on the southern side of the picnic area leads down to the creek.

Head up again to Blaxlands Ridge and take this back to the Putty Road where a steep, winding and narrow descent takes you back to the car at Colo. For anyone who is interested, a shorter but similar round trip can be made east of Colo, heading to the right and following the southern bank *down*-stream until it joins up with Blaxland Ridge. This is only 21 km long and all that's needed is the Lower Portland map. However the national park does not feature here, although some dramatic sandstone cliffs line the Colo River as the trail follows it down.

RIDE 50:   MOUNTAIN LAGOON

FROM: Kurrajong
TO: Bilpin (return)
VIA: Wheeny Creek
LENGTH: 55 km
TIME: 1 long day
RIDE/TRACK GRADE: 6/4
WALKING: None
HEIGHT VARIATION: 540 m
TRANSPORT: Private transport to Kurrajong or bike from Richmond Station
FACILITIES: Picnic ground at the Wheeny Creek Recreation Area
MAPS: CMA Kurrajong and Mountain Lagoon 1:25 000 topographicals

Few people realise that the massive Wollemi National Park that stretches almost to Muswellbrook starts as far south as Kurrajong Heights. This ride features the Wheeny Creek Picnic Ground and a very good cycling road along the Mountain Lagoon Fire Trail. Start by parking your car at the most convenient place nearest to the intersection between Bells Line of Road and Comleroy Road. Cycle north and the national park is entered at Mount Butler (175 m) although the official national park boundaries aren't yet marked on the topographical map.

Head down a great decline to Wheeny Creek where its banks have been developed into a very popular picnic ground. Unfortunately trail-bikers have discovered it and often use it to practise creating noise pollution. Head up again with excellent views of the gorge becoming apparent the higher you get. Turn a sharp left at the top of the ridge. The road here is quite rocky but is ideal for the new mountain biker and allows one to practise one's skills: honking, spinning, jumping rocks, and most important maintaining a fast even rhythm. It leads back to the Bells Line of Road via Mountain Lagoon. Simply follow the main road downhill back to the car.

RIDE 51:   TOOTIE RIDGE

FROM: Itchenstoke, Mount Tootie
TO: Tootie Ridge (lookout over lower Wollangambe River Creek)
VIA: Mount Tootie, Tootie Fire Trail
LENGTH: 33 km (split into 2 days)
TIME: 2–4 days
RIDE/TRACK GRADE: 6–7/7
WALKING: Optional 8 km bush-bashing to Colo River gorge (3rd and 4th days required)
HEIGHT VARIATION: 190 m
TRANSPORT: Private transport to Itchenstoke, Mount Tootie
ACCESS: A short section of private property must be crossed to access the beginning of the fire trail. By contacting the NPWS ranger's station at Blackheath on (047) 87 8878, they will be able to give the landowner's phone number.
FACILITIES: None (complete self-sufficiency required)

SPECIAL EQUIPMENT: Five litres of water per person each 2 days
MAPS: CMA (LIC) Mount Wilson, Wollangambe, Mountain Lagoon, & Colo Heights 1:25 000 topographicals (Mount Wilson and Wollangambe are not needed for cycling, only for vehicular access to starting point).

Tootie Ridge leads all the way to the Colo River gorge at its confluence with the Wollangambe River. The terrain in this area is very rugged, isolated, and wild and the Mountain Lagoon 1:25 000 topographical map is essential, as is complete self-sufficiency. The purpose of this tour is cycle the ridge as far the trail allows you and camp in a clearing at the end with views over this spectacular eroded sandstone terrain. The hard-core walker has the option of following a very minor foot pad along the centre of the remaining four kilometres of the ridge and either camping directly over the Colo River or walking down and camp by the water. Since there is no water available anywhere along the ridge, it is imperative that at least 5 litres is brought along for the cycling component and another 5 litres for the walking. Another word of warning: the Colo Heights 1:25 000 topographical displays the Tootie Ridge trail as extending all the way to the Colo River gorge. This is incorrect, the trail ends about 4 km before.

Private vehicle access to the starting point is via the Bells Line of Road through Richmond and Bilpin to the Mount Tootie Road. About 4 km along this road you come to a large stone sign on the left that says Itchenstoke. Drive as far as you can and park the car on the side where the private property starts. Assuming you've got permission, proceed to the right, skirting around the base of Mount Tootie (794 m). Despite much of it being cleared, the vegetation is quite rich here and even has palms prospering in the volcanic soil. The road continues to contour around to the north. Leave all gates as found and do not disturb the cattle. The road ascends the ridge again and heads down and across the saddle between Mount Tootie and Little Tootie to the north. After passing across some cattle grids and circumventing Little Tootie to the south, a final gate is passed and then you are in the Wollemi National Park. It is good cycling from here with the trail undulating only very gently through dry Aussie bush. Most of the turn-offs to the right and left are not of good quality and only require a quick confirmation on the map. About an hour after passing into the national park, a clearing marks the final turn-off. Ignore the left, which quickly becomes a dead end and head right. The trail deteriorates here and erosion gullies have destroyed one downhill necessitating actually *walking* the bike down. Very embarrassing. We also came across a tiger snake here sunbaking in the middle of the trail.

There are occasional views where the bush opens up, and it is generally easy going to the end. The trail suddenly comes to a halt at a flat clearing with good views to the north-west. Excellent acoustics resulting from echoing coo-ees are also a feature. Do not walk around barefoot—at the very end of the clearing is something worth seeing: a nest with some gigantic red ants. The clearing is firm-packed, ideal for several self-supporting tents. Some rock platforms a few dozen metres before the end on the left also provide some unobscured views over the dissected canyons of Bowens Creek, and Wollangambe River, and the Colo River gorge in the distance. At night, the lights from Sydney can be seen. The nearest people are almost 20 kilometres away!

The next day, one can opt to proceed along the ridge. We tried this but ran out of water about half way. What I can relate is that there is a very minor foot-pad that hard-core bushwalkers must have formed. If it has just rained, water may be available from gullies down to the east. Despite being only 4 kilometres from the end, the rugged terrain makes progress very slow and you should allow at least three hours with packs. Avoid the hottest part of the day. Although the NPWS rangers at Richmond tell me one can directly access the Colo River from here, it remains to be seen whether cliffs would bar your way. If they do, you still have the reward of camping over the gorge. Backtrack to the car via the same route.

RIDE 52: MOUNT WILSON
(VIA BOWENS CREEK)

FROM: Bilpin
TO: Mount Wilson
VIA: Bowens Creek
LENGTH: 44 km

TIME: 1 long day
RIDE/TRACK GRADE: 6/3–4
WALKING: None
HEIGHT VARIATION: 600 m
TRANSPORT: Private transport to Bilpin
FACILITIES: Picnic area opposite the Cathedral of Ferns
MAPS: CMA (LIC) Wollangambe and Mount Wilson
1:25 000 topographicals

The most direct access to Mount Wilson from Sydney is via the Bowen Creek Road but for motorists it is of too poor quality to drive on, especially after rain, meaning that they are forced to take the Bells Line of Road for another 24 km before they can turn off. Cyclists however can ride to Mount Wilson through two national parks: Wollemi and the Blue Mountains via a relatively unused road down a sandstone gorge cut through by Bowen Creek. Rather than proceeding down a ridge like most trails do in the area, it winds down giving a long enjoyable ride and also making cycling possible up the other side for the fit.

Drive to the turn-off just after Bilpin, officially called Warawaralong. Park the car here. One can either cycle to Mount Wilson and come back the same way, or return via Bells Line of Road making a round trip. Start early for the day's distance is quite long.

The dirt road is of good quality and along the way there are good views of the steep gorge. Indeed one wonders how the road can actually lead to the bottom and up the other side, yet still be so gentle. What is especially dramatic is that sheer cliffs line the water, but the road somehow manages to avoid these. There are a number of incredibly sharp corners where the cyclist almost has to stop before turning on the loose surface. Enter each curve from the outside to maximise the turning circle.

At the bottom is a small resting area with a sign warning that the following road is suitable for four wheel drives only. Basically it is still a 2WD road but a good clearance is needed. I've seen many a daring driver use a modern conventional car to climb up to Mount Wilson. A walking track leads from the western side of the bridge down to the water. There are some swimming spots at the back of the rest area, but the water is fairly shallow and because of the vegetation the banks are overgrown meaning there are few sunny grassy spots to dry off.

238

Climb up to Mount Wilson passing a turn-off to Mount Irvine. The road is very steep in some sections and pushing the bike might become necessary for all but the ultra-fit. Mount Wilson is a prominent mountain capped by a 90 m thick layer of basalt. The cyclist will notice the sudden change in vegetation as he rides up the mountain, changing from dry eucalypt to what can almost be described as rainforest. Many of the wealthier residents of the metropolis down below have their secret hideaways here. Huge estate houses and country villas are secluded by tall hedges and huge beautiful gardens. In fact you could almost believe you were cycling through an old English country town here. The place has been described as timeless. It is as if a shell has been placed over the community that cuts it off from civilisation, much of it surrounded by impassable wilderness On the west and southern edges of the mountain are two lookouts over truly wild country. There are no coal mines, railway tracks, fire trails, or even walking tracks in much of the wide expanse around the Wollangambe River. Places to see are the Cathedral of Ferns, Du Faurs Lookout, and Wynnes Lookout in that order.

At the Cathedral of Ferns, there is a very large picnic ground on the left and the entrance to the ferns is directly opposite on the right. A sign nailed to a tree warns of the penalties for removing any vegetation. The walk through the Cathedral of Ferns can be ridden with a bike, but is not recommended due to the soft nature of the soil. However, I see no problem in wheeling it up the slope, then taking the 4WD track back to the Du Faurs Rocks Lookout. The Cathedral of Ferns is a very dense patch of vegetation dominated by sassafras, coachwood trees, and of course, ferns.

On the way to Wynnes Rocks are some fine and new examples of the well-to-do's second or third residences. At the very end is an unmarked fork and you should keep left and cycle down a small embankment to a car-park. A short walk over rocks leads to the lookout itself. The horizon is broken by such prominent features as Mount Hay, Mount Tomah, and most of all, the massive Mount Banks which looks quite close but is about 7 km away. Returning to Bilpin via Bells Line of Road, the road descends off the south-western side of the basalt-capped mountain before joining up with the main road. Watch out for high speed traffic along here.

RIDE 53: CANOE CREEK
(COLO RIVER)

FROM: Putty Road
TO: Colo River (Canoe Creek) (return)
VIA: Grassy Hill
LENGTH: 20 km (10 km each way)
TIME: 1 day (option for overnight camping by or over Colo River)
RIDE/TRACK GRADE: 4/6 (mostly 3/4)
WALKING: Short steep walk to the Colo River
HEIGHT VARIATION: 80 m
TRANSPORT: Private transport to Putty Road
FACILITIES: None
MAPS: CMA (LIC) Colo Heights 1:25 000 topographical

This is perhaps the best mountain bike ride available in the eastern half of Wollemi National Park. The track is flat, short, and of reasonable quality. There are two objectives: (1) a dramatic lookout over a sharp bend in the rugged Colo River gorge, and (2) a short walk down to a beach around which sweeps the wide Colo River, ideal swimming.

Access to the starting point is along the Putty Road via Windsor. The turn-off on the left is signposted as Wollemi National Park, with a Vehicles must be registered sign. The track cuts back to the south. A hundred metres into the bush is a turning circle and the car should be parked here. The trail is open to four wheel drives, so beware.

There are some initial uphills when cycling, punctuated by some sand patches to keep you on guard. The trail then gently undulates with occasional partially obscured views to the left and right. The turn-offs to the right and left present no navigational hazards as they are very minor. A long very flat section makes easy riding, through open country with many wildflowers and the odd cesspit. The rocky sections are mainly on the slopes. Vegetation along the last sections is predominantly dry sclerophyll forest, sometimes alternative to wet forest where sheltered.

After a particularly enjoyable downhill, you suddenly emerge in a large clearing with a track descending to the left and another track descending gently to the right. This is not marked on the map. Four wheel drivers sometimes camp here. The left track is quite steep and soon turns into a walking track heading straight down to Canoe Creek. From here it is about a 70–80 minute walk scrambling over slippery boulders downstream to the confluence with the Colo River.

It is suggested to head along the right option from the clearing. The bike can still be ridden for most of this section although there occasional large large, waterfilled pot-holes and overgrown sections. The objective is to attain the southerly U-shaped bend in the road underneath a cliff before Alidade Hill. Where the trail swings from west-south-west to north-east (just uphill from a particular overgrown muddy section, and the most southerly point on the entire track) is another smaller clearing and makeshift campsite. Leave the bikes and walk along the well-defined footpad to the left. Do not attempt to circumvent Alidade Hill. Although the topographical map shows the trail continuing on for another 5 km, it actually peters out in only 2 km amidst a tangle of vines.

The footpad descends to the edge of the Colo River gorge, emerging among a series of rock platforms. For dramatic views, head to the right over the platforms. The vegetation is fairly dispersed here and trackless walking is relatively easy. Some rock ledges about 200 m upstream give particularly fine unobscured views over a strange phenomenon. Because of the very sharp angle that the Colo River bends, you see two gorges, one behind the other.

Head back to the track. It drops very steeply and directly to Canoe Creek from where it is only ten minutes to Colo River. A trail from the northern bank leads up to a spectacular viewing area over the sweeping bend and beach allowing you to look into both gorges.

One can either camp here or spend the middle hours of the day before heading back to the bikes and then the car. Fresh water can be obtained from Canoe Creek.

RIDE 54:   SIX BROTHERS
(COLO RIVER)

FROM: Putty Road
TO: Colo River gorge

VIA: Six Brothers, Culoul Range
LENGTH: 34 km (17 km each way)
TIME: 1 day (option for overnight camping over Wollemi Creek or by Colo River)
RIDE/TRACK GRADE: 4/6
WALKING: Rough footpad to Wollemi Creek/Colo River lookout
HEIGHT VARIATION: 120 m cycling, 80 m walking
TRANSPORT: Private transport to Putty Road via Windsor
FACILITIES: None
MAPS: CMA (LIC) Six Brothers 1:25 000 topographical

This ride resembles the previous one in many ways: cycling along a ridge through wild terrain to access a remote part of the spectacular Colo River gorge. This tour, however, is longer and also allows walkers to camp by the longest watercourse in the national park, Wollemi Creek. Although it can be done in one day, it is recommended to camp overnight either on the ridgetop where the trail ends, or walk with packs down to Wollemi Creek and then the sandy banks of the Colo River.

Access to the starting point is along the Putty Road via Windsor. The turn-off is on the left about 19 km from Colo Heights and is signposted as Wollemi National Park, with a Vehicles must be registered sign. The trail climbs briefly before coming to a junction. Ignore the left option which leads to a bit of a shooters' playground with shotgun shells everywhere. Keep right, paralleling another track up on the left embankment. It is fairly level cycling and a good rhythm can be maintained, spoiled only by occasional sand patches. You soon comes to a prominent saddle where the track deteriorates into rocky sections due to the slope.

There is nothing of interest at the Six Brothers Trig Point. A good downhill past some abandoned dams takes you to Hollow Rock. Here is another turn-off not marked on the map. Keep right—the left option descends quickly to Boorai Creek. The right track descends along the centre of the ridge to a prominent saddle where a steep uphill takes you to another junction. Keep right here, contouring around and climbing a knoll from the north-east. On top is a makeshift camping area set on a bed of pine needles. Two trails branch off here, also not marked on the topographical. Although the left option seems like the way to go, head right. The trail immediately deteriorates and because of the downhill nature cycling is still possible, even enjoyable in parts. The vegetation becomes more stunted as the ridge narrows, giving more views to the north and south.

Suddenly the track peters out just past a turning circle/ clearing. This place is a possible option for a camp site if you only have panniers. Cycling is no longer practical past this point. The trail continues west along the centre of the ridge. There was evidence of trail bikes along this part. It becomes an orthodox footpad as the vegetation closes in again. The track then heads north off the ridge on to a spur and is marked by rock cairns across several flat rock platforms. Despite being an unofficial walking trail, it is fairly well defined.

At the edge of Wollemi Creek the track descends very steeply and some pack hauling may be necessary to reach the bottom. For day trippers just interested in the view, do not descend, but instead head left (north) down a small embankment to another spur. This shortly emerges amidst some rock ledges. Negotiate these to reach an extensive rock platform perimeter around the lower Wollemi Creek/Colo River area giving extensive views over the t-intersection confluence between the two long well developed water courses. The gorge here is incredibly steep—almost 90 degrees.

Backtrack to the bikes and then the car. If camping by the water, allow half a day to reach the Colo River from where the bikes must be left at the end of the ridge track.

2. WESTERN WOLLEMI NATIONAL PARK

RIDE 55: THE GLOW WORM TUNNEL

FROM: Bell Station
TO: Lithgow
VIA: Glow Worm Tunnel
LENGTH:
    Day 1: Bell to Glow Worm Tunnel glen 49 km
    Day 2: Glow Worm Tunnel glen to Lithgow 40 km
    Total distance is 89 km

RIDE/TRACK GRADE: 3/3–4
WALKING: Through the tunnel
HEIGHT VARIATION: 320 m
TRANSPORT: Rail (Blue Mountains Line)
FACILITIES: None
SPECIAL EQUIPMENT: A torch, water, fuel stove
MAPS: CMA (LIC) Mount Wilson, Wollangambe, Lithgow, Cullen Bullen, and Ben Bullen 1:25 000 topographicals (it is possible to do without the first two if you have the Wallerawang 1:100 000 Natmap)

The Glow Worm Tunnel was built by the Commonwealth Oil Corporation Limited as part of a 52 mile railway link between Newnes Junction and the Wolgan Valley mines at Newnes. For 20 years carriages full of oil shale passed through the tunnel until the mines were closed down after the stock market crash of 1929. Today the tracks have been dismantled but the tunnel still remains, now inhabited by a small insect called a glow worm.

Because the tunnel is curved, it is possible to walk in until there is no light visible from either end. When your eyes adjust to the darkness, myriad pale blue pinpoints of light cover the walls. The glow worms are minute and harmless, being about 2 cm long with a luminous bulb on one end. But they are not really worms at all but simply the larval stage of a fungus gnat. The sight is quite amazing and certainly beats the Bundanoon equivalent.

Cycling to the tunnel is largely through the Newnes State Forest with the national park being entered just a few kilometres before the tunnel. Bell Station is the most convenient start of the ride. It is an unattended platform and cyclists must travel to the rear of the train and notify the guard of their intention to stop at Bell.

From Bell Station, take the unsealed Sandham Road on the north side of the railway line to Newnes Junction where the Clarence Colliery is situated. On the right along this road is a continuation of the Blue Mountains National Park and the beginning of the Wollangambe River wilderness area. Continue past Newnes Junction, to Clarence where you should turn right on to the Old Bells Line of Road and then north through Newnes State Forest.

The 1:25 000 series maps of this area are fairly poor quality compared to other parts of NSW. The contour interval is only 20 m instead of 10 m, and a lot of the lines are quite vague. Further north, many of the contour lines are approximations only as is the charting of watercourses.

The Old Bells Line of Road meets the Glow Worm Tunnel Road in the Newnes State Forest just before the Bungleboori Picnic Area. Tall pine trees make this area quite pleasant to ride through, giving an unusual contrast to the clutter of the ordinary Australian bush. Head north, following the abandoned rail line. Ignore two turn-offs to the right: one to Galah Mountain, the other about 30 km along to Newnes called the Old Coach Road. Just after this second turn-off you enter the Wollemi National Park and the scenery begins to get quite spectacular. The road passes through a narrow tunnel. The road deteriorates from here on, and you soon come to a carpark where drivers have to walk. Fortunately cyclists don't need to leave their transport behind.

A walking track leads to some pagodas. Large sections of the road have been washed away down the embankment of Tunnel Creek. Here the bikes have to be pushed across a bridge for some of the way to get around these obstacles. There is some really wet country here, and the final approach to the tunnel is rideable and completely surrounded by thousands of ferns. The narrow shallow canyon here and across the reservoir makes perfect mountain biking country, pursuing destinations that motorised vehicles can't reach.

The tunnel soon appears ahead of you, a dark hole through the ferns, reminiscent of Indiana Jones movies. You can't actually cycle through the tunnel, even with dynamo or battery powered headlights because of the large rocks on the floor, especially near the far end. Therefore the bikes must be left at the entrance. Get out your torch and walk about two hundred metres in where it becomes pitch black. Allow about 10 minutes for your eyes to adjust before you can fully appreciate the spectacle. Even though you are under a mountain, it looks as if you are staring at a cloudless nightsky with millions of blue stars. Close inspection of the glow-worms will reveal that they have spun silk cocoons in which they attach themselves to the wall and ceiling. Their scientific name is *Arachnocampa richardsae*, belonging to the order of flies. The cocoons and webs contain many minute droplets of a sticky silky substance, used to trap small insects such as mosquitoes. The worm's glow is formally called bioluminescence, and is the result of a chemical reaction between the larvae's body waste and oxygen. The glow comes from the enlarged tips on the insect's four excretory outlets. The more oxygen that is supplied to these outlets, the brighter the glow. Shining torches directly on them will have their light go out. From the larval stage, the insect develops into a pupa. After 12 days, they become adults and also glow until they mate. Three weeks after the eggs are laid, the larvae hatch and the cycle starts over again.

Since this is an historic site, a small history lesson is appropriate at this stage. Having discovered oil shale in the Capertee Valley 'next door', Campbell Mitchell opened up a kerosene shale mining pit in 1873. The first road into the valley was built in 1897. It was not called Newnes until the Commonwealth Oil Corporation began operations in 1906, and named the mine sites after one of its company directors. The oil shale itself was similar to coal but burns more readily. The high grade ore, called torbanite was heated causing the oil inside to evaporate. The fumes were retrieved through condensation. Subsequent refining allowed all sort of liquids to be derived from the rock: paraffin wax, fuel, acids, tar, pitch, kerosene, and lubricating oils.

The township itself was very crude and consisted of a few shoddy houses, some shops, and a school. The industrial complex included numerous mine shafts, refineries, tanks, a reservoir, a power house, a distillation area, and even a brickworks. The greatest engineering feat however was the small 32-mile railway that wound its way through (and under) the rugged mountains delivering the products of the complex to Newnes Junction where it could be transported to Sydney. Under the supervision of Henry Dean, the railway cost about £130,000 to build or £4,000 per mile, the most expensive part being the tunnel drilling through the sandstone. The second tunnel is longer than the first, and was constructed in November 1907. This was first called Bell's Grotto before the name changed to Glow Worm Tunnel.

The area was closed in 1911 due to poor returns, but World War One revived operations and mining was spasmodically carried out throughout the 1920s before the buildings were dismantled and moved to nearby Glen Davis in 1934. All locomotives used on the railway, Shay numbers 1 to 4 were dismantled and used for spare parts or scrap metal.

A pretty little glen exists just on the other side of the tunnel. There aren't as many ferns here but the place is very sheltered. One would have to bring your own water because the stream here is saturated with rust from the remains of the railway. A walking track heads upstream to the left where you should make camp. The area here is quite picturesque, but very sensitive due to soft wet soils. To the right, following the railway, lies Newnes. What firewood there is, is most likely to be wet and fuel stoves are recommended if you want to be guaranteed a warm meal.

Head to Lithgow the next day by following the Glow Worm Tunnel Road back to the Bungleboori Picnic Area. Head right avoiding the Old Bells Line of Road and you quickly drop down into State Mine Creek valley where it is downhill nearly all the way to Lithgow. Keep an eye out for the unusual pagoda formations during the descent.

RIDE 56: WOLGAN LOOKOUT (DEANES CREEK GORGE)

FROM: Bell Station
TO: Lithgow Station
VIA: Newnes State Forest
LENGTH:
   Day 1: Bell Station to Wolgan Lookout 54 km
   Day 2: Wolgan Lookout to Lithgow 48 km
   Total distance is 102 km
RIDE/TRACK GRADE: 3–4/6 (mostly 3/3)
WALKING: None
HEIGHT VARIATION: 320 m
TRANSPORT: Rail (Blue Mountains Line)
FACILITIES: None
SPECIAL EQUIPMENT: Water, camera
MAPS: Mount Wilson, Wollangambe, Lithgow, Cullen Bullen, Rock Hill and Mount Morgan 1:25 000 topographicals

This is the best ride in the western part of Wollemi National Park. Its destination is a spectacular lookout that presides over a box canyon where three gorges collide: Deans Creek, Rocky Creek, and the mighty Wolgan River. The cycling is largely flat and easy, the surface being well compacted. Unlike tours of Wollemi, one doesn't need to walk away from the bikes to access the lookout, and consequently one can carry panniers instead of a backpack. Remember to take plenty of water for none is available at or near the lookout.

From Bell take the unsealed Sandham Road on the north side of the railway line to Newnes Junction where the Clarence Colliery is situated. On the right along this road is a continuation of the Blue Mountains National Park and the beginning of the Wollangambe River wilderness area. Continue past Newnes Junction to Clarence where you should turn right on to the Old Bells Line of Road and then north through Newnes State Forest.

The 1:25 000 series maps of this area are fairly poor quality compared to other parts of NSW. The contour interval is only 20 m instead of 10, and a lot of the lines are quite vague. Further north, many of the contour lines are approximations only as is the charting of watercourses.

The Old Bells Line of Road meets the Glow Worm Tunnel Road in the Newnes State Forest just before the Bungleboori Picnic Area. Tall pine trees make this area quiet pleasant to ride through, giving an unusual contrast to the clutter of the ordinary Australian bush. Head north, following the abandoned rail line.

About 6 km on to the Cullen Bullen 1:25 000 topographical map you begin to parallel a road just to the right. In between the two roads is a clearfelled section, often attracting kangaroos. Where the parallel road ends is a turn-off to the right. Navigation aids include a sudden swing to the left of the Glow Worm Tunnel Road and an initial downhill of the right hand road. To the left is the very upper headwaters of Deanes Creek which you will see later as a massive canyon. The creek was named after Henry Dean, the supervisor of the railway construction shipping shale ore from Newnes to Newnes Junction.

There are many minor turn-offs along this section, with frequent grading incursions into the left and right embankments. You soon come to a major fork with an anthill on the right. Keep left here and you soon leave the Newnes State Forest to enter Wollemi National Park. This is signposted with a fence. Some large waterfilled pot holes also exist along here as well as the odd sand patch making. Nevertheless, a nice cycling rhythm can be maintained.

You are then presented with a wide t-intersection after a particularly flat section. Once again head left for more flat cycling until the vegetation closes in and you start to climb. The ridge that you are on starts to narrow and become more predominant as the tracks gets rockier and more undulating. Finally the trees give way to heath and you pass down through a saddle and up the other side with occasional views to the east and west. The track narrows here as the vegetation once again closes in and you pass over a series of knolls before coming to a turning circle at the end.

A walking track then continues over two more knolls for about 200 m before you arrive at a sight that will take your breath away. The bikes can be wheeled along this section with a minimum of lifting. A rock platform gives fairly unobscured views over a majestic box canyon lined with 300 m high cliffs all around. If you use your imagination, there's an armchair formation to the right. The photographer has to be careful how to frame his shots. During the middle of a hot day, there'll be a lot of haze, while the rock platform viewing area doesn't allow one to get back far enough to take in the whole sight. Directly below you is the confluence of Deanes and Rocky Creeks. Deanes Creek then flows into the Wolgan River. There is a tour outlined to this destination in Ride 58, accessible from Newnes. Together with the Capertee River, the Wolgan forms the Colo River than flows in the Hawkesbury River at Lower Portland.

It is suggested to pitch your tent either at the car-park turning circle, or just 30 m back on the track, or on the edge, depending on your preferences. Be very careful when building a camp fire as the surrounding vegetation is extremely dry. In the morning, if you are lucky, the floor of the canyon will be covered in cloud—just when you thought the view couldn't get any better.

Head to Lithgow the next day by following the Glow Worm Tunnel Road back to the Bungleboori Picnic Area. Head right avoiding the Old Bells Line of Road and you quickly drop down into State Mine Creek valley where it is downhill nearly all the way to Lithgow. Keep an eye out for the unusual pagoda formations during the descent.

RIDE 57: NEWNES

FROM: Bell Station
TO: Lithgow Station
VIA: Newnes
LENGTH:
  Day 1: Bell to Glow Worm Tunnel Glen 49 km
  Day 2: Glow Worm Tunnel Glen to Newnes 18 km
  Day 3: Newnes to Wolgan Lookout via Old Coach Road 41 km
  Day 4: Wolgan Lookout to Lithgow 48 km
  Total distance is 156 km
RIDE/TRACK GRADE: 6–7/7
WALKING: Through the tunnel, exploration of Newnes ruins
HEIGHT VARIATION: 730 m
TRANSPORT: Rail (Blue Mountains Line)
FACILITIES: None
SPECIAL EQUIPMENT: A torch, water, fuel stove
MAPS: CMA (LIC) Mount Wilson, Wollangambe, Lithgow, Cullen Bullen, Ben Bullen, Rock Hill and Mount Morgan 1:25 000 topographicals (it is possible to do without the first two if you have the Natmap Wallerawang 1:100 000 topographical)

This ride has it all—the famous Glow Worm Tunnel, the historic Newnes oil shale ruins, the Wolgan River gorge, and the most spectacular lookout in Wollemi National Park. The majority of the 156 km distance is on the well graded Glow Worm Tunnel Road through the Newnes State Forest. However there are also many sections which are quite rough and steep. In fact the bike will have to wheeled in some sections: part of the descent from the Glow Worm Tunnel to Newnes and the uphill from the Wolgan via the Old Coach Road. Nevertheless the sheer variety and rugged beauty of the terrain will long live in the cyclist's memory.

From Bell Station, take the unsealed Sandham Road on the north side of the railway line to Newnes Junction where the Clarence Colliery is situated. On the right along this road is a continuation of the Blue Mountains National Park and the beginning of the Wollangambe River wilderness area. Continue past Newnes Junction to Clarence, where you should turn right on to the Old Bells Line of Road and then north through Newnes State Forest.

The 1:25 000 series maps of this area are fairly poor quality compared to other parts of NSW. The contour interval is only 20 m instead of 10 m, and a lot of the lines are quite vague. Further north, many of the contour lines are approximations only as is the charting of watercourses.

The Old Bells Line of Road meets the Glow Worm Tunnel Road in the Newnes State Forest just before the Bungleboori Picnic Area. Tall pine trees make this area quite pleasant to ride through, giving an unusual contrast to the clutter of the ordinary Australian bush. Head north, following the abandoned rail line. Ignore two turn-offs to the right: one to Galah Mountain, the other called the Old Coach Road about 30 km along to Newnes. Just after this second turn-off you enter the Wollemi National Park and the scenery begins to get quite spectacular. The road passes through a narrow tunnel. The road deteriorates from here on, and you soon come to a carpark where drivers have to walk. Fortunately cyclists don't need to leave their transport behind.

A walking track leads to some pagodas. Large sections of the road have been washed away down the embankment of Tunnel Creek. Here the bikes have to be pushed across a bridge for some of the way to get around these obstacles. There is some really wet country here, and the final approach to the tunnel is rideable and completely surrounded by thousands of ferns. The narrow shallow canyon here and across the reservoir makes perfect mountain biking country, pursuing destinations that motorised vehicles can't reach.

The tunnel soon appears ahead of you, a dark hole through the ferns, reminiscent of Indiana Jones movies. You can't actually cycle through the tunnel, even with dynamo or battery powered headlights because of the large rocks on the floor, especially near the far end. Therefore the bikes must be left at the entrance. Get out your torch and walk about two hundred metres in where it becomes pitch black. Allow about 10 minutes for your eyes to adjust before you can fully appreciate the spectacle. Even though you are under a mountain, it looks as if you are staring at a cloudless nightsky with millions of blue stars. Close inspection of the glow-worms will reveal that they have spun silk cocoons in which they attach themselves to the wall and ceiling. Their scientific name is *Arachnocampa richardsae*, belonging to the order of flies. The cocoons and webs contain many minute droplets of a sticky silky substance, used to trap small insects such as mosquitoes. The worm's glow is formally called bioluminescence, and is the result of a chemical reaction between the larvae's body waste and oxygen. The glow comes from the enlarged tips on the insect's four excretory outlets. The more oxygen that is supplied to these outlets, the brighter the glow. Shining torches directly on them will have their light go out. From the larval stage, the insect develops into a pupa. After 12 days, they become adults and also glow until they mate. Three weeks after the eggs are laid, the larvae hatch and the cycle starts over again.

One of the greatest engineering feats of pre-First World War Australia was the small 52 mile railway that wound its way through (and under) the rugged mountains, delivering the products of the Newnes complex to Newnes Junction where it could be transported to Sydney. Under the supervision of Henry Dean, the railway cost about £130,000 to build or £4,000 per mile, the most expensive part being the tunnel drilling through the sandstone. The second tunnel is longer than the first, and was constructed in November 1907. This was first called Bell's Grotto before the name changed to Glow Worm Tunnel.

Newnes was closed in 1911 due to poor returns, but World War One revived operations and mining was spasmodically carried out throughout the 1920s before the buildings were dismantled and moved to nearby Glen Davis in 1934. All loco-motives used on the railway, Shay numbers 1 to 4 were dis-mantled and used for spare parts or scrap metal.

A pretty little glen exists just on the other side of the tunnel. There aren't as many ferns here but the place is very sheltered. You would have to bring your own water because the stream here is saturated with rust from the remains of the railway. A walking track heads upstream to the left where you should make camp. The area is quite picturesque, but very sensitive due to soft wet soils. To the right, following the railway, lies Newnes. What firewood there is, is most likely to be wet and fuel stoves are recommended if you want to be guaranteed a warm meal.

The next day, continue along the old railway line. Tunnel Creek has to be crossed and the bikes will have to be lifted along this section. After this the track remains flat and if the bikes can't be ridden, they can at least be walked comfortably. Some sections, especially at the start are quite overgrown and muddy due to the sheltered nature of the cliffs. As the track continues north-west along the base of the cliffs, the vegetation becomes more exposed and therefore drier. The cycling also becomes easier as the trail swings around to the north-east. Turn left at the first intersection, heading straight down past the old colliery to the Wolgan River. Ford here and then head right on to the Lidsdale to Newnes Road. It is flat and easy cycling along here, but watch out for holiday traffic.

Just before you reach Newnes, there's an old hotel on the left which has now been reopened as a kiosk. Here one can buy soft drinks and get some information leaflets on the ruins. The camping ground is quite extensive and sites are scattered. The ruins are best accessed by crossing the shallow Wolgan River and cycling downstream for about ten minutes. This is quite a popular walk and mountain bike ride. Featured among the pre-World War One ruins are:

• Newnes Railway Station precinct
• Coke ovens and coal mines
• Works reservoir
• Shale storage bins
• Wax production area
• Paraffin storage sheds, stock tanks
• Workshop complex
• Water separator and powerhouse
• Distillation area

It is incredible to think heavy industry occupied such a beautiful valley. Since this is an historic site, a small history lesson is appropriate at this stage. Having discovered oil shale in the Capertee Valley 'next door', Campbell Mitchell opened up a kerosene shale mining pit in 1873. The first road into the valley was built in 1897. It was not called Newnes until the Commonwealth Oil Corporation began operations in 1906, and named the mine sites after one of its company directors. The oil shale itself was similar to coal but burns more readily. The high grade ore, called torbanite was heated causing the oil inside to evaporate. The fumes were retrieved through condensation. Subsequent refining allowed all sort of liquids to be derived from the rock: paraffin wax, fuel, acids, tar, pitch, kerosene, and lubricating oils. The township of Newnes itself was very crude and consisted of a few shoddy houses, some shops, and a school. Not much is left of the residential area today.

Head back to the camping area to complete an eventful day's exploration. The next day, cycle back up the Lidsdale to Newnes Road and cross over the Wolgan River. This time head up the signposted Old Coach Road. The track is very washed out in places and the bike will have to be pushed most of the 400 m uphill. This used to be the only vehicular access in the entire Wolgan valley. After several kilometres, the road levels out and becomes easy cycling through pagoda country to meet up with the Glow Worm Tunnel Road at Deanes Siding. Cycle south for 5 km before coming to a turn-off on the left. It is marked by the start of a parallel road on the left hand side. Other navigational aids to locate the turn-off are a sudden curve in the road from east to south and an immediate downhill on the turn-off. To the left are the upper headwaters of Deanes Creek which you will see later as a massive canyon. The creek was named after Henry Dean, the supervisor of the railway construction shipping shale from Newnes to Newnes Junction.

There are many minor turn-offs along this first section, with frequent grading incursions into the left and right embankments. You soon come to a major fork with an anthill on the right. Keep left here and you soon leave the Newnes State Forest to enter Wollemi National Park. This is signposted with a fence. Some large waterfilled potholes also exist along here as well as the odd sand patch making progress challenging. Nevertheless, a nice cycling rhythm can be maintained.

You are then presented with a wide t-intersection after a particularly flat section. Once again head left for more flat cycling until the vegetation closes in and you start to climb. The ridge that you are on starts to narrow and becomes more predominant as the tracks get rockier and more undulating. Finally the trees give way to heath and you pass down through a saddle and up the other side with occasional views to the east and west. The track narrows here as the vegetation once again closes in and you pass over a series of knolls before coming to a turning circle at the end.

A walking track then continues over two more knolls for about 200 m before you arrive at a sight that will take your breath away. The bikes can be wheeled along this section with a minimum of lifting. A rock platform gives fairly unobscured views over a majestic box canyon lined with 300 m high cliffs all around. If you use your imagination, there is an armchair formation to the right. The photographer has to be careful how to frame his shots. During the middle of a hot day, there'll be a lot of haze, while the rock platform viewing area doesn't allow one to get back far enough to take the whole sight in. Directly below you is the confluence of Deanes and Rocky Creeks. Deanes Creek then flows into the Wolgan River. There is a tour outlined to this destination in Ride 58, accessible from Newnes. Together with the Capertee River, the Wolgan forms the Colo River than flows into the Hawkesbury River at Lower Portland.

It is suggested you pitch your tent either at the car-park turning circle, or just 30 m back on the track, or on the edge, depending on your preferences. Be very careful when building a camp fire as the surrounding vegetation is extremely dry. In the morning, if you are lucky, the floor of the canyon will be covered in cloud—just when you thought the view couldn't get any better.

Head to Lithgow the next day by following the Glow Worm Tunnel Road back to the Bungleboori Picnic Area. Head right avoiding the Old Bells Line of Road and you quickly drop down into State Mine Creek valley where it is downhill nearly all the way to Lithgow. Keep an eye out for the unusual pagoda formations during the descent.

RIDE 58: WOLGAN RIVER (DEANES CREEK)

FROM: Newnes
TO: Deanes Creek
VIA: Wolgan River
LENGTH: 26 km (split into 2 days of 13 km)
TIME: 2 day
RIDE/TRACK GRADE: 5/8
WALKING: Option walk up to a Wolgan valley lookdown via the Pipeline Track
HEIGHT VARIATION: 150 m
TRANSPORT: Private transport to Newnes

FACILITIES: None
MAPS: CMA (LIC) Ben Bullen and Mount Morgan 1:25 000
topographicals

For those cyclists who detest crowds, here's the perfec
getaway. While Newnes is becoming an increasingly popula
tourist destination for walkers, motorists, cyclists, and fou
wheel drivers, hardly anyone ventures down the river! The
road is too washed out in places for vehicles, but for mountain
bikes, this is the perfect venue. Since the entire trail is along
side a river, there are no great uphills or downhills and all the
way are views up to the spectacular cliffs that line this majestic
valley.

Access to Newnes is through Lithgow and Lidsdale. Cross
the river and cycle east into the Wollemi National Park
Located here are the ruins from the old oil shale works that
had their heyday before World War One. It is incredible to
think should a heavy industry occupied such a beautiful
valley. Since this is an historic site, a small history lesson is
appropriate at this stage. Having discovered oil shale in the
Capertee Valley 'next door', Campbell Mitchell opened up a
kerosene shale mining pit in 1873. The first road into the valley
was built in 1897. It was not called Newnes until the Commonwealth Oil Corporation began operations in 1906, and
named the mine site after one of its company directors. The
oil shale itself was similar to coal but burns more readily. The
high grade ore, called torbanite was heated causing the oil
inside to evaporate. The fumes were retrieved through condensation. Subsequent refining allowed all sort of liquids to
be derived from the rock: paraffin wax, fuel, acids, tar, pitch,
kerosene, and lubricating oils. The township of Newnes itself
was very crude and consisted of a few shoddy houses, some
shops, and a school. Not much is left of the residential area
today.

Leaflets available from the old hotel before the camping
ground give information on the historic features. Featured
among the derelict works are:

• Newnes Railway Station precinct
• Coke ovens and coal mines
• Works reservoir
• Shale storage bins

Kanangra Walls (Ride 46)

Wollemi wilderness from Tootie Ridge (Ride 51)

The Colo Gorge from its confluence with Canoe Creek (Ride 53)

- Wax production area
- Paraffin storage sheds, stock tanks
- Workshop complex
- Water separator and powerhouse
- Distillation area

This is as far as most people go. On the opposite side is the start of the Pipeline Track that leads over the dividing ridge to the Glen Davis in the Capertee. For those with some energy who are willing to leave their bikes behind can cross the river and climb up to an spectacular lookdown over the Wolgan gorge to survey the area they have just come through and are about to enter. The reverb acoustics arising from coo-eeing from this point are particularly impressive. It takes about an hour each way and the vertical rise to the top pagoda is some 300 m. The walking track uses a gully to access the top of the cliffs, where it then doubles back to reach the edge to the east.

After the walk, continue east on the southern bank. You are confronted with some turn-offs initially but keep left when in doubt. The right turn-offs usually end in mineshafts or quarries. One section of the track here is completely washed out and the bikes will have to be wheeled carefully along above the river. Cycling conditions then improve again as the water course curves to the north. Some small uphills and downhills must be negotiated as well as some particular rocky and sandy sections. Everywhere are gigantic boulders that have crashed down to the river from the massive sandstone cliffs. This is real hard-core mountain biking and the reason why the track condition is rated a maximum 8. Just when you think progress is becoming very frustrating, the track improves again through old private property not marked on the map. There are some old huts here where some earlier pioneer had built a farm. They are long abandoned and the artefacts have been souvenired.

This peaceful pastoral setting is interrupted by some lengthy uphills and downhills as the Wolgan River swings to the south-east and the cliffs open up as the Deanes Creek gorge becomes visible. The track finishes at the exact confluence between the two watercourses with a pleasant grassy clearing on the right being available for camping. Fresh water can be obtained from Deanes Creek. The cliffs to the south can be accessed from a tour from the Newnes State Forest—Ride 56.

The river is not quite deep enough for orthodox swimming but nevertheless provides cool relief on a hot day. If time is available why not stay a couple of days here relaxing. I've heard rumours that the trail actually continues as far as Annie Rowan Creek. ...

Simply backtrack to Newnes when exiting the area.

RIDE 59: GLEN DAVIS
(CAPERTEE RIVER)

FROM: Glen Davis
TO: Capertee River
VIA: Oil shale refinery ruins
LENGTH: 22 km (11 km each way)
TIME: 2 days
RIDE/TRACK GRADE: 5/6–7
WALKING: None
HEIGHT VARIATION: 80 m
TRANSPORT: Private transport to Glen Davis
FACILITIES: None
MAPS: CMA (LIC) Gospers Mountain and Mount Morgan 1:25 000 topographicals

Glen Davis is another historic mining town set in a very rugged gorge that is claimed to be the second largest in the world after the Grand Canyon. Those who've seen the Australian film *The Chain Reaction* will remember the beautiful Australian scenery. The movie was shot on location at Glen Davis using the ghost town and industrial ruins as a backdrop.

Since recent 'upgrading' rail services, bikes can no longer be transported to Capertee. The easiest way would be to drive to Glen Davis and park at the popular well developed camping ground. Toilets, barbecues, bins and tables are all provided here. I've spoken with the caretaker of the museum and he says the place is absolutely packed full on public holidays so try to avoid these days. For those cyclists who detest crowds here's the perfect getaway. While Newnes is becoming an increasingly popular tourist destination for walkers, motorists, cyclists and four wheel drivers, hardly anyone ventures down the river! The road is too washed out in places for vehicles, but for mountain bikes this is the perfect venue. Since the entire trail is alongside a river, there are no great uphills or downhills and all the way are views up to the spectacular cliffs that line this majestic valley. If you opt for this type of bush camping, you can cycle right down the Capertee River past the ruins and away from the crowds. The only hitch is that the owners' permission has to be asked for in order to pass through into the national park.

It was Cox's companion, Blackman, who first discovered the Capertee Valley in the early nineteenth century. By 1821, the first settlers were moving into Glen Alice nearby. The surrounding area was populated when the Mudgee rail line was built. By 1873, oil shale was discovered at Glen Davis and was worked in a number of individual leases a decade later. This first tunnel was sunk but it was not until 1940 that commercial operations began. The Second World War kept it briefly alive when the demand for fuel was high. In its shortlived heyday, the township had hundreds of buildings, a bank, churches, and even a cinema, and crude oil production was an incredible 23,500 gallons a day. But in the 1950s, the main seam had reduced to 1 foot across and the high costs of production couldn't compete with imports. The plant was some £5 million in debt, and by 1952 all the miners and their families had moved.

As you drive in, there are some ruins on both sides of the road, and it is curious to see lonesome chimneys sticking out of grazing land. The actual major industrial ruins are in private property but the owners have no problem in letting you inspect them if permission is asked. A tourist drive takes you up through the old township to a museum (a quaint old shed at the end called 'Metulah'. Here exhibits of the shale can be viewed as well as photographs of the township in its heyday. The caretaker has spent a lot of time producing souvenirs for purchase, and inquiries about the area can be made by phoning the Glen Davis Museum on (063) 79 7251.

In the morning, head down to 'The Poplars' station at the end of the road. The signs at the large white gate warn trespassers and the consequences that shall befall them should they think about passing through. However the owners live in a large old estate house behind you. Their main concern is souveniring of the piles of equipment that remain amidst the ruins. Once you obtain permission, cycle straight through the property heading left and then right on to a concrete road resembling a runway. This passes in between the derelict refinery ruins—a ghost complex with towering orange cliffs in the background. At the end of this tarmac is a giant black slag heap. If you manage the scramble to the top, you'll be rewarded with fine views over the Capertee Valley framed by Mount Gundangaroo (789 m) in the background. This is a perfect place for photographs. The low grade dross shale that you are standing on here burns quite brightly in a camp fire. It is a difficult choice what to call the main attraction. Certainly the derelict industrial complex and mining town is a central feature but so to is the steep gorge that Glen Davis is located in.

As you round the northern side of the slag heap, the Aussie bush closes in and you are soon in the Wollemi National Park. Continue east paralelling the Capertee River to the left. The cycling here is quite easy, the surface being dominated by more examples of black oil shale. Collect a few samples for the night's campfire. It burns brighter than wood.

You soon come to a gate signposted as Goorangooba Station. Pass through a large cleared area where some horses roam. It appears that no one lives here on a permanent basis. Sometimes the army use this valley for field training. To the left Goorangooba Creek gorge joins with the Capertee. Some of the cliffs visible here are massive. Old farm tracks head down to the water.

Keep right, passing by some fences and cycling uphill to the south-eastern corner of the cleared area. The trail continues climbing here quite steeply. Sandstone rocks dominate the surface. After the short climb, the track contours over a spur past some huge boulders before descending to the river again. There are some great grassy clearings here—some have evidence of previous campfires. There is also a large pool further along, just before a block-up which makes an ideal location for lunch and a swim.

From here, the basic idea is to camp anywhere you want, either by the pool or explore as far downstream as the trail allows. Fresh water can be obtained from the appropriately named Freshwater Creek soon after the Capertee River has swung south. You are virtually guaranteed to get the entire section of the valley for yourself. Why not stay a couple of days relaxing by the water before heading back to the car?

RIDE 60: DUNN'S SWAMP
(GLEN ALICE CIRCUIT)

FROM: Rylstone
TO: Glen Alice
VIA: Kandos Weir
LENGTH:
   Day 1: Rylstone to Dunn's Swamp 30 km
   Day 2: Kandos Weir to Rollen Creek 19 km
   Day 3: Rollen Creek to Glen Davis 43 km
   Day 4: Glen Davis to Rylstone 55 km
   Total Distance is 147 km
RIDE/TRACK GRADE: 7/6
WALKING: None
HEIGHT VARIATION: 450 m
TRANSPORT: Private transport to Rylstone via Lithgow
FACILITIES: Official camping areas with facilities at Dunn's Swamp and Glen Davis
MAPS: CMA (LIC) Olinda and Coorongobba 1:25 000 topographicals, Wollemi National Park 1:150 000 Tourist Map

The township of Rylstone is off the road from Lithgow to Mudgee, 257 km from Sydney. It lies on the point where Cudgegong River is crossed by the Wallerwang Highway. The lookouts marked on the street map of Rylstone on the western side of the river don't exist, but the most significant point about the township from a cyclist's perspective is that it is the starting point of the only two fire trails through the Wollemi National Park.

A round trip from Rylstone can be conducted camping at Dunn's Swamp (formerly called Kandos Weir), Rollen Creek, and Glen Davis, where only a small 5 km and a 3 km section must be backtracked. The majority of the trip is along well maintained roads; however the section between Rollen Creek and Glen Alice is quite rough and a good bike and tyres are needed. This tour highlights the major features of the central western Wollemi National Park including much variety in terrain and places of interest. Complete self-sufficiency is required. Water is available at Dunn's Swamp and Glen Davis and intermittently at Rollen Creek.

Although there's a train station at Rylstone, no trains run

there any more and bikes are usually not allowed on CountryLink coaches. You may be lucky if the driver is cool and the coach is not full—it is up to his discretion. Otherwise, you must drive to Rylstone via Lithgow. You can leave the car at the Rocky Picnic Area. From the main street, cycle left up Fitzgerald Street which leads into Narrango Road. This remains fairly flat for the next 25 km. Keep left past the signposted turn-off to Glen Davis. This is the road you'll be coming back on. A very large cemetery is passed on the left and there are good views to unusual shaped knolls in the foothills of the Great Dividing Range. Narrango Road then passes through pastoral land that is littered with granite boulders. The road contains occasional dips. Just past a ranch, the surface becomes unsealed and the country consists of low mountains. The road momentarily joins up the with the Cudgegong River before it heads north. On the other side of a cattle grid is a wildlife refuge with an old cabin called Birds Hut on the right. On the opposite side of the road are rock formations that will remind Budawang enthusiasts of the Monolith Valley. As you proceed, the valley gets quite narrow before you climb to a narrow rocky pass. The entrance to Wollemi National Park is signposted by the usual NPWS sign. The rock here resembles conglomerate rings, and lines both sides of the road during a good downhill. The turn-off to Dunn's Swamp is on the left and is signposted by a small white sign.

The road to Dunn's Swamp is sandy in parts and one section crosses a small tributary of Ganduddy Creek creating a permanent waterfilled pothole in the road. However, it is rarely deep. The roads around the lake are very sandy, but the worst patches can be skirted. Kangaroos and wombats are quite abundant through here. At the lake there is a whole network of trails to various secluded camping spots. The road emerges at one such on the right but there are others accessed by heading left to a very open flat clearing besides the water next to a boat-ramp. The camping ground is well equipped, with even recycling bins installed allowing you to not only dispose of your rubbish, but classify it as well. Graffiti on some rocks indicate that the place has visited by idiots. Camp anywhere you want. The choice is good: from rocky overhangs in the hills to a peninsula jutting into the lake. I've found the firewood to be in good supply. The valley where the lake is situated contains more of the domed rock formations. The weir itself only recently came under the National Parks and Wildlife Service's administration from Rylstone Shire where it incurred a name change from Kandos Weir to Dunn's Swamp. The lake is popular for passive water sports and is well visited by locals on summer weekends. Some Aboriginal sites exist around the lake but many have been spoilt by graffiti and the national parks authorities are reluctant to reveal the location of more. One prominent site is behind the boat ramp close to the pit toilets and is marked by an information sign—however it has been severely vandalised by people breaking off part of the rock, presumably to take home.

The next morning, head out again to the main road and turn left. You leave the national park boundaries again and cycle through pastoral land for about 10 km. At Red Hill, a sign-posted turn-off on the right indicates an army 4WD trail leads to Mount Darcy and thence to the Putty Road via the Wirraba Range. Straight ahead, the Rylstone–Narrango Road becomes a 4WD track at the Kelgoola homestead and proceeds through the national park along the Hunter Range to emerge in the Putty state forest.

Follow the army road south-east and then east. There is a gate at the beginning which must be left as found. The next 8 km are quite flat but unfortunately sand does cause problems. Sometimes the cycling is better just off the track on the leaves. The best cycling is experienced on the gradual uphills and downhills which are usually firmly packed. Ignore an initial turn-off on the right and a large clearing. Soon you come to another unlocked gate which is usually closed. This is not marked on the map, but after going through this you are into the Coricudgy State Forest. The Glen Alice trail is well sign-posted on the right and should be ignored. The next day you will use this route to access Glen Davis. Another sign points left confirming that you're on the army road.

Continue on to the base of Mount Darcy where the trail suddenly climbs steeply to the left. Ignore this—a tour to Gospers Mountain along this road is outlined in Ride 61. Instead head right behind the signpost on a short trail and climbs slightly and coming out at a beautiful grassy clearing. For wilderness enthusiasts, sometimes natural bush clearings can be better campsites than developed camping grounds. This is a fine example. According to the map there is supposed to be a hut here, but we couldn't find one. Water may be obtainable from a track that climbs to the north up the slope of Mount Darcy. This is the very headwater of Rollen Creek that eventually flows into the Cudgegong River and then into South Australia via Bourke. Believe it or not, but the low hills less than a kilometre to the south form part of the Great Dividing Range. Water falling on the other side of them flows into the Capertee River, thence the Pacific Ocean via the Hawkesbury.

The next day, rise early for this is the true mountain biking leg. Head back to the signposted Glen Alice Trail on the left passed the previous day. A sign says 'No Through Road' due to private property on the other side. After remaining flat for 2 km, the trail immediately deteriorates as it climbs steeply up to the Great Dividing Range to the left of the prominent Mount Coorongooba (1067 m). It then roughly follows the centre of ridge to Grassy Mountain before descending down to the upper Glen Alice valley. This place contains the oldest settlements north of Lithgow. The valley is very green and I found a lot of the trees filled with large flocks of cockatoos. The road immediately improves as it emerges from the Wollemi National Park and then parallels Umbiella Creek southwards. Owner's permission has to be asked to pass from the national park to the Umbiella Creek road, but once at the bottom of the valley it is a public road and proceeds gently downhill to the main Rylstone to Glen Davis road. The old houses here were originally pioneering Scottish families, namely the Macleans and the Innes. At the southern end of the valley are the original homesteads that were purchased from these families by Sir John Jamison, the Swedish knight and close friend of Governor Macquarie. Watch out for the numerous cattle grids here; some are quite wide, being made of railway track I beams and could cause a nasty accident if approached too slowly.

Turn left and cycle to Glen Davis, about 13 km away. A good, well developed camping site exists on the southern side of the road just up from the old township. Glen Davis is an historic mining town set in a very rugged gorge that is claimed to be the second largest in the world after the Grand Canyon. Those who have seen the Australian film *The Chain Reaction* will remember the beautiful Australian scenery. The movie was shot on location at Glen Davis using the ghost town and industrial ruins as a backdrop. It was Cox's companion, Blackman who first saw the Capertee Valley in the early nineteenth century. By 1821, the first settlers were moving into Glen Alice nearby. The surrounding area was populated when the Mudgee train line was built. By 1873, oil shale was discovered at Glen Davis and was worked in a number of individual leases a decade later. This first tunnel was sunk but it wasn't until 1940 that commercial operations began. The Second World War kept it briefly alive when the demand for fuel was high. In its shortlived heyday, the township had hundreds of buildings, a bank, churches, and even a cinema and crude oil production was an incredible 23 500 gallons a day. But in the 1950s, the main seam had reduced to 1 foot across and the high costs of production couldn't compete with imports. The plant was some £5 million in debt, and by 1952 all the miners and their families had moved.

As you cycle in, there are some ruins on both sides of the road, and it is curious to see lonesome chimneys sticking out of grazing land. The actual major industrial ruins are in private property but the owners have no problem in letting you inspect them if permission is asked. A tourist road takes you up through the old township to a museum (a quaint old shed at the end called 'Metulah'). Here exhibits of the shale can be viewed as well as photographs of the township in its heyday. The caretaker has spent a lot of time producing souvenirs for purchase, and inquiries about the area can be made by phoning the Glen Davis Museum on (063) 79 7251.

In the morning, head down to 'The Poplars' station at the end of the road. The signs at the large white gate warn trespassers of the consequences that shall befall them should they think about passing through. However the owners live in a large old estate house behind you. Their main concern is souveniring of the piles of equipment that remain amidst the ruins. Once you obtain permission, cycle straight through the property heading left and then right on to a concrete road resembling a runway. This passes in between the derelict refinery ruins—a ghost complex with towering orange cliffs in the background. At the end of this tarmac is a giant black slag heap. If you manage the scramble to the top, you'll be rewarded with fine views over the Capertee Valley framed by Mount Gundangaroo (789 m) in the background. This is a perfect place for photographs. The low grade dross shale that you are standing on here burns quite brightly in a camp fire. It is a difficult choice what to call the main attraction. Certainly the derelict industrial complex and mining town is a central feature but so too is the steep gorge that Glen Davis is located in.

When ready to leave, simply follow the main road back to Rylstone via Glen Alice and the Capertee River.

RIDE 61: GOSPERS MOUNTAIN (ARMY ROAD)

FROM: Red Hill
TO: Gospers Mountain (return)
VIA: Mount Darcy, Wollemi Range, Army Road
LENGTH:
   Day 1: Drive to Red Hill and 8 km cycle to camp site by Rollen Creek
   Day 2: Rollen Creek to Gospers Mountain 30 km
   Day 3: Gospers Mountain to Red Hill 38 km
   Total distance is 76 km
TIME: 2 days
RIDE/TRACK GRADE: 7/7
WALKING: None
HEIGHT VARIATION: 340 m
TRANSPORT: Private transport to Red Hill
FACILITIES: None
SPECIAL EQUIPMENT: Provision for at least 6 litres of water per person for the round trip, especially if expecting hot weather.
MAPS: CMA (LIC) Coorongooba and Gospers Mountain 1:25 000 topographical. Use the CMA Wollemi National Park 1:150 000 Tourist Map to access the starting area by car

This ride penetrates deep in the one of the wildest and most inaccessible areas in the state. The object is to camp on top of Gospers Mountain, a bald basalt-capped residual where 360 degree panoramic views are obtainable from the tent. The mountain is the most prominent peak of western Wollemi with views as far east as the coast, as far north as the Barrington Tops, and as far south as the Bells Line of Road ridge. In the foreground is the endless maze of canyons and gorges that makes up much of Wollemi National Park. At night the steel

266

works of Newcastle are clearly visible as well as a few million stars.

There is no public transport anywhere near the area so one must drive to Red Hill via Lithgow, Rylstone, and the Narrango Road. The turn-off on to the Army Road is well signposted on the right hand side. There is a gate initially which you must leave as found. Drive as far as you can. A clearing on the right about 1–2 kilometres along is a good place to park.

Follow the Army Road south-east and then east. The next 8 km are quite flat but unfortunately sand does cause problems. Sometimes the cycling is better just off the track on the leaves. The best cycling is experienced on the gradual uphills and downhills which are usually firmly packed. Ignore an initial turn-off on the right. Soon you come to another unlocked gate which is usually closed. This is not marked on the map, but after crossing through this you are into the Coricudgy State Forest. The Glen Alice trail is well signposted on the right and should be ignored. Another sign points left confirming that you are on the Army Road.

Continue on to the base of Mount Darcy where the trail suddenly climbs steeply to the left. Ignore this—a tour to Gospers Mountain along this road is outlined in Ride 61. Instead head right behind the signpost on short trail and climbs slightly and comes out at a beautiful grassy clearing. For wilderness enthusiasts, sometimes natural bush clearings can be better campsites than developed camping grounds. This is a fine example. According to the map there is supposed to be a hut here, but we couldn't find one. Water may be obtainable from a track that climbs to the north up the slope of Mount Darcy. This is the very headwater of Rollen Creek that eventually flows into the Cudgegong River and then into South Australia via Bourke. Believe it or not, but the low hills less than a kilometre to the south form part of the Great Dividing Range. Water falling on the other side of them flows into the Capertee River, thence the Pacific Ocean via the Hawkesbury.

The next day, rise early for what lies ahead is true mountain biking territory. Backtrack to the signposted Mount Darcy ascent (Army Road) and begin the gruelling climb up to the 1079 m peak. The road here is quite rocky, making cycling very difficult if not impossible. A pannier-laden bike will almost definitely have to be pushed up here by all but immortal supermen. On the first bend is a quarry pit which has been converted into a trail-bike obstacle course with big jumps and banked corners. If you have any energy left, you might like to do some timetrials around the circuit. Otherwise continue up the slope as it bends south-east and then north. Just when you thought it couldn't get any steeper—it does. The surface is so slippery here that even pushing becomes technically difficult.

The vegetation changes on top, becoming more moist due to the volcanic soils supporting denser stands of timber. Despite being on the highest point of the trip, the views are not that great. The road curves around to the right of the summit and you see a height indicator by a grassy clearing on the left—a good place for a rest. The road continues to climb slightly become accessing the centre of the ridge and then down to a saddle between Mount Darcy and Mount Duran Duran. The cycling is quite pleasant here, marred only by the occasional waterfilled pothole. There are limited views to cleared agricultural land to the north.

All of a sudden the road heads right and plummets down a 300 m hill into the Wollemi National Park. Some former private land is passed on the right. The trail is very steep and constant braking pressure is required. Quite dramatically the green vegetation is left behind and you are into very dry Aussie bush—dominated by heath and sandstone. As we cycled through this section we nicknamed it 'the wasteland'. You are now travelling south along the approximate centre of a ridge which undulates considerably, slowing progress. Fortunately there is not too much sand on the track. Sometimes there are reasonable views, mainly to the east of domes and pagodas. This is truly desolate country, unsuitable for any commercial activity. Its only inherent value is as pure wilderness.

If it is a cloudless day, a lot of water will have to be consumed along this section for there is little cover. Cyrils Rocks is a nice place for lunch. There are taller trees and a prominent sandstone monolith. Don't bother climbing it for the views are limited by trees on top. The road momentarily branches in two here. To the left leads up an extremely steep spur by the monolith to join up with the right branch. After doing both, I recommend going right as the easier option. The trail gets quite rough after this before improving as it passes through some pleasant open woodland.

Continue south to the top of the ridge once more where it is easy cycling to a deep saddle. Push up the other side and around the base of three knolls which peak at 812 m. There is a short steep climb to the top, exiting the 'wasteland' where it is back to orthodox cycling conditions. A level well graded road with little surface rock leads south through pleasant bush until the turn-off to Gospers Airstrip at the Geebung Ground. To the left leads to the Putty Road through private property on the eastern side of the national park. Head right and then soon left again. Gospers Mountain is not visible at this stage, being shielded by a knoll to its west. The trail contours around this knoll to a saddle between the two peaks. A rough trail heads right to the Capertee Valley (see Ride 62).

With Gospers Mountain looming ahead, the trail heads east, circumventing the mount to the north. Everywhere is evidence of former private property. Located here is a Water Board rain gauge and an old shed containing a old tractor. A steep track heads straight up to the summit trig point. Camp wherever you want. We pitched our tent right by the trig survey marker (847 m). The mount is bare, covered only by grass and cow pats. It's windy but the views are superb. Besides the cleared land in the very foreground, try to spot anything man-made in the panoramic vista around you. To the south-west is the Capertee River gorge, claimed as the second largest in the world after the Grand Canyon. Within its walls is the historical township of Glen Davis. The last of the great bushfires of early January 1994 originated near Gospers Mountain area and spread all the way to the Putty Road.

A simple retrace of the route leads back to the cars at Red Hill. See the next ride for a possible extension to the Gospers Mountain tour.

RIDE 62: CAPERTEE RIVER
(GOSPERS MOUNTAIN extension)

FROM: Gospers Mountain
TO: Capertee River gorge (return)
LENGTH: 32 km (16 each way)
TIME: 2 days
RIDE/TRACK GRADE: 7/8

WALKING: To the edge of the cliffs
HEIGHT VARIATION: 160 m
TRANSPORT: Extension of Ride 61 (see Ride 61 for details)
FACILITIES: None (complete self-sufficiency required). No water is available
MAPS: CMA (LIC) Gospers Mountain and Mount Morgan 1:25 000 topographicals

A two day extension of the previous ride is to cycle south from Gospers Mountain along an abandoned fire trail in order to access the edge of one of the largest gorges in the world—the Capertee. Three hundred cliffs line a majestic river as it winds its way through the largest forest area in Australia. This trail is the only one that accesses the top of this gorge.

From the summit of Gospers Mountain (847 m), head back down to the saddle and left. The trail follows a very gently sloping ridge south and then south-west and ends about 2 km short of the cliff edge where you can either wheel the bikes or walk to the edge. There are many fallen trees and towards the end, it gets quite narrow. About 6 litres of water must be carried for this overnight extension.

The best vantage points are to the right, camping almost directly opposite Freshwater Creek. The bushbashing on the final section here is not too bad due to the dry open nature of the vegetation. However all allow a full day to travel from Gospers Mountain to the Capertee Gorge due to the difficult terrain. Make sure to mark the end of the trail in your memory for the return trip, as it can be difficult to find.

OTHER RIDES IN WOLLEMI NATIONAL PARK

Because of the wilderness nature of Wollemi, there is not much more that one can explore by bicycle. What trails there are, are blocked by private property. Most end on ridgetops requiring backtracking. Descents into valleys are extremely difficult in most places due to the exposed sheer cliffs. Rockclimbing skills are essential if this sort of cycling, walking, abseiling, camping combination is to be done. The northern part of the national park, featuring the Wilden, Baerami, and Martindale Valleys contains only agricultural land and the access roads are all dead ends or private property. The only exception is the Narrango-Main Access Road from Rylstone to Three Ways. The Hunter Range can then be followed north-east to Raspberry Junction. The best exit from the park is via Sheepskin Hut (camping allowed here) along the Electricity Commission service road to Appletree Flat and then to the nearest railway station at Singleton. From Lithgow Station to Singleton would require about 10 days without so much as a general store for resupply.

Other extended tours follow the Hunter and Wollemi Ranges. However these are generally too long to do without access to water.

For mortals, Deep Pass is an interesting destination. Set in the Wollangambe Wilderness area, it can be accessed by fire trail from Newnes Junction, or Bell Station. For details, see Neil Paton's *Walks in the Blue Mountains*.

FURTHER INQUIRIES

Regional Office: National Parks and Wildlife Service
    Govetts Leap Road, Blackheath (047) 87 8877
  Other District Offices:
    Musellbrook Branch, Bridge Street (065) 43 3533 (North and east Wollemi)
    Oberon Branch (063) 36 1972
    Richmond Branch (045) 88 5247
    Wilberforce Branch (045) 75 1671
  Lithgow Tourist Information Bureau (063) 51 2307

GRASS
TREE

7
Morton National Park

Size: 170 297 hectares including Budawang National Park
Enactment: 1938 Morton Primitive Area
           1967 Declared a National Park
           1970 Major extensions
           1981 Budawang National Park created
Visitors: In the north, many casual sightseers frequent Fitzroy Falls, Bungonia Caves, and Tallowa Dam. In the south, visitors are restricted by the wilderness nature of the Budawangs. Experienced walkers and clubs are the main users of this end of the Park. The exception is Pigeon House, a popular lookout for coastal holidayers.
Aboriginal Sites: An interesting well preserved bora ground exists on Quintly's Mountain in the mid-south. Humans have occupied the region for about 20 000 years. In the heart of the Clyde Valley, carbon dating has found remains about 3500 years old. Cave paintings and sharpening grooves have also been found.
Flora: With its great variation in altitude and habitats, Morton National Park has one of the most diverse vegetation covers in Australia. The tablelands have a thin cover of heath, while forests, swamps, woodlands, and rainforests all occur within the park.
Camping: In the south, no facilities are provided, and apart from Monolith Valley, camping is permitted almost anywhere. In the north there are several developed camping areas. Gambells Rest (Bundanoon—reservations required), and Fitzroy Falls both allow for car camping, and a developed campsite also occurs at Bungonia Caves in the Bungonia State Recreation Area near Goulburn.
Fauna: Dingoes, brumbies, grey kangaroos, native mice, pygmy possums, koalas, gliders, dragons, and pythons among others.
District Office: Berry Street, Nowra. Visitors centre at Fitzroy Falls
Adjoining Parks: Budawang National Park adjoins the south, together with adjoining state forests which include Macdonald, Croobyar, Yadboro, Flat Rock, Clyde, Currawan, and

272

Monga. To the west, various plots of freehold, leasehold, and crown land separate the national park from the more built up areas of Braidwood and Goulburn.

Those wishing to experience one of the truly great national parks of Australia can do much worse than visit the incredibly scenic Morton. The park is basically divided into three general sections: the northern end and the southern end with a core of inaccessible wilderness in between. The majestic Shoalhaven River cuts a 500 m gorge through the north of the park, and its tributaries have also cut narrow deep canyons where swimming or canoeing are popular pastimes. Just nearby, the Bungonia Caves provide an interesting display of limestone sculpture. Further east, lies the wonderful Glow Worm Glen.

Around to the north lie 80 m high Fitzroy Falls which are quite impressive after heavy rain and only about 2 hours from Sydney. From there, an exciting cliff pass leads down into the Kangaroo Valley, across the historic Hampden Bridge, and the picnic area at Tallowa Dam lies only a short drive to the west in the middle of the national park.

But the south of the park provides even more sights for the visitor. Here the main attraction is the double-cliff lined Clyde Gorge with the famous Castle and Pigeon House standing at the opening. A strenuous three hour walk will take one to the mecca of bushwalkers in NSW: the Monolith Valley. People come from all round Australia to explore the maze of eerie domes and narrow ravines that distinguish this place from all others. Unfortunately the bike has to be left behind here, but there is an intricate network of logging roads that extend through the state forests to the south of the park that will satisfy any keen cyclist. Two of these forests, Yadboro and Flat Rock, are rivalled only by the Barrington Tops and Myall Lakes State Forests for aesthetic beauty.

Access to the northern end is via the Southern Freeway from Sydney. Between Mittagong and Marulan, numerous roads enter the park all finishing on the northern side of the Shoalhaven River. The centre of the park is accessed from Nowra via the unsealed road to Sassafras and Nerriga along the Pigeon House Range. To the south, access is via the Princes Highway turning right at Milton.

Despite its isolated location, access by public transport is still possible. Bundanoon on the Goulburn line is just 2.5 hours from Central. Along the coast, the Illawarra line terminates at Nowra and one can cycle directly into the park via the HMAS *Albatross* navy base, or catch the connecting bus service to Milton where the base of Pigeon House is some 3 hours of cycling to the west.

In order to fully appreciate the splendours of Morton, an overnight camping trip is a must. Backtracking can be avoided by taking full advantage of the old fire trails that interlace the park, and round trips from railway station to bus stop are perfectly possible with plenty of time for walking trips such as the exploration of the Monolith Valley. However, for those who aren't prepared for camping, one day rides around the Bungonia Caves, Bundanoon, and Fitzroy Falls are enjoyable and are becoming increasingly popular. Already the Southern Highlands is proving itself one of the most popular cycling areas in Australia.

The grading of the trails in Morton is just as varied as the terrain. Some are little more than walking tracks with fallen logs, rocks, and deep mud patches. Others are standard 2WD roads that are regularly graded. One should be careful after rain where one can be cut off from the coast as the park's fast flowing rivers have been known to flood extremely rapidly. Gradients are generally very good as few trails actually transcend the cliffs that separate the valleys from the plateau tops. In the north, all roads concentrate on the lookout circuit following the Shoalhaven River gorge, and therefore remain relatively flat. In the south, the foothills of the Budawangs create gently undulating hills with rises of no more than 200 m.

Please note that on overnight rides, it is recommended by the park authorities that you leave details of your intended trip with either the Rangers at Fitzroy Falls (048) 87 7270 or the Park authorities at Nowra (044) 21 9969.

RIDE 63: BUNDANOON

FROM: Bundanoon Station
TO: Lookout circuit
LENGTH: 22 km (half of which is walking)
TIME: Easy day
RIDE/TRACK GRADE: 3/3

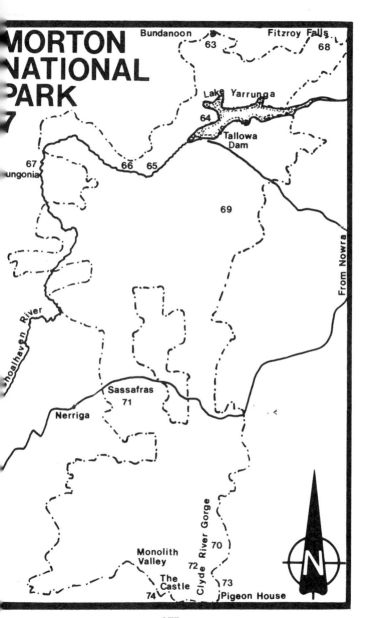

MORTON
NATIONAL
PARK
7

Bundanoon
63
Fitzroy Falls
68

Lake Yarrunga
64
Tallowa Dam

67
ungonia
66 65

69

From Nowra

Shoalhaven River

Sassafras
71

Nerriga

Clyde River Gorge
70

Monolith
Valley
72
The
Castle
74
73
Pigeon House

N

WALKING: Cliff walks, Nicholas pass, Glow Worm Glen
HEIGHT VARIATION: 50 m cycling, 300 m walking
TRANSPORT: Rail (Goulburn line). Approximately 2.5 hours
from Central
FACILITIES: Shops and bike hire (from 'Ye Olde Bicycle
Shoppe on Church Street) at Bundanoon. General picnic
facilities are scattered among the various lookouts. There are
almost a dozen developed campsites in the vicinity
SPECIAL EQUIPMENT: Torch and bike lock
MAPS: CMA (LIC) Bundanoon 1:25 000 topographical (or
NRMA Southern Highlands holiday map)

For those sick of lookouts, this is not the ride for you. The
lookout circuit described in this section includes a sample of
the dozens of scenic vantage points over Bundanoon Gorge.
Myriad cliffs greet the sightseer, as does the maze of ravines
and canyons cut by water over millions of years. A number of
walking tracks lead from the lookouts down through cliff
passes. Features of interest here include an 1860s coal mine,
wet forest, fern-choked gullies, an amphitheatre, and most
popular of all—a glow worm glen with its natural light show.
    One can leave Sydney in the mid-morning and be at Bun-
danoon by lunch time. It is recommended that one spends the
afternoon exploring the lookouts by both bike and foot. In the
evening, one can follow the short track to the glow worm glen,
for it is only at night that the insects are visible. A torch is
needed to see the way.
    From Bundanoon Station, head down Constitution Hill
which is far steeper than it looks on the map. Gullies Road
then leads all the way to the first lookout on Mount Carnarvon. This plateau marks the southern limit of Hawkesbury
sandstone. Morton National Park is renowned by geologists
for its vast exposure of all types of stone, and the Shoalhaven
River itself has cut right through the various layers revealing
ancient Ordovician quartzites, over half a billion years old!
    About half way along Echo Point Road, a walking track
leads to the Erith Coal Mine on the right hand side. It was
operated over a century ago by the Sydney Melbourne Land
and Coal Company, which managed to bore a tunnel almost
half a kilometre into the mountain. The walk is steep, but only
takes 10–15 minutes each way.
    From Echo Point, there is another short walk along a ridge

to the tops of the second set of small cliffs overlooking Bundanoon Creek. On returning, one can then proceed to Bonnie View Lookout and Beauchamp Cliffs Lookout which are all just a few metres from the road. As the Bundanoon topographical map indicates, another gravel road can be taken to Gambells, Tooths, and Sunrise Point Lookouts, all within the general area and all giving variations of the same view of the dissected plateaus to the south.

From here a number of walks leave the road. It is recommended that bikes be locked up due to the popularity of the area. The most challenging is the Grand Canyon walk down to the creek, dropping 300 m in little more than a kilometre. Steps take you steeply down, past a track junction to the bottom. The return trip is up and right to Fairy Bower Falls. By means of some ladders, the track negotiates the cliffs up to more lookouts before reaching the road again. The whole journey takes about 90 minutes and is very strenuous but rewarding. An extension of this walk is to continue along the base of the cliffs at the bottom of the falls. This is called the Nicholas Pass and contains many ferns which thrive on the dripping moisture from the cliffs. Steps then lead out on Amphitheatre Lookout. To return to the bikes, one either has to take the Riverview Road to Gambells Rest or backtrack.

Cycle to Riverview Lookout Picnic Ground in the late afternoon and chain the bikes up. The sunset can be viewed from the Mark Morton Lookout, named after the parliamentarian who first instigated the idea of preserving this rugged wilderness. It was a pioneering parliamentary move, as the Tallowa Primitive Reserve was the first declared wilderness area in Australia. Continue back along the 4WD track to the walking trail turnoff. This follows the national park boundary fence to the Glow Worm Glen Track. Turn right down some steps for just over 100 m before entering the moist glen on Dimmocks Creek. Simply retrace the route back to the bikes and then cycle to the station. Be careful not to miss the last train as services finish early.

RIDE 64: PURNOO LOOKOUT

FROM: Caoura Road (turn-off with Cedar Road)
TO: Purnoo Lookout and Lake Yarrunga
VIA: Cedar Road
LENGTH: 42 km including 6 km walking
TIME: 1 day (option for overnight camping)
RIDE/TRACK GRADE: 5/7 (long steep uphill from Lake Yarrunga)
WALKING: None
HEIGHT VARIATION: 672 m cycling
TRANSPORT: Private transport starting point via Mittagong and Tallong
FACILITIES: None
MAPS: CMA (LIC) Caoura and Burrier 1:25 000 topographicals

Looking at the Caoura topographical map tells the whole story of this ride. The contour lines depicting the Shoalhaven River gorge are so close together that the entire depression looks like one solid red mass. Descending the 500 m to the bottom is a geologist's paradise, for one passes through a dozen different types of rock: Hawkesbury sandstone, Illawarra coal measures, Berry formation shales, tuffs, Nowra sandstones, Conjola siltstone, conglomerate, and the oldest of all: quartzite of the Carboniferous age. For the tourist, this is a paradise also, but for different reasons. One can spend hours relaxing by this great river far away from cars and civilisation. If you have one, bring an air-mattress along.

The first stop however is Purnoo Lookout, opposite Tallowa Dam. The starting point can be accessed from Mittagong through Mossvale and Bundanoon on the Wingello Road. Nine kilometres past Wingello turn left at Tallong and drive about 20 km through pastoral land. Park your car at the turn-off on to the Cedar Road. It is marked by an unofficial metal sign saying 'River Road to Lookout'.

Start cycling along a relatively flat surface before the topography closes in and soon you find yourself dropping off a narrow ridge. This is a spectacular section for cycling as track maintenance procedures have created many drainage humps hat assist in sending you airborne if you resist braking for a split-second.

This downhill deposits you on a flat ridge where it is easy cycling through pleasant terrain where a good average can be maintained. Due to the dry open nature of the vegetation, there are limited views to the north and south. We disturbed a large goanna when pedalling through this section. He unfortunately didn't hang around long enough to pose.

It doesn't take much more than an hour to reach the lookout. Near the end, you must ignore a turn-off to the right to Pauls Lookout. This will be explored on the return. Continue east to the very end. It's not possible to cycle exactly to the end due to gaps between several large rock platforms. However it's not much of a hassle to manhandle the bikes to the edge for photographs. You are presented with excellent views to the east over Lake Yarrunga and its tributaries. This is the very end of the Shoalhaven River's natural flow. It started some 250 km earlier at on the slopes of Big Badja Hill (1362 m) in the southern Deua National Park.

Next, head back up to the turn-off on the left. It was informally marked as 'service trail'. The northern part of the bush here has been burnt out. Another navigational marker is an old gate. The track drops immediately, the trail deteriorating as it becomes rockier and more slippery. We found cycling momentarily impossible due to the rough grade, but it soon gets better. After the short dramatic descent, it suddenly levels out as it curves west and enters pleasant forest, sheltered by the cliffs overhead. The rocks have almost completely disappeared, being replaced by leaves. There are many overhanging branches and little logs to jump on the 350 m descent and you must remember that one is entering the official Lake Yarrunga Catchment Area so all the normal conditions of the Water Board must be complied with: no fires, shooting, fishing, etc.

Pauls Lookout is little known and one would be unlucky to find anyone else there. It is accessible from the prominent hairpin bend which leads to a round-about. The track is very overgrown here. The view is of Tallowa Dam and part of Lake Yarrunga. Continuing on to the lake, there is a brief uphill before an extremely steep eroded final down hill. Cyclists with clipless pedals might want to release their feet for stability during this descent.

The tracks then emerges behind a wide camping ground

often used by canoeists. You are out of sight of the dam here and there are great views of the cliff-lined gorge. There are also heaps of firewood for anyone contemplating staying overnight. The water and the Cedar Road are the only way to get to this area. Swimming is great here, as is camping.

From here it is about two to three hours back to the car.

RIDE 65: BADGERY'S LOOKOUT

FROM: Tallong Station
TO: Badgerys Lookout (return)
VIA: Caoura Ridge Road
LENGTH: 16 km (8 km each way)
TIME: 1 day (option for overnight camping)
RIDE/TRACK GRADE: 2/3
WALKING: Medium–hard grade 4 km return walk down to Shoalhaven River
HEIGHT VARIATION: 40 m cycling, 490 m
TRANSPORT: Rail (Goulburn Line)
FACILITIES: Picnic area at Badgerys Point
SPECIAL EQUIPMENT: Day or overnight pack, bike lock
MAPS: CMA (LIC) Wingello and Caoura 1:25 000 topographicals

A ride for the walkers. The objective is quite simple. Catch a CityLink train (no bookings required—just hop on) to Tallong Station. The journey is about 3 hours from Central on weekends. Then it is a half hour bike ride to a dramatic lookout over the spectacular Shoalhaven River gorge when you can lock up the bikes and walk straight down to the water for a swim before returning to the bikes.

From Tallong Station, simply head south along the Caoura Ridge Road and turn right at the signposted Badgery Lookout turn-off. The cycling here is easy and fast. The walking track is easy to follow and will cause no navigational problems. However the climb back up from the river will cause some exhaustion problems as its direct route is very steep. Why not camp by the sandy beaches at the bottom before returning to the station the next day?

RIDE 66:   LONG POINT

FROM: Tallong Station
TO: Long Point Lookout (return)
VIA: Long Point Road
LENGTH: 16 km (8 km each way)
TIME: 1 day (option for overnight camping)
RIDE/TRACK GRADE: 2/3
WALKING: Hard grade 8 km return walk down to Shoal-
haven River via Kingpin Mountain
HEIGHT VARIATION: 40 m cycling, 490 m
TRANSPORT: Rail (Goulburn Line)
FACILITIES: Picnic area at Long Point
SPECIAL EQUIPMENT: Day or overnight pack, bike lock
MAPS: CMA (LIC) Wingello and Caoura 1:25 000
topographicals

Here's another ride for the walkers. Once again, the objective
is quite simple. Catch a CityLink train (no bookings required—
just hop on) to Tallong Station. The journey is about 3 hours
from Central on weekends. Then it's a half hour bike ride to
a dramatic lookout over the spectacular Shoalhaven River
gorge when you can lock up the bikes and walk straight down
to the water for a swim before returning to the bikes.

From Tallong Station, simply head west along the Wingello
Road for 2 km. Turn left at the signposted Long Point Lookout
turn-off. The cycling here is easy and fast. The walking track
is easy to follow and will cause no navigational problems.
However the climb back up from the river will cause some
exhaustion problems as certain sections are very steep. Why
not camp by the sandy beaches at the bottom before returning
to the station the next day?

RIDE 67:   BUNGONIA

FROM: Marulan Station
TO: Bungonia Lookdown (return)
VIA: Bungonia
LENGTH:
   Day 1: Marulan to Bungonia State Recreation Area 30 km

Day 2: General exploration of area including walking
5–10 km
Day 3: Bungonia State Recreation Area to Marulan 30 km
Total distance is 60 km
RIDE/TRACK GRADE: 3/3
WALKING: Round circuit half-day hard-grade walk through
Bungonia Canyon
HEIGHT VARIATION: 95 m cycling, 400 m walking
TRANSPORT: Train (Goulburn Line)
FACILITIES: General picnic and good camping facilities
(capacity of 600) at Bungonia State Recreation Area
MAPS: CMA Wingello, Bungonia, Towrang and Caoura
1:25 000 topographicals (The first three can be dispensed
with if you have the NRMA Southern Highlands Holiday
Map. Caoura 1:25 000 is needed for the walk)

Although this ride isn't through the Morton National Park
itself, it covers much the same type of area and has the added
bonus of dozens of caves, and a narrow limestone canyon
where Bungonia Creek joins the Shoalhaven River. The state
recreational area is 3836 hectares in size, and forms a very new
extension to the Morton National Park, although people have
been visiting the caves for a long time. Today the caves themselves can only be explored with a permit from the ranger,
Bungonia State Recreation Area, Bungonia 2580. Otherwise
phone (048) 48 4277 for details. The Bungonia cave reserve is
known among conservation historians as the oldest non-utilitarian reserve in the world. In 1872, Water Reserve No. 27 (for
Public Recreation and Water Supply) was gazetted. Prior to
this, land had only been reserved for commercial purposes:
timber reservations, water catchment stabilisation, etc.—not
for public recreation. About 50 000 people visit the lookdown
each year.

The cave entrances are scattered around the state recreation
area; some are only small holes in the ground, while others
are gaping entrances in the sides of hills. Some are named (e.g.
Hogans, Fossil, Drum), but most are simply numbered. The
dominant vegetation here is sparse, dry eucalypt forest.

Commence at Marulan (about 3 hours from Sydney) and
cycle south-west along the Hume Highway to the marked
Bungonia turn-off (3 km from the railway station). Pass
through cleared pastoral land on a typical country road before

meeting with another major road. Turn left, cross Bungonia Creek (notice how tame the watercourse is here) and pass through the quiet village of Bungonia. It is another half hour along relatively flat land to the entrance of the state recreation area. A large camping area is located to the left. The road proceeds to the very cliff tops, marked on the map as Bungonia Lookdown. There are actually two lookdowns, and both have walking tracks down to the canyon. The guard rails here were erected in 1891. Opposite is one of the most controversial mining locations in Australia—the South Marulan limestone quarry. Not only do its operations stand out like a sore thumb in this beautiful area directly opposite the lookout, but the constant noise of the trucks and explosions only adds to destroying the wilderness atmosphere. The quarry principally extracts limestone for use in Portland cement. It eventually plans to lower the level of the main pit to only 100 m above the level of Bungonia Creek. If it is late in the day, head back to the camping area and set up for the night.

Cave	Depth	Length	Comments
Acoustic Pot	68 m	104 m	Strange reflection and reverb effects. 30+ m vertical pitch.
Argyle Hole	97 m	274 m	Hard graded cave with many vertical pitches ending in a couple of pools.
Blowfly Cave	152 m	84 m	Many pitches, stale air. One of the deepest caves on the Australian mainland.
Drum Cave	125 m	412 m	Entry requires a very long 50 m vertical descent. Known for stale air.
Fossil Cave	131 m	1800 m	Known for stale air. Connects with Hogans Hole. Entrance can be blocked by water during protracted rain periods.
Grill Cave	127 m	610 m	Commonly known as Bungonia Cave. This was well visited by tourists during the pre-war years.

Cave	Depth	Length	Comments
Mass Cave	21 m	49 m	Easy access for walkers with a torch. No ropes needed. Catholic church services used to be held here.
Odyssey Cave	148 m	412 m	Experienced cavers only. High, decorated chambers. Accesses a subterranean watercourse.

The next day, it is suggested that the bikes be locked up back at the Lookdown and an interesting and scenically spectacular walk be done down to the canyon, through it and then up the other side. Despite the small distances involved, the walk is quite strenuous due to the considerable height variation but not technically difficult. All the walks around here are colour coded. For example, the white walk will take you to the Shoal-haven River. However, the red walk allows the most direct access to the bottom of Bungonia Creek. Good views of the canyon entrance are available on the descent. Some sections on the loose rock are quite slippery. Once you are down by the green coloured creek, you will see many large warning signs explaining what the sirens mean in relation to blasting. People should not be in the area if the mine intends to blast due to the danger of rubble crashing down the steep slopes.

The creek can be followed upstream to the canyon where massive boulders slow progress. The entrance to the canyon has a 300 m cliff on the left hand side known as Troy Walls. It is difficult to follow the track as you scramble over and under the giant limestone boulders. In addition your hands will get very white. If you lift a rock up you will notice that it is very dense.

Finally you emerge from the boulders on to a pebble strewn floor and you are into the canyon. Where has the creek gone? It is now subterranean, surfacing only during particularly pro-tracted rain. The canyon walls are very narrow here and because of their alignment, sunlight rarely reaches the bottom. With all the rock here, it is hard to figure out why the Abo-riginals called this creek 'Bungonia' meaning 'sandy creek'.

On the other side, you meet up with the creek again and

he track heads up a gully on the left climbing steeping via
he Efflux Track and a rocky slope to reach the top. It is then
asy walking east back to the bikes.

Once you have a rest from the climb, you could spend the
est of the day exploring the other lookouts. Adams Lookout
as very good views over a western amphitheatre containing
ome waterfalls. You can also explore some of the cave
ntrances to the south-east, before heading back on the third
ay. Make sure you have a torch.

RIDE 68: MERYLA PASS

ROM: Moss Vale Station
O: Nowra (Bomaderry Station)
IA: Fitzroy Falls and Kangaroo Valley
ENGTH:
   Day 1: Moss Vale to Fitzroy Falls Camping Area 21 km
   Day 2: Fitzroy Falls to Wombat Hill Lookout 20 km
   Day 3: Wombat Hill Lookout to Yarrunga Creek 17 km
   Day 4: Yarrunga Creek to Kangaroo Valley 45 km
   Total distance is 103 km
RIDE/TRACK GRADE: 6/7 (4WD tracks in this area are gen-
erally of reasonable quality)
WALKING: Short walks to various lookouts
HEIGHT VARIATION: 670 m
TRANSPORT: Rail (Goulburn and Illawarra Lines)
FACILITIES: Visitor Centre and picnic area at Fitzroy Falls
SPECIAL EQUIPMENT: Water provisions for overnight cliff-
top camping.
MAPS: CMA (LIC) Moss Vale, Bundanoon, Kangaroo Valley
and Berry 1:25 000 topographicals

Those wishing to explore the wilder parts of the north-eastern
Morton National Park would find this ride quite rewarding.
The route starts at Moss Vale and simply follows the Moss
Vale to Nowra Road before stopping at Fitzroy Falls to view
this very popular attraction. From here the going gets tough
with strictly 4WD tracks being taken through the Meryla State
Forest, dropping 500 m, and crossing the beautiful Yarrunga
Creek. From here the Water Board catchment area is entered,

and soon after historic Hampden Bridge is passed on the wa to Nowra where a train can be taken home again.

From Moss Vale Station, follow the road south to Nowr (Throsby Street and Yarrawa Road). Fitzroy Falls are 19 kr away on a sealed road through woodland with a reasonab' traffic load. This is the start of the Morton National Park, an a rangers headquarters, visitors centre, car park, toilets, an picnic tables are located here. Just before the main facilities ar reached, a turn-off on the right leads to Gwen Road and a fir trail that leads to Starkeys Lookout. Just south of this lookou a walking track leads to Renown Lookout. Of all of the doze or so lookouts around the two rims, this is by far the best fo it allows the several drops of the 300 m falls to be seen, includ ing the Lady Harden Falls at the very bottom. The largest o the falls, the very top one, is 81 m. If one feels fit one can tak the valley walk to the base of the falls where lush rainfores grows and the roar of the water is deafening. Opportunitie: for photography are limitless here if the sun just happens t be shining on the spray. The vegetation at the base include: red cedar, silver top ash, and turpentine. About 30–60 minute: has to be allowed for getting back up again, via a 7 m ladder

It is recommended to camp at the official camping grounc on the eastern side of the falls. This day is kept purposely shor to allow for the train journey and some exploration of the fall: area from various lookouts.

The next day, head back to Starkeys Lookout and follow the Redhill Fire Trail through private property and turn right a' Redhills Road. You are trespassing here at the goodwill of the landowners and as yet they haven't refused access. This is strictly a thoroughfare and should not be used for picnics, camping, or anything else. Pass more private property on both sides when travelling north along Redhills Road before turning left at the Gunrock Creek Fire Trail. This joins up at a junction and one should take the south-west option called the Links Fire Trail. Ignore turn-offs on the right and head down a flat ridge until cliffs force the trail to swing west. Turn left along cliffs until one comes to a junction with a road that doubles back and down. From here one continues to the right, proceeding along the cliff tops to Wombat Hill Lookout. The track peters out on a ridge some 5 km later. There are fine views here over Lake Yarrunga and upper Yarrunga Creek, but unfortunately the Fitzroy Falls themselves are obscured by

iffs. Set up your camping gear overnight. If you are fortunate
n the morning, you might be rewarded with a cloud covering
f the gorge below you.

Backtrack to Meryla Pass and check both brakes and your
anity. From the lookout, the old private property at Gales Flat
s clearly visible. What follows is a hair-raising, non-stop
escent to Crankeys Creek along a fairly rough, windy road.
his pass was used over 160 years ago by an explorer named
Charles Throsby on his way to Jervis Bay from Sydney. Be
ure not to overshoot the junction about half way down. The
ake Yarrunga catchment area is entered via a gate, and one
ollows Yarrunga Creek upstream along the Griffins Fire Trail
ast an abandoned farm. It is pleasant cycling along here. Just
ooking at the derelict remains, the property owner must have
ad a peaceful existence in this tranquil isolated valley, shel-
ered from the outside world. Camp anywhere you want along
Yarrunga Creek, preferably as close to the crossing as possible
n order to minimise the distance on the final day. 'Yarrunga'
s the Aboriginal word for 'large trees'.

The next morning, rise early and ford the creek, before
scending 150 m heading south. At another gate, the catchment area is exited and a dirt road leads to the Bundella Power
Station where a sealed road takes you to Kangaroo Valley. For
ome reason I had several punctures in a row on this road, so
don't know if there were tacks scattered along the surface,
r if it was plain bad luck.

Check out the historic Hampden Bridge to the left before
ncading east and then south to Nowra along sealed roads. Just
ollow the road signs to Bomaderry Train Station.

RIDE 69: YALWAL

FROM: Nowra (Bomaderry Station)
TO: Yalwal (Danjera Dam) (return)
VIA: Yalwal Road, Yarramunmun Creek
LENGTH:
   Day 1: Nowra to Yalwal 32 km
   Day 2: Yalwal to Yarramunmun Creek (Fletchers Flat)
14 km
   Day 3: Yarramunmun Creek to Nowra 39 km

Total distance is 85 km
RIDE/TRACK GRADE: 6–7/7 (steep uphill from Yarramun-mun Creek to Deans Gap Road)
WALKING: None
HEIGHT VARIATION: 330 m
TRANSPORT: Rail (Illawarra Line)
FACILITIES: None
MAPS: CMA (LIC) Nowra and Yalwal 1:25 000 topographicals

Yalwal has long been popular with four wheel drivers as long weekend destination. Much of the area is through stat forest and restrictions on driving and camping are limited. A the time of writing, the NSW state government is considerin the reservation of a wilderness area centred on Yalwal wit possible restrictions on motor vehicle use.

For the same reasons as four wheel drivers enjoy the area mountain bike riding at Yalwal is good fun due to the larg number of open scenic trails through the valley. The lan immediately surrounding Lake Danjera has many features c historical interest and the second day of riding has been pur posely kept short to allow time to check out all the sights.

The directions are quite simple. From Bomaderry, heac south to Nowra and then south-west on to Albatross Road This leads to the HMAS *Albatross* base. However, you shoul turn right on to Yalwal Road and travel west into the Shoal haven State Forest. The road gradually climbs to Bamaran; Reservoir and then descends to Cleymea Creek where you ar almost at sea level once more. Yalwal Road then branches lef climbing steeply to meet power lines which it parallels south west to Deans Gap Road. Head right here, keeping to th centre of the plateau, still gradually climbing almost all th way to Yalwal Gap.

From the top of the plateau, it is a radical direct descen down to Yarramunmun Creek. Watch out for vehicles comin; the other way. Cross the creek and head south to the campin; area by the lake. Yalwal was once a gold mining establishment The original station was first bought by Dr McKenzie in 1841 Twelve years later, the Commissioner for Crown Land, M A. Mackay notified government authorities that there was a possibility of gold in the area, a claim later supported by the geologist responsible for surveying the area, Rev. W. Clarke

Wolgan Lookout (Ride 56)

The Wolgan River downstream from Newnes (Ride 58)

The Capertee River downstream from Glen Davis (Ride 59)

Glen Davis and the Capertee Gorge (Ride 59)

Three prospectors in the 1870s found gold at Bundundah and Danjera Creeks. By the 1890s, mining operations were in full swing and Yalwal had its heyday—shops, houses, bank, school of arts, and hotel. By World War I, all viable gold had been extracted and the town became deserted. In January 1939 the area was wiped out by savage bushfires.

The next day, after exploring the ruins, head south and then right over the Jinkbilly Range, past the old Telecom transmitter tower, and down to Deans Flat at Yarramunmun Creek. Ford the water and turn right cycling along the bottom of the valley to Fletcher Flat where camp should be made for the second night. On the opposite side of the valley is the Yalwal plateau lined by partially broken cliffs.

On the final day, Nowra can be accessed by the rough Wombat Flat Road (marked on the map as Mintbush Trail) to the Deans Gap Road. It is a very steep climb reflecting the terrific descent you had the first day from Yalwal Gap. Deans Gap Road should be followed north back to Yalwal Road. Many maintenance trails branch off to the left and right, servicing the overhead power lines.

Another option for exploration is to follow Ettrema Creek up a spectacular gorge. Four wheel drivers have cut through the road, removing many fallen trees and allowing deep penetration into the core wilderness of the central Morton National Park.

RIDE 70:   TIANJARA PLATEAU

FROM: Nowra Station (Bombaderry)
TO: Milton
VIA: Porters Creek Dam
LENGTH:
   Day 1: Nowra to Tianjara Falls 45 km
   Day 2: Tianjara Falls to Porters Creek Dam 42 km
   Day 3: Porters Creek Dam to Milton 28 km
   Total distance is 115 km.
RIDE/TRACK GRADE: 4/6
WALKING: Optional overnight walking to Gadara Point, Mount Talaterang and Pigeon House Creek Canyon
HEIGHT VARIATION: 670 m

TRANSPORT: Rail (Illawarra Line), Bus (Pioneer Coach service from Milton to Bomaderry/Sydney)
FACILITIES: None
MAPS: CMA (LIC) Nowra, Yalwal, Sassafras, Tianjara and Milton 1:25 000 topographicals (one could get by with an NRMA road map of the south coast, e.g. 'Central Coast and Illawarra', and the Northern Budawang 1:50 000 sketch map)

Those wishing to visit the gentler parts of the Budawangs can be advised to consider this suggestion. Despite the considerable height variation, most of the cycling on the first day is along the top of a flat plateau to a very good camping area by Tianjara Falls. The second day is along an eastern plateau in the Budawangs that gives good views not only to the spectacular Clyde River gorge but to the coast as well. The last day simply involves a downhill ride to Milton where a bus can be taken back to Nowra or Sydney. This takes some organisation and tickets can be booked in advance. An extra freight fee is charged for the bikes and the front wheel has to be taken off, so make sure you have the right tools. For details, contact the Ansett Pioneer Motor Service on (044) 21 7722. Tickets can also be bought at the bus company's agent in Milton (the white service station on the eastern end) although you are not guaranteed a seat.

Cycle north once you leave Bomaderry to Nowra, crossing the wide expanse of the Shoalhaven River. Turn right at Kalandar Street and left at Albatross Road. Follow the signs to the HMAS *Albatross* naval base. The road becomes unsealed when passing the runway. Stay on this road for another 35 km gradually rising up on to the Turpentine Range. Tianjara Falls are on the right, but are often dry in summer due to lack of rain. The views over the Yarramunmun valley are quite good. Your own water is needed here on the first night as fresh water can't be guaranteed unless it has just been raining heavily.

The next day, head east for one kilometre. The start of Twelve Mile Road is not very well marked. You can also use the runway to get there. The turn-off is a fairly low-key affair surrounded by dry eucalypt forest and standard bush scrub. What distinguishes it from the other service trails is the better quality of the road for it is essentially a dry weather road for conventional vehicles. You will know you are on the road for you immediately cross under the power lines with excellent views east to the coast. The two right turnoffs to the landing ground which are marked on the map are basically overgrown dead-ends and should be ignored.

This part of the trail can be very muddy at times and I had the bad luck of cycling along here after a lot of rain. Consequently there were places where I wanted to remount after taking some photographs but only found the handlebars sticking out. It is 7 km along a gradually undulating good quality road to the turn-off on to the Tianjara Fire Trail. Be warned that this is sometimes used as a military range and there are apparently many unexploded shells in the vicinity. At the t-intersection at the base of a grass covered hill, turn right on to a very rocky 4WD track along the side of the Kangaroo Hill. To the right there are glimpses of the upper Clyde Gorge. The trail undulates through open heath country and one extremely steep but short slope is encountered when cresting the Tianjara ridge. Once past the prominent mountain, the road swings east in a gradual arc and fast easy cycling can be maintained on the flat smooth parts. There are also distant views of Pigeon House and part of the Castle, but the mountain that dominates the south is the Talaterang massif. The walls of the plateau momentarily close in on the track, forming a sort of narrow-neck. It is 16 km from the previously mentioned t-intersection to here and it might be worthwhile having lunch here. Good views are obtained particularly on top of the eastern cliffs looking north to Jervis Bay and east to Conjola Lakes. But what steals the show are the numerous incredibly deep crevasses on either side of the road. One can very readily imagine that soon there'll be a rift where the Tianjara Plateau will become separated from the Little Forest Plateau.

The trail becomes rockier past here with long patches of loose pebbles and even some small pools to cross. One hugs the eastern cliffs before ascending to the landing strip. Once past this there are more views to Mount Talaterang but these are obscured as the road enters forest with a lot of green regrowth just after a junction. There is a gradual but long downhill. Be careful of traffic however as this part of the Porters Lake is frequently visited by the locals. The road gets better before it gets worse. Climb up to a junction and a locked gate which isn't marked on the map. Bikes don't have to lifted over however as there is an embankment on the side where one can simply ride over. The track then swings around to the north before descending down a very gradual slope to the Porters Creek Dam wall itself.

The road actually continues below the dam until it ends at a collapsed bridge across Porters Creek. On the other side one can see the remains of a very old trail swinging around to the left. Before the bridge, on the way down to this unmarked road, there is a small clearing on the left which makes an excellent campsite with a reasonable amount of firewood. The dam was built in 1967 to supply Milton and Ulladulla with water. The rule here is that there is no swimming in the lake. Be on your best behaviour, for rangers regularly come down to inspect the lake.

The third day can either be spent walking or cycling down to Milton. Good trails in the area include a round circuit to the very wild Pigeon House Creek Gorge. It should be stressed that the Budawang terrain is for experienced walkers only and good navigational skills are essential. The trails are sometimes indistinguishable from the bush. Dozens of parties have been lost around the Talaterang mountain and the descent in and out of the Pigeon House Creek Gorge requires good climbing skills. Ropes aren't usually needed but are recommended for people who are less confident on rock. Less demanding walks are out to Florence and Rusden Heads and these trails are marked on the map. Both can be done in a leisurely pace within a few hours leaving the rest of the day to relax at the campsite.

The Pigeon House Creek Gorge is a challenging hike involving two long days. Cross what is left of the bridge below the dam. The trail soon thins out and one should make one's own way along the cliffs to Gadara Point. There is no track. Towards the end there is a broad plain that must be crossed containing thousands of prickly stunted bushes that will lacerate bare legs, so make sure trousers are worn. To make matters worse, there are many water-filled 'contour-trenches' that demand more concentrated walking. However this obstacle course ends with fantastic views over the Clyde River Gorge which has fully matured in size since it was previously seen from the Tianjara Plateau. The double-cliffs of the unmistakable Castle contrast strongly to the forest covered slopes of the massive Mount Talaterang in the foreground. The cliff tops are then followed to a cairned route down through a crevice and a pleasant ridge top walk around a knoll ends up at Pallin

Pass. Walkers here should have the Budawang sketchmap as standard equipment as well as having read Chapter 2 from *Pigeon House and Beyond*, both available from camping stores such as Paddy Pallin. And to speak of the devil, the way up to the summit of Talaterang is via Pallin Pass named after the man himself when he discovered the route in 1956. A visitors book can be signed on top and then one hugs the western cliff tops, passing across a sea of ferns, and dropping through a rocky gully on to a ridge that leads to Warre Head. Needed here is the Corang 1:25 000 map. If one has left early enough from the dam, it is possible to make the gorge in one day. If not, one can camp by one of the many creeks that plummet over the edge of Warre Head. Full tracknote descriptions are given in the Pigeon House book mentioned above. The bottom of the gorge is a spectacle in itself: huge trees, numerous wind-cut caves, falls, and natural conglomerate arches and domes. There are camping sites along the bottom but not much dry firewood due to the lack of any prolonged period of sunlight. The climb out again basically involves ascending the series of rock rings up a very steep slope. Once up the top, a fire trail is reached and a rocky pass leads up a chimney on to Rusden Head.

When you've had enough, or time is limited, ride down Pointer Gap Road. The lookout is not really worth seeing as it repeats what was seen on the first day, although there are views to the south here. The obvious way out is to cross over Pointer Mountain and thence to the highway, but unfortunately this is private property and the owners are quite protective of their land. Therefore the normal road must be followed, which was just being sealed the last time I rode down. It passes through uneventful rural country. One moderately steep hill is climbed once Currowar Creek is crossed, but is basically downhill once on the Princes Highway to the township of Milton.

RIDE 71:   SASSAFRAS
(THE VINES CIRCUIT)

FROM: Sassafras
TO: The Vines

VIA: Tanderra Camp, Endrick River
LENGTH:
   Day 1: Sassafras to The Vines via Tanderra Camp 18
   Day 2: The Vines to Endrick River via Nerriga 27
   Day 3: Endrick River to Sassafras via Bulee Gap 20 km
   Total distance is 65 km
RIDE/TRACK GRADE: 6/7 (steep uphill to Bulee Gap)
WALKING: Limitless options. The best walks include Quiltys
Mountain Bora Ground, Folly Point, and Hidden Valley
HEIGHT VARIATION: 760 m
TRANSPORT: Private transport to Sassafras via Nowra
FACILITIES: None
MAPS: CMA (LIC) Sassafras, Nerriga, Tianjara and Endrick
1:25 000 topographicals. If walking, the *Northern Budawang
Range and Upper Clyde River Valley* 1:50 000 Sketchmap pub-
lished by the Budawang Committee is essential as it shows
major negotiable routes and camping spots through the area.
It is available at camping stores such as Paddy Pallin.

For more adventurous mountain bikers, this ride follows
disused fire trails in the central Morton National Park. The
territory is extremely wild and the cyclist has to be totally self-
sufficient for the duration of the trip. Since this is wilderness
area, camping is allowed anywhere and the streams and creeks
here are all unpolluted. Because of the rugged terrain and var-
iable condition of the tracks, progress is slow and even the
fittest cyclists will be pushing to average 15 kph.
   However the benefits are worthwhile. This country is where
the mountain bike comes into its own. Trails pass through
dense rainforest in cliff lined valleys, open heathlands on
plateau tops, dry tall forest, and rocky mountain passes.
Walking sidetrips include the sacred Aboriginal bora ground
with its well preserved stone arrangements, weird rock formations in narrow gorges, and various lookouts over the coast
and waterfalls.
   Drive to Nowra and then inland on the Sassafras (Nowra to
Braidwood) Road via HMAS *Albatross*. Continue past Tianjara
Falls and park the car at the start of a small private property
road between an old house and a large iron shed (marked on
the map). There is an old farmhouse on the opposite side of
the gate which is marked 'hut' on the map. This is the
Newhaven Gap Road and the national parks authorities have

purposely made it a low key affair to discourage overuse. Near the start is a sign explaining that you're entering the Morton National Park through private property. Cycle south through private property over undulating country. The road here deteriorates further (Grade 4–5) and follows a ridge that marks the beginning of the Budawang Range. Leave *ALL* gates as you found them. There are five which you have to open and close. Water falling on the right of the road will end up in the Shoalhaven River and eventually find its way north to Nowra, while water falling on the left contributes to the Clyde River that flows south to Batemans Bay.

Once on the Tianjara 1:25 000 topographical map, the national park is entered and the occasion is marked by a gate. The road gets quite rough from here on and it is quite hard to imagine some people bringing conventional 2WD vehicles in here. A kilometre to the east, the Clyde River has already begun to cut its famous gorge into the rock. On the other side of the river is the Tianjara Plateau which is sometimes used as a military training ground and artillery range. There are apparently many unexploded shells within this area and cyclists and walkers should not venture off formed tracks.

After about 11 km along this road, a sign and gate prevents further progress by cars. From here on only pushbikes and walkers are permitted. This is Tanderra Camp (Aboriginal for resting place) set amongst open scrub at the confluence of Strang Creek and another smaller stream. The car-park is often used as a camping area. No water or other facilities are available. One can either have the option of camping here or slightly further on in the densely forested Vines area. Two large overhangs exist here: Camp Rock and Red Johnny's Cave. These are 2 caves with historic significance. Near the second one, a copy of the *Sydney Morning Herald* dating back to 1919 was found in recent times which had been left there by John Rolfe. This man, nicknamed Red Johnny because of his red beard, had occupied the cave when he was grazing cattle in the area. However he was also suffering from cancer and spent most of his last days there before dying in Nowra Hospital a few weeks later. The other cave, marked on the map as Camp Rock, was also used by a grazier and his family well over 100 years ago. Along the way from Newhaven Gap to The Vines are occasional views over the desolate rocky terrain with some unusual rock formations.

The second day can be spent exploring this region. The Vines is a central place in the Budawangs within easy walking of the Bora Ground on Quiltys Mountain or the pretty Hidden Valley inside Sturgiss Mountain. A popular circuit from here is through the rainforest to the upper Kilpatrick Creek and thence around Sturgiss Mountain to the spectacular Pagoda Rocks, through the pass alongside Mount Elliot, across the top of Sluice Box Falls and finally up Watson Pass to Folly Point where a visitors book can be signed. A proper track then leads back north past Mitchell Lookout to the trail from Newhaven Gap. This is a very long day of difficult walking and is best broken into two by camping in Hollands Gorge where water is readily available. Good navigation and experience is essential as this area is primary wilderness country with relatively few walkers. Once you leave the 4WD trail, the track is a negotiable route which sometimes involves using your imagination. For more information, get hold of the information-packed *Pigeon House and Beyond* published by the Budawang Committee. Chapter 2 outlines tracknotes for walks in this region.

A much shorter walk however is to the Aboriginal bora ground on Quiltys Mountain. From Red Johnnys Cave proceed west until you come to the junction of the two trails. The right one leads north exiting the area via the old Wool Road while the left one curves around Quiltys Mountain via Styles Creek. Take the left one up to a crest where a reasonably good quality walking track heads right. The place is marked by a huge fallen tree. The bikes must be left here and you should have no problem hiding them. Neither the walking track nor the bora ground are marked on the map but it is fairly easy to follow up a short rocky slope to the heath and scrub country which is so characteristic of the plateau tops of the Budawangs. The track is marked by a combination of cloth tied to scrubs, rock cairns, and arrows. There are a small series of rock ledges to negotiate but they present no technical difficulty. The track can be followed through here by a series of rock cairns. Once to the top of the plateau head left along various rock platforms. Please remember that the rock formations are not to be touched or disturbed in any way. It is also interesting to note the profusion of large quartzite boulders scattered over the plateau. The views over the Vines Creek gorge are quite good.

This is by no means the only bora ground in the Budawangs.

The region has a rich pre-European history with evidence of ceremonial grounds being found on Mount Kingiman in the eastern region and in the Ettrema wilderness area to the north. The local tribes would gather for occasions such as initiations and end the ceremony by trading all sorts of goods: rugs, paint, medicines, tools, weapons, hunting implements, baskets, and furs.

Make sure you locate the rock cairns before descending through the rock ledges back to the bikes, and proceed north by Vines Creek to open cleared land which used to be grazing land a century ago. Along the way one passes the ruins of Michael Dowlings Hut, built in 1880. Although not marked on the map, other old miners, loggers, and graziers huts are scattered throughout the area. However, not much is left these days.

Several gates are passed on the way out to the small settlement of Nerriga. Once on the Sassafras road again, you are on the other side of the Budawangs. To get back to your car at Sassafras, you must head north and then east and cross the range again. Some supplies can be bought at Nerriga if the service station is open. Camp down by the Endrick River on the other side of the town.

On the last day, there is a long 200 m climb up again to Bulee Lookout, with views over the country you've just passed through. The cycling here becomes very easy as the terrain is flat and through relatively uneventful country back to Sassafras.

RIDE 72: CLYDE RIVER

FROM: Yadboro
TO: Tinga Clearing (return)
VIA: Clyde River
LENGTH: 18 km
TIME: 1–2 days
RIDE/TRACK GRADE: 3–4/7
WALKING: None
HEIGHT VARIATION: 80 m
TRANSPORT: Private transport to Yadboro via Milton
FACILITIES: None
MAPS: CMA (LIC) Corang 1:25 000 topographical

Mountain bikers who have 'graduated' from a few rides in the Blue Mountains might like to progress to other parks. Here's an introduction to the grandeur of the magnificent Budawang mountains. All that's involved is a short ride along the beautiful Clyde River where the massive Byangee Walls plateau shields you from civilisation. The objective is to camp south of Tinga Clearing in the middle of the spectacular Clyde River Gorge. The size of the clearing by the river allows you unobscured views to the surrounding double-cliff formations.

Drive to Milton via Nowra. The Crooybar Road heads west and then south. According to the map, it branches off to the right but you should drive straight, continuing south until it turns to dirt. Soon after, head right following the signs to Yadboro and Pigeon House. Keep right on Clyde Ridge Road at the next intersection and ignore the next turn-off right to Pigeon House. The road undulates through various creek valleys before a steady descent down to the Clyde River at Yadboro. Park just after the bridge on either side in the Yadboro State Forest camping ground. Cycle back across the bridge and head left on Deadman's Gulch Road paralleling the river towards the impressive cliffs of the Byangee Walls plateau. A locked gate at the beginning is signposted, warning that this track gives access to private property. The track rises gradually, giving partially obscured views over the camping areas on the other side of the river, as well as to The Castle. After a gradual ascent, the track comes to another locked gate where it exits the Yadboro State Forest.

A portion of this track ride is through the 'Byangee View' property. The former landowner used to allow genuine bushwalkers to pass through to Tinga clearing. However the property has recently changed hands and it is advisable to ask permission or to take the trail to the right after crossing a paddock and a deep ditch. The landowner is conscious of the fact that property could be stolen by trespassers. Every attempt should be made to respect the property and privacy of the landowner. If the road is taken to the right, you should be into the national park within 10 minutes of leaving the Yadboro State Forest. This tracks parallels a perimeter fence until it comes to a gate where a Morton National Park sign prohibits vehicles. The track then climbs as it winds its way around several prominent spurs before a steep descent down to the Clyde River. It should have taken about an hour to get to this crossing from Yadboro. If the day is hot, why not swim in one of the pools downstream?

The track continues on the other side, first through open forest with some fallen logs, and then up a steep rocky hill that crosses a spur from Pickering Point. The bikes will probably need to be pushed up this 80 m hill before a great descent takes you into the wilderness. The forest opens up and you are in the upper Clyde River gorge! Cliffs line the river valley on all sides. Occasionally reminders of the pioneering past exist here: old water tanks, stock yards, etc.

The clearings marked on the topographical map are now largely overgrown with bracken fern, causing even the track to be sometimes indistinguishable from the undergrowth. It is only when it climbs spurs that it again resembles a road.

The first large flat gives unsurpassed views to the surrounding cliffs. Pigeon House stands behind you while the entrance to the eerie Pigeon House Creek Gorge is just to the right. One can camp where one wishes. For example, on the northern side of the first open fern covered clearing, a minor foot pad heads right straight to the river. Some grassy flats and direct access to the water makes this an ideal bush camping site. Other sites exist where the track crosses the Clyde River further upstream.

There is evidence to suggest that Tinga Clearing is not natural. Theories about its formation include consistent controlled Aboriginal backburning. Despite the short distance to the upper headwaters, the Clyde River is very well developed at this stage and many swimming holes exist. Simply return the next day or two by the same route. If you'd like some walking exploration, why not follow the river upstream to the spectacular Hollands Gorge. Many natural campsites exist along here. Other possible walking destinations include the deep sandstone caves of Pigeon House Creek Gorge, or attaining the top of the Byangee Walls plateau for impressive views over the Clyde River Gorge.

RIDE 73: PIGEON HOUSE

FROM: Milton
TO: Yadboro Flat

LENGTH:

Day 1: Milton to Yadboro Flat via Pigeon House plateau
33 km

Day 2: Yadboro Flat to Milton 45 km

Total distance is 77 km

TIME: 2–3 days

RIDE/TRACK GRADE: 7/8 (mainly 4/2–3)

WALKING: To Pigeon House summit by means of ladders.
Easy–Medium grade

HEIGHT VARIATION: 480 m

TRANSPORT: Rail to Nowra (Illawarra Line), and a connecting bus to Milton. Alternatively a car can be taken to
Yadboro Flat

FACILITIES: Shops at Milton, and a good camping ground at
Yadboro

MAPS: CMA (LIC) Milton, Corang, Brooman and Tabourie
1:25 000 topographicals

This ride takes you around one of the most famous landmarks
on the south coast. First sighted by white man in 1770 when
Captain Cook noted in his diary 'a remarkable peaked hill
which resembled a square dovehouse with a dome on top and
for that reason I called it Pigeon House'. The view from the
stone-capped summit (720 m) ranks as one of the best in the
state. To the north and south are nothing but unblemished
mountains. The rugged Clyde River gorge dominates the view.
At the end of Byangee Walls the legendary Castle beckons to
anyone with a sense of adventure. Walking up to the summit
is attained by means of steel ladders for convenience. Pigeon
House is a very popular tourist walk along a well maintained
track.

If using public transport, catch the train to Bomaderry where
a Pioneer bus leaves for Eden. Bookings are recommended and
the number to contact is (044) 21 7722. Get off at Milton which
is a small coastal south between Conjola Lakes and Ulladulla.
Head right (south) off the highway by taking any one of the
four roads down. Turn right at the bottom of the hill on to
Croobyar Road which curves around south and then west. A
long stretch through boring agricultural land has to be
endured before the forest is entered just a little further on. Any
one of the several fire trails can be taken up a spur to the
Kingiman ridge. It is recommended that the trail marked as

the Croobyar Creek Fire Trail be taken as this doesn't infringe on private property but instead passes through beautiful state forest. It's a steady climb of 200 m to the ridge. If one wants to climb the summit of the prominent Mount Kingiman (390 m), it can be attained by a short scramble from the eastern side. This mountain had a special significance to the Aborigines for it was a central meeting place on festive occasions where tribes from the local area would meet. The main tribes in the Budawangs were the Walbangas and the Wandandians, who occupied an area from the Shoalhaven River in the north to Moruya in the south: about 1000 people spread throughout 9000 square kilometres!

From Mount Kingiman, one can either continue descending down the ridge and taking two right turns to reach the Jindelara Creek road, or one can back track and drop down a steep spur on to the same road. In any case they're both downhill and lead to the same place through dense, wet forest. Although not marked on the map, there is a gate here just before the creek preventing vehicular access up on to the Pigeon House plateau. It is recommended that one has a small rest here and fills up with water for it is a long strenuous climb over the plateau before the next water at the Clyde River.

Jindelara Creek marks the entrance to the Morton National Park. Commence the steep climb along the Pigeon House Fire Trail (Grade 7). The gradient gets less steep as time goes by but it still is a non-interrupted uphill trudge. Good views back to the coast are obtained once sufficient height is reached to clear the Kingiman Ridge. In total, some 400 m must be gained. When you reach the t-intersection on Wombat Ridge turn left heading directly towards the looming mass of Pigeon House. This trail is marked as a walking track but in reality was an old fire trail which followed an Aboriginal track down Longfella Ridge spur. The track quality here is the worst of the two days and makes for some challenging mountain bike riding. Continue climbing up to the very base of Pigeon House. The suggestion is that you actually climb the mountain tomorrow via the return route on Yadboro Road, but for those who can't wait there is a small track that swings around the mountain on the eastern side before joining up with the main tourist walk at the base of the cliffs. If one loses the track it is a simple matter of scrub bashing up to the base of the cliffs and following them around to the other side where the ladders are. At least an hour return should be allowed for.

The track continues west through open dry woodland rising slightly before the spectacular descent down to the Clyde River. It might be wise to tighten or at least check the brakes before this descent and make sure all panniers are secured and closed. Lean back whilst descending to increase pressure on the back wheel thus maximising braking power on the loose rock. Be warned that this is an extremely steep and long descent and because of the trail's disuse expect fallen logs and erosion gullies.

The trail comes out on the Yadboro Road just before the Clyde River. Cross the bridge and the camp sites are immediately on the right and left hand sides. This is no longer national park but the expansive Yadboro State Forest which comprises the foothills of the Budawangs to the west and south. There is private property close to the campsite and one can expect cows to come wandering through the camping ground. The place is reasonably popular due to its car access and the beauty of the Clyde River gorge and the Byangee Walls plateau, but there are numerous sites available in secluded clearings along the western bank of the river.

The next day return to Milton via the heavily undulating Yadboro Road. Along the way is the turn off to Pigeon House and the picnic area in Flat Rock State Forest. The walking track is 4.8 km return and is divided into three sections. The first is a very steep climb straight up a spur, the second is left along a flat ridge, and the third involves another steep climb to the summit. The bikes would have to be left at the bottom for about 3 hours, giving one plenty of time to enjoy the incredible and unobscured views on top.

Back on the Yadboro Road one should proceed westerly on to Clyde Ridge Road and thence to Woodburn Road. It is predominantly downhill to Milton where the bus can be caught back to Nowra. Make sure you have organised times before you leave so as to avoid an unexpected extra night. There's a schedule of bus routes in the back of the Illawarra Line timetable.

RIDE 74:   THE CASTLE

FROM: Milton
TO: The Castle
VIA: Yadboro
LENGTH:
   Day 1: Milton to Yadboro via Pigeon House 33 km
   Day 2: Yadboro to Yadboro River via Western Distributor
6 km
   Day 3: Yadboro River to The Castle summit: 12 km
walking
   Day 4: Yadboro River to Milton via Clyde Ridge Road
51 km
   Total distance is 102 km
RIDE/TRACK GRADE: 7/7
WALKING: The Castle. Option for extra days spent exploring
the Monolith Valley and Mount Owen
HEIGHT VARIATION: 450 m cycling, 790 m walking
TRANSPORT: Rail (Illawarra Line), bus to Milton
FACILITIES: After Milton, none
MAPS: CMA (LIC) Brooman, Milton, Corang and Tabourie
1:25 000 topographicals (the Northern Budawang 1:50 000
sketchmap is not as accurate as the topographicals due to its
smaller scale, but it shows the tracks through the Monolith
Valley)

The Castle wasn't climbed until 1947. Several attempts were
made throughout the early part of this century but its double
layer of sheer cliffs caused many to say it was unconquerable.
Today, thanks to the pioneers of the fifties and sixties, it's a
popular Sunday 'stroll' to the summit. The views obtainable
rival Kanangra Walls and Govetts Leap for scenic beauty.

   This is a four-day journey where the first is spent cycling to
the base of the Castle from Milton. Excellent camping sites
exist along the Yadboro River. The bikes are left behind the
next day. The conquest of the summit and descent again takes
a good five to six hours. Additional days can be spent exploring the fascinating and eerie Monolith Valley. This is a won-
derland of domes, narrow chasms, moss covered walls, and
pockets of rainforest set in an art gallery of natural rock sculp-

ture. It is an easy day's cycling back to the coast again where a bus can be caught north to Sydney.

Like all walking in the Budawangs, the ascent of The Castle is extremely strenuous and people who are used to the wide open bushwalking tracks of the more popular Royal and Ku-ring-gai National Parks are best advised to join one of the many walking clubs that frequent the area such as the Coast and Mountains Walkers of NSW.

If using public transport, catch the day's first train to Bom-aderry where a Pioneer bus leaves for Eden. Bookings are rec-ommended and the number to contact is (044) 21 7722. Get off at Milton which is a small coastal south between Conjola Lakes and Ulladulla. Head right (south) off the highway by taking any one of the four roads down. Turn right at the bottom of the hill on to Croobyar Road which curves around south and then west. A long stretch through boring agricultural land has to be endured before the forest is entered just a little further on. Any one of the several fire trails can be taken up a spur to the Kingiman Ridge. It is recommended that the trail marked as the Croobyar Creek Fire Trail be taken as this doesn't infringe on private property but instead passes through beautiful state forest. It's a steady climb of 200 m to the ridge. If one wants to climb the summit of the prominent Mount Kingiman (390 m), it can be attained by a short scram-ble from the eastern side. This mountain had a special signif-icance to the Aborigines for it was a central meeting place on festive occasions where tribes from the local area would meet. The main tribes in the Budawangs were the Walbangas and the Wandandians, who occupied an area from the Shoalhaven River in the north to Moruya in the south: about 1000 people spread throughout 9000 square kilometres!

From Mount Kingiman, one can either continue down the ridge and take two right turns to reach the Jindelara Creek road, or one can back track and drop down a steep spur on to the same road. In any case they are both downhill and lead to the same place through dense, wet forest. Although not marked on the map, there is a gate here just before the creek preventing vehicular access up on to the Pigeon House plateau. It is recommended that you have a small rest here and replenish your water supply for it is a long strenuous climb over the plateau before the next water at the Clyde River.

Jindelara Creek marks the entrance to the Morton National Park. Commence the steep climb along the Pigeon House Fire Trail (Grade 7). The gradient gets less steep as time goes by but it still is an uninterrupted uphill trudge. Good views back to the coast are obtained once sufficient height is reached to clear the Kingiman Ridge. In total, some 400 m must be gained. When you reach the t-intersection on Wombat Ridge turn left heading directly towards the looming mass of Pigeon House. This trail is marked as a walking track but in reality was an old fire trail which followed an Aboriginal track down Long-fella Ridge spur. The track quality here is the worst of the two days and makes for some challenging mountain bike riding. Continue climbing up to the very base of Pigeon House. For those wanting to climb Pigeon House, there is a small track that swings around the mountain on the eastern side before joining up with the main tourist walk at the base of the cliffs. If one loses the track it is a simple matter of scrub bashing up to the base of the cliffs and following them around to the other side where the ladders are. At least an hour return should be allowed for. It is not recommended if there are few hours in the day left.

The track continues west through open dry woodland, rising slightly before the spectacular descent down to the Clyde River. It might be wise to tighten or at least check the brakes before this descent and make sure all panniers are secured and closed. Lean back while descending to increase pressure on the back wheel thus maximising braking power on the loose rock. Be warned that this is an extremely steep and long descent and because of the trail's disuse expect fallen logs and erosion gullies.

The trail comes out on the Yadboro Road just before the Clyde River. Cross the bridge and the camping sites are immediately on the right and left hand sides. This is no longer national park but the expansive Yadboro State Forest which comprises the foothills of the Budawangs to the west and south. There is private property close to the campsite and one can expect cows to come wandering through the camping ground. The place is reasonably popular due to its car access and the beauty of the Clyde River gorge and the Byangee Walls plateau, but there are numerous sites available in secluded clearings along the western bank of the river.

The morning or afternoon on the second day can be spent

relaxing from the long first day. The distance is quite short and shouldn't take more than two hours before you've got your tent set up again by the Yadboro River. Ascend briefly up the Western Distributor Road, turn right, and then right again ignoring the signposted private property track. Descend to Yadboro River with good but brief views of Byangee Walls, The Castle and Mount Owen. Indeed one may wonder looking at the next day's destination how it is possible to climb it with anything but ropes.

Once at the end, there are informal camping spots for vehicles to the right. If there are people there, one can follow the road left to the car park. A sign here tells walkers that 10 m of rope are needed on the 8 hour return walk. Beyond the barrier posts is an old jeep track that continues for a few hundred metres before coming to a large grass and fern covered clearing between Yadboro River and a steep slope up to the road. There is a good camping site in the middle here and plentiful firewood and fresh water just half a minute away. A signpost points the way to The Castle and Monolith Valley walking tracks. Be wary of black snakes in the area during summer.

The next day, hide the bikes and cross the Yadboro River. A good track leads up Kalianna Ridge through pleasant forest to a rocky bluff. It is overgrown at first due to the sheltered nature of the terrain but it opens out as you gain altitude. The conglomerate at the end of the ridge can easily be climbed and a rope has been installed for convenience. At the base of the bluff is the Morton National Park entry sign, marking the southern boundary of this great national park. Once on top, enjoy the view over the Budawang foothills. The easy leg is over, and it is tough walking following the base of the western cliffs along a small rocky undulating track. You pass several overhangs and water is available from a pool enclosed by gigantic boulders. Almost an hour further, a short steep slope is climbed to a large conglomerate overhang. The track then contours around and a short footpad detour on the left leads out to some conglomerate rock platforms where there are superb views over the Oakey Creek valley, up to Mount Owen and the Yadboro State Forest. From this point, the track immediately ascends up a muddy creek. Close to the top a junction is reached marked by three arrows on the rock. The track forks between a 'T' for tunnel, and 'MV' for Monolith Valley. The slope between the two cliffs has suffered from much erosion due to walkers and the NPWS is presently installing steps to help stabilise the track.

Follow the tunnel track up directly to the base of the second cliffs and turn right. White chalked arrows lead to the tunnel itself and some scrambling is involved in negotiating more large boulders. Keep an eye out for arrows. The narrow chasm that leads into the tunnel gets smaller and one has to crawl. However there is plenty of light from gaps in the roof. One then descends down some ledges on to the forest-covered eastern side of The Castle. Turn right and follow a good track south along the base of the second-tier cliffs. Just after a large camp overhang, you reach the start of the climb which is marked by white arrows that point upwards. Two large rocks need to be scrambled over almost straight away and the arrows must be followed around the 'tail' of The Castle. The final ascent is on the western side with fantastic views of hundreds of unusual shaped domes on the side on Mount Mooryan. Good photographic opportunities also exist here, and on one section, Byangee Walls, Pigeon House, and the coast provide a spectacular backdrop to the rugged cliff of The Castle in the foreground. This shot however, has become something of a cliché. There is one particular tricky part where a steep wall has to be ascended to the left of a chimney. Climbing up is not so difficult, providing you have good tread on your shoes. However getting down again can be a problem if the rock is wet and therefore it can help if a short 10–15 m length of rope is taken along. This is the worst section for walkers and recently rope has been installed to assist people. Above this ledge it is an easy climb to the flat top of The Castle. A walking track leads through low scrub to the southern tip where there are expansive views to the Deua National Park in the distance. There is usually a visitors book in the large rock cairn near the very end on the left.

Descend via the same route taking care on the steep ledge and the Kalianna bluff at the bottom of the first set of cliffs. Take the road back to Yadboro Flat the next day and then follow the previous ride's tracknotes along Yadboro and Clyde Ridge, and Woodburn Roads back to Milton.

For those who want to spend an extra day up in the mountains exploring the Monolith Valley, it is best to consult the book *Pigeon House and Beyond* for route descriptions up the summits of the Shrouded Gods Mountain, and Mount Cole. The Monolith Valley has been closed to camping for some time, and it is likely that this restriction will remain in force due to the large number of people who are continuing to break this rule. Primitive camp sites can be found at Meakins Pass (named after Reg Meakins whose life ambition was fulfilled when he made the first recorded ascent of The Castle), and in an overhang just before Nibelung Pass. Other sites exist on the other side of the Monolith Valley in caves at the base of Mount Cole. Many of the names of the Monolith Valley were given by Major Jim Sturgiss, a local pioneer. They either stem from Richard Wagner's opera cycle, *Der Ring des Nibelungen*, or directly from the Nordic legends.

The highlight of my excursions in the Budawang area was camping on the very end of Mount Owen and watching the sun rise over The Castle in the morning. Almost a kilometre below was a complete blanket of clouds. Walking access to Mount Owen is through the Monolith Valley to a creek crossing marked by a small footbridge. Turn left here and you soon end up at an impressive open amphitheatre. The start of the Mount Owen climb is on the right and is signposted. You climb up a steep slope to a saddle. Here you should not head left, but scramble down the other side to a rocky creek. Cross over and a root-dominated climb takes you up to the base of rocks. The trail splits here and you should keep right as it ascends around the corner and up to some rock ledges. Access to the top is aided by vines and roots, making excellent foot and hand holds. Overnight packs will probably have to be manually hauled up.

The vegetation changes on top, becoming immediately drier. Head up to the base of giant rocky spurs and keep right. The track enters one gully between two rock spurs and disappears. Continue up to the saddle where it's a short scramble to the top of rock platforms. The worst part is now over. Now it's a matter of following rock cairns over rock platforms to the back of Mount Owen almost to Mount Cole. Here the trail swings to the left and it is easy walking south over more rock platforms connected by muddy grassy and heath-enclosed footpads. At the end, a deep gully separates you from the visitors book with outstanding views to the coast and the Budawang National Park. There is no real wood or water here so campers have to be totally self-sufficient.

OTHER RIDES IN THE MORTON NATIONAL PARK

By far the best area for further mountain bike pioneering is in the central part of the park between the Shoalhaven River and the Nowra to Braidwood Road. There are many abandoned fire trails centred on the Yalwal district, known only to locals and hard-core four-wheel drivers. The best access would be through Nowra and setting up a base camp in the Yarramunmun Creek valley. Walking in the Ettrema Gorge area will be particularly rewarding to wilderness enthusiasts.

The northern and southern ends of the park offer little more opportunities for mountain biking. Rides in the north are limited due to the uncrossable 500 m Shoalhaven River and Lake Yarrunga while the southern Budawang end is dominant by rugged impenetrable cliff-dominated wilderness.

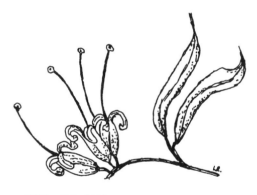

RED SPIDER FLOWER

8
Southern Ranges

As opposed to the northern half of New South Wales, the southern national parks cling to the Great Dividing Range which is relatively close to the coast. The principal national park in this chapter is Deua. Its boundary is less than two hours ride from the Moruya beaches. Also significant in this region are the extensive Batemans Bay state forests that stretch from Jervis Bay in the north right to the Victorian border. Because of this close relation between highland and ocean, the land is very moist and green. Sanctuary from the summer heat can be sought either in cool mountain streams, or on the empty beaches. Fishing is also popular here where the Clyde, Deua, and Tuross Rivers flow into the Pacific.

To the west of Deua National Park, the ACT contains Namadgi National Park, which takes up some 75% of its area. The most spectacular part of Namadgi is the Brindabella Range, a northern extension of Kosciusko National Park. Thus Canberra is quite a good city to live in if you enjoy mountain biking due to proximity of spectacular mountain ranges within a few minutes drive of Parliament House. The only disadvantage is that it is preferable to get dropped off at a high altitude on top of the Brindabella Range, rather than having to climb. There is no public transport at all to these parts.

NAMADGI NATIONAL PARK

Size: 94 000 hectares
Enactment:
   Gudgenby Nature reserve: 26 April 1978
   National Park: 3 October 1984 (formerly called 'Gudgenby' or 'Kelly' Wilderness)
Visitors: Unknown
Flora: Sub-alpine woodlands and heaths, montane savanna woodland, wet sclerophyll forest, and grassland swamps.
Fauna: Platypus, bogong moth, koala, river blackfish, broad-toothed rat, gang gang cockatoo

Camping: Official site at Clear Hill
Adjoining Parks: Kosciusko National Park, Tidbinbilla Nature
Reserve

RIDE 75:   BRINDABELLA RANGE

FROM: Mount Ginini
TO: Mount Gingera
VIA: NSW–ACT state border
LENGTH: 18 km
TIME: 1 day
RIDE/TRACK GRADE: 3–4/6 (some short steep uphills)
WALKING: No
HEIGHT VARIATION: 340 m
TRANSPORT: Private transport to Mount Ginini
FACILITIES: None
MAPS: CMA (LIC) Corin Map 1:25 000 topographical

Here's a short, very scenic mountain bike ride suitable for
beginners in the southern Brindabellas. From the summit of
Mount Ginini, accessible by 2WD about an hour from Canberra, one can cycle south past a locked gate barring all motor
vehicles to the high summit of Mount Gingera (1857 m). On
both starting and destination summits are outstanding views
over the Canberra hinterland, the northern Kosciusko National
Park hinterland, Brindabella Range, and Namadgi National
Park. There is no higher peak north of this point on the Australian continent.

   Access to Mount Ginini is through Cotter Dam, taking the
Brindabella Road up to Piccadilly Circus and then 22 km
south, passing Mount Franklin and Aggie Gap on the way.
The road is closed in winter months as the Brindabellas are
often snow-bound. At Mount Franklin is a 1938 two-storey
chalet that has been refurnished by the local ski club. After
Mount Franklin, the road deteriorates slightly, especially on
the final ascent up to the Mount Ginini summit. The wilderness atmosphere is spoiled slightly by a CAA relay station on
top but the views are fantastic to the east and west. To the
south one can also survey the territory you'll be cycling

through as Mount Gingera dominates the skyline. One can be unlucky, however, and get a white-out due to low clouds. The car should be parked up here on the border between NSW and the ACT. This is quite a popular area for Canberran mountain bikers.

Start cycling back down from the summit back to the main road and turn right. Within 300 m you'll come to a gate which bars all motorised transport. It is downhill all the way to the Stockyard Gap saddle in between the two mountains. On the right are remains of private property in the Namadgi National Park.

It is uphill as you round Little Ginini to the east, ignoring a left hand turn-off. The trail contours to Pryors Hut and an arboretum before rising gradually around the eastern flank of Mount Gingera. It is a steep uphill push through the snow-gums to the trig point on the summit. Bikes can be left at the bottom if you find the gradient too hard. However you might like endure the pain, being rewarded by great photographic opportunities. As the altitude of Mount Gingera is partially above the tree-line, the views are largely obscured. In summer, expect large fields of alpine wildflowers. Return via the same route.

RIDE 76:   NAMADGI NATIONAL PARK

FROM: Clear Hill Camping Ground
TO: Mount Clear (return)
VIA: Naas River, Horse Gully Hut
LENGTH: 35 km
TIME: 1 day
RIDE/TRACK GRADE: 5/6
WALKING: None
HEIGHT VARIATION: 760 m (several short uphills)
TRANSPORT: Private transport to Clear Hill Camping Ground via Boboyan Road and Tharwa
FACILITIES: General camping facilities included toilets, fire-wood, etc at Clear Hill Camping Ground
MAPS: CMA (LIC) Bredbo & Colinton 1:25 000 topographicals

Those of you wishing to explore the remote south of the magnificent Namadgi National Park can do much worse than drive to Clear Hill, hop on your bike and complete a marvellous circuit through the alpine mountain ranges. A nice feature of the ride is that it does not involve backtracking and can be done comfortably in one day by a reasonably fit cyclist. The majority of the terrain is through gentle rolling hills and spurs.

Clear Hill Camping Ground is set in former private south in far south of the ACT. Access is via Boboyan Road, south of Tharwa passing the Namadgi National Park visitors centre and administrative headquarters on the way. The drive from Canberra should take no longer than 80 minutes. The camping ground is on the left. At the end of a short dirt road, turn left again. To the right leads to some paddocks which abound with rabbits. The camping ground too is situated next to flat grassy fields in the Naas River valley. The camping area is structured so that you can't camp next to your car if you're arriving late.

If the day is early, start cycling by travelling back out to the first junction and heading left down to a paddock with many rabbits. You will notice that some of the following tracks do not appear on the Colinton map, but do continue on the more recently printed Bredbo topographical. Cross Grassy Creek and head right, following the signposts to Mount Clear summit via the Long Flat. At one point, you are very near the southernmost extent of the ACT border before heading north, following the ridge of the Clear Range to the Clear Range Fire Trail. On the summit, views of Namadgi's granite mountain ranges capped by many rocky tors (stacks of boulders formed by freezing and erosion) is very spectacular. Below you is the pretty upper Naas River valley. Its headwaters run off the southern slopes of Mount Gudgenby.

The descent is perilous in nature due to the loose stone surface and steep gradient. Head left towards Left Hand Creek and eventually Horse Gully Hut. Cycle almost due south here back to the cars. This ride could also be done clockwise if you prefer a steep uphill and gentle downhills.

DEUA NATIONAL PARK

Size: 81 158 hectares

Enactment: February 1979

Visitors: Less than 10 000 a year, most of whom travel along the Deua River road to Araluen. The upper Deua River valley centred on Bendethera Caves is popular among four wheel drivers. Caving is also popular with hard-core speleologists.

Aboriginal Sites: No survey yet conducted. Due to the rich wildlife that exists in the area, many examples of past occupation are expected.

Flora: Mainly wet and dry sclerophyll forest depending on altitude and proximity to water. The rare leaning *Eucalyptus fraxinoides* grows in isolated patches here.

Fauna: Over 90 species of birds, and many hundreds of mammals, reptiles, and invertebrates.

Camping: Since the area is a designated wilderness zone, no facilities are provided. The advantage is that bush camping is allowed anywhere.

District Office: Narooma, Princes Highway.

Adjoining Parks: Wadbilliga National Park as well as numerous state forests right around its perimeter: Buckenbowra, Wandera, Dampier, and Tallaganda. These 'buffers' comprise a land area twice as large as the park itself!

Few people know of the relatively new Deua National Park. There are many fascinating attractions waiting for anyone willing to make the five hour drive from Sydney. Within its boundaries lie the Bendethera Caves, Hanging Rock, the Big Hole, Marble Arch, pristine catchment areas, a river that rivals the Kowmung for beauty, and the impressive Wyanbene Caves. Most are accessible by bike, if not, a short walk from a fire trail.

Like the Budawangs, the national park is primarily a wilderness area and some experience with camping in the bush is recommended. In places like these, one has to be totally self-sufficient and trips of up to one week duration are necessary in order to see the main features. This is enjoyable but tiring as a lot of climbing is required. The fire trails are very rough n places with erosion gullies and rocky sections that keep the cyclist working.

Access is via the Princes Highway to Moruya, about 20 minutes south of Batemans Bay. Public transport, a coach service, follows the same route from Nowra. The full journey from Central to setting up camp along the grand Deua River takes just under a day. Journeys can be conducted any time but one must be prepared for rapid weather changes when cold winds from the Snowy Mountains mix with the moist coastal air.

Note: The Pioneer Bus service to Moruya, Narooma, and Bateman's Bay runs 3 times a day. A schedule is reproduced in the Illawarra Line train timetable. For details ring (044) 21 7722.

RIDE 77:   DEUA RIVER (LOWER)

FROM: Moruya
TO: Araluen (return)
VIA: Deua River
LENGTH:
   Day 1: Moruya to Deua River camping area 41 km
   Day 2: Deua River camping area to Araluen (return) 40 km
   Day 3: Deua River camping area to Moruya 41 km
   Total Distance is 122 km
RIDE/TRACK GRADE: 3/3
WALKING: None
HEIGHT VARIATION: 180 m
TRANSPORT: Bus service or private transport to Moruya
FACILITIES: Basic camping facilities: toilets, wood, barbecues
MAPS: CMA (LIC) Araluen, Burrembela, Bendethera and Moruya 1:25 000 topographicals

The Deua River is one of the most pristine in the state. Its upper catchment area comes from a total wilderness area. The object of this ride is to follow the river from where it runs into the sea at Moruya to the northern end of the Deua National Park to the Araluen valley. The camping grounds along the

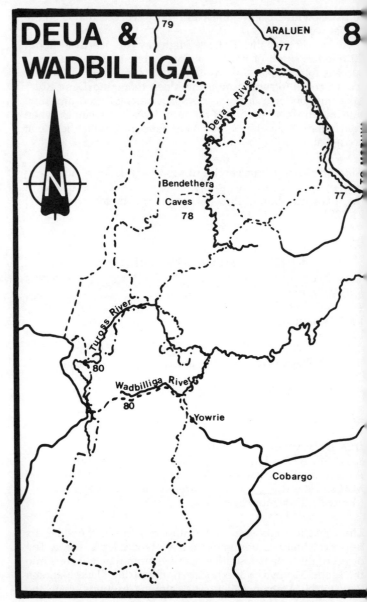

DEUA & WADBILLIGA

79

ARALUEN
77

8

N

Deua River

Bendethera
Caves
78

77

Tuross River

80

Wadbilliga River

80

Yowrie

Cobargo

Araluen to Moruya Road are very beautiful with large grassy clearings by the water.

Campbell Street, in the centre of the township, turns into the Araluen Road and this leads all the way through the national park to Braidwood. The old country town style post office is passed as well as a museum on the left. A number of buildings here have been built from local granite quarried nearby. Moruya means a 'water crossing' in Aboriginal. Indeed the major obstacle in settling the south coast was fording the huge rivers like the Shoalhaven near Nowra, the Clyde at Batemans Bay, and the Tuross. Most transport had to be by sea, and in fact the first bridge was only built at Moruya as recently as 1876.

Cross the wide river at Kiora and head up into the Wandera State Forest where the road becomes unsealed. Along the river is a narrow corridor of private agricultural land that separates the state forest from the national park. The cycling and scenery is pleasant. The road is quite windy and one should watch out for tourists who don't watch the road and locals who cut corners. For most of its length, the road runs about 30 or 40 m above the northern bank of the river and occasionally comes down to meet it where Casuarinas or river oaks can be found. There are good views throughout the trip.

Soon after passing the 'Deua National Park' sign, two camping options become available, both on the left hand side. The first is more informal with a couple of tracks leading from the road to grassy sites with barbecues. The right option is particularly attractive. The river has lots of flood-wood that sits high on the banks and is usually dry and ideal for campfires.

The second of the two camping options is just over the hill and is the official NPWS camping ground with pit toilets. Try your luck at fossicking in the river: gold was discovered here in 1851.

The next day can be spent cycling to Araluen. The township's name means the 'place of water lilies'. More important to the early pioneers was that gold was discovered there in 1851. Araluen once housed 1600 people who found almost 3000 kg of gold! Because of the temporary nature of gold rushes, few permanent buildings are left standing. Yet the place is still worth a visit. Directions are simple—just keep following the road north-west, leaving the Deua River and entering a pleasant wide valley surrounded by large forested mountains. It's one of those townships that has the mystique of timelessness about it, and many examples of run-down overgrown buildings and rusted machinery exist. There is a shire camping ground on the northern side of town at Apple Tree Flat by Majors Creek. Nearby are some peach orchards and a cemetery. However, it is suggested to camp by the Deua River again on the second night.

One can return via the same route or go 'off-road' for a round circuit. This entails hard-core mountain biking on extremely rough trails with a murderously steep uphill of 700 m. For those masochists wishing to do this option, cycle south to Jimmys Hill where a trail runs down to the river where it is forded. On the other side, and slightly upstream, begins the Dry Creek Fire Trail which connects to the main Oulla Creek Trail via the Merricumbene Fire Trail. It rises very steeply up before turning south and heading over a heavily undulating ridge through the Deua National Park. The highest point on the ridge is Mount Merricumbene at 748 m where there are fantastic views of the Deua River valley both to the east and west. This section is extremely rocky and the utmost care must be taken. The many steep uphills will prove very exhausting and unless the trail has just been recently graded will require walking the bike uphill. Take plenty of water for there is none along the ridge. Follow the Oulla Creek Fire Trail south, steadily losing altitude until you are almost at sea level when you ford the Deua River again. The trail joins up with Donalds Creek Road, where it is only 13 km back to Moruya.

RIDE 78:   BENDETHERA CAVES

FROM: Deua River (upper)
TO: Bendethera Caves (return)
VIA: Little Con Creek
LENGTH: 12 km
TIME: 1 easy day
RIDE/TRACK GRADE: 4/7
WALKING: Short uphill scramble to cave entrance and walk through cave
HEIGHT VARIATION: 160 m

The Walk Bendethera Caves are highly decorated, and have been well visited by tourists for a long time. The main cave, Bendethera, is open to visitors and a path exists along a relatively flat incline through several chambers and past some excellent formations including some massive columns. The walk through the cave is not technically difficult, involving one tight squeeze and negotiating some slippery slopes. Wear old clothes, for you will get quite dirty. It also helps if every member of the party has their own torch.

The Drive Access is by four wheel drive from Moruya via Little Sugarloaf Road. The track is not that rough and when recently graded, can be down in a 2WD. The rain receives a lot of rain and therefore the roads can get quite slippery. During long weekends and holidays, the upper Deua River valley can turn into a 4WD regatta while during the off-season, you can have the whole valley for yourself. The location is, in my opinion, one of the best in Australia. The river is very pristine and totally pure, much cleaner and better tasting than Sydney drinking water. It is fast flowing so it replenishes itself quite quickly even with a few people swimming there. Furthermore, the camping opportunities are virtually limitless. As the area was once private property, there are many clearings by the river, some are quite secluded. Everywhere is wildlife—kangaroos, wombats, and birds.

The Ride Start cycling from your camping area to the middle of the valley where some old stockyard fences exist. The track to Bendethera Caves is to the west and signposted. The first section to a barrier is easy flat cycling along an old jeep track. A sign warns of a rare species vegetation in the area, the Bendethera Wattle, an unusual silver-blue tree that is quite prominent along the way. The track is basically overgrown and sometimes the bike will have to be manhandled across the many creek crossings as you head up the Little Con Creek gully and then a tributary to the right.

There are some pleasant flat parts before a final steep uphill to the cave entrance. The bikes will have to left at the bottom of this uphill because it's extremely slippery and is impossible

to cycle down anyway. This is only one of the caves in the
Bendethera karst area. Another is the 59 m deep Windlass
Cave. This limestone region was first discovered in 1875 and
by 1890 an 1180 hectare reserve had been established through
Benjamin George.

The track through the cave keeps to the left and two chains
are installed through tricky sections. Tiny bats will zoom in
and out of your torch beam, but they're nothing to worry
about. At the end is a large cavern, but the best attractions are
some gigantic columns and stalagmites. The return walk
should take about an hour. Return to the Deua River via the
same route. Why not spend the afternoon exploring the many
trails in the valley, to the north and south? When swimming
watch out for huge long-legged spiders which hunt on the
rocks in or near the water—they're quite impressive.

RIDE 79:   WEST DEUA KARST AREAS

FROM: Berlang Camping Ground
TO: The Big Hole, Marble Arch, Wyanbene Caves
VIA: Shoalhaven River
LENGTH: 39 km
TIME: 1 day
RIDE/TRACK GRADE: 4/5 (first section involves pushing
bike along a 1.5 km walking track)
WALKING: To Marble Arch (2 km), Wyanbene Cave (1 km)
HEIGHT VARIATION: 110 m cycling, 140 m walking
TRANSPORT: Private transport to Berlang Camping Ground
via Braidwood or Captains Flat
FACILITIES: General camping facilities at Berlang Camping
Ground
SPECIAL EQUIPMENT: Torch, old clothes as you will get
dirty in Wyanbene Cave
MAPS: CMA (LIC) Krawarree and Kain 1:25 000
topographicals

The western Deua National Park, despite having no direct
access from the coast, is surprisingly more approachable. The
terrain is gentler and features of scenic interest are closer
together. This ride combines all the main features of the north-

A campsite with a view—the summit of Gospers Mountain (Rides 61 & 62)

Overlooking Lake Yarrunga from Purnoo Lookout (Ride 64)

western karst area, the protection of which is one of the primary reasons why the Deua National Park was declared.

The Big Hole This is a gigantic 50 m wide hole created when an underground cave system collapsed. Vegetation and rubble can be seen almost 100 m below sheer Devonian sandstone walls. A solid wooden platform gives visitors safe viewing directly into the hole.

Marble Arch A limestone tunnel through which flows Reedy Creek.

Wyanbene Caves One of the longest river caves in the state can be found here being almost 2 km long and 112 m deep. They are very popular wild caves and one large cavern is open to the general public. It is a water cave and visitors have to expect the occasional wades to get from cavern to cavern. Not for people who suffer from claustrophobia! Permits are required to deeper parts of the cave.

Access to the Berlang Camping Area is via the Braidwood to Nimmitabel (Krawarree) Road that runs north-south along the western perimeter of the Deua and Wadbilliga National Parks. The camping area is just off the road on the left hand side (turn-off signposted next to a cemetery) about 40 km south of Braidwood. A notice board tells of The Big Hole and its formation, while a walking track heads east to the Shoalhaven River. Many people are surprised to know that the Shoalhaven River, which is normally associated with the Nowra/Illawarra region, has its catchment area south of Moruya. The source of the Shoalhaven River on the left was first discovered by Robert Hoddle in 1828. He also was responsible for much of the surveying of Morton National Park. A geologist and reverend by the name of Clarke noted that the plateau swamplands around the Mount Dampier area were important sources of water for the Shoalhaven.

Start the tour by walking your bikes down to the river and crossing it via some rocks. The river is not quite mature at this stage, having no deep swimming holes during normal flow. If there have been recent heavy rains, however, then wading through the current will be necessary. On the other side, the walking track undulates briefly before heading up a gully to a wide open bald hill where fine views of the huge valley to the west can be obtained. The mountains on the horizon are the Great Dividing Range. On the other side lies the Monaro Highway and the southern ACT.

Cycling is possible here as the track rounds the bald hill and enters woodland. It is not far along here to a viewing platform and a sight that'll be remembered for a long time. The hole is gigantic, having maximum parameters of 114 m by 53 m. The ferns at the bottom, looking like small bracken fern, are actually tree ferns 2–3 m high. If you're lucky you'll see small birds flying in and out of the hole catching insects. The information sign tells of a lyrebird that's in residence at the bottom.

The next stage of the ride is accessed by dropping straight down the hill to the east to reach the Bettowynd-link Fire Trail can be followed further into the karst area to Marble Arch. You pass through predominantly flat terrain on a good quality surface and high averages can be maintained. Just to the north is private property. The turn-off right at the 747 m spot height (indicated on the map) is a low key affair which was not signposted when last visited. In the upper catchment of Neringla Creek to the north are Cleatmore Caves, a significant bat breeding ground.

The track comes to a car-park with a visitors-survey canister where cyclists can make notes as to how they got here, number of people in their party, improvements to better access Marble Arch, etc. The bikes will have to be left at the top. A well defined walking track straight down the steep hill into the Reedy Creek valley to Marble Arch.

Return via the same route to the Big Hole. Unfortunately both exits to the north and south are barred by private property so the bike will need to be pushed once more to the Berlang Camping Ground. Head out to the main Krawarree Road and turn south to the Wyanbene turn-off. This road has recently been widened and improved. It is easy cycling as you cross the Shoalhaven River once more and south-east and then south to a huge camping area, re-entering the Deua National Park. Continue cycling south and the cave entrance is a short scramble up the slope.

Wyanbene Cave is a water cave with the caverns being separated by narrow entrances where wading and crawling is required. It helps if your torch is waterproof. A lot of the formations are mud or silt based. The cave kinks to the left where vertical pitches make further progress without equipment impossible. Park authorities would like as little disturbance as

322

possible and advise not to souvenir formations. In sunlight, limestone becomes a dark grey, losing its underground beauty. It's also surprisingly heavy, despite its vulnerability to rapid erosion.

Head back to the Berlang via the same route.

RIDE 80:   WADBILLIGA NATIONAL PARK
(Cascades Rest Area)

FROM: Wadbilliga Crossing
TO: Tuross Falls (return)
VIA: Badja State Forest
LENGTH: 80 km (2 days of 40 km)
TIME: 3 days (1st and 3rd cycling, 2nd walking)
RIDE/TRACK GRADE: 7/5
WALKING: 4 km negotiable route to Tuross Falls
HEIGHT VARIATION: 1300 m (1st day involves long uphill)
TRANSPORT: Private 2WD (sometimes 4WD access) to Wadbilliga Crossing
FACILITIES: Basic camping facilities at Wadbilliga Crossing and Cascades Rest Area in the Wadbilliga National Park
MAPS: CMA (LIC) Yowrie, Belowra, Numeralla, Kybeyan 1:25 000 topographicals. The Forestry Commission's Batemans Bay and Eden 1:125 000 State Forests Maps will also come in handy for vehicle access.

Almost identical to Deua National Park, Wadbilliga occupies the same type of area and contains similar vegetation, wildlife and geology. It was dedicated at the same time as its northern twin, and is of similar size (73 399 hectares), and is of similar importance in preserving pristine catchment areas. Three main rivers dominate the national park: the Tuross, Wadbilliga, and the Brogo. Also like Deua National Park, it is relatively undisturbed and undeveloped, being primary wilderness area. A NPWS survey has sighted 122 native bird species in the park and other fauna commonly found include swamp wallabies, eastern grey kangaroos, wombats, possums, platypus and echidnas.

Fortunately for the cyclist, some roads dissect the park allowing long bushcamping excursions. This ride covers only

the north-western section. Access to start central is through
Cobargo and Yowrie via Yowrie and Bourkes Road. The
nearest bus station, Narooma is about 7 hours from Sydney.

For this ride, the main attraction is the Tuross River, with
the cascades and falls making interesting detours. Although
not that high (only 35 m), the Tuross Falls are quite heavy but
most spectacular is the dramatic 5 km gorge made of vertically
jointed granite where the Tuross River falls into.

Drive to the Wadbilliga Crossing via Cobargo and Yowrie.
The road is unsealed as you pass through private property
and many cattle grids into the Wadbilliga National Park. A
small range is crossed before you drop down into the Wadbilliga River valley. The road is rated as 2WD but can get a
little rough between gradings. On the right the station of
'Wadbilliga' can be seen, an oasis of civilisation in a sea of
wilderness.

Some small creeks are crossed before the road fords the
Wadbilliga River via a concrete causeway. This is another
beautiful river to rate with the Kowmung and Deua as the
purest in the state. The small camping area is on the other side
and contains a visitors survey canister. A large fire pit should
be the only location of your campfire. Toilets exist up the back
and a track heads upstream. Park your car here.

The road that continues up the other side of the valley is
graded as four-wheel drive. The next day, start early for it is
a gruelling climb up to a height of 1100 m above sea level to
the Great Dividing Range. This will involve extended pushing
for a large part but one can look forward to a classic descent
on the third day. Take plenty of water. The road emerges
through private property (public thoroughfare access is legal)
on to the Kybeyan–Tuross Road (Braidwood to Nimmitabel)
after crossing the infant Tuross River.

Head right, cycling north through pleasant country. It is
easy riding and good progress can be made from Two River
Plain to Countegany. Head right on to the signposted Badja
Forest Road leading to the Tuross Cascades. You soon enter
the Badja State Forest, back on the Great Dividing Range. At
another turn-off head right on to the Tuross River Road. The
trail becomes four-wheel drive (good quality) and the Wadbilliga National Park entrance sign is passed before the final
short descent to the Cascades Rest Area. This is quite a nice
place, being adjacent to the river and is gaining in popularity

nce the NPWS and Forestry Commission jointly developed
e access road.

The next day involves some relaxing by the river, perhaps
en a swim if the weather is appropriate. There's a walk for
ose who are interested, first to the cascades, then to the falls
d gorge. It's along a negotiable route, meaning that there is
well defined walking track. The walker should be armed
ith the Belowra 1:25 000 topographical map, compass, water,
d camera. Start by heading up the road and turning right
the short trail that leads to a turning circle. A short track
eads straight down the slope to some rock platforms where
e rugged three-tiered cascades can be surveyed. The water
usually stained brown due to tea tree upstream. Time expo-
re shots might be appropriate if there is low light or you
ave slow film.

Backtrack to the carpark at the top and head east, finding
e path of least resistance. There is a footpad of sorts,
though sometimes you have to use your imagination. The
ute crosses over a few gullies, tributaries of the Tuross River.
hen in doubt, keep right so that you parallel the river. Pretty
on it begins to sink in a steep vertical canyon while you are
aintaining the same height. You come out on some over-
rown rock platforms with terrific views over a deeply dis-
ected gorge of the wildest geometry. The columnar basalt and
e twisted nature of the terrain provides an extremely pho-
genic background. The falls are partially obscured by rocky
eninsulas and you have to scramble around the end to find
he best vantage points. On the other side is a walking track
hich leads down to the falls. This can be accessed from a
ail near the original crossing of the Tuross River you made
e previous day or by rock-hopping all the way along the
iver from the cascades.

Head back to the camping area via the same route. The next
ay should be spent re-tracing the route to the Wadbilliga
rossing completing a fantastic tour of some of the most
ugged wilderness this state has to offer.

RIDE 81:   NELLIGEN

FROM: Batemans Bay
TO: Nelligen (return)
VIA: Benandarah State Forest
LENGTH: 30 km
TIME: 1 day
RIDE/TRACK GRADE: 3/3
WALKING: None
HEIGHT VARIATION: 200 m
TRANSPORT: Private transport to Batemans Bay
FACILITIES: Picnic area at Nelligen
MAPS: CMA (LIC) Batemans Bay 1:125 000 State Forests
Map

This is the pick of one day mountain bike rides in the southe'
state forests. Locals and holiday makers can spend a perfe'
day cycling inland as a break from the lovely beach resorts
the area. Batemans Bay was named after a friend of Capta'
Cook, Captain Nathaniel Bateman who sailed with him on
former ship. Today, it is a popular tourist city and holida
resort due its many beaches. Murramarang National Park
just to the north, where fishing is popular.

The object of this ride is to skirt the large inlet created whe'
the Clyde River flows into the sea. There are not many bridg'
over the massive Clyde River but one is located at histor'
Nelligen. Like many other towns in the south coast hinterlan'
it was a gold mining city in the 1860s. It managed to surviv
because of diversification into other areas: oyster growin;
tourism, saw milling, and wattle-bark stripping.

From the northern side of the long bridge, head up alon'
the Braidwood Road to Nelligen through state forest. There :
some traffic on this road, but it is left behind once you tur'
south from the town along the Runnyford Road which lead'
back to the highway on the southern side of Batemans Ba'
Along the way is Holmes Lookout just off the Braidwood Roa'
on the left and the Round Hill Fire Tower Lookout. The centr'
feature though is the beautiful Clyde River which has i'
source in the southern Morton National Park. Its upper valle'
is one of the most spectacular in Australia. Many of the road'

the area are signposted differently from the Bateman's Bay ate Forests Map.

OTHER RIDES IN THE SOUTHERN RANGES

he Batemans Bay district contains some expansive state orests that fill in the green belt between the Morton and Buda-ang National Parks to the north and the Deua and Wadbil-ga National Parks to the south. Some state forests even begin mmediately on the coast and extend inland almost to Can-erra. As a consequence, the southern state forests represent he greatest potential for extended off-road mountain bike pio-eering in New South Wales. The total area is over 300 000 ectares, larger than the Blue Mountains! Unlike the local ational parks, the state forests have unlimited logging roads nd fire trails that are open to the public with camping llowed anywhere. Attractions include pockets of rainforest, npolluted beaches, ghost mining towns, and wilderness. Another advantage for the casual sightseer is the provision of icnic and camping facilities such as at Nelligen along the anks of the scenic Clyde River.

BUSH RAT

9
The Coast

About a third of the New South Wales coast is protected b
public land reservations. Most of these are national park
extending from Broadwater and Bundjalung National Parks
the far north to Nadgee Nature Reserve in the far south. N
only do these parks protect the beaches and sand dunes, b
the hinterland which often comprises swampland and marir
estuaries. Many of these parks contain coastal ranges whei
an astounding variety of vegetation is present due to the dive
sity in landform and climate.

RIDE 82:   JERVIS BAY (CAVE BEACH)

FROM: Nowra (Bomaderry Station)
TO: Cave Beach
VIA: Jervis Bay
LENGTH: 96 km (2 days of 47 km)
TIME: 2 days cycling (plus any days spent at beach)
RIDE/TRACK GRADE: 3/2
WALKING: None
HEIGHT VARIATION: 70 m
TRANSPORT: Rail (Illawarra Line)
FACILITIES: Good camping facilities at Cave Beach Campinŋ
Ground
MAPS: Natmap Kiama and Jervis Bay 1:100 000 topographi-
cals (NRMA touring road map will also be sufficient).

Jervis Bay is one of the most attractive and well visited coasta
reservations in the state. It is actually Commonwealth terri
tory, being managed from the ACT and officially you ar
leaving NSW when entering the bay area. A nice walk-ir
camping ground offers overnight camping opportunities righ
next to a pleasant beach on the south side of the peninsula iı
the Jervis Bay Nature Reserve. The area has been the subjec
of much controversy between conservationists who highligh
the marine environment as a harbour for whales and dolphins

hile the Commonwealth government would like to keep the
rea as one of Australia's major naval bases.

From Bomaderry Station, cycle south through Nowra along
he Princes Highway, crossing the wide Shoalhaven River.
outh Nowra is an industrial area which also contains some
opular fast food outlets such as McDonalds. Continue south,
urning left about 13 km from the Shoalhaven. Continue south-
ast along Jervis Bay Road into the nature reserve and right
ast the airfield to the signposted Cave Beach at Wreck Bay.
A barrier prevents vehicle owners from car-camping on the
vell maintained ground. The beaches in the entire vicinity are
amous for their white sands. Because of their popularity, theft
s a problem so beware. Spend a day or two by the water
efore heading back to Nowra. Further cycling can be under-
aken to the Point Perpendicular lighthouse.

MYALL LAKES NATIONAL PARK

Size: 34 500 hectares (10 125 of which are water)
Enactment: 1972
Visitors: 100 000 per year, many of whom are boaters
Aboriginal Sites: Piles of discarded shells, bones, and other
waste, called 'middens' are the primary reminder of occupation by the Gaddhang tribe.
Flora: The range of flora is quite extraordinary: from the standard sand-dune spinifex to the tallest trees in the state. Aquatic
plants also play a dominant role in the park's maritime atmosphere. A thin corridor of spectacular dunes separate the five
large lakes from the Pacific Ocean. On the western flanks,
beautiful temperate rainforests cover the low coastal ranges.
Fauna: 33 species of mammals, 280 bird species, and 36 species
of freshwater fish.
Camping: Most of the dune-belt is closed to campers due to its
sensitivity. In fact camping is only really authorised at developed camping sites, and fees apply. The most common places
are Legges Camp at Bombah Point and Mungo Brush. Both
are on the shores of Bombah Broadwater Lake. Other camping
sites exist near Violet Hill and Yagon.
District Office: NPWS District Office: (049) 87 3108
                  Legges Camp Bookings: (049) 97 4495

Adjoining Parks: Nerong, Bachelor, Wallingat and Bulahdela
State Forests, Booti Booti State Recreation Area and Suga
Creek Flora Reserve

RIDE 83: MYALL LAKES

FROM: Bulahdelah
TO: Seal Rocks
VIA: Myall Lake
LENGTH:
  Day 1: Bulahdelah to Yagon Camping Area 59 km
  Day 2: Yagon Camping Area to Mungo Brush 33 km
  Day 3: Mungo Brush to Bulahdelah 28 km
  Total distance is 120 km
TIME: 3 days
RIDE/TRACK GRADE: 6/4
WALKING: Short walk to the tallest tree in NSW
HEIGHT VARIATION: 180 m
TRANSPORT: Private transport to Bulahdelah
FACILITIES: Camping ground at Legges Camp
MAPS: CMA (LIC) Seal Rocks, Myall Lake, Bulahdelah and
Bombah Point 1:25 000 topographicals

Although boating is the recreational activity in Myall Lakes
National Park, many opportunities for cycling exist. To traverse the small coastal ranges and overlook the huge expanses
of water is truly rewarding. Access by public transport is by
means of a joint rail-bus service from Sydney to Bulahdelah
via Newcastle. State Rail coaches stop there but bikes cannot
be carried meaning they have to be sent as freight, causing a
few problems in synchronising arrival times. The trip takes
approximately four hours. From Bulahdelah, it is just an hour
to the park entrance through the very beautiful coastal forests
that were nearly threatened by logging.

Indeed the struggle to save the national park was very
nearly lost. The Caloola Club, a bushwalking-turned-conser-
vationist group first proposed the idea of a fauna reserve.
Threatened by sand mining, timber-felling, real estate development, and local council projects, the struggle escalated until
the state government intervened and accepted a reservation

lan first proposed by the Myall Lakes Committee in 1968. Today the damaged forests are being re-generated. Clear evidence of this can be seen in the overwhelming majority of younger, smaller strands of white *eucalyptus grandis* that predominate in the north-west.

Most of this small national park can be seen on this trip and the 4WD tracks on the second day makes some scenic and interesting riding. The basic outline of the route skirts the border of the largest lake in the park, Myall Lake, and includes the best of the state forests. A small detour on the first day leads to the tallest tree in the state, well worth seeing for its own sake and for the pocket of rainforest which it resides in. Thick, knobbly tyres are needed for traction, as the eastern trails in the park contain quite a high sand content.

From the Pacific Highway, head up the Lakes Road to the beginning of the beautiful wet state forests. The road climbs briefly and some traffic will be encountered as this is the main access route to the northern part of the national park. As you head over the range the turn-off to 'The Grandis' tree is on the left and is well signposted. The distance is 11 km return, taking about an hour in all through some beautiful lush woodland. The road gets rocky around the Branch Creek area. A high proportion of the trees here have bright red bark and are quite thin. This is because the entire area was logged in 1977 and is now undergoing regeneration. A wide bend in the road (which serves as a car park) marks the start of the short 100 m walking trail through the rainforest on the right. At the beginning is a data table on the tree, giving the following statistics:

Age: 400 years
Species: *Eucalyptus grandis*
Height: 76.2 m
Volume: 122.76 cubic metres

Unless you have a 180 degree fish-eye lens, photographing the tree from the wooden viewing platform presents a problem due its sheer size and encroaching forest. A number of other similar size trees nearby have survived the logging. A nature trail on the way back leads up the stream on the right.

Back on the main road, head down the other side of the range with good views of Myall Lake. Follow the signs along the Lake Way to Seal Rocks entering the national park a short distance after the Seal Rocks Road turn-off. After some small hills, the road gets quite flat and becomes unsealed once again. At the end is a lighthouse with some strict visiting hour Tuesday–Thursdays 10.00–12.00 a.m., and 1.00–3.00 p.m. There is small community on the peninsula and a beach on the left hand side has been specifically zoned off for camping. Many of the houses are a are holiday houses, owned by residents of Newcastle and Sydney.

When you've taken a look around Sugarloaf Point, head back along the Seal Rocks road and turn left along a track which leads down to the Yagon Camping Area. There is a very newly developed camp ground with clivus multrum auto dry composting toilets, the latest in pit toilet technology. A windmill-driven pump supplies the camping ground with water. Signs prohibit generators. Although this isn't the most popular camping area in the park, its relatively recent development has been responsible for a sudden increase in the number of visitors here. A walking track leads over sand dunes to a long winding beach.

On the second day, head south-west past Middle camp to the Hawks Nest–Seal Rocks Road. This was recently closed for vehicular traffic due to its bad condition but its still remain a very useful thoroughfare for mountain bikers. I don't know why they call it a road though—I've seen better walking tracks. Some sections are very sandy and will involve pushing. Rainy weather is actually the best time to trasverse sand for it compacts it, making it rideable.

The track eventually joins up with Mungo Brush Road which has been recently upgraded to a sealed road at a cost of $500 000. Head right until you come to the ferry. A clearing just to the right has a 'No Camping' sign and a parks service road runs just behind it. A gong hanging from the tree on the right signals the ferryman who lives on the other side. It might help to time your arrival here with a car because we waited for an hour here on our bikes, and it was only when a car came that the ferryman bothered to come out. It ceases running at 7.00 p.m. so those leaving Yagon Beach late have to make good time. $2 are charged to users. On the other side is Legges Camp, the best developed site in the park, and indeed in any park I've visited since Wilsons Promontory in Victoria. School-children frequent this place but you would have to be unfortunate indeed to find it completely full. It sits on the foreshore on Bombah Water and has a good amenities

lock and specific sites. It was the site of an upgrade project
n the early 1990s as part of the national park's $1 000 000
levelopment program.

The alternative camping option on the second night is to
continue south down the Mungo Brush Road to the popular
camping area of Mungo Brush in the south of the national
park. This was also targeted for major upgrading in the early
1990s, with an expansive system of car-camping facilities being
provided. There are several new car-parks exclusively zoned
for overnight parking.

The next day, simply head north west up the Lakes Way
through rural property back to Bulahdelah to complete a
round trip.

OTHER RIDES ON THE COAST

The places accessible by bicycle on the coast are too numerous
to mention, and I have only listed the 'pick of the crop'. The
national parks and state forests stretch right up and down the
coast. The following is a list of the most scenic coastal parks:

Bundjalung (northern and southern sectors)

Yaraygir

Crowdy Bay

Murramurang

Ben Boyd

Nadgee Nature Reserve

10
Kosciusko

Size: 690 000 hectares
Enactment: 1944: State Park
         1967: National Park
         1977: World Heritage Listing
Visitors: 2.5 million a year (most of whom are skiers)
Aboriginal Sites: Little evidence of Aboriginal occupation, though they visited the area in summer mainly to feed on the Bogong moths.
Flora: The variety of plants in the park is enormous, with the area divided into four different zones related to altitude. Snow gums and other eucalypts dominate the vegetation, while shrubs and herbs add colour to the alpine meadows above the treeline (1850 m).
Fauna: 202 bird species, 21 species of reptiles, 35 species of mammals, and over 300 types of invertebrates. Feral animals include cats, dogs, rabbits, foxes, pigs and trout. But perhaps the most popular are the wild brumbies that roam the highlands.
Camping: Campers are recommended to register at the visitors centre at Sawpit Creek on their way into the park, or at the various rangers' stations on other access routes. Camping is not permitted in resort areas (e.g. Perisher, Thredbo). Permits and fees are not required.
District Office: Sawpit Creek, 14 km from Jindabyne
Adjoining Parks: Cobberas-Tingaringy National Park in Victoria, Namadgi National Park in the ACT, and numerous state forests on the western flank.

Even though the Snowy Mountains are the highest in the country, the cycling is among the easiest as grades are generally very gentle. Most of the highest peaks on the Main Range are accessible by bike, and there is a trail right up to the summit of Kosciusko itself. Because of its remote locality and its huge size, the park is suited for overnight expeditions. However, rough camping is not always required. Due to the development of the region since last century, many forms of overnight accommodation are available: from primitive huts to youth hostels to expensive hotels.

The recession has reduced incomes for many lodges during the peak winter seasons. Accordingly they have tried to recoup the foregone revenue by attracting tourists in the summer months. Thredbo has led the way and now caters extremely well for summer visitors with a whole range of activities: bushwalking, horse-riding, mountain-bike riding, golf, tennis, swimming, fishing, even oriental meditation. In other resorts, ski lodges are starting to open in summer and bookings are just as essential as in winter. The late summer is the ideal time to go, but the park is notorious for its 'killer' flies, so take plenty of repellent. A greater degree of map reading skills are also required as the CMA hasn't bothered to produce a 1:25 000 series for the region, meaning that the less detailed 1:50 000 scale maps are the best available.

A list of activities conducted in the park reads like a run-down of a Sunday TV sports program: hang-gliding, rafting, horse-riding, cycling, caving, fishing, walking, climbing, canoeing, cross-country and downhill skiing, and abseiling. The authorities have traditionally been very relaxed about the heavy recreational use of the park and it is only now that stricter rules are in force. For cyclists, this means that walking trails cannot be used as thoroughfares. The rocks and soil are very fragile and easily subjectable to erosion.

However, the hundreds of fire-trails and SMA service roads that exist within the park boundaries are all open to cyclists and camping is permitted anywhere off the roads. Some of the greatest variations between high and low points exist in the park (height variations are sometimes more appropriately expressed in kilometres rather than metres), but because of the gradual slopes, can often be ridden up or down comfortably. The quality of the tracks is mostly good although some of the older 4WD trails consist mainly of two overgrown tyre-tracks which sometimes are barely discernible. Everywhere, the cyclist could encounter herds of brumbies. The many old stockmen's huts scattered throughout the park help generate an atmosphere of timelessness. Twisted snow gums and graceful mountain ash set among one of the largest wilderness tracts in the state make this park one of the best.

A unique feature of the park is the Snowy Mountains Hydro-electric Scheme, by far the largest engineering project in Australia's history. Most of the trails used by cyclists in the park were built by the Snowy Mountains Authority (SMA) and are still maintained by them. Everywhere evidence of the project is apparent; in pipelines that appear and disappear dozens of huts, overhead lines, dams and power stations. It defied the Great Dividing Range, diverting the water from the east-flowing rivers, and pumping them over the mountains to the Murray River for irrigation. As the water plummeted down through subterranean pipes, losing over 1000 m in height, electricity would be generated that today serves Sydney and the rest of NSW, the ACT, and Victoria. Sixteen dams were built, one of them submerging the old township of Jindabyne. During the construction, which lasted a quarter of a century, vast tunnels were driven through the mountains costing many men's lives. Bulldozers were airlifted into remote places, whole townships were built, and huge trucks crawled up the mountains carrying massive concrete pipes. But it wasn't just an Australian project; contracts for various sections were awarded to companies from all around the world. Foreign corporations, like Norwegian Selmer Engineering, had to import most of their labour and technology. Over 600 West German tradesmen were recruited and they worked side by side with Americans, Italians, and the Dutch. The restoration work was equally impressive; about half a million trees had to be planted to cover the scars of earth removal. The rehabilitation program was moderately successful.

The ideal way to visit the park is to stay at Jindabyne and catch the ski-tube up to Blue Cow for day rides around the main range. This saves climbing 700 m and allows one the enjoyment of a free ride down the mountain. The train operates all year. The cost is not cheap, but very convenient, leaving every hour. Bikes can be hired from Bullocks Flat, the Thredbo activities desk, or the Paddy Pallin store at Jindabyne. A Pioneer Bus service to Thredbo operates from Sydney via Canberra and Jindabyne. There is an additional charge for bikes, and the front wheel has to be taken off.

It is recommended that all overnight rides be registered with the park rangers at the visitors centre by filling out a route form.

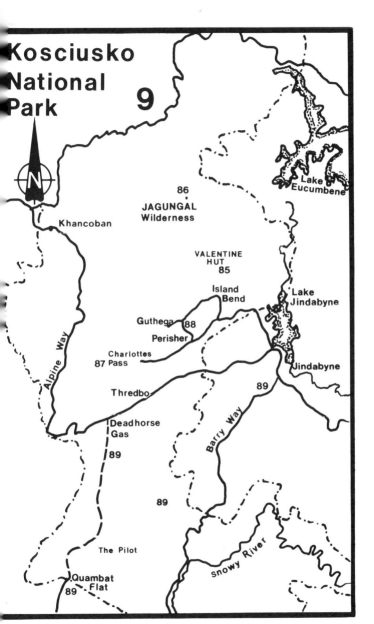

Kosciusko
National
Park

9

N

JAGUNGAL
Wilderness
86

Khancoban

VALENTINE
HUT
85

Island
Bend

Guthega 88

Perisher

Lake
Jindabyne

Charlottes
87 Pass

Jindabyne

Thredbo

89

Deadhorse
Gas

89

Barry Way

89

The Pilot

Quambat
Flat
89

snowy River

Lake
Eucumbene

Alpine Way

RIDE 84:   BLUE WATERHOLES
(NORTH KOSCIUSKO TOUR)

FROM: Canberra
TO: Yarrangobilly Caves
VIA: Brindabella Range
LENGTH:
  Day 1: Canberra to Cotter Dam Camping Area (Paddys River) 25 km
  Day 2: Cotter Dam to Mount Coree 37 km (via Brindabella and Curries Road)
  Day 3: Mount Coree to Goodradigbee River 47 km
  Day 4: Goodradigbee River to Blue Waterholes 32 km
  Day 5: Rest day at Blue Waterholes, walking exploration of limestone canyon
  Day 6: Blue Water Holes to Long Plain Hut 28 km
  Day 7: Long Plain Hut to Yarrangobilly Caves 20 km
  Total distance is 189 km
TIME: 6 days cycling, 1 or more rest days as preferred
RIDE/TRACK GRADE: 7–8/5
WALKING: Short walk through limestone canyon
HEIGHT VARIATION: 1310 m
TRANSPORT: Private or public transport to Canberra, private transport from Yarrangobilly Caves
FACILITIES: None
SPECIAL EQUIPMENT: Waterproof clothing and tents, several litres of water per person for the second day.
MAPS: CMA (LIC) Cotter Dam, Brindabella, Tidbinbilla, Peppercorn, Rules Point and Yarrangobilly 1:25 000 topographicals

Presented here is one of the most scenic long distance mountain bike tours imaginable. Included in the package are camping beside some beautiful pristine streams, hut camping, and mountain-top lookout camping. There are caves, a dramatic limestone canyon, fantastic views, great swimming, long downhills, and generally great cycling. The destination is Yarrangobilly Caves—no camping is permissible here. The closest accommodation is Long Plain Hut. It is recommended that you arrange to be picked up here either by pre-arrangement or by phoning out. Otherwise you will have to cycle along the

Snowy Mountains Highway to Adaminaby and then Cooma to the train back to Canberra. The only factor that could potentially spoil the trip is bad weather. Reaching the destination involves crossing the 1400 m high north Brindabella Range. In winter this is usually snow-bound, but even in summer, blizzard conditions are be experienced. The ride also involves super uphills, especially on the second day. Rarely is the grade exceptionally steep (except for the Mount Coree summit) so a steady pace and low gear should enable one to avoid pushing the bike from Cotter Dam to the Brindabellas. Due to the long distances and considerable height variations, a very good degree of fitness is required. In addition, the cyclist needs to be entirely self-sufficient with good quality lightweight camping gear. Preferably a party of 3–5 should spread out the weight, allowing good progress to be made.

From Canberra head west to Cotter Dam crossing the Murrumbidgee River via a narrow bridge and camping on the left hand side just upstream from the confluence with Paddys River. A developed camping ground exists here, the most civilised of the journey. If you have left early in the day, then a side trip up to Mount Stromlo Observatory in the Stromlo pine forest on the way might interest astronomy fans. The turn-off is on the right and signposted.

Day 2 is the most difficult and involves perhaps the longest ascent in any of the rides in this guide. Just to the west, Brindabella Road heads up the left contouring around the prominent Mount McDonald pinnacle before levelling out. The cycling conditions along this section are probably the best on the ride. Head left at the t-intersection where you see some signs on various roads which are closed during winter.

Soon after you enter state forest agin, the road starts to climb and climb and climb. On the way are notices explaining that you are in the catchment area for Canberra's water supply. At Thompsons Corner, the road follows a small watercourse called Wombat Creek. All water containers should be filled here. Where Brindabella Road then leaves this watercourse, head right on to Curries Road. This leads across Blundells Flat up to Two Sticks Road at the base of the Mount Coree massif.

The final 300 m climb to the saddle on the NSW–ACT border is extremely gruelling and will require pushing by all but steroid-pumping super-athletes. Head right, contouring around the left of the ridge to a turn-off to the right. A fire-dam is passed as you descend slightly before the final ascent to the day's goal—the summit. The track is quite rocky as it hair-pins through the snow gums climbing constantly to the fire-tower at 1421 m. The exhausting effort is well worth it for the views are outstanding. Campers will especially enjoy watching the sunset and sunrise in the morning over the expansive radiata pine state forests that lie between the Brindabellas and Canberra.

The third day is a lot easier, with most of the height gained the previous day being lost as the drop down the western flank of the Brindabella Range to the Goodradigbee River in Kosciusko National Park. Backtrack to the saddle and head south along Two Sticks Road to Piccadilly Circus. Turn right, rejoining the Brindabella Road and follow it all the way down to the virtually non-existent township of Brindabella. Continue south into the Kosciusko National Park where a number of grassy camping areas exist on the left in pleasant clearings between the road and the river. Keep an eye out for wombat holes.

Day 4 sees you continuing through the Kosciusko National Park. SMA power lines are followed as you climb on to Long Plain plateau via some more hair-pin corners and head left at the signposted Blue Waterholes turn-off. This area was formerly known as Cooleman Caves. The access road into the karst area used to be extremely rough but has been upgraded and makes pleasant cycling. The camping area at the end fortunately bars vehicles. It is right beside a brook that has its subterranean origins just upstream.

The next day should be spent exploring the limestone canyon by following a foot pad downstream and to the right. The walk ends at some waterfalls on Cave Creek. Some fording will be necessary, so your shoes may have to be sacrificed to the cold water. The caves were discovered in 1922 and range in length from just a few metres to a maximum of 784 m. There are 96 of them in all. The most interesting are the Murray, River, Easter, Cooleman and Barbers Caves.

The sixth day to Long Plain Hut is fairly uneventful. The plain seems to go on and on. You can almost see your destination for the great part of the day. Along the way are the swamps that form the very headwaters of one of Australia's great rivers, the Murrumbidgee. A great eyesore are the power-lines that follow the open plain. The turn-off to Long

Plain Hut is on the right just before you reach the Snowy Mountains Highway. The hut presides in pleasant snow-gum forest. Four-wheel drivers often stay here. There are several open rooms and one fireplace. Toilets exist out the back. A visitors book allows you to tell of your experiences.

The last day is quite simply. From the Snowy Mountains Highway, one can turn either right or left to reach Yarrango-billy although the left option is the safest as you would be moving with the traffic to the station. A number of tours can be conducted here as well as your own explorations of Glory Hole. A big hit is the Thermal Pool which is always a mild 27 degrees. This part of the park is made of a huge block of heavily eroded limestone 12 km long and 2500 m deep. Water has carved 60 caves with 205 entrances into the limestone, but only four of them are open to the public: the Glory Hole Cave, the North Glory Cave, Jersey Cave, and Jillabenan Cave. The main feature is the first one: the massive Glory Hole with its gigantic arch entrance and extreme depth of 330 m. It was discovered in 1834 by a stockman who was looking for stray cattle. Inside is a self-guided tour with pre-recorded information and push-button lighting controls on various viewing platforms. Features of interest include a natural skylight, the sacrificial altar, a Grand Dome 55 m high. North Glory Hole contains enormous stalactites, while the Jersey Cave is noted for its extensive deposits of flowstone. Guided tours are available through the Jillanbenan Cave with its 200 million year old calcite formations. Other caves of note are Restoration, East Deep Creek, Easter, and Janus Caves. The East and West Eagles Nest system form the third longest cave in NSW being 3.6 km long and 174 m deep. The beautiful Mutmut Cave was discovered as recently as 1986. There is also a 2 km walk to other caves such as the Castle and Harry Wood which were badly vandalised last century together with the Coppermine Cave and they are now closed.

The caves area has quite good facilities and one can phone here to be picked up or cycle to Adaminaby and Cooma. Bush camping areas exist along the way.

RIDE 85:   VALENTINE HUT

FROM: Guthega Power Station
TO: Valentine Hut
VIA: Schlink Pass
LENGTH: 40 km (20 km each way)
TIME: 2 days
RIDE/TRACK GRADE: 5/5
WALKING: Medium grade walk to Valentine Falls
HEIGHT VARIATION: 590 m
TRANSPORT: Private transport to Guthega Power Station via Jindabyne
FACILITIES: None (hut has firewood, pot belly stove). Accommodation in the hut can not be relied upon.
SPECIAL EQUIPMENT: Warm clothing, e.g. gloves. Thorn-proof tubes are highly recommended. Also carry plenty of spare tubes and patches.
MAPS: CMA (LIC) Mount Kosciusko and Khancoban 1:50 000 topographicals

The destination of this ride is one of the most picturesque huts in the Kosciusko National Park. There is no vehicle access, so the SMA service trails belong to the cyclist, and indeed, this is becoming as popular a cyclist's destination in summer, as it is a cross-country skier's goal in winter. If using private transport, a car-park exists at the Guthega Power Station. People driving from Sydney from Kosciusko can car-camp the first night at Island Bend on the Snowy River.

The Guthega Power Station is responsible for pumping water from the Snowy River up over the Great Divide to the Geehi Reservoir. The car should be left here. A sign gives distances to various locations and warns to boil all drinking water. This road is the main access for walkers and cyclists to the central part of the national park and one of the only entry points into the Jagungal wilderness.

A long steep climb takes you to Horse Camp Hut. The road temporarily follows a large pipeline where some great views are obtained over the Snowy River valley. Some 400 m have to be gained, and this takes around an hour before the slope becomes gentle enough to allow bikes to be ridden. If you are lucky you might be able to hitch a ride up in the back of a

Hydro-electric Commission truck—we weren't. The road branches off right to follow the Munyang River valley north. Horse Camp Hut is situated on a hill to the left of the track after crossing a small concrete bridge. The track up to the hut is signposted. It is an old stockman's hut with an iron roof and walls, containing a table, benches, and even a small stove.

When cycling, be careful of the granite on the trails in the area. The volcanic rocks are much harder than sandstone and there is consequently a higher frequency of punctures. Avoid skidding on loose rock going downhill as this will lead to erosion problems if done too often by too many cyclists. Ideally one needs a bike with anti-lock brakes in the Snowies.

Continue climbing up to Schlink Pass (1800 m) through some open hills topped by rocks. Another hut is situated close to where the powerlines cross the track on the left hand side. It is un-named and partly obscured by the trees, approximately marking the position of the underground pipelines from Island Bend to Geehi. To the right is the massive Gungartan pinnacle, and the Great Dividing Range. At the crest of the prominent pass, water falling south flows into the Snowy River and eventually into Victoria, while water falling on the other side of the ridge flows north into the Murray and heads for South Australia.

Once over the crest of Schlink Pass, it is a gradual and enjoyable downhill through an almost identical valley where the well graded road curves in and out of side gullies. Ever present are the powerlines, which are one of the few reminders of the industrialisation of this national park. On the left is the 'Schlink Hilton' which has a wooden floor and toilets, making it one of the more luxurious accommodation venues in the area. The building is quite big, but half of it is closed off, being reserved for the SMA. Access for the public is around the back. A visitors book can be signed here, and included on our visit were some interesting tales of adventures by cross-country skiers. I recall one account of a man warning readers not to ski down Gungartan while on acid!

The turn-off on to the Valentine Fire Trail is not well marked but since it is the only one on the right hand side it isn't hard to recognise. The trail consists of two overgrown tyre tracks and undulates considerably while meandering north to the Valentine River. A small pretty valley is traversed, and then it is a steep uphill through a magnificent patch of pure white snow gums. The track is littered with loose rock in places, making climbing in low gear difficult. A makeshift bridge marks the crossing of Duck Creek and from here it is only a short distance to Valentine Hut. Despite its small size, the hut is even better than the 'Schlink Hilton'. Inside is a pot belly stove, furniture, bunks and a visitors book. Pre-cut wood and a toilet are out the back. Due to its good condition, the hut is well frequented and it is rare indeed that you will find it vacant. It was built by the SMA, but is now owned by the NPWS and is maintained by the Coast and Mountain Walkers and the Kosciusko Huts Association.

If there is no accommodation available inside the hut, then one can also camp on the grassy clearings down the slope by the Valentine River. The next day, one can walk to the falls by following the northern bank. Large swimming holes exist about 100 m downstream among some cascades. The Valentine Falls themselves are quite high and can best be seen close up from the bottom but the walk is about two hours return.

RIDE 86:   MOUNT JAGUNGAL

FROM: Guthega Power Station
TO: Mount Jagungal (return)
VIA: Schlink Pass
LENGTH:
    Day 1: Guthega Power Station to Valentine Hut 20 km
    Day 2: Valentine Hut to Mount Jagungal 23 km
    Day 3: Mount Jagungal to Valentine Hut 23 km
    Day 4: Valentine Hut to Guthega Power Station 20 km
    Total distance is 86 km
RIDE/TRACK GRADE: 5–6/6
WALKING: To the summit. About 2 km return
HEIGHT VARIATION: 590 m cycling, 400 m walking
TRANSPORT: Private transport to Guthega Power Station
FACILITIES: Various old huts along the way
SPECIAL EQUIPMENT: Warm clothing, e.g. gloves. Thorn-proof tubes are highly recommended. Also carry plenty of spare tubes and patches.
MAPS: CMA (LIC) Mount Kosciusko and Khancoban 1:50 000 topographicals

Mount Jagungal is the highest mountain in the central and northern Kosciusko National Park and is the only 2000 m peak that stands apart from the main range. The views from its prominent bald summit are quite photogenic and will be remembered for a long time. No higher mountain exists to the north. As public vehicle access is prohibited, the SMA service trails belong to the cyclist, and indeed, this is becoming as popular a cyclist's destination in summer, as it is a cross-country skier's goal in winter. If using private transport, a car-park exists at the Guthega Power Station. People driving from Sydney to Kosciusko can car-camp the first night at Island Bend on the Snowy River.

The Guthega Power Station is responsible for pumping water from the Snowy River up over the Great Divide to the Ccchi Reservoir. The car should be left here. A sign gives distances to various locations and warns to boil all drinking water. This road is the main access for walkers and cyclists to the central part of the national park and one of the only entry points into the Jagungal wilderness.

A long steep climb takes you to Horse Camp Hut. The road temporarily follows a large pipeline where some great views are obtained over the Snowy River valley. Some 400 m have to be gained, and this takes around an hour before the slope becomes gentle enough to allow bikes to be ridden. If you are lucky you might be able to hitch a ride up in the back of a Hydro-electric Commission truck—we weren't. The road branches off right to follow the Munyang River valley north. Horse Camp Hut is situated on a hill to the left of the track after crossing a small concrete bridge. The track up to the hut is signposted. It is an old stockman's hut with an iron roof and walls, containing a table, benches, and even a small stove.

When cycling, be careful of the granite on the trails in the area. The volcanic rocks are much harder than sandstone and there is consequently a higher frequency of punctures. Avoid skidding on loose rock going downhill as this will lead to erosion problems if done too often by too many cyclists. Ideally one needs a bike with anti-lock brakes in the Snowies.

Continue climbing up to Schlink Pass (1800 m) through some open hills topped by rocks. Another hut is situated close to where the powerlines cross the track on the left hand side. It is marked on the marked but is un-named and partly obscured by the trees, approximately marking the position of the underground pipelines from Island Bend to Geehi. To the right is the massive Gungartan pinnacle, and the Great Dividing Range. At the crest of the prominent pass, water falling south flows into the Snowy River ane eventually into Victoria, while water falling on the other side of the ridge flows north into the Murray and heads for South Australia.

Once over the crest of Schlink Pass, it is a gradual and enjoyable downhill through an almost identical valley where the well-graded road curves in and out of side gullies. Ever present are the powerlines, which are one of the few reminders of the industrialisation of this national park. On the left is the 'Schlink Hilton' which has a wooden floor and toilets, making it one of the more luxurious accommodation venues in the area. The building is quite big, but half of it is closed off, being reserved for the SMA. Access for the public is around the back. A visitors book can be signed here, and included on our visit were some interesting tales of adventures by cross-country skiers. I recall one account of a man warning readers not to ski down Gungartan while on acid!

The turn-off on to the Valentine Fire Trail is not well marked but since it is the only one on the right hand side it isn't hard to recognise. The trail consists of two overgrown tyre tracks and undulates considerably while meandering north to the Valentine River. A small pretty valley is traversed, and then it is a steep uphill through a magnificent patch of pure white snow gums. The track is littered with loose rock in places, which makes climbing in low gear difficult. A makeshift bridge marks the crossing of Duck Creek and from here it is only a short distance to Valentine Hut. Despite its small size, the hut is in even better condition than the 'Schlink Hilton'. Inside is a pot belly stove, furniture, bunks, and a visitors book. Pre-cut wood and a toilet are out the back. Due to its good condition, the hut is well frequented and it is rare indeed that you will find it vacant. It was built by the SMA, but is now owned by the NPWS and is maintained by the Coast and Mountain Walkers and the Kosciusko Huts Association.

If there is no accommodation available inside the hut, then one can also camp on the grassy clearings down the slope by the Valentine River. The next day, one can walk to the falls by following the northern bank. Large swimming holes exist about 100 m downstream among some cascades. The Valentine Falls themselves are quite high and can best be seen close up from the bottom. The walk is about two hours return and can either be done on any of the four days. The last day would be preferable as the terrain is predominantly downhill and the distance is the shortest, allowing more time for exploration.

Follow the road across the Valentine River and up and around through open and relatively flat country. There are good views south-west to the main range, and every now and then the massive bulk of Mount Jagungal looms over the gentle hills in the foreground. On the way down the slope to Back Flat Creek are views across the valley to the Valentine Falls on the far left. Three fords must be crossed in a gigantic wide valley that once supported gold mining activities. Grey Mare Hut was built in 1949–50 with iron walls and a wooden floor. Inside are six bunks plus benches and a table. Like the Valentine Hut, it is heavily used and has been known to house rats living off food scraps.

Head north and up a low hilly range. Those looking for the Strawberry Hill Fire Trail will find it very overgrown, making walking let alone cycling difficult. A good downhill leads to another huge wide valley containing the swampy headwaters of the Tooma River. It is easy and fast cycling along the bottom. Mount Jagungal will now have come into full view and because of its sheer size will appear quite close although it is still some 5 km distant. Its name is derived from an Aboriginal term meaning 'mother of waters'.

Turn right at the signposted intersection marked on the map. Woodland is entered again as the foothills of the mountain are reached. Climb briefly before coming to a left-hand curve in the trail. Straight ahead is a flat grassy area which is ideal for camping as water is located nearby in the form of the young Tumut River. This is also the start of the only defined track to the summit, making it a convenient place to stay. Its only disadvantage is that it is exposed. For those who prefer something closer to home, O'Keefe's Hut can be reached by following the trail around the mountain for another 3 km. It was built in 1934 and has a wooden floor with iron walls 8 m long and a metal roof. It is one of the larger huts in the highlands, containing three rooms and four bunks. Water can be obtained from Hut Creek, one of the feeder streams of the Tumut River. Depending on time and energy, the mountain can be climbed either on the first day or early on the second. The bikes must be hidden in the scrub at the bottom. Allow about three full hours including a lengthy stay at the top.

Any route can be taken up, but the lower slopes of the mountain are choked with thick scrub, making slow progress. However, as previously mentioned, a small track begins at the first camping ground by the prominent bend in the road. The start of it is on the left where tall grass marks the boundary of the clearing. Frequent use has made the track fairly easy to follow. After ascending through the dense forest, one suddenly emerges into open grassland and some rock scrambling leads on to an enormous spur. The track disappears here but it is easy to make your own way up through the final rocky obstacle to the summit. A concrete column marks the actual peak. Because there are no trees here, the view is unobscured for 360 degrees. Particularly prominent is the main range and Gungartan to the south, the Munyang Range to the east and Tabletop Mountain in the north. The colourful rock that characterises the summit is a metamorphosed basalt called diorite-gabbro which has its source in ancient lava flows throughout the entire region. To the east is wide open slope containing many species of alpine grasses.

Returning to Guthega can be done by simply backtracking, or taking a longer more visually interesting detour via Geehi Reservoir. On the fourth day, remember to check your brakes before the final steep descent and be careful of service vehicles coming the other way.

RIDE 87: MOUNT KOSCIUSKO

FROM: Charlottes Pass
TO: Mount Kosciusko and Mount Twynam
VIA: The Summit Road
LENGTH: 17 km
TIME: An easy day
RIDE/TRACK GRADE: 3/5
WALKING: Final easy-grade ascent to the summit
HEIGHT VARIATION: 508 m
TRANSPORT: Private transport to Charlottes Pass
FACILITIES: None
MAPS: CMA (LIC) Mount Kosciusko 1:50 000 topographical

348

Tibetans would laugh if they could see Mount Kosciusko. Our highest peak is a bald knob that isn't even a mountain by world standards. Furthermore, a road leads right to the summit which dampens any feeling of conquest and achievement. Many lower peaks in Australia offer the climber a much greater sense of accomplishment than Kosciusko: for example Federation Peak in Tasmania, Mount Barney in Queensland, or Balls Pyramid off Lord Howe Island. But still none of these are mountains in the conventional sense of the word: ice picks and oxygen tanks are very out of place in Australia. I don't want to sound like a spoilsport but technically Kosciusko is not our highest mountain. Part of Australia includes Heard Island in the southern Indian Ocean, on which sits a massive active volcano called Big Ben. It is more than half a kilometre higher than Mount Kosciusko. Even higher is Australian administered Antarctica where the ice cap is almost 4000 m above sea level qualifying peaks there as true mountains.

However the reason for cycling up to Mount Kosciusko is the scenery. The large white patch on the Mount Kosciusko 1: 50 000 topographical map approximately follows the 1800 metre contour line around its circumference indicating that no trees grow past this point. Large granodiorite boulders are strewn all around this region, having been deposited some 20 000 years ago during the Pleistocene ice age.

The road to the summit, built in 1909, is open to the public as far as Charlottes Pass and this is where private transport must be left. If this is not possible, one can take a bus to Thredbo and ride up the Ramsheads approaching Kosciusko from the south. Alternatively, a train/coach service allows public transport from Sydney to Jindabyne via Canberra. From here the ski tube can be taken up to Blue Cow. Another author of an Australian cycling book, Julia Thorn, actually started from Cooma and cycled all the way to Seamans Hut in one day: a rise in altitude of nearly 2000 m! The advantage of making use of the Pioneer Bus service to Thredbo (which runs in summer) is that you can make a round trip from Thredbo to Jindabyne. This is a distance of about 66 km with quite long downhills, but unfortunately containing some traffic on weekends.

From Charlottes Pass (1840 m), the summit is just over 8 km away. Park the car and continue along the management trail as it climbs gradually to the upper Snowy River. Then cycle up the deteriorating road to Seamans Hut which wa built as a memorial to Laurie Seaman who died of hypothe mia nearby in 1928. It offers good shelter from sudden change in the weather and there is no higher accommodation in a of Australia. Snowdrifts sometimes exist around here i summer.

The track traverses around Etherridge Ridge, with som gentle climbing. At Rawsons Pass, the bikes have to be left a the large turning circle for the final ascent. This is a very nev policy by national parks authorities and is probably related t previous cyclists who were removing the road's cover b using low gears that caused the tyres to slip. Examining th rock on the road here will reveal that there is not the coars grained granite that is so common in the Snowies but a met amorphosed sedimentary rock that resembles slate. Lookin around, it is a very bare landscape with piles of granite boul ders or tors dominating the summits of all the peaks in th area. These were exposed by a 'periglacial' erosion proces whereby the original covering of the mountains was remove by saturation from snow and melting ice. The whole surround ing landscape is evidence of the only glacial activity on main land Australia, the only other being in Tasmania.

The road takes you to within a few metres of the summi It always gives people an ego boost when they know that the can go no higher, and a clear summer day will find many people on the summit; mainly walkers from Thredbo who us the metal grid from the top of the Crackenback chairlift. Th entire highlands were uplifted in stages about 12 million year ago, with the greatest rise occurring very recently: only 2 million years. Since then, periodic Ice Ages saw glaciers carv out mountain sides creating hollows called carries and depos iting rocks into large piles called moraines. The best exampl of these, the beautiful Blue Lake can be explored in the after noon if you have left early enough. The elements have indee been cruel to this land: since 400 million years ago, the lanc has been folded, uplifted, covered by lava, eroded, flooded and fractured. And puny little mankind can destroy such a landscape with just a few bulldozers.

To the south lies Lake Cootapatamba which is Aborigina for 'the place where eagles drink'. It is blocked by a moraine deposited by a Pleistocene glacier. It is slowly being filled in again due to erosion. To the west lies the Murray River in a

350

eep valley and 1500 m below. It was from here that Count aul Edmund de Strzelecki climbed and named Kosciusko on 5 February 1840. Australia's highest mountain was named 'ter a Polish patriot, Tadeusz Kosciuszko (1746–1817), ecause it reminded Strzelecki of his tomb in Krakow. A metal laque on the summit tells of this feat. Some historians aimed that he actually climbed nearby Mount Townsend ecause it resembles the shape of the tomb more closely and at should have been named Mount Kosciusko. Don't leave our gear if you go off wandering. Someone stole my camera nd bike computer near Kosciusko Lookout on the Thredbo pproach. It was unattended for less than 30 minutes.

When you've enjoyed the view, head back down to Charottes Pass. If you still have time and energy left, why not walk to Blue Lake. From Charlottes Pass, one heads down a steep rick-surfaced trail to the Snowy River and up the other side. lthough the entire walk can be done by mountain bike due the excellent nature of the pavement, park authorities unfornately prohibit bikes because of conflict-of-use problems. It akes any mountain biker envious that such an excellent well urfaced scenic trail is restricted to walkers only.

The road then climbs steeply up and up and up towards Mount Twynam. There is one downhill where the road sudenly changes to dirt and rock before a steep paved ascent to lue Lake lookout. The lake is a large glacial pool and an excelent spot to have a rest. Surprisingly swimming is possible in ummer due to a constant water temperature.

Between December and March, wildflowers such as the entian bloom in abundance. The tracks here are strictly for valking and were built by the Soil Conservation Foundation n the 1950s and 1960s. Much of the initial erosion has been alted by mulching the immediate track borders with straw nd seeding them. To the south, metal walkways have been onstructed so walkers don't even have to touch the ground, vhile the road to Blue Lake has been revegetated by a system f drains, benches, and terraces.

Retracing your route is the long way back to Charlottes Pass. The final ascent from the Snowy River to your car will half ill you due to its unrelenting steep grade. Surprisingly, the aved walkway is more tiring on your leg muscles than a ormal dirt track because you feet and ankles are always nclined in one direction for long periods of time. On an ortho-

dox bushwalking track, variation of foot position constantl
relieves different muscles.

RIDE 88:   SMIGGIN HOLES

FROM: Smiggin Holes
TO: Island Bend (return)
VIA: Guthega Power Station
LENGTH: 29 km
TIME: 1 day
RIDE/TRACK GRADE: 5/4
WALKING: None
HEIGHT VARIATION: 400 m
TRANSPORT: Private transport to Smiggin Holes or ski tube
to Blue Cow
FACILITIES: None
MAPS: CMA (LIC) Mount Kosciusko 1:50 000 topographical

From Sydney, the Kosciusko National Park is about 6 to ?
hours driving via Goulburn, Canberra, Cooma, and Jindabyne
An entry fee is charged for vehicles just after Jindabyne as you
cross the Thredbo River. Further up is Sawpit Creek where the
rangers headquarters and visitors centre are located. All sorts
of souvenirs can be bought here. Smiggin Holes, a very
popular ski resort is just a few minutes further up the road
and it is suggested that this be the starting point of a one day
round circuit.
   This is one of the few day tours in Kosciusko National Park
that the cyclist can do all year round. The backroad from
Smiggin Holes to Guthega is extremely beautiful with snow-
gums, and a small running creek providing some tranqui
relief from the hustle and bustle of the ski resorts. Park your
car at the large tar-sealed northern car-park at Smiggin Holes
and the road continues, passing a chalet on the right and up
into the snow gums. Along the way are views to the right over
an unblemished landscape around Pipers Creek. The road is
perfect for cycling as there are no steep inclines. It progresses
steadily down to meet Perisher Creek where another road
forks left to service the large chair lift that was built in 1987
(not marked on the map). This massive mountain is Blue Cow

The Bungonia limestone canyon (Ride 67)

Porters Creek Dam (Ride 70)

Approaching The Vines from Newhaven Gap, Budawangs, Morton National Park (Ride 71)

Pigeon House (Ride 73)

pon which there are views north to the Snowy River and
long the main range. An early lunch on the large piles of
ocks and snowgums on the right is recommended. Although
: wasn't operating when I was last here, the chairlift can now
·e taken to the summit to avoid a strenuous walk. Another
·reat lunch venue along this ride is Island Bend down by the
nowy River. The road continues to follow the creek down-
tream until a signposted T-junction is reached. Left is to the
mall alpine village of Guthega. Seen in winter, this village is
bout as close to Europe as you are going to get. Turn right
nd head down past the large Guthega Power Station to Island
3end. The road undulates here and some traffic might be expe-
ienced. At Island Bend, a rough stony road takes you down
o the Snowy River. In summer this is a fantastic place to swim
nd the water is surprisingly mild. By the river is a grassy
learing with a fireplace. The spot is popular for fishing, and
n unmarked walking track leads upstream along the southern
·ank past some shallow cascades. Return to Smiggin Holes by
·ejoining the Guthega Road and turning left up Diggers Creek.
t is here where most of the lost height has to be regained and
he grade is steep at times. On reaching the Summit Road, turn
ight and it is easy riding back to the carpark at Smiggin Holes.

RIDE 89: PILOT WILDERNESS

FROM: Thredbo
TO: Jindabyne
VIA: Quambat Flat (marked Cowombat Flat on the map)
LENGTH:
   Day 1: Thredbo to Carters Hut (Tin Mine) 37 km
   Day 2: Carters Hut to Quambat Flat 27 km
   Day 3: Quambat Flat to Pinch River 42 km
   Day 4: Pinch River to Jacobs River 19 km
   Day 5: Jacobs River to Jindabyne 45 km
   Total distance is 171 km
RIDE/TRACK GRADE: 6/6
WALKING: Optional walk up The Pilot
HEIGHT VARIATION: 1080 m

TRANSPORT: Pioneer bus service to Thredbo and/or ski-
tube from Jindabyne
Fees: $10 for bikes
FACILITIES: General tourist facilities at Thredbo and
Jindabyne
Several stockmen's huts. No developed
campsites
MAPS: CMA (LIC) Thredbo, Suggan Buggan, Numbla Vale,
and Berridale 1:–50 000 topographicals

Kosciusko National Park allows cyclists few opportunities to
exploit height differentials by starting at a higher altitude than
the end point. This, however, is one of them. The destination
is the NSW–Victorian border, leaving Thredbo at 1400 m and
ending at Jindabyne at 930 m four days later. Along the way
are some great sights: old mines, wild rivers, a plane crash
site, the very start of the Murray River, and some great down
hills. The Cascades Trail follows the top of the Great Dividing
Range south of Thredbo into the Pilot Wilderness. This region
is well known for its rugged isolation. Characteristic of the
region are the numerous brumbies that inhabit the sub-alpine
meadows. Along the way are examples of the high country's
rich history: stock yards, old wooden cabins, and mines.

More than in other areas, the southern Snowy Mountains
are very susceptible to sudden weather changes. Snow and
frost in summer are not uncommon, and it is necessary that
one brings a waterproof parka, and at least one woollen
jumper. Down sleeping bags are also strongly recommended.
Another factor to take into consideration is the presence of
tiger snakes in the southern region. If walking, wear gaiters
and thick long pants. The cycling is generally easy, but gradients can get steep at times, requiring long periods of
pushing.

From Thredbo, ascend west along the Alpine Way to Dead
Horse Gap. Just before you cross the Thredbo River (also
called Crackenback River), there is a clearing on the left with
a signpost indicating the start of the Cascades Trail. There is
a gate at the very beginning which isn't marked on the map,
and just to the right of the gate is a Backcountry Register,
where it is strongly advised to leave details of your route. A
large carpark here is often full, evidence that this is the starting

354

oint of extended tours into the southern Pilot wilderness—
horse-riding, walking, and cycling are all popular here.

Continue climbing along the river until you come to a ford.
From here, the trail leaves the river and it is a 200 m climb to
Bobs Ridge. Here, the open woodland allows fantastic views
looking north to the Ramshead Range. In the warmer months,
wildflowers cover the heathlands. The trail here alternates
between a wide flat road and two small ruts, and at no time
will the bike need to be carried due to poor surface condition.
You may, however, experience spoke trouble due to twigs and
small branches being kicked up by your wheels.

From Bobs Ridge, you descend into the Cascade valley
through mountain ash and snow gums. Once you cross the
Cascade Creek, it is only a short walk left to the hut which is
worth inspecting. It was built in the 1930s by Harry Nankervis,
who leased the surrounding area off the government. For 40
years the quality of the hut deteriorated until the Illawarra
Alpine Club restored the interior to its present condition. Just
behind the hut, there is a small walking pad to a creek where
a pipe enables one to easily obtain water. Within the hut itself
are usually emergency food rations and pre-cut firewood. On
the left wall is a wooden platform, raised above the dirt floor,
which serves as a makeshift bunk.

From the hut, the trail continues south predominantly
downhill. Ahead, the granite-covered Pilot dominates the
horizon. From here it is relatively easy cycling along the Great
Dividing Range to Tin Mine, where Charlie Carters Hut can
be inspected. Like Cascades Hut, it was built in the interwar
years and served the miners and brumby runners. It is generally in good condition and contains bunks, a fireplace and a
toilet. It was named after the man who built it. Carter was the
last true hermit of the Snowies, catching brumbies for a living.
His life history is a strange mixture of fact and myth. For
example he would emerge into civilisation about three times
a year selling hides and socialism articles to the Cooma newspaper. A popular theory of his death relates to his strange
activity of self-applying exotic concoctions for 'healing' purposes; such as petroleum jelly and copper sulphate. Spend the
first night here, preferably outside on the meadow.

At Tin Mine, the trail forks into the Cowombat and Ingee-
goodbee Fire Trails. Take the right trail west past the actual
abandoned tin mine. After crossing the bridge over Tin Mine

Creek, the trail climbs to another junction where either option can be taken. If the option of climbing The Pilot is to be taken then it is recommended that you go left for a kilometre and hide the bikes at the base of the mountain. It is a moderately easy climb taking approximately an hour. On top there are very rewarding panoramic views. Visible here is the main range and the Victorian alps in the south. On clear days, the coast may be just visible.

Back on the trail, it is about 30 minutes of easy downhill riding to Quambat Flat. There are good campsites on the northern side of the infant Murray, right on the Victorian border. Before the junction of the trails, there is a fire place on the left hand side. One would be unfortunate indeed to find this place crowded. Clean drinking water is available from the Murray River and if you are quiet you have a very good chance of seeing the herds of brumbies that populate this region.

The next morning can be spent investigating the wreckage of the plane that crashed here in 1954. Despite being marked on the map as Southern Cloud, park authorities say that it was in fact an RAAF DC-3 that ploughed into the ground during an unsuccessful emergency landing. Out of the four crew members, one was killed. The survivors had food air-lifted in to them until a ground-based search-and-rescue party located them. Unfortunately most of the remains have been souvenired over the last few decades. Pieces of the fuselage were once used to construct a makeshift hut nearby. The Southern Cloud crashed to the north. To the east is Forest Hill upon which a control point marks the switch from the irregular Murray River state border to the straight line that goes directly to the coast at Point Hicks.

Leave in the early morning, for much of this day will be spent retracing the trail back to Tin Mine. From the campsite, turn right and head up a 400 m slope to the scenic Cowombat Ridge and thence back to the Cowombat Fire Trail. Backtrack through Tin Mine, up the Cascades Trail for 4 km, and then a signposted turn-off on the right leads on to the Tin Mine Fire Trail to the Pinch River and the former site of Flanagans Hut. This building was burnt down by a bushfire in December 1972. Camp in a pleasant clearing several kilometres after fording Pinch River where the track and one of the Pinch River's tributaries meet up again. A navigational aid is the 1385 m spot eight on the map. The clearing is to the north-east of this point.

The third day is relatively short, partly to recover from the lengthy distance on the second, and partly because it involves a long uphill over Stockwhip Hill. Follow the Tin Mine Fire Trail east as it winds over the Charcoal Range. The trail undulates quite dramatically, first up to 1620 m before a descent of almost 12 km interrupted by just one small uphill. The total drop in elevation is 800 m and should take about 20 minutes until you are by Jacobs River. It is suggested you make a rough campsite here, perhaps upstream.

Begin the last day with an hour's climb to get out of the Jacobs River valley and then it's another climb after crossing Tuross Creek. After Thatchers Waterhole, the trail still climbs and you should keep left at the fork with the Native Dog Trail and left again on to the Barry Fire Trail where you finally get a short descent down to Kings Arms Creek. The Golden Age Fire Trail is the only exit to the Barry Way that doesn't pass through private property. It is then easy cycling north to Jindabyne.

FURTHER CYCLING IN KOSCIUSKO NATIONAL PARK

This massive national park offers great opportunities for extended mountain bike pioneering. Because of the Snowy Mountains Scheme, there are many service trails to dams, power stations, pipelines, and overhead electric powerlines. Camping restrictions are generally pretty relaxed and most watercourses rising from the Great Dividing Range are reasonably pure. Much of the north-western part of the park has not been covered in this guide: the Bogong Peaks wilderness area and Talbingo Reservoir in particular. Due to the isolation and long distances involved, cyclists need to be entirely self-sufficient and well-prepared for extra days needed to brave out incipient conditions.

11
Barrington Tops

Size: 39 121 hectares (72% of which is wilderness)
Enactment: 1969
Visitors: 215 000+ per year
Aboriginal Sites: Limited pre-European use of the park. Little evidence of permanent occupation.
Animals: Kangaroos, platypuses, bandicoots, gliders, possums, bats, koalas, and large varieties of aquatic fauna, rare invertebrates, and many hundreds of species of birds. Brumbies also live within the park and adjacent state forests.
Plants: Most notable are the ancient, and beautiful *Antarctic or Negrohead* beech trees, in the highest rainforests. The Barrington and Gloucester Tops areas have a wide range of plant communities, including sub-tropical rainforests, eucalypt forests and woodlands, and the largest areas of peat swamps outside the Kosciusko National Park. The introduced bright yellow Scotch broom has become quite a major pest in the northern half of the plateau.
Camping: There are a number of developed campsites around the Allyn River in the south, on the Gloucester river in the east, and the Polblue Swamp area in the north. Permits are now required for primitive bush camping.
District Office: Raymond Terrace
Adjoining Parks: Large and numerous state forests including Avon River, Chichester, Barrington Tops, Mount Royal, Stewarts Brook, and Masseys Creek which together comprise an area twice the size of the park itself!

Snow often falls on this extremely beautiful national park within an hour's drive from Newcastle. The peaks are among the highest outside Kosciusko (1555 m) and the forests among the oldest and most lush.

Before the Barrington Tops were formed, the region north-west of Newcastle was chiefly composed of sedimentary rocks such as limestone and mudstone. Then volcanic rock rich in quartz was forced up through jointing and folded in the original layer, forming a lofty range that was subsequently eroded away leaving only a small residual area of some 300 square kilometres. Volcanic basalt flows occurred about 50 million years ago although much of it has been washed down via the rivers. Today little evidence remains of the original limestone and less still of the basalt. The former is confined to the spurs and rim walls around the plateau while the latter is evident on isolated caps.

The volcanic soils however support dense forests of thousands of species of plants, which in turn once supported an active logging industry, and therefore literally hundreds of mountain trails now exist throughout the upper Barrington and Gloucester River areas. Most of these are well graded and open to cyclists. However public transport is limited to Dungog and Gloucester which are unfortunately at an altitude of only 100–200 m with a long climb in store for anyone intending to camp on the tops. Alternatively, one can drive to the Polblue Rest Area in the centre on the park where there are fine opportunities for round trips.

Because of the park's popularity, especially during holidays, the cyclist will have to contend with many other users of the park: four-wheel drivers, canoeists, walkers, and horseriders. Visitors in school holidays, especially during good weather, will find the lower Barrington Tops bustling with sightseers. Empty spots will be hard to find, and avoiding running over tourists will be the cyclist's main preoccupation.

Dungog is just three hours by XPT from Central, and the national park just another three hours further by bike. From there, one can cycle up to the tops, amidst the snow gums, beech trees, and rainforest. Any number of days can be spent exploring the mountains before descending back to civilisation where the XPT provides a service back to the coast.

RIDE 90:   ALLYN RIVER

FROM: Allyn River Forest Park
TO: Mount Allyn Forest Park (return)
VIA: Chichester State Forest, Mount Allyn
LENGTH: 30 km
TIME: 1 day
RIDE/TRACK GRADE: 5/5 (long steep uphills)

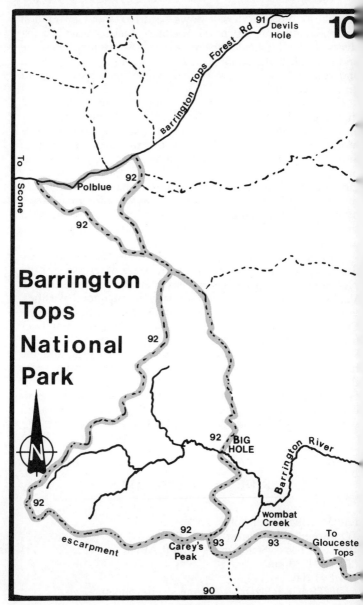

Barrington
Tops
National
Park

WALKING: Burraga Swamp and the Allyn River Rainforest Trail
HEIGHT VARIATION: 790 m
TRANSPORT: Private transport to Allyn River Forest Park via Dungog
FACILITIES: Basic picnic facilities: tables, bins, etc
MAPS: CMA (LIC) Carrabolla, Barrington Tops 1:25 000 topographicals. Also useful is the Barrington Tops and Gloucester Districts 1:100 000 Tourist Map which has a detailed and up-to-date 1:30 000 map on the reverse side of the Allyn River area.

The Barrington Tops are famous for their very old beech trees—some were alive during Biblical times. Fossils of them have been found in South America and Antarctica, helping to prove that these three continents were once joined. They grow only in moist cool conditions very similar to rainforests. One such dense stand of mature trees lies on the border between the Barrington Tops National Park and Chichester State Forest. This ride suggestion takes the cyclist through this beautiful area, up a 1135 m high mountain, and down along the attractive Allyn River valley with its rainforest, swimming holes, and numerous popular picnic and camping areas. Another positive feature of this ride is that it involves no backtracking. Due to the considerable height variation, some degree of fitness is necessary to enjoy the ride, although the ride can be done comfortably in one day by most cyclists.

A train service runs from Sydney to Maitland and thence to Brisbane. Along the way is Dungog, a reasonably large town on the Williams River north of Maitland. From here one can cycle to Salisbury and thence to the White Rock Camping Ground. Alternatively one can drive up the Allyn River Forest Road from Dungog, camping on any of the numerous clearings along the river.

From the Allyn River Forest Park, head upstream along the river, keeping on the Allyn River Forest Road. The road heads north along a consistently uphill slope. The track is poor and in patches is quite rough for conventional vehicles despite its grading on the map. However cycling along trails like these can be a very enjoyable experience in the Barrington Tops. The scenery and vegetation do much to distract from the long uphill slopes along the way.

The Allyn River Forest Road swings around after a partic
ularly steep climb and continues south along the base of th
prominent sharp-peaked Mount Lumeah (1200 m). It join
with the better quality Mount Allyn Forest Road at a sand
clearing sometimes used as a rough campsite. Turn sharp righ
and head down a short slope to an entrance way on the righ
This is the start of a fascinating walk through a wet negrohead
beech tree forest (*Nothofagus moorei*) with huge red and greer
leaved trees, some 1000 to 2000 years old. The average thick
ness of the trunks are 1.5 m and just after this isolated patcl
there is a dramatic change again to the standard dry eucalyp
of the Australian bush. An equally fascinating walk is the 15-
20 minute stroll to Burraga Swamp at the western foot o
Mount Lumeah. The walk is marked on both the tourist anc
topographical maps. The destination is an ancient depressior
in the ground that has accumulated sediments for millions o
years. Compression has forced these sediments into a soft pea
some 2.65 m deep with a high water table. However walking
on the tree less swamp itself is perfectly possible and quite ar
interesting experience. The peat compresses beneath the foot
step and springs back up again, giving you the impression tha
you are walking on a mattress. Another unusual aspect of the
swamp is that it is perfectly square, just like a gigantic tram-
poline. From the explanatory park information sign at the edge
of the swamp, a small walking track continues across the
middle. In the background towers Mount Lumeah and bor-
dering the swamp are the beech and rainforest trees.

The rest area at the beginning of this short walking track
contains one picnic table and an old fireplace. The bikes can
be hidden in the undergrowth to the left or along the walking
trail. Just another few hundred metres down the road another
more developed picnic ground is on the left. This is called the
Mount Allyn Forest Park. Here are covered tables and a water
tank situated next to a massive eucalypt tree. All around are
the beech trees which make good photographic subjects either
in low clouds or in bright sunlight.

The next stop along the way is the Mount Allyn Lookout.
Take the bikes back up the slope to the ridge top where a
signpost leads straight up a rough road. The bikes are better
left in the scrub at the bottom if you prefer walking. Ascend
steeply up circling the mountain twice. At the end is car park
and a short walking track to a concrete column at the summit,

ome 1135 m above sea level. This is the highest stage of the journey. Panoramic views are obtainable all around, particularly along the narrow ridge line of the Allyn Range. To the south, cleared agricultural land predominates.

For the walkers with a day to spare, a lengthy and challenging hike originates at the bottom of Mount Allyn. It is called the Gillwinga Walk and basically follows the roller coaster ridgeline of the Allyn Range over Mount Lumeah and Mount Gunama (where a visitors book can be signed). The track was opened by the Minister of Conservation, Mr Gordon, on 30 March 1980 and was constructed by local 4WD clubs in conjunction with the Forestry Commission. It marks the border between Chichester State Forest and Barrington Tops National Park and authorities recommend about five to six hours should be allowed. It finishes back at the White Rock Camping Area.

From Mount Allyn, it's good cycling back to the Allyn River. Return to the Forest Park via any combination of downhill roads. Take the well marked Mount Allyn Forest Road (called the Paterson Forest Road on the topographical map) down past altitude indicators to a junction and turn left. Other alternatives, if one wants to avoid traffic, are the Bungari Road or the nearby unnamed 4WD road. They all lead eventually to the Allyn River via a small holiday house called Gunyah where a well equipped cabin is available for rent.

Once reaching the river after an enjoyable 700 m drop, merely turn left and cycle through the numerous pleasant campsites along the Allyn River.

Optional days can be spent exploring other tracks in the immediate vicinity. For example on the eastern side of the river is a short rainforest walking trail described as 'educational' on the tourist map. A longer walk through wet sclerophyll forest is the Main Track to the guest house. From here, a short diversion can be taken to the upper Williams River such as the Pool of Reflections.

RIDE 91:   MANNING RIVER LOOP
(Northern Barrington Tops State Forest)

FROM: Devils Hole Camping Area
TO: Manning River (return)
VIA: Dilgry River, Gummi Falls
LENGTH: 34 km
TIME: 1 day
RIDE/TRACK GRADE: 4/4
WALKING: Short walk to see Gummi Falls
HEIGHT VARIATION: 380 m
TRANSPORT: Private transport to Devils Hole Camping
Area via Gloucester or Scone
FACILITIES: General picnic and camping facilities
MAPS: CMA (LIC) Cobark and Moonan Brook 1:25 000
topographicals. Also useful is the Barrington Tops and
Gloucester Districts 1:100 000 Tourist Map for vehicle access
to staging area.

While the south of the Barrington Tops contains many features
and is accordingly well visited, the northern section is often
by passed. The sheer aesthetic quality of dense lush beech tree
forests is no less. Featured on this one day circuit of the Barrington Tops State Forest is a lookout over the wild Moppy
River valley, pristine mountain rivers, and a waterfall.

Start by driving to the Devils Hole Camping Area which is
located just off the Barrington Tops Forest Road and links
Gloucester with Scone. If arriving late, one can car-camp here
at the nearby Polblue Camping Area. In the morning, check
the lookout over the only pure wilderness area in the Barrington Tops—the upper Moppy River valley. From here, one can
see a clear distinction between the wet beech forest on the
slopes and dry eucalypt bush on the plateau. Start the cycling
by travelling east to the signposted Honeysuckle Picnic Area.
Turn left here directly opposite the picnic ground on to Pheasant Creek Road which leads down to Dilgry River. The small
camping and picnic areas are set in open forest, while the
Dilgry River itself is lined by a corridor of moss-draped beech
trees.

Head up the other side and left at the top, then cycle west
until you reach a turn-off. Keep right here still following the

heasant Creek Road. The turn-off to the Manning River Camping Area is on the right. This is quite a beautiful ground, making it the ideal venue for lunch. When you're finished, head back up to the road and right, crossing the river. The Pheasant Creek Road then leads up on to the Mount Royal Range and over 200 m of height need to be gained here.

Turn off the Pheasant Creek Road on to the Tubrabucca Road and then left again on to the Bullock Brush Road which leads down via a great descent to the Gummi Falls on the Infant Manning River. Although they're more like a cascade, they still make nice photographic material due to the lush green vegetation surrounding the rocks. A tripod might be handy for slow exposures.

To attain the Devils Hole Camping Area, simply head up the other side where the trail curves south and directly accesses the Barrington Tops Forest Road via Thunderbolts Trail. Of course, this ride could also be done in reverse.

RIDE 92: THE BARRINGTON TOPS

FROM: Polblue Camping Area
TO: Barrington Tops (return)
VIA: Careys Peak, The Big Hole
LENGTH:
   Day 1: Polblue Camping Area to The Big Hole via Careys Peak 35 km
   Day 2: The Big Hole to Polblue Camping Area via Beean Beean Plain 18 km
   Total distance is 53 km
TIME: 2 days (recommended extra day by The Big Hole)
RIDE/TRACK GRADE: 3/5
WALKING: Short easy grade 200 m walk to Careys Peak summit
HEIGHT VARIATION: 155 m
TRANSPORT: Private transport needs to be taken to the Polblue Camping Area via Scone or Gloucester. The nearest station is Gloucester, but it is 1.4 km lower than the camping ground and the best part of a day is needed to cycle there via the Scone Road.

FACILITIES: General camping facilities at Polblue, and some authorised fire places are located on the plateau itself.
SPECIAL EQUIPMENT: Extra warm clothes
MAPS: CMA (LIC) Moonan Brook and Barrington Tops 1:25 000 topographicals. Also useful is the Barrington Tops and Gloucester Districts 1:100 000 Tourist Map.

This is the best ride in the park and one of the best in the state. It is easy as there are none of the big uphills that characterise the Barrington Tops, and it covers the most visually attractive scenery including features of interest such as spectacular look outs, the highest peak, swimming holes, good mountain bike tracks, beech trees, and sub-alpine vegetation.

The Polblue Camping Area can best be reached from Sydney via Gloucester and Newcastle and takes about four to five hours from the metropolitan area. Two ways lead from Gloucester to the national park. The short one simply goes north through flat uneventful agricultural land. The local names are equally unoriginal: the road is first called the Barrington Road which passes through the township of Barrington, crosses the Barrington River before entering the Barrington Tops State Forest and then it becomes the Barrington Tops Forest Road which soon leads to the Barrington Tops National Park. A better road, which gives almost total relief from the word 'Barrington', and incidentally passes through some lovely country side is the Gloucester Tops–Rawson Vale Road. Turn left 9 km before Gloucester on to Bucketts Way and drive along the river upstream for about 45 minutes. Turn right up on to Rawson Vale Road that climbs up to a crest where a spectacular panoramic valley lies spread before you. At the very horizon are the mountains that are your destination. Cross Kerripit River and turn left soon after. The road follows Cobark River for several kilometres before climbing continuously until it finds a ridge about 1500 m above sea level. This road is another 200–300 m higher than the tallest peaks in the Blue Mountains. The camping area is close to the road on the left hand side in the Stewarts Brook State Forest. Water, fireplaces and toilets are provided. This area is located on the western edge of the Devils Hole Wilderness area, some 2330 hectares of the rugged catchment area of the upper Moppy River, totally unblemished by human interference.

If some time is available after setting up all the camping

ear from the car, the rest of the day can be spent exploring the swamp which surrounds the camping area. It is not the conventional swamp usually associated with stagnant water and rotting vegetation, but a pleasant environment where distinctive border communities grow such as sub-alpine grasslands and wildflowers.

The basic outline of the circuit is to circumnavigate the western and southern edge of the plateau before cutting in by an alpine plain to the Big Hole. Along the way is Careys Peak, where a short track leads to the summit with impressive views over the upper Allyn River.

On the first day of cycling, go back up to the main road, turn left and take the first track on the left. This is the Polblue Trail which connects with the Barrington Trail at a t-intersection on the base of Mount Polblue (1577 m) on the edge of the national park. Turn right and head south-east down a long slope to the Little Murray Picnic Area. The track is well graded and good progress can be made. You are now inside the national park. Turn right where the trail heads around two large mountains which mark the Mount Royal Range. Brumlow Top is the highest peak in the entire Barrington Tops area although it resembles a wooded hill. There are some pleasant stream fordings along the way, ideal for rest breaks. In summer, the yellow-leafed weed, Scotch broom, is very predominant in the undergrowth and actually is visually quite attractive.

On the way is a turn-off to Junction Pool which should be ignored. Keep right, following the Barrington Trail along the Mount Royal Range. A minor detour is up to the summit of Mount Barrington (1555 m) where you obtain reasonable western views. The Middle Ridge Trail which is passed is used by 4WD clubs as an entry and exit to the plateau. I was here once when an entire convoy of Range Rovers were leaving.

The trail swings to the east, always following the rim of the escarpment. It is now called the Careys Peak Trail and it is very easy and pleasant cycling to a spur just before Careys Peak. The trail deteriorates here and it is a difficult short uphill slog to the picnic ground on the right. An old hut marks a clearing right on the very southerly edge of the plateau. A walking track on the western end leads up for 200 m to the top of the lookout. A fence prevents sightseers falling down the steep slope. To the right is a stark dark green/light green line between dense moist beech rainforest and dry eucalypt bush on the plateau. The prevailing winds are from the south west, dropping most of their moisture on their way up the slopes.

Most of the Hunter Valley can be seen from this lookout. At night, even the lights of Sydney and Newcastle are visible. On a clear day, one can see as far south as Gospers Mountain in the Wollemi National Park, but usually warm days produce haze limiting views. Even worse is a white-out which often occurs, especially in the early morning. This is a perfect place for lunch. However no water is available here.

Head back out to the Careys Peak Trail and continue east to a turn-off. A gate on the right bars vehicle access to The Corker and the Wombat Creek Camping Area. A sign tells you that The Big Hole is to the left. What follows are good down hills on a reasonable surface. On the way is Black Swamp, an open alpine plain surrounded by white eucalypt trees. Just before you cross a creek that flows out of the swamp, an infor mal picnic/camping area exists on the right hand side. After the creek, it is a bit of an uphill before more pleasant level cycling. The trail then drops into the Barrington River valley where it is downhill all the way to The Big Hole. This is one of my favourite camping areas in Australia. The cleared camping area is separated from the end of the trail by a barrier. The hole itself is a very deep wide bend in the river set in open pleasant woodland.

If the place is crowded, one can access another place slightly downstream from the boulders at the end of the road. This is a much smaller clearing with a rough walking track that takes you around some rapids to directly access The Big Hole. The water is chilly but well worth the effort. You are swimming in a large pool on top of a plateau over a kilometre higher than the rest of the Hunter Valley area. There is a rare species of native pepper (*Tasmannia purpurascens*) among the snow gums here which are found nowhere else in the state.

Spend one or more days here, lazing around. Exit the area via Bobs Crossing upstream and then the Watergauge Trail up to Beenan Beenan Plain joining back up to the Barrington Trail. A lot of Scotch broom and snow gums are passed through this section, and Beenan Beenan Plain itself must be one of the best sub-alpine off-road cycling environments in New South Wales due to its level gradient.

Sunrise over The Castle from Mt. Owen (Ride 74)

The view from Mt. Ginini, Brindabella Range, ACT (Ride 75)

Returning from Bendethera Caves, Deua National Park (Ride 78)

To complete the round trip head right after the large uphill
Mount Polblue, coming out on the Barrington Tops Forest
oad to the east of the Polblue Camping Area. This minimises
ny backtracking.

This tour can also be done in reverse (clockwise) direction
you wish to have the shorter day first.

RIDE 93: GLOUCESTER TOPS
(WOMBAT CREEK)

ROM: Gloucester Tops (Kerripit Road)
O: The Barrington Tops
IA: Gloucester Tops Walking Track
ENGTH:
   Day 1: Gloucester Tops to The Big Hole 18 km
   Day 2: The Big Hole to Wombat Creek via Mount Barring-
on 31 km
   Day 3: Wombat Creek to Gloucester Tops 13 km
   Total distance is 62 km
IDE/TRACK GRADE: 5–6/8
VALKING: Short easy 200 m walk up to Careys Peak
HEIGHT VARIATION: 310 m
RANSPORT: Private transport to Gloucester Tops via
Gloucester
ACILITIES: None
MAPS: CMA (LIC) Barrington Tops, Gloucester Tops and
Moonan Brook 1:25 000 topographical. Also useful is the Bar-
ington Tops and Gloucester Districts 1:100 000 Tourist Map.

The beautiful Barrington Tops area can also be accessed from
the Gloucester Tops via a ridge-track that links the two pla-
eaus. The second day involves classic mountain biking
through terrain described in the previous ride, but the first
nd third days contain a 6 km section where the trail is very
overgrown with many fallen trees that frustrate rapid progress, hence the maximum '8' grading for the track condition.
The ride should only be attempted by cyclists expecting to
manhandle the bikes through this difficult part. This is the
pain one has to endure to reap the reward of unparalleled
mountain biking action around the Barrington Tops.

It is suggested that you drive to the Gloucester Riv
Camping Area on the first day and car-camp. It is accesse
from The Bucketts Way south of Gloucester and involves
few fordings that are no problem unless it has just been rainin
heavily.

The next day, drive up to Gloucester Tops and do th
Gloucester Falls short walk at the end before backtracking t
Kerripit Road. Head left and drive as far as you can. A gat
bars all vehicle access. From this point cycle west, making
brief detour to Munro Hut. The track to this building is th
first on the right. It heads down through messmate and mour
tain gums, skirting around a large swamp. The road ends a
a camp clearing. However a short walking tracks heads north
west to the hut which is hidden in the bushes on the edge c
an escarpment. A small stream provides water to hut resi
dences. The condition has deteriorated considerably and it i
no longer very hygienic. There are many bunks, even jus
under the rafters!

When you've finished checking out the hut, head back u
to the road and continue west. After a downhill the roa
comes to another barrier and a sign again bars all vehicl
access. This section is very overgrown due to the soft rich soils
high rainfall, and sheltered topography. The bikes will hav
to be walked up the hill here as many mossy beech trees hav
fallen over.

The vegetation soon opens out into eucalypt forest as yo
climb but there are still fallen trees to negotiate. Some can b
ridden over, some can be skirted, but most simply involv
lifting the bike over requiring constant mounting anc
remounting. It is then good cycling across a couple of creeks
The trail swings from south-west to north-west avoiding th
beech tree stands. Although marked as a walking track on th
map and signposted as such, this is clearly not the case. In th
1960s, four-wheel drives used this road to travel between th
two plateaus. Today this involves over 100 km of detours.

The vegetation generally gets moister in nature as you com
to a turn-off. Keep right—the trail ascends a ridge climbing
from 1300 to nearly 1400 metres. Although it is not far unti
you are off the edge of the Gloucester Tops topographical map
this is the slowest progress of all. The track gradually get
worse—mud, vines, rocks and more fallen beech trees all pro
viding problems. Many short sections however can still b

dden. The geology here is dominated by granodiorite, a granular rock with large visible mineral crystals.

The final uphill is particularly bad and you will indeed wonder what you're doing with a bike in almost jungle terrain. This is the worst. At the top a massive tree forms a barrier just east of a metal chain. The terrain and vegetation improves considerably as you emerge on to the Barrington Tops plateau. The beech trees suddenly disappear, the snow gums return, and no fallen trees! The track undulates over a good surface and it's a terrific downhill to Wombat Creek where you can refill your water bottles. The turn-off is signposted on the right and the camping area is set in pleasant wet sclerophyll forest just between the road and the creek. This is where you'll be camping on the second night.

Continue west, where you soon come to a barrier blocking vehicles from the western end who wish to access Gloucester Tops. The road option at the junction here leads down to the Allyn River and Dungog. Head right from up a very steep hill to another turn off with the Careys Peak Trail. Another gate exists here. A sign points north to the Big Hole.

What follows are good downhills on a reasonable surface. On the way is Black Swamp, an open alpine plain surrounded by white eucalypt trees. Just before you cross a creek that flows out of the swamp, an informal picnic/camping area exists on the right hand side. After the creek, it is a bit of an uphill before more pleasant level cycling. The trail then drops into the Barrington River valley where it is downhill all the way to The Big Hole. This is one of my favourite camping areas in Australia. The cleared camping area is separated from the end of the trail by a barrier. The hole itself is a very deep wide bend in the river, set in open pleasant woodland.

If the place is crowded, one can reach another place slightly downstream from the boulders at the end of the road. This is a much smaller clearing with a rough walking track that takes you around some rapids directly to The Big Hole. The water is chilly but well worth the effort. You are swimming in a large pool on top of a plateau over a kilometre higher than the rest of the Hunter Valley area. There is a rare species of native pepper (*Tasmannia purpurascens*) among the snow gums here which are found nowhere else in the state.

The next day involves a round circuit of the Barrington Tops. Exit the Barrington River valley via Bobs Crossing upstream and then the Watergauge Trail up to Beenan Beenan Plain joining up to the Barrington Trail. A lot of Scotch broom and snow gums are passed through this section, and Beenan Beenan Plain itself must be one of the best sub-alpine off-road cycling environments in New South Wales due to its level gradient.

Head left, travelling south on the Barrington Trail. This track heads around two large flat mountains which mark the Mount Royal Range. Brumlow Top is the highest peak in the entire Barrington Tops area although it resembles a wooded hill. There are some pleasant stream fordings along the way, ideal for rest breaks.

On the way is a turn-off to Junction Pool which should be ignored. Keep right, following the Barrington Trail along the Mount Royal Range. A minor detour is up to the summit of Mount Barrington (1555 m) where you obtain reasonable views west. The Middle Ridge Trail which is passed is used by 4WD clubs as an entry and exit to the plateau. I was here once when an entire convoy of Range Rovers were leaving.

The trail swings to the east, always following the rim of the escarpment. It is now called the Careys Peak Trail and it is very easy and pleasant cycling to a spur just before Careys Peak. The trail deteriorates here and it is a difficult short uphill slog to the picnic ground on the right. An old hut marks a clearing right on the very southerly edge of the plateau. A walking track on the western end leads up for 200 m to the top of the lookout. A fence prevents sightseers falling down the steep slope. To the right is a stark dark green/light green line between dense moist beech rainforest and dry eucalypt bush on the plateau. The prevailing winds are from the south west, dropping most of their moisture on their way up the slopes.

Most of the Hunter Valley can be seen from this lookout. At night, even the lights of Sydney and Newcastle are visible. On a clear day, one can see as far south as Gospers Mountain in the Wollemi National Park, but usually warm days produce haze limiting views. Even worse is a white-out which often occurs, especially in the early morning. This is a perfect place for lunch. However no water is available here.

Head back out to the Careys Peak Trail and continue east to the turn-off where you were yesterday with a barrier barring vehicular access to the south. Head right down the eep hill retracing the first day's ride to Wombat Creek. Since ou have seen both Wombat Creek and The Big Hole on the rst day, it's up to you where you want to camp. Even though he Big Hole is the nicer area, Wombat Creek has been rec- mmended for variety purposes.

The third day simply involves backtracking to the car on .erripit Road, negotiating the 6 km 'hell' section on the way.

URTHER CYCLING IN THE BARRINGTON TOPS

he rides described in the preceding pages cover the high- ghts of the main plateau area. Plenty of opportunities exist or variations of these rides including different access points or people who (a) are willing to endure a 1200 m climb to each the tops, or (b) can organise a car-shuttle to eliminate ack-tracking. The general idea would be to start at the top, .g. Polblue, tour the Barrington Tops, and cycle down either ia The Corker to the Allyn River, or The Mountaineer to)ungog. Over a kilometre of altitude would be lost in one of he longest, steepest downhills possible in the country.

One sector of the Barrington Tops not described in this ection is the south-east, centred on the Chichester State Forest. There are many camping areas here with great mountain look-)uts, streams, and rainforest vegetation. This section happens o be the most easily accessible from public transport through)ungog. Consult the CMA Chichester 1:25 000 topographical.

GUM NUTS

12
The North

For the off-road cyclist who can't be satisfied, there are som very rugged, wild national parks scattered throughout th northern region of the state which offer some unique and spe tacular country. These parks are very isolated, usually devoi of facilities, and with difficult access on predominantl unsealed roads. Furthermore much of the access has to be b car: there are no train tracks here.

Personally I regard the northern parks such as Gibralt Range, New England, and Cathedral Rock to be among th wildest in the state. Rainforest is abundant and the scener easily distracts from any of the rigours of cycling. The follow ing rides and walk descriptions will cover such divers domains as the Warrumbungles where gigantic volcanic plug tower above a tiny oasis in the featureless wheat belt. Beec trees stand side by side with snow gums in the clouds nea Point Lookout on the escarpment of New England Nationa Park, while huge stacks of granite boulders that make u Cathedral Rock National Park remind the visitor of a cit skyline.

The rivers of the state's north fall from the ranges into dee rainforested gorges—Wollomombi Falls are the highest i Australia, and are within easy cycling distance of Armidale o New England National Park. Further north, another hig plateau is dissected into rounded domes and spires of granit in the Gibraltar Range, and yet another by the untamed Guy Fawkes River, while cool valleys abound with lush rainfores in the Washpool National Park. All these places are just acces sible by bike.

NEW ENGLAND NATIONAL PARK

Size: 29 500 hectares
Enactment: 1931: State Reserve
1935: Public Recreation Reserve
1967: National Park

Visitors: About 77 000 a year: mostly casual tourists to Point Lookout

Aboriginal Sites: Presently, little is known. The Aboriginals that resided in the area were mobile, using the many freshwater streams as transitional base-camps on journeys from the coast and the tablelands.

Flora: Over 500 species in 11 communities, determined by the soils, aspect, climate and exposure, to name a few. Rainforest and wet sclerophyll are the most common vegetation forms in the park. Three types of rainforest occur in the park: sub-tropical rainforest, warm temperate rainforest and cool temperate rainforest. Distinct division of the flora types occurs at 1200 m where the communities change from beech trees to snowgums. Heathlands are restricted, but rich in species. Weeds, mainly Lantana, pose few problems.

Fauna: Because of the rugged wilderness nature of the park, little is known about the fauna. However, so far 113 species of birds have been recorded and some 30 species of animals. Not many of the potential reptiles and insect species have been recorded. Rare species includes the sphagnum frog that is found in the higher swamps.

Camping: Camping is permitted anywhere off roads, and permits are not required. Several excellent cabins are available at a price, but bookings are required well in advance. The Thungutti Camping Ground is the main developed camping area for visitors and can be used as a base camp from which cycling and walking tours may be conducted. It comes with showers and toilets. Sites are secluded and bookings aren't necessary.

District Office: Dorrigo

Adjoining Parks: Numerous state forests surround the southern perimeter of the park, including Nulla Five Day, Styx River and Lower Creek. Also adjacent are nature reserves such as Georges Creek and Serpentine. Nearby lies the large Guy Fawkes River National Park and its associated state forests. To the north and west lies the striking Cathedral Rock and Oxley Wild Rivers National Parks.

New England is popularly approached from Armidale where tourists can inspect Point Lookout and walk to the base of the cliffs through magical beech tree rainforest that could be straight out of the pages of a fantasy novel.

Nevertheless, few people decide to venture out into the landscape they are viewing at Point Lookout. Several trails extend from the 1563 m high ridge down to the Georges River through the extensive Styx River State Forest. This forestry commission administered area is larger than some national parks. On the way, side trips can be taken to Wrights Plateau and the wild cascades that make up the headwaters of Five Day Creek. The ideal situation would be to travel to New England with another party in another car. A car shuttle before the ride then allows effortless cycling among some of the best forests in the state.

Unless lengthy tiring climbs are not minded by the cyclist, the park is better suited to overnight rides with the main access to the southern end of the park by the Macleay River Road (Kempsey–Armidale Road). This means the return route to the main plateau can be taken slowly. It sometimes takes three days to regain what is lost in one. The closest public transport is by means of a rail service to Armidale, or alternatively, the rail service to Kempsey or Coffs Harbour.

The park is notorious for its misty weather. In fact, there's a 1 in 3 chance that Point Lookout will be a 'white-out' increasing to 1 in 2 in the summer months. However the visitor need not despair if this occurs, because conditions for photography in the beech tree rainforest just below become perfect so take plenty of film. A tripod is also recommended.

Accommodation for caravans and car camping is located just outside the park in the Thungutti Camping Ground. Toms Cabin, The Residence, and the Chalet at Banksia Point require bookings. Here facilities include beds, stoves, gas lights, hot water, and perhaps best of all: four walls. Below the ridgeline primitive camping is available anywhere in the park. The only major trail into the heart of the park starts from near the park entrance and extends down past the base of Wrights Plateau to Killiekrankie Mountain and out through Horseshoe Road.

To the north Cathedral Rock National Park is only now coming into its own. Gigantic tors, like those in Gibraltar Range National Park, make up the principal attraction. The Barokee and Native Dog Creek Rest Areas and their associated swamp plains and boulder strewn grasslands, make pleasant green scenery that comprises some of the highest land north of the Kosciusko main range

The park is a refuge for eagles and yellow-tailed cockatoos.

stroll around the principal camping area at Barokee in the
late afternoon will often result in sighting grey kangaroos and
swamp wallabies. The only access is via the Round Mountain
Road, about 8 km long and not far from Ebor on the Armidale
to Grafton Road.

RIDE 94: STYX RIVER
(Wattle Flat)

FROM: Thungatti Camping Area
TO: Styx River camping ground (Wattle Flat) (return)
VIA: Styx River Forest Way
LENGTH: 40 km (20 km each way)
TIME: 2 days
RIDE/TRACK GRADE: 5/3
WALKING: None
HEIGHT VARIATION: 520 m
TRANSPORT: Private transport to the Thungutti Camping
Area
FACILITIES: Firewood, barbecues, and pit toilets at Wattle
Flat. Good well developed camping ground at Thungatti.
MAPS: Hyatts Flat and Jeogla 1:25 000 topographicals. The
Armidale and District 1:150 000 Tourist Map will come in
handy.

The topography of New England National Park means that
you have almost endless downhills lasting the best part of a
day where well over a kilometre of altitude is lost, and the
harsh alternative: a long upward push to regain the camping
and accommodation spots along the main entrance road to
Point Lookout.
   At 29 000 hectares, the Styx River State Forest is almost as
large as the national park itself. Within its boundaries are
pockets of rainforest, beech trees, blackbutt, coachwood, and
sassafras. The first part of this trail involves a terrific descent
from the entrance to the national park (about 4 km from Point
Lookout) down the Styx River Forest Way to Wattle Flat. This
camping area is located on the Styx River and the turn-off is
signposted. On the way is an eastern lookout over the rugged
Georges River valley.

Wattle Flat is a very pleasant camping area. Many old jee▯ tracks can be followed upstream allowing you to camp wher▯ you like. Due to the predominantly down▯hill nature of th▯ day's ride, it will not have taken long to get here and the re▯ of the day can be spent swimming in the many tranquil swim▯ ming holes in the river. One time we were here, a platypu▯ was feeding in a prominent pool to the north-east of the form▯ camping area. Rainbow trout introduced from the nearb▯ hatchery can be legally caught here. Graziers allow their catt▯ to roam here at times.

Some backtracking can be avoided the next day by takin▯ The Loop Road some of the way back up to Thungat▯ Camping Area. Naturally, the second day is predominantl▯ uphill, the punishment for the fantastic downhill experience▯ on the first day.

RIDE 95:   NEW ENGLAND
(WRIGHTS PLATEAU)

FROM: Thungatti Camping Ground
TO: Point Lookout, Wrights Plateau
VIA: Toms Cabin
LENGTH: 13 km
TIME: 1 day
RIDE/TRACK GRADE: 4/5
WALKING: Many short walk options: Eagles Nest, Wrights Plateau, the Cascades.
HEIGHT VARIATION: 510 m
TRANSPORT: Private transport to the Thungutti Camping Area
FACILITIES: Good well developed camping ground at Thungatti.
SPECIAL EQUIPMENT: Bike lock, day pack
MAPS: CMA (LIC) Hyatts Flat 1:25 000 topographical. The Armidale and District 1:150 000 Tourist Map might also come in handy.

This cycling/walking combination tour features the best and most accessible highlights of the New England National Park.

he cycling distance is short and easy, with some steep uphills. However, the majority of the day can be spent walking the many tourist tracks to various places of interest.

From the main road, keep along the unsealed park entrance road to Point Lookout. It is basically uphill all the way. At Toms Cabin, the road is sealed for the final steep ascent to the car-park. The views from the two platforms are quite good. From the top of the escarpment, you can survey the whole of the New England National Park looking as far east as the coast. Before you are the green forested ridges and hills of one of the largest wilderness areas in the state's north. Quite often the lookout is in the clouds, but you can still do one of the short beech-forest walks from the end.

It is suggested you lock your bikes and do the Eagles Nest Walk. From the car-park the walking track starts on the left behind the large shelter. It descends to the base of the first set of cliffs and contours around before climbing up again. It is not very long (90 minutes), but winds its way through some of the most beautiful beech tree forest there is; containing lichen-covered rocks, creaking cliffs, waterfalls, a weeping rock, and hundreds of types of moss and fungi. Tolkien fans will especially love the magical 'fairytale' atmosphere the moss covered beech trees generate.

The track leads back to the Point Lookout car-park via snow gums. Once you are back on you bike, head down, briefly checking out The Chalet and Residence near the Banksia Point ranger station for more views. Cycle back to the main camping ground and head left to Wrights Plateau. Another branch to the left leads down Cliffs Trail to Five Day Creek.

Keep on the left trail. You pass a gate and the track heads steeply down to a junction with a walking track. On the right, signposts point out the Cascades Walk and the Wrights Plateau. The bikes should be left here. The old road keeps descending to Robinsons Knob in the centre of the park.

The walking track to Wrights Plateau climbs immediate and ascends via a short rocky scramble to the very flat plateau that will remind Budawang enthusiasts of a miniature version of The Castle. Signs warn you to stay on the path. The track sometimes disappears due to the rock. From the end, more panoramic views of the New England National Park are obtained including views up to the Point Lookout escarpment. Insects are common here in summer so take plenty of repellent. If there is mist still blocking out views, don't be disappointed. Instead, why not do the Cascades walk?

The start of the track is located where you left your bike at the western base of Wrights Plateau. Proceed down through open forest to the water. Some beautiful mountain pools are separated by low waterfalls as the upper Five Day Creek races down a steep chasm. Be careful down by the water; I saw two snakes in the moist undergrowth lying right on the path, camouflaging themselves quite well. Because of the terrain there was no way around them, so I just had to stamp my feet until they finally disappeared.

A much shorter walk is the Tea Tree Walk which leaves at the back of the camping area where it soon joins up with the Little Styx River before coming out opposite Toms Cabin. It takes only 30 minutes and pamphlets are available from Banksia Point.

RIDE 96: CATHEDRAL ROCK

FROM: Thungutti Camping Area
TO: Cathedral Rock (return)
VIA: Barokee Rest Area
LENGTH: 48 km (24 km each way)
TIME: 2 days
RIDE/TRACK GRADE: 3/3
WALKING: 6 km to the top of Cathedral Rock
HEIGHT VARIATION: 300 m
TRANSPORT: Private transport to the Thungutti Camping Area
FACILITIES: Firewood, barbecues, and pit-toilets at the Barokee Rest Area. Good well developed camping ground at Thungatti.
MAPS: CMA (LIC) Ebor and Hyatts Flat 1:25 000 topographicals (Maiden Creek covers much of the views overlooked from the tor)

In my opinion, the view from the top of Cathedral Top is amongst the best in the state. From the top of the boulder stack, one can see the coast, the Armidale district, and the New

ngland escarpment. Cathedral Rock National Park contains
he highest point north of the alps.

From the camping ground near Point Lookout, head back
bout 12 km past the Trout Hatchery to the Armidale to
Grafton road. Turn right and then left 5 km later. A rough dirt
oad leads up a hill through grazing land on both sides. It is
km to the entrance of the national park and another 5 km to
he actual starting point of the walk at the Barokee Rest Area
also called the Snowy Creek Picnic Area). The Round Moun-
ain Road goes further but a locked gate prevents access to the
rominent Round Mountain itself as it is owned by the Civil
Aviation Authority who have installed a microwave/radar
otating dish built in the late 1960s. Wallabies can be found
verywhere around here, especially in the early or late hours
ear the swamp at the base of Cathedral Rock.

The camping ground is very pleasant but not very large.
ortunately not too many people yet know of or visit the park.
A numerous system of small walking trails leads around the
principal water supply of the camping ground: a small creek
on the northern side which runs through the swamp. The
vater is very clean and fresh. The sphagnum bogs and peat
swamps around the area are quite unusual and make interesting study for the botanist, containing ground orchids, lilies,
nintbushes, bottlebrushes and heath.

The start of the walking track is well marked. A NPWS 'let-
terbox' contains free information leaflets concerning the track
and the park in general. The track heads out across the swamp
and up into a gully between Cathedral Rock and Round
Mountain. Ignore a track to the right as this is where you come
out on the return. Along the way are gigantic boulders that
have crashed down from the top. About half way around the
mountain, a signposted trail heads up to the rock stack itself
about 400 m away. It involves some scrambling. The last
section is entirely over rock where the visitor has to crawl
under and over rock. A chain provides assistance up a small
steep slope. At the top is an amazing display of wildflowers
on the southern end. You can't actually get to the very top
because of the sheer roundness of the highest boulders but
they make an interesting foreground for anyone willing to
drag a camera up there. Another rock stack is visible across
the gully opposite, while to the south-east it will not be
unusual to see clouds scraping the ground near the Point

Lookout area. Even though Cathedral Rock is higher, it is much drier because it doesn't sit on the edge of the escarpment.

The boulders are pink adamelite granite formed by weathering and often arranged in lines, running north-west to south-east due to the vertical jointing of volcanic dykes. Some of the tors are 30 m high.

Return to Barokee by continuing on the trail around the mountains and passing more giant boulders.

RIDE 97:   WOOLPACK ROCKS

FROM: Thungutti Camping Area
TO: Woolpack Rock (return)
VIA: Native Dog Creek Rest Area
LENGTH: 56 km (28 km each way)
TIME: 2 days
RIDE/TRACK GRADE: 3/3
WALKING: 7.5 km to the top of Woolpack Rocks
HEIGHT VARIATION: 300 m
TRANSPORT: Private transport to the Thungutti Camping Area
FACILITIES: Firewood, barbecues and pit-toilets at Native Dog Creek Rest Area. Good well developed camping ground at Thungatti.
MAPS: CMA (LIC) Ebor and Hyatts Flat 1:25 000 topographicals (Maiden Creek covers much of the views overlooked from the tor)

In similar style to the previous ride, one can cycle to another camping ground in the Cathedral Rock National Park and do a short scenic walk to the top of some gigantic granite tors with superb views. One can see the coast, the Armidale district, and the New England escarpment. Cathedral Rock National Park contains the highest point north of the alps.

From the camping ground near Point Lookout, head back about 12 km past the Trout Hatchery to the Armidale to Grafton Road. Turn right and then left 7 km later. The camping ground turn-off is on the left about 8 km from the Armidale–Grafton Road turn-off. Several sites are scattered throughout he ground. In winter this area often receives snow due to its high altitude.

The walking track is well signposted and basically skirts all the way around the base of Woolpack Rocks, ascending the boulders from the south. A parka might be handy for it does get very windy on top because of its exposure to south-westerlies. The boulders are pink adamelite granite formed by weathering and often arranged in lines, running north-west to south-east due to the vertical jointing of volcanic dykes. Some of the tors are 30 m high.

Return via the same route.

RIDE 98:   GUY FAWKES RIVER

FROM: Thungutti Camping Area
TO: Ebor Falls
VIA: Armidale to Grafton Road
LENGTH: 46 km
TIME: 1 day
RIDE/TRACK GRADE: 2–3/2
WALKING: None
HEIGHT VARIATION: 300 m
TRANSPORT: Private transport to the Thungutti Camping Area
FACILITIES: Firewood, barbecues, and pit-toilets at the Barokee Rest Area. Good well developed camping ground at Thungatti.
MAPS: CMA (LIC) Ebor and Hyatts Flat 1:25 000 topographicals (Hernani covers much of the views overlooked from the Guy Fawkes River National Park viewing area)

For such a small catchment area, the Ebor Falls are extremely impressive. They are located in a southerly pocket of the Guy Fawkes River National Park near the small township of Ebor (population 100). It was given its named after the Roman translation for the English city of York, Eboracum, where the original Guy Fawkes lived. The river falls 96 m in two stages but even more spectacular is the sheer volume of water. Furthermore no walking is involved as you can cycle right to the very lookout platform. From the Thungutti Camping Ground, make your way back to the main road and head right and then right again 7 km later to Ebor. The turn-off to the falls is just before the township and is marked by the usual national parks brown roadsign. A flower covered cemetery is passed before the first of three lookouts on the right. The first wooden platform on the right gives views over the first set of falls. It is difficult to imagine when looking at these that the second set are twice as high. Notice also the symmetrically jointed basalt gorge that the river falls into. The stone resembles hundreds of tall regular columns. The second lookout further down the sealed road to the rest area involves some rideable steps but overlooks both falls. There is a short track along the cliff edge to another wooden platformed vantage point which gives views over the upper Guy Fawkes River Valley. Notice how incredibly steep the gorge sides are. Most of the national park is inaccessible to all but the toughest walkers and canoeists. The vast majority of the national park starts about 25 km downstream. Return via the same route.

FURTHER CYCLING ON THE NEW ENGLAND TABLELAND

About 150 km of gravelled roads run through the Styx River State Forest and this would be the main focus for one day and overnight rides due to its scenery, campsites, and proximity to the main access road to the New England National Park. It is possible to traverse the park by keeping to the Robinsons Knob Fire Trail until it becomes Horseshoe Road. But this definitely involves a major car shuttle if backtracking and altitude gain is to be avoided. Numerous other trails start from agricultural land in the south and enter the foothills of the national park and these remain to be explored. To the east lies Dorrigo National Park and to the north lies the bulk of the Guy Fawkes River National Park which are largely wilderness areas and beyond the scope of a cycling book. The other major scenic attraction to the west is the highest waterfall in Australia: Wollomombi Falls in the Oxley Wild Rivers National Park.

GIBRALTAR RANGE
NATIONAL PARK

Size: 17 273 hectares
Enactment: March 1963: Public Recreation Reserve
　　　　　　1967: National Park
Visitors: Possibly 4000
Aboriginal Occupation: Bora grounds, sacred ceremonial sites, stone arrangements, axe grinding grooves, and art sites are all examples of previous occupation by three tribes: the Badja-ong, the Jukambol, and the Kumbaingiri.
Flora: Gibraltar Range has a diverse variety of plant communities, including heathland, swamps, dry sclerophyll and rain-forests. Among the notable plants are waratahs (found here at their northernmost limit), giant elkhorns and orchids, and large grasstrees.
Fauna: 34 species of mammals, 225 bird species, 19 frog species, and 248 moth and butterfly species. The park is famous among zoologists for the occurrence of the rare tiger cat. The wallabies around Mulligans Hut are quite tame.
Camping: Primitive camping anywhere and everywhere off trails. Mulligans Hut Camping Ground provides all basic facilities.
District Office: The visitors centre is at the entrance to the park at the start of Mulligans Road. The actual District Office is located in Grey Street, Glen Innes.
Adjoining Parks: Washpool National Park to the north, and Gibraltar Range State Forest to the south and west.

RIDE 99:　TREE FERN FOREST

FROM: Mulligans Hut Camping Area
TO: Tree Fern Forest (return)
VIA: Twin Bridges
LENGTH: 18 km
TIME: 1 day
RIDE/TRACK GRADE: 3/6–7 (1 km of ride including push the bike along a well defined walking track)
WALKING: Optional short side detour to The Needles

HEIGHT VARIATION: 110 m
TRANSPORT: Private transport to Mulligans Hut Camping
Area via Gwydir Highway from Glen Innes or Grafton
FACILITIES: Car camping ground at Mulligans Hut where
pit toilets, firewood, barbecues, and a shelter are provided.
There are also fireplaces and picnic tables.
MAPS: CMA (LIC) Cangai 1:25 000 topographical

This ride is one of the few one-day mountain bike tours avail
able in the magnificent Washpool–Gibraltar rainforest region
The ride is a round trip, involving no backtracking with the
highlight being a forest comprised almost solely of giant tree
ferns, some growing as high as 9 m.

From the Mulligans Hut camping ground, cross Little Dandahra Creek and walk up through eucalypt forest until you
come to a four-wheel drive track. On the way are some fine
specimens of grass trees. If you want to see The Needles, head
right. The bikes will soon have to be dumped where a walk
through thick undergrowth takes you over a crest to the
viewing area. This is rather obscure and you are forced to
scramble to obtain the best vantage point. The pointed rock
stacks are reminders of the park's volcanic origins.

From the junction with the walking track from Mulligans
Hut, head left where the vegetation closes in and within 400 m
you come to Twin Bridges, which is simply a couple of old
planks over the infant Richardsons Creek. Apparently there is
an usually dense concentration of ferns in this vicinity with
over twenty recorded at this one spot alone.

The trail climbs steadily and steeply for 2 km from here, and
the surface can be quite muddy after recent rain. A turn-off
left leads down to the Tree Fern Forest. Four ferns dominate
here: the soft *Dicksonia antarctica*, the prickly *Cyathea leichhard-
tiana*, the rough *Cyathea australis*, and the more orthodox
Coopers tree fern, *Cyathea cooperi*. Take some photos and head
up again, turning left following the rough graded trail through
rainforest to the Gwydir Highway near the visitors centre.
Then simply follow the well graded Mulligans Drive back to
the camping area to complete a round trip.

NPWS pamphlets and leaflets at the visitors centre give
information about short walks in the national park such as
Dandahra Falls, Barra Nula Cascades, Anvil Rock, and Dandahra Crags.

WARRUMBUNGLE NATIONAL PARK

Size: 20 914 hectares
Enactment: 30 October 1953: State Reserve
1967: National Park
Visitors: 140 000+ a year
Aboriginal Sites: Kamiloroi people, though there is limited evidence, possibly due to dispersed occupation. The mountainous area was probably not particularly productive.
Flora: 530+ species of plants are known from the park, in a variety of communities. These include dry eucalypt woodland, heath, and damper forms of forest. The central area is mainly grassland—cleared of forest many years ago for grazing purposes.
Fauna: 12+ mammal species, 46 reptile species, 170 species of birds
Camping: A variety of camping is permitted in the park, though it is mainly restricted to the central area. Checking in at the visitor centre is required, for permits and information on the current conditions. Pre-cut firewood is obtainable from the side of the road just before Camp Blackman on the other side of Mopra Creek. A coin donation cylinder stands nearby.
District Office: The visitors centre and rangers station is just 10 minutes from the entrance at Camp Elongery.

The volcanic hotspot which formed the Nandewar Range and Mount Kaputar also formed the Warrumbungle Volcano about 15 million years ago. Erosion of this has resulted in the distinctive domes and spires of this park. The volcanic trachyte (a rock-like basalt) is not the only rock in the park—sediments of a similar age to the sandstones of the Sydney Basin, including coal, have been found beneath the volcanic layer.

The Warrumbungles (Aboriginal for 'jump-up' mountains), would be by far the most frequently visited national park west of Lithgow. For years, the Breadknife and Crater Bluff have had cameras pointed at them, and the walking tracks are accordingly very well defined. Both walking and cycling are relatively easy and camping facilities are well developed (showers and laundry are provided at Camp Blackman). For the less experienced with camping, a caravan site is available at the same place. For those who can't do without the finer

things in life, numerous hotels and motels lie between Coon
abarabran and the national park.

The main attraction of the park is its geology. In addition
the Warrumbungles is one of the few parks where tame kan
garoos and emus will approach humans and actually eat ou
of your hand! The rest of the biology is just as exciting, as the
area's vegetation is representative of flora from all points o
the compass.

Bike riding is limited to the central road (John Renshaw
Parkway) and its tributaries. Many of the campsites on the
base of the park's highest peak, Mount Exmouth (1206 m) are
directly accessible by bike.

Another interesting aspect to the park is the seven telescopes
situated at the Siding Spring Observatory. The largest, a 3.9 m
optical telescope, run jointly by the Australian National Uni
versity and CSIRO, is the second in size only to Moun
Palomar in California. Tours are conducted before 4.00 p.m
on all days except public holidays.

RIDE 100: MOUNT EXMOUTH

FROM: Camp Wambelong
TO: Mount Exmouth (return)
VIA: Burbie Camp
LENGTH: 20 km
TIME: 1 day
RIDE/TRACK GRADE: 6–7/4–5
WALKING: 7 km return walk to the summit of Mount
Exmouth
HEIGHT VARIATION: 400 m cycling, 346 m walking.
TRANSPORT: Private transport to Wambelong Camp on
John Renshaw Parkway from Coonabarabran.
FACILITIES: None along route. Well developed camping
ground at Camp Blackman. Water available at Camp Burbie
(except drought periods)
MAPS: CMA (LIC) Warrumbungles National Park 1:30 000
Tourist Map

Mount Exmouth is the highest peak in the national park and
from its summit are views over the entire area. Bring a packed

lunch along and a water bottle for it is very dry on top. From Camp Wambelong, follow the Burbie Spur Trail south. It initially is very flat as it parallels a dry creek bed to the left to a turning circle and a walking track start to Belougery Split Rock.

The trail starts to rise from here on, deteriorating slightly as it passes through dry Australian bush. A good downhill made interesting by some large drainage humps leads to a flat grassy open section where the last pleasant cycling can be enjoyed before a non-stop uphill. As the trail hits the beginning of the slope, the surface becomes very rocky. There are occasional half-obscured views to the east on the ascent.

There is a brief interruption from the grinding uphill at Burbie Camp. A barrier here prevents further travel by any vehicle. Distances are also given to various points of interest accessed from this road. Burbie Camp is a wide open camping ground containing a large water tank amidst some trees on the other side. Pit toilets are also located here, a good place for a break.

A walking track leads up to Mount Exmouth, but you should keep to the trail where the barrier is. The track still climbs varying between steep and very steep. Some short sections, however, can be ridden. To the south, the bulk of Mount Exmouth dominates the horizon. The final slog to Danu Saddle is painful, rocky and slippery. From the prominent crest, there are good views to the south of the park. The road continues here to Gunneemooroo Camp, and is quite rough. Walking tracks lead to the left and right of the saddle. The left track, near an unusual volcanic vent formation leads to the Grand High Tops. Take note of how large Bluff Mountain looks now. At the top of Mount Exmouth, it will appear quite small.

Stash the bikes and take the right track as it zig-zags its way up an initial crest to a spur on Mount Exmouth. As you get higher the views get better. The track passes through pine-dominated woodland and contours to the south of the second tier of cliffs, where grass-trees take over as the dominant plant. There are some tricky sections over ledges before the track climbs again to attain the top of the plateau from behind. One simply walks west along the rocky top to the height marker and panoramic views. From here, the Grand High Tops area looks very insignificant.

Retrace your route to Camp Wambelong, enjoying a long terrific descent that'll test all your mountain biking skills.

WALKING IN THE WARRUMBUNGLES

No visit to the Warrumbungles National Park is complet
without a walk up to the Grand High Tops. Three things mak
this walk unique: the Breadknife, Belougery Spire, and th
unsurpassable view to Crater Bluff. The Breadknife itsel
cannot be legally climbed. All along the walk, Belougery Spir
dominates the eastern horizon. From the Grand High Tops
walking tracks continue to Bluff Mountain and Moun
Exmouth. For a comfortable 1 day walk, the other side of th
Breadknife can be passed on the way down again via a hu
(tankwater available) from Dagda Saddle to rejoin the trac
above Spires Creek. Navigation is not difficult as all trails ar
well marked and rock scrambling is minimised. For variation:
and longer walks in the park, consult Tyrone Thomas' 10(
Walks in New South Wales.

Make sure your bikes are securely locked when walking ir
the park for theft is a problem.

INDEX TO RIDES

Ride	Region	Length (km)	Time (days)	Grade Ride/track	Page
Capertee River	Glen Davis, Wollemi	22	2	5/6–7	258
Capertee River	Gospers Mountain	32	2	7/8	269
Castle, The	Morton (Budawangs)	102	4	7/7	303
Cathedral Rock	New England	48	2	3/3	380
Clyde River	Morton (Budawangs)	18	1–2	3/6	297
Colo River (lower)	Wollemi (south-east)	45	1	4/3	233
Colo River (upper)	Wollemi (east)	34	1–2	4/6	241
Cooleman Caves	Kosciusko (north)	189	7	7–8/5	338
Cliff Drive	Katoomba, Blue Mountains	16	1	2/1	197
Deanes Creek	Wollemi (Wolgan River)	26	2	5/8	255
Deanes Gorge	Wollemi (Wolgan River)	102	2	3–4/6	247
Deua River	Deua NP	122	3	3/3	315
Dunn's Swamp	Wollemi NP	147	4	7/6	261
Ebor Falls	Guy Fawkes River	46	1	2–3/2	383
Erskine Creek	Lower Blue Mountains	34	1	4/3	156
Evans Lookout	Upper Blue Mountains	19	1	2/3–4	203
Euroka Clearing	Lower Blue Mountains	15	1	4/2	152
Faulconbridge Point	Lower Blue Mountains	29	1–2	3/4	168
Garie Beach	Royal NP	41	1	4/1	124
Glenbrook Creek	Lower Blue Mountains	16	1	3/4	159
Glen Alice circuit	Wollemi NP	147	4	7/6	261
Glen Davis	Wollemi NP	22	2	5/6–7	258

de	Region	Length (km)	Time (days)	Grade Ride/track	Page
Gloucester Tops	Barrington Tops	62	3	5–6/8	369
Glow Worm Tunnel	Wollemi NP	89	2	3/3–4	243
Gospers Mountain	Wollemi NP	76	2	7/7	266
Govetts Leap	Upper Blue Mountains	24	1	3/4	204
Grand Canyon	Blackheath	19	1	2/3–4	203
Great Old North Rd	Dharug NP	130	2	5/6	127
Grose Head South	Lower Blue Mountains	37	1	4–5/5–6	164
Grose River	Lower Blue Mountains	29	1–2	3/4	168
Grose River Gorge	Mount Banks	42	1	4/6	217
Grose River Gorge	Perrys Lookdown	24	1	2/3–4	204
Guy Fawkes River	New England	46	1	2–3/2	383
Hawkesbury Lookout	Lower Blue Mountains	28	1	2/1	163
Heathcote NP	Heathcote	33	1	3/3	125
Ingar	Lower Blue Mountains	29	1	2/4	180
Jervis Bay	Nowra (south)	96	2	3/2	328
Kanangra Walls	Kanangra Boyd	24	1	4/6	221
Kandos Weir	Wollemi NP	147	4	7/6	261
Kowmung River	Kanangra Boyd	32	2	6–7/7	227
Lady Car-rington Drive	Royal NP	32	1	3/3	121
Lake Burragorang	Lower Blue Mountains	48	1–2	3/4–5	189

Ride	Region	Length (km)	Time (days)	Grade Ride/track	Page
Lake Yarrunga	Morton (north)	42	1–2	5/7	278
Lawson Ridge	Lower Blue Mountains	25	1	4/7	178
Long Point	Morton (north)	16	1–2	2/3	281
Lost World	Lower Blue Mountains	39	2	5/7–8	173
Manning River	Barrington Tops	34	1	4/4	364
Marble Arch	Deua NP	39	1	4/5	320
Martins Lookout	Lower Blue Mountains	12	1	2–3/3	166
Megalong Valley	Upper Blue Mountains	31	1	6/6	208
Meryla Pass	Morton (north)	103	4	6–7/7	285
Mountain Lagoon	Wollemi (south-east)	55	1	6/4	234
Mount Banks	Blue Mountains	42	1	4/6	217
Mount Clear	ACT	35	1	5/6	312
Mount Exmouth	Warrumbungles	20	1	6–7/4–5	387
Mount Gingera	ACT	18	1	3–4/6	310
Mount Hay	Upper Blue Mountains	39	1	3–4/4	195
Mount Jagungal	Kosciusko (central)	86	4	5–6/6	344
Mount Kosciusko	Kosciusko (main range)	17	1	3/5	348
Mount Wilson	Upper Blue Mountains	44	1	6/3–4	237
Murphys Glen	Lower Blue Mountains	22	1–2	3/4	176
Myall Lakes	Bulahdelah	120	3	6/4	330
Nattai River	Blue Mountains foothills	63	2–3	3/3	149
Namadgi	ACT	35	1	5/6	312
Narrow Neck	Upper Blue Mountains	35	1	3/4	199
Newnes	Wollemi NP	156	4	6–7/7	250

Ride	Region	Length (km)	Time (days)	Grade Ride/track	Page
Tianjara Plateau	Morton (Budawangs)	115	3	4/6	289
Tobys Glen	Lower Blue Mountains	30–59	1	3/5	173
Tootie Ridge	Wollemi NP	33	2–4	6–7/7	235
Tree Fern Forest	Gibraltar Range	18	1	3/6–7	385
Tuglow Caves	Kanangra Boyd	51	2	6/6	225
Tuross River	Wadbilliga NP	80	3	7/5	323
Vale Lookout	Blue Mountains foothills	40	1	4/3	139
Valentine Hut	Kosciusko NP	40	2	5/5	342
Victoria Falls	Upper Blue Mountains	15	1	2/3	216
Vines, The	Morton (Budawangs)	65	3	6/7	293
Wadbilliga River	Wadbilliga NP	80	3	7/5	323
Warrumbun- gles	Coonabarabran	20	1	6–7/4–5	387
Watershed Road	Lower Blue Mountains	109	4	5/4–5	184
Wattle Flat	New England (Styx River)	40	2	5/3	375
Wentworth Creek	Lower Blue Mountains	25	1	4/7	178
Wentworth Falls	Upper Blue Mountains	17	1	2/2	193
West Head	Ku-ring-gai Chase	66	1	2/1	109
Wolgan River	Wollemi NP	26	2	5/8	255
Wollemi Creek	Wollemi NP	34	1–2	4/6	241
Wombat Creek	Barrington Tops	62	3	5–6/8	369
Woolpack Rocks	Cathedral Rock	56	2	3/3	382
Wyanbene Caves	Deua NP	39	1	4/5	320

YCLING THE BUSH:
)0 RIDES IN VICTORIA

t 444 pages, *CYCLING THE BUSH: 100 RIDES IN VICTORIA* one of the most comprehensive guidebooks ever published Australia. It contains detailed tracknotes for one hundred the best bicycle rides in the state. The rides include short ne-day trips around Melbourne and the Dandenongs to xtended overnight mountain biking/walking expeditions in .e rugged wilderness of Victoria's magnificent Alps, the)astal ranges of the Otways and Wilsons Promontory, the ndstone mountains of the Grampians, and many other cations.

From mountain lookouts to fishing lakes, from pristine vers to limestone caves, from secluded coves to ancient)rests, all major national parks are covered as well as a selec-on of the most scenic state forests and other nature reserves etween the rainforests of East Gippsland and the desert parks f the Mallee.

Each ride in the guide incorporates data on distances, trans-ort, access and ride grades, facilities, map references and pecial equipment needed. Extensive research has provided iformation on geological, biological, and historical aspects of atural, Aboriginal, and colonial features along the rides. 'here are chapters devoted to the development, mechanics, nd maintenance of the mountain bike, in addition to sections overing accessories, riding techniques, first aid, food, equip-nent, photography, and camping.

'Klinge's excellent ride description, his attention to detail and iis beautiful photography make this book a most enjoyable ead.'

John Trevorrow, Melbourne *Herald Sun*

CYCLING THE BUSH:
100 RIDES IN TASMANIA

This 348 page guide outlines the best tours in the most scen
areas of this beautiful island. Already one of Australia's mo
popular areas for cycling, Sven Klinge's book is the most con
prehensive guide available for both touring and mountain bil
cyclists. The range of rides includes one 'dayers' of historic
interest around the major cities, as well as coastal rides, ar
extended overnight mountain biking/walking expeditions i
the rugged wilderness that Tasmania is internationally famou
for.

From mountain lookouts to fishing lakes, from pristir
rivers to limestone caves, all National Parks are covered a
well as a selection of the most scenic State Forests, Recreatic
Areas, Forest Reserves, and Bass Strait islands. Mountai
biking is an excellent way of exploring one of the largest an
most spectacular parks systems in Australia.

Each ride in the guide incorporates data on distances, trans
port, access and ride grades, facilities, map references an
special equipment needed. Extensive research has provide
information on geological, biological, and historical aspects c
natural, aboriginal, and colonial features along the rides. Ther
are chapters devoted to the development, mechanics, an
maintenance of the mountain bike, in addition to sections cov
ering accessories, riding techniques, first aid, food, equipmen
photography, and camping.

'… it offers everything the would-be rider needs to know …
                    Heather Kennedy, *The Sunday Herald Su*